Amazing Soy

Other books by Dana Jacobi

The Joy of Soy

The Best of Clay Pot Cooking

Amazing
Soy

DANA JACOBI

A complete guide to buying

and cooking this nutritional

powerhouse, with 240 recipes

wm

WILLIAM MORROW

75 YEARS OF PUBLISHING

An Imprint of HarperCollins Publishers

HarperCollins books may be purchased for educational, business, or sales promotional use. For information please write: Special Markets Department, HarperCollins Publishers Inc., 10 East 53rd Street, New York, NY 10022.

FIRST EDITION

Designed by Nicola Ferguson

Library of Congress Cataloging-in-Publication Data
Jacobi, Dana.
    Amazing soy : a complete guide to buying and cooking
this nutritional powerhouse, with 240 recipes / Dana Jacobi.—1st ed.
        p.   cm.
    Includes index.
    ISBN 0-06-093381-X
    1. Cookery (Soybeans)   2. Soyfoods.   I. Title.
TX803.S6 J3296   2001
641.6'5655—dc21   00–066210

01 02 03 04 05   QW   10 9 8 7 6 5 4 3 2 1

Dedicated to Joan Emery
and William Shurtleff

contents

acknowledgments

Creating this book required the support of experts in science, technology, culinary arts, and nutrition. It has been a joy working with these members of the soy community. I love you all for your vision, passion, and the humanitarian, ecological, and spiritual commitment underlying your work. Your generous help has been essential for keeping up with the flood of new soy products and for understanding the amazing history of soy, its profound potential for our health and its myriad personalities. For creating recipes, I bless my culinary elders and peers; your life's work and expertise are deep waters from which I draw knowledge and inspiration. I am also eternally grateful to a small village of enthusiastic fellow cooks, professional and amateur, and to the assistants who provided support.

In particular, my deepest thanks go to: William Shurtleff's Soyfoods Center of Lafayette, California, Peter Goldbitz of Soyatech, and Nancy Chapman et. al. at SANA for an abundance of information and insight. Billy Bramblett and Jeremiah Ridenour of Wildwood Natural Foods, Chia Collins and Michael Cohen of Lightlife Foods, Steve Demos and James Terman of White Wave, Ted Nordquist of The WholeSoy Company, Christian Elwell of South River Miso, Yvonne Lo of Vitasoy USA, Inc., and Raj Gupta of ProSoya Inc., for insight into how soyfoods are made and how the soy community developed. Stephen Barnes, Ph.D., of the University of Alabama at Birmingham, Clare M. Hasler, Ph.D., of the University of Illinois at Chicago, and Julie Freyman at Protein Technologies, Inc., for scientific and medical information.

Jean Anderson, Rick Bayless, Shirley Corriher, Ken Hom, Harold McGee, Nick Malgieri, Julie Sahni, Barbara Tropp, and Paula Wolfert for the work that has nurtured my own. Oldways Preservation and Exchange Trust, the International Olive Oil Council, Nancy Harmon Jenkins, Anna Tasca Lanza, Fred Plotkin, and Nancie McDermott for infinitely enriching my ethnic culinary perspective.

Chefs Quian Minghua of Evergreen, Michel Nischan of Heartbeat, Tadashi Ono of Sono, Ahmed Reda of Pyramida, and Jean-George Vongerichten of JoJo in New York City, Tanya

Petrovna of Native Food in Los Angeles, Sandy Sonnefelt of The Pasta Shop in Oakland, California, for recipes shared. Elaine Jacobi (thanks, Mom), Martha Casselman, Eileen Guastella, and Judith Prince for unexpected recipes. Elizabeth Andoh, Jackie Newman, and Susan Purdy for your expertise on Asian soyfoods and on baking.

Carol Durst at NYU, Jane Feinstein, Ellen Fried, Mona Lombardi, Robin Mendelwager, Kathy Moore, and Mindy Schreil for recipe testing. Beth Shepherd, Susan Dunnington, Alonna Smith, and Sara Purcell for road-testing recipes. Susan Miller, R.D., for incomparable recipe analysis. Soy milkmaids Carol Guber, Regina Ragone, Vicki Caparullo; San Jose's tofu team—Mona Onstead, Jackie and Gerry Pagnini, Michael Hamilton, Mickey Benson, Christi Welter, Genevieve Torresala, Theresa Brooks, and Bonnie Walters for rigorous tasting.

Barney Stein and Linda Murray Berzok for typing and preliminary editing. Iris Carulli for editing and proofreading.

Harriet Bell for totally getting it and for refining *Amazing Soy* with your thoughtful genius. Roberto De Vicq De Cumptich, Ellen Silverman, and Anne Disrude for the perfect cover. Nicola Ferguson for the beautiful interior pages. Angela Miller, my agent, for making a perfect marriage. Karen Ferries for answering every question.

Nadine Elleman, Joan Emery, Muriel Miller, and Susan Purdy for helping me hold it together, and to fellow soy bitches Askasha Richmond and Patricia Greenberg.

Amazing
Soy

introduction

Soy is amazing because it offers outstanding nutrition along with protective health benefits. Foods made from soy are good, not just for us but for the planet, too, because cultivating soybeans uses land most productively and maximizes our ability to feed everyone.

Soy is also delicious. The recipes in *Amazing Soy* prove how easily soyfoods can fit into any style of eating and any lifestyle, even that of the most particular eaters.

The soybean itself is amazingly versatile. Beyond its use in cooking, including oil and soy sauce, I could write another, fatter book about soy used industrially, in plastics, ink, glue, and other products. (I do not include soy sauce or soy oil either, because this book concentrates on foods rich in soy protein and in the biologically active compounds known as phytochemicals.)

Healthy Soy

When you eat soy, you are being good to your body. This amazing bean provides such significant health benefits that eating soy has gained almost mythical status. Though we still have a great deal to learn about the nature and extent of these benefits, and it will take time to separate fact from wishful thinking, there are many compelling reasons to include soy in your diet.

Study after study confirms that a plant-based diet is the most healthful choice. However, this does not mean you have to be vegetarian. (I enjoy eating fish, poultry, and occasionally even meat.) Soyfoods just make it easier to serve meatless meals so varied and exciting they satisfy everyone. Soyfoods are also useful if you follow Jewish or Islamic dietary laws. (Many soyfoods are kosher, as noted on their labels.)

Soy provides high-quality protein, equal to that of poultry, milk, and other animal foods. Not all soyfoods are low in fat, but most are cholesterol-free. They do not contain saturated fat unless it is added during processing or soy is combined with ingredients that contain saturated fat.

Because many forms of soy, including those imitating meat and dairy foods, are modest in total fat or fat-free, they help you eat leaner. For those of us who cannot resist the great flavor that comes with fat, using soy products leave room to add a bit of butter or cream to dishes while keeping them low in cholesterol and saturated fats.

Consuming at least 25 grams of soy protein a day may reduce blood cholesterol levels and thus the risk of heart disease. We know this with such certainty that in October 1999, the Food and Drug Administration began allowing foods containing at least 6.25 grams of soy protein per serving to be labeled with this claim, and the statement that they should be part of a diet low in saturated fat and cholesterol. The American Heart Association officially recommends eating 35 to 50 grams a day of soy protein. In November 2000, they added it to their list of foods people should eat every day to lower cholesterol and the risk of heart disease. A study conducted by Clare Hasler, Ph.D., executive director of the Functional Foods for Health Program at the University of Illinois, and a leader in researching the effects of eating soy, determined that even 20 grams of soy protein a day is effective in lowering blood cholesterol.

If no other health benefit is conclusively proven, this alone makes it worthwhile to eat enough soy every day to total 25 grams or more of soy protein. (In this case, more soy is good, up to a total of 50 grams, according to some clinical studies.)

Many people assume eating soyfoods also reduces their risk of cancer. Epidemiological studies of Asian populations appear to support this. In Japan, where people have eaten soy every day for centuries, including tofu and miso, women have the lowest rate of breast cancer in the world. The low rate of active prostate cancer in Asian men might also be attributable to soyfoods they eat regularly. (In Japan, men are diagnosed with prostate cancer as often as in the United States, but it progresses much more slowly, causing less mortality. Soybeans contain a number of components that have demonstrated anticancer activity in animal and human tissue studies. Evidence suggests this is because of the phytochemicals in soy.

To date, there are no clinical studies that conclusively confirm the relationship between preventing or treating cancers and eating soy. Scientists are, however, looking closely at isoflavones, naturally occurring plant components in which soybeans are particularly rich. These isoflavones have both estrogenlike and anti-estrogen properties. Results of various clinical studies, while promising, have not yet proven the ability of isoflavones to reduce the risk of various cancers. In the case of breast cancer, these studies have produced mixed results; they look more optimistic regarding prostate cancer.

Along with attention focused on the possibility of soy to reduce cancer risk, questions have been raised about its effect in women with estrogen-receptor positive tumors. These types of tumors are stimulated by estrogen and therefore might be stimulated by soy isoflavones. Given the mixed research results and limited data, women who have estrogen-receptor positive cancer should consult with their physician before assuming that eating soy, particularly in substantial amounts, is advisable.

The health benefits of soy are more clearly demonstrated in helping to prevent osteoporosis. Again, scientists are looking at isoflavones in soy protein as the active agent. They seem to help reduce the loss of calcium from bones. Eating isoflavone-rich soy has even been shown to enhance bone mineral density. There is also much interest in the effect of eating soyfoods on menopausal symptoms. Research, as well as the personal experience of some women, suggests that soyfoods containing naturally occurring isoflavones may help in reducing the severity and number of menopausal symptoms.

For isoflavones, scientists are not yet certain what amount is optimal. It appears to be in the range of 40 to 60 milligrams a day. A study conducted by Dr. Clare Hasler has demonstrated that more is not necessarily better. In this study, women who consumed 100 milligrams of isoflavones a day did not fare better than those getting a lesser amount. Many soy products state the amount of isoflavones they provide per serving, so you can keep track.

Soy is also being studied for the way it affects the stability of blood sugar levels, which may prove beneficial for diabetics.

Although we are not yet certain which components of soy, in what combination and at what levels, provide desirable benefits, many health care professionals recommend eating soyfoods. While eating soy is good, to be healthy, you cannot, as Peter Goldbitz of SoyaTech, an industry consulting firm, says, just add it to the other four basic American food groups—pizza, hamburgers, chocolate, and beer—and you can be assured that you will stay healthy. You need to follow a sensible diet that includes soy. Getting proper exercise is important as well.

Delicious Soy

With all these known and possible benefits, it is easy to see soy as a health food. Unless it's well prepared and tastes good, however, that doesn't matter. I would rather have food that is 75 percent healthy and 100 percent delicious than the other way round. Taste rules!

Appealing soy products abound. They are the result of a trend to Westernization that took off in the 1970s. As Peter Goldbitz recounts, the entrepreneurs at companies like Turtle Mountain, Inc., and Lightlife Foods, Inc., said, "You like your ice cream and meat. We will make them for you out of soy, and tasting as close as possible to the real thing."

Despite this commitment, it took a couple of decades to eliminate the flat, pronounced soybean taste in soymilk that Asians like but Western palates find unpleasant. With tofu, too, a more neutral taste took some time to achieve.

Now, thanks to hard work and technological innovations, nearly every group of soyfoods includes good-tasting choices. Without question, soymilk and tofu have entered a new era. Some of the best improvements in soyfoods are recent, including creamy yogurt made with live cultures.

For this book, I conducted a tofu tasting of forty-three items. Comparing the results to those of a tasting I did for my previous soy cookbook, in 1996, the differences were remarkable. At that time, many products tasted less than pleasant; some were chalky, others dreadfully beany. One even tasted burned. Today, most tofu is mild and fresh-tasting, with only subtle differences among brands. The main differences are in texture.

For the soymilk tasting I gathered thirty-seven items. More than half of them were not even available in 1996. Of the soymilks that did exist, most have been improved during those five years, some more than once. As a result, soymilk today tastes better than ever before.

Soy cheese is a rapidly improving category. Further along, I explain which ones are good, and how to use soy cheeses to best advantage.

Meat alternatives show how companies keep working to improve products. Only a few years ago, the only meat replacement products worth talking about, except to committed vegetarians, were a few veggie burgers. Now, however, there are easily a dozen brands of delicious burgers, along with a rapidly growing selection of soy chicken, sausages, and other meat alternatives. I also enthusiastically recommend meatlike soy crumbles, crisp bacon strips, pepperoni, and chorizo made with soy.

Among soymeat products, cold cuts and hot dogs have come a long way, although children and some dedicated vegans remain their prime fans. At the rate they are improving, check out the franks and sliced bologna every six months or so. Soon there may be ones you will like.

Soyfoods vary noticeably both in taste and in texture from one brand to another. This is true even with tofu, which is made from just soybeans, water, and mineral salts. For this reason, if you do not like a particular soyfood the first time you taste it or cook with it, try another brand.

To see how much their differences in texture and taste affect the results of a recipe, I prepared batches of taco filling using Ground Boca Burger Recipe Basics, Morningstar Farms Burger Recipe Crumbles, Lightlife's Smart Ground, and Veggie Ground Round from Yves. The Boca crumbles taste grilled and are softer than the other products, a plus for some dishes, not for others. Morningstar's crumbles taste clean and mild; they go well in most dishes. Both the Lightlife and Yves products are closest to cooked meat in texture, which is useful when combining them with ground turkey or beef.

For predictably good soy dishes, settle on brands that please you, particularly for soyfoods you use regularly, like soymilk, tofu, and soy crumbles. After cooking with them a few times, you will know how they work.

To make sure each dish in *Amazing Soy* is outstanding, after developing a recipe, I always shared it. Some of the people I fed were ultra-fussy foodies. Other tasters regularly eat at McDonald's and Taco Bell, and their idea of cooking is to heat up a Weight Watchers or Lean Cuisine frozen entree. Some of them liked the idea of eating soy. Few did it on their own. I even dragooned people who openly disliked eating soy. Only when these tasters gave me thumbs up, and even took seconds, and told me their husband or children liked it, too, did I consider a recipe good enough to include here.

Global Soy

Tofu, miso, soymilk, and tempeh are the original soyfoods. All four originated in Asia, where there are still tofu shops as well as those making miso and tempeh, producing them traditionally, using only the heat from a fire, primitive forms of mechanical pressure where needed, and the natural process of fermentation in the case of miso and tempeh. Today, these ethnic foods are used around the world. We think of them not only for making authentic Asian dishes but also for tofu cheesecake and creamed soups.

Using Asian soyfoods in Western recipes was inevitable once they traveled outside Asian communities in America. If a Dominican missionary in the seventeenth century described tofu as "like cheese," it could hardly take long for the hippies of the 1960s to experiment beyond using it for stir-fries. And milk is milk, so why not soy white sauce? They also had earlier American models, in cookbooks like *The Soybean Cookbook* by Dorothea Van Gundy Jones (1963) with its vegetable soy soup, soy cheese croquettes (soy cheese being another name for tofu), and soy date bars.

The ultimate globalization of soy has been the creation of decidedly non–Asian foods, such as hot dogs, burgers, sour cream, breakfast cereals, and other dairy and meat ingredient imitators like ground meat, bacon, cream cheese, and ice cream. Now making a great bowl of hearty Texas chili, or decadent tiramisù using soy cream cheese is a reality.

The flexibility of what a cook can do with soy is as dazzling as the range of foods we get from soybeans. These soyfoods make possible a world of dishes, from Japanese miso soup to tiramisù and fajitas. You can use them to make an elegant, meatless pot pie or combine them with meat for a more healthful meat loaf. If you are constantly on the go, you will appreciate the quick dishes possible with soy that you can eat on the run. The four traditional soyfoods

Eastern Spirit, Western Style

Many of today's successful soy companies were founded by counterculture hippies in the 1970s and early 1980s. Wanting to create "right livelihood" that would support their belief in universal love, peace, and vegetarianism, they started out making tofu, tempeh, or soymilk.

As times changed and their customers matured, these granola-heads realized that to stay in business, they had to improve their product along with following their heart. Focusing their efforts, many of the companies that began with a mission to save the world and end world hunger, including White Wave, Lightlife Foods, and Eden Foods, have ended up among the most successful natural foods companies by giving the public what they want—palatable, familiar foods—while standing by their principles in making them natural, often organic.

are particularly adaptable. As you will see in the recipes that follow, tofu alone can take the place of poultry, meat, seafood, eggs, milk, cheese, mayonnaise, or fats in recipes from savory to sweet.

Tofu comes in four textures, and you can vary it further if you puree it, compact it into cutlets, freeze then crumble it into grainlike bits, fry it into chewy croutons, and much, much more.

Historic Soy

The soybean originated in China and spread from there to other parts of Asia, then to Europe, and finally, to the New World. Piecing together the picture from geographical, historical, and linguistic evidence, we think the soybean was probably domesticated during the Shang Dynasty (1700–1100 B.C.) in northern China. By the first century A.D., soybeans were cultivated widely in China and had most likely reached Korea. Soybeans gradually arrived in Japan and most of Southeast Asia, including Thailand, Vietnam, Burma, north India, Indonesia, and the Philippines, either traveling with tribes as they migrated or being transported along the Silk Road and other trade routes.

The earliest Europeans to visit Asia ate miso and tofu without making the connection between soybeans as a plant and as the source of these foods. Finally, Engelbert Kaempfer, a German who had lived in Japan, grasped their relationship. He even described accurately how to make miso in *Amoenutatum Exoticarum,* the book he published in 1712.

In Europe, soybeans were first cultivated in Holland and at the Jardin des Plantes in Paris in 1739, strictly for display as botanical specimens. In North America, however, Samuel Bowen, a seaman who had been to China with the East India Company and brought the first soybeans to the American colonies in 1765, saw their potential as food. He planted these beans at Greenwich, his plantation in Thunderbolt, Georgia, near Savannah, then proceeded to obtain a patent for inventions used to produce "vermicelli," soybean noodles, and soy sauce from them. In 1770, Benjamin Franklin sent soybeans from London to John Bartram in Philadelphia.

After this, soybeans were cultivated primarily as an Oriental curiosity in the United States until World Wars I and II spurred interest in them as a crop. Ultimately, by the 1970s we were growing 76 percent of the entire world's soybean crop. Today, many Asian countries buy seed from the United States.

Any history of soy in America has to mention the Seventh-day Adventists, who have been leaders in the use of soyfoods in America. "The first seven Caucasian tofu-makers in this country were Seventh-day Adventists," says William Shurtleff. "They were the first to do many things with soy." John Henry Kellogg's work making meat alternatives in the 1890s eventually led to the founding of Worthington Foods, the largest American company making these products. Ironically, Kellogg's, the food giant founded by John's brother to make breakfast cereals, now owns Worthington Foods, which produces Morningstar Farms meatlike products.

Genetically Engineered (GMO) and Organic Soy

In 2000, about 50 percent of the U.S. soybean crop was genetically engineered. This was nearly 10 percent less than the previous year's yield. It reflected some movement by major food companies, under pressure from the public, to use beans that are not genetically engineered.

These companies were actually following the lead of the smaller soyfoods companies, nearly all of whom oppose genetically engineered foods because they care about the health of our planet. These natural food companies led the demand for seed stock that is not genetically engineered. They also support public consciousness of this issue, which can help force the bigger companies to fall in line.

You can buy soy products made from non-GMO soybeans, including soymilk, tofu and some meat alternatives, like those made by Lightlife Foods and Yves Veggie Cuisine. If a product you like does not state on the label whether the beans it uses are non-GMO, call the company and ask, as some companies that do avoid the modified beans do not list this on the package. The list of soyfood companies (page 339) provides information for contacting them. Only if the public voices a continued preference for non-genetically engineered foods will companies make the effort to provide them, and to stay with the program.

For organic products, the industry shows an interesting split. Most soymilk, soy dairy products, and tofu are made with beans that are both organically grown and non-GMO. Makers of many other products are also offering products, from breakfast cereals to protein bars, from organically grown, non-GMO soybeans.

Meat alternatives are a different story. Most of these products use soy isolate, a concentrated form of soy protein. Not much of this bland powder is being made from organic soybeans because of the expense. People who care will have to make it clear to companies that

Organic Soybeans

There are products made using organically grown soybeans, although the product itself is not labeled "organic." This reflects the USDA regulation that 95 percent of the ingredients in a product must be organic in order to call the product itself organic. Products made using organic beans may claim their use in the ingredients list even if the other ingredients are not also organic.

they will pay the premium it takes to manufacture meatlike products using organic soybeans. (Many companies do use organic products for the other ingredients.)

Some major companies also use organic soybeans for other products, including General Mills for Sunrise Breakfast Cereal. The bottom line is that in nearly every category of soyfoods, there are brands offering the choice of organic ingredients. As the use of organic ingredients in products from mainstream companies increases, this will include soy.

Nearly every day some information about how soy benefits our health appears. Based on all the studies under way, we will keep learning how to gain from eating soy and how much is best. In the meantime, we are certain that eating soy, for its solid protein and as a healthful food, makes sense for most of us.

Nutritional Analysis

Gemini R&D, Version 6.6 (2001) from Estra Research, Inc., Salem, Oregon, was used to calculate the nutritional analyses for the recipes in this book. Calculations were based on a recipe's individual ingredients, using data from the United States Department of Agriculture (USDA) and manufacturers. Where information was unavailable, substitution of similar ingredients was made. Optional ingredients and those without a specific amount are not included. Where a choice is given, the first ingredient or size listed was used. The values for soy protein and other nutrients in soy products can vary from brand to brand; this information is intended as a guide.

ingredients and techniques

Here is a primer on the many soyfoods used as ingredients in cooking. Some can also be eaten as is, like cream cheese and baked tofu. Most are available at your supermarket and local natural foods store, including edamame, tofu, soymilk, miso, tempeh, and meat alternatives, as well as remarkable products to use for baking and desserts. This chapter discusses Asian soyfoods that are easy to use and add excitement to your cooking. These ethnic products are increasingly easy to find, thanks to the growing number of Asian markets and Internet sites selling ethnic foods. You will learn what these ingredients are and what you can do with them. In all, here is information on over thirty different soyfoods, including where to buy them and how to store them. When it matters, I suggest which brands are best.

Ingredients
Dairy Foods

Tofu does a nice job replacing eggs, cheese, and cream in recipes, but soy dairy products really lift the bar on what you can do in savory dishes, baking, and desserts. They help you to reproduce the creamy textures of dairy foods and some impart a similar, fresh, tangy taste.

Soy Cheese

Soy cheeses let you enjoy cozy macaroni and cheese, cheese-laden pizza, a chef's salad, or veggie cheeseburger without cholesterol. Many of them are lean, some are fat-free. If you are lactose-intolerant, they are a boon. Though good when eaten out-of-hand, they are fine for cooking.

Most soy cheeses contain casein, a milk protein that helps it melt. These are not dairy-free. There is vegan soy cheese, which gets soft but doesn't flow like real cheese when heated.

Flavor-wise, I recommend the Good Slice by Yves Veggie Cuisine, in all flavors. The Tex-Mex jalapeño and smoked cheeses from Soya Kaas are good in recipes. Lisanetti also offers good Cheddar. All soy mozzarella resembles white plastic, in my opinion. Lite & Less grated soy Parmesan from Soyco, though nothing like imported Parmigiano-Reggiano, is quite useful if you can't eat the original.

Soy cheese comes in wrapped, individual slices, blocks, and shredded. The sliced and shredded forms are worth using, since soy cheese is quite soft and hard to slice or grate. An ounce of shredded soy cheese produces a different volume than dairy cheeses do, and this can vary by brand, so go by volume in recipes, not by weight.

Cream Cheese

You won't reduce the fat in recipes by much if you use soy cream cheese in place of dairy cream cheese, but it is cholesterol-free and pareve (meaning, under Jewish dietary laws, it contains neither meat nor milk). It is one of the most useful ingredients around for dairy-free dessert-making. You can also combine it with regular dairy cream cheese to reduce the cholesterol in your favorite cheesecakes and blintzes. Soy cream cheese does not provide much soy protein benefit, but it adds the richness of true cream cheese to many dishes.

As a spread, soy cream cheese, which by law must be labeled "imitation cream cheese," is as good as most commercial dairy versions on bagels and sandwiches. In fact, it passed unnoticed by my godmother, who had no interest whatsoever in eating soy when I slipped it onto her toasted bagel.

There is tremendous variation of flavor and texture among different brands. Tofutti's Better Than Cream Cheese is excellent. Soya Kaas cream cheese was like rubber the last time I tried it. (Every soy company reformulates products, so dogs can turn into winners. Take a look occasionally at brands not recommended, as they might have changed.)

Soy cream cheese is highly processed and keeps as well as cream cheese.

Sour Cream

You can have fun using soy sour cream on tacos, in a baked potato, or in a dip. It enriches a stroganoff or paprikash nicely, too. Mainly a non-dairy substitute, it has little soy protein value. It is cholesterol-free but not fat-free (2 tablespoons add 5 grams of fat to a dish).

Soy sour cream can also replace dairy sour cream in baking, where it works well in muffins and cookie dough. However, in cheesecake, it can cause a grayish tinge.

I recommend Tofutti's Sour Supreme for the best flavor and texture.

This highly processed food keeps as well as dairy sour cream.

Dairy Creamer

Soy dairy creamer was created specifically to use in hot beverages. It gives dairylike richness to coffee and other drinks while adding a minimal amount of fat and no cholesterol. It is not intended for use in cooking. I have only used soy creamer successfully to make one dish, an exquisite creamed spinach.

Yogurt

Officially called cultured soy because it is not made from animal milk, soy yogurt demonstrates how well a soy dairy product can replace the conventional kind. Today's soy yogurt is beautifully creamy, contains live cultures, and comes in an array of flavors, from lemon (my favorite) to exotic apricot mango and rich cappuccino, as well as the berry flavors. Plain soy yogurt can be used in some cooking, as explained in the section "Cooking with Soy Yogurt." The only tipoff that a cup of luscious WholeSoy Creamy Cultured Soy or Silk Cultured Soy (the brands I prefer) are different from what you may be used to is a slightly more grayish color. In time, the manufacturers will probably fix that.

Edamame

It is hard to believe these lovable, mild-tasting green vegetable soybeans, nestled two or three beans inside each fuzzy pod about the size of a sugar snap pea, are the same as the dried, yellow soybeans used in making soymilk, tofu, tempeh, and other soyfoods. One reason for their sweetness is they are picked at the moment of full maturity and before they can start to dry out.

William Shurtleff, author of *The Book of Tofu* and *The Book of Miso*, likens edamame to fresh sweet corn. He says they should be rushed from the field to the pot, like corn, and boiled or blanched when they are at peak sweetness, before the natural sugars in them start turning to starch. Playing up this sweet taste, and to avoid the negative association Americans have had with soybeans, some American companies call edamame sweet beans or sweet soybeans.

For many of us, eating enough servings of vegetables every day is difficult. Since edamame can easily be added to salads, soups, and pasta dishes, or eaten out of hand as an appetizer or snack, they are an ideal way to eat your vegetables and add soy to your diet.

The Chinese have eaten edamame since the third century A.D., calling them *mao dao* or "hair bean," because of their fuzzy pods. By the tenth century, the Japanese were also eating green vegetable soybeans. They named them edamame, meaning branch beans.

When fresh edamame are in season, from late May to early September, the Japanese and Chinese eat them at least five times a week. In Japan, they are served in bars and at home as a snack accompanying a frosty beer. My friend Wangsheng Li, who comes from a town near Shanghai, recalls eating them as a snack, by the handful, and having them stir-fried with dried watermelon rind.

Most edamame are imported from East Asia. They are grown on Taiwan, in Mainland China, Thailand, and, more recently, Vietnam. According to Takuji Kimura, aka Edamame Dude!, who imports edamame, these crops are all non-genetically engineered. Farmers in Asia, he says, cannot afford to buy the more expensive seed stock, even if they were interested

Fresh Edamame

You may find fresh edamame at farmers' markets, mainly during the summer months. They should be sold as whole plants that were pulled from the ground, with their roots on. This keeps the plants and their beans moist. When the stalks are cut, the plants loose moisture quickly, so that within a few hours the beans are not as sweet and tender.

in them, which they are not. For them, flavor is everything, and they use only the time-tested varieties that they know grow best in their fields. These produce the biggest, sweetest beans, which Asians harvest by hand, so they will not be bruised.

Buying and Storing Edamame

Supermarkets, natural foods stores, and Asian markets all sell edamame, in the pod and shelled. Some are organically grown. Refrigerated edamame in plastic containers are cooked and ready to eat. Frozen edamame sold in bags have been blanched, so they need only a few minutes in boiling water. In my experience, the beans imported from China are bigger, plumper, and sweeter than edamame grown elsewhere. This includes those sold at farmers' markets. A number of brands offer frozen organic edamame, including Seapoint Farms and Cascadian Farms.

Meat Alternatives

Soy products imitating meat should be called speedy soy because of the time they save. Many are already cooked and can be added to a dish toward the end, just in time to imbue them with flavor and heat them through. Other products benefit from being crisped or need enough time to soak up deeper flavor.

Many of these products are fat-free and kosher. All are cholesterol-free. Those sold in natural food stores are generally made with non-GMO soybeans. (Check with the manufacturer as this is not always indicated on the label.)

These meatlike products can ease the transition from eating meat to following a vegetarian diet. Simple to cook with, they help you make dishes that feel more authentic, hence more satisfying, than if you used chopped tofu in, say, chili. These meatlike choices are particularly popular with children, because they let them eat like their friends at a cookout, and with people just cutting back on or giving up meat, because they seem familiar.

Meat alternatives are made from soybeans processed until nearly all that is left is their protein. Reading the ingredients, you will notice similarities in the combination of soy protein, soy protein concentrate, textured soy or vegetable protein, and soy protein isolate used in most of them. The primary difference among these high-tech, highly processed foods is the level of soy protein they contain, between 70 and 90 percent. Other common ingredients in soymeat products are wheat gluten, the protein in wheat, which adds chewiness, egg whites, and yeast for flavoring.

While soymeat alternatives are generally protein-rich, you must read the label attentively. In some products, soy may account for only 6.25 grams of their protein, with the rest coming from wheat, eggs, and sometimes cheese.

These products have so much in common, yet are so varied in appearance and texture. That is where art and technology meet. Each is the result of different degrees of heat and pressure, applied in different ways. Some are extruded, much like dry pasta. Others are made from soy spun into fibers, then bunched together to resemble the muscle of animal meat. This variety of forms makes soymeat useful in a remarkable variety of dishes, where it can stand in for ground meat, chicken cutlets, kebabs, sausages, and more. When converting a non-vegetarian recipe, simply pick the form of soymeat closest to the cut of meat called for in your recipe.

Soy Crumbles

Resembling browned ground meat, this meat alternative is cooked and ready to turn into meat loaf, tacos, chili, sloppy Joes, and homemade burgers.

The main choice you face when buying crumbles is between those in a refrigerated vacuum-sealed plastic pouch and those sold frozen. Frozen crumbles are smaller, firmer, and browner than the refrigerated brands. The refrigerated ones are more tender, ruddier, and more easily blended with meat in recipes, particularly in a 50/50 chili or meat loaf. Boca's soy crumbles have a pronounced grilled taste. Morningstar Farms soy crumbles taste meaty in a clear, neutral way. Some brands offer Italian and Tex-Mex flavored crumbles, which taste artificially seasoned. Soy crumbles are much improved when you enrich their flavor by browning them with seasonings (see page 43).

Refrigerated and Frozen Soymeats

My favorite soymeats are made from spun fibers. Veat's Gourmet-Bites, Nuggets, and Fillet are prime examples. What you can do with them is amazing, in stews, as kebabs, in Asian dishes, and in Western sautés. In recipes, I refer to these as frozen soymeat. All they need is brief cooking and they soak up great flavor easily. Other soymeats, including meatballs, chicken-like cutlets, and sausage (breakfast links and patties, pepperoni for pizza, and amazing chorizo), are truly heat-and-eat. There is also crisp bacon, soft tempeh bacon, and lean Canadian bacon rounds. The bacon bits sprinkled on salads are made from soy as well.

Burgers, hot dogs, and cold cuts made from soy are other popular meat alternatives. Many of the tenders and burgers are remarkable. If you can work them into a Parmigiana, by all means do. I do not yet like any of the franks and do not cook with them, even sliced in soup or baked beans. Cold cuts are the other soymeat I refuse to eat until they are a lot better tasting. But if you need sandwiches for school lunches, they are adequate buried in with lettuce, tomato, and mayonnaise. And you can be certain that new, improved versions are in the works.

Textured Soy Protein (TSP)

These dry, kibbled bits have been around for decades, mainly used like ground meat in chili, pasta sauces, and other dishes. I have found some interesting new ways of using this rather old-fashioned form of soy, including as a crunchy topping for yogurt and cereals. Larger pieces of TSP, imitating meats and chicken, go into stews, soups, and kebabs like Tanya Petrovna's Rockin' Moroccan Skewers. For the size that makes kebabs, I like SoSoy+, sold in natural food stores.

Only a few companies make this highly processed soyfood, including Archer Daniels Midland (who owns the trademark for TVP) and Cargill. They sell it to other companies. Most of it is used in making prepared foods. For cooking, it is usually sold in bulk, and you have no way of knowing whose product you are getting.

All sizes of TSP, from the small, kibbled bits to big chunks, keep for a year, in a tightly sealed container in a cool, dry place. Some sources, including The Farm in Summertown, Tenn., and Dixie Diners Club (see Sources, page 339), sell various sizes, intended to imitate meat and poultry cut in different ways. They also offer it flavored, though I think it best to add your own seasonings in the course of cooking.

Miso

Thanks to recipes using miso as a marinade and in seasoning pastes for grilled foods, we are getting to know this savory, fermented bean paste as more than the main ingredient in miso soup. While it is the body and soul of this classic soup, which many Japanese sip every day, it is also indispensable in dengaku, grilled tofu topped with a miso paste, which has been served in Japan since the 1600s. The Japanese use miso in many other dishes as well, primarily for seasoning. And oh, what flavor it adds, to everything from stews and sauces to salad dressings and desserts.

When people ask me about miso, I describe it as soy sauce squared—or even cubed. If soy sauce offers a trio of brightness, salt, and yeasty flavor, miso is a culinary orchestra, offering a profound harmony of complex flavors, including evanescent top notes, a sweet or dry body that lingers, and unique grace notes. Miso also adds a creaminess and body to the texture of dishes. Finally, it offers health benefits, both as a fermented food rich in enzymes that aid digestion and as a soyfood containing protein, which soy sauce and tamari do not.

Miso is a blend of soybeans, grain, salt, and *Aspergillis orzyae*, a benevolent mold. It ranges in color from creamy ivory and pale yellow to soft ochre, burnt sienna, and earth-black. Often compared to peanut butter in texture, miso can be dry and pasty, moist and smooth as apple butter, crumbly as potting soil, or nubbly with bits of bean and grain. In flavor, miso ranges from decidedly sweet to meatlike with coffee or cocoa notes. The layers of flavor, the result of fermentation, are what make miso an ideal enrichment in meatless dishes, where it instantly adds the kind of depth a good stew develops only after it has simmered for hours.

When produced the way it has been for centuries in Japanese farmhouses and miso shops, where it is allowed to ferment as nature takes its course, no two batches of miso are alike. Their differences come from the specific qualities of the soybean crop in a given year, the specific qualities of an equally variable crop of grain, usually barley or rice, and the variations of temperature and humidity that take place while enzymes from friendly bacteria are busy digesting the sugars in the soybeans and grain. This is not true of industrially manufactured miso, where artificially controlled temperatures and careful monitoring assures uniformity as well as faster fermentation than by the traditional method.

Miso has qualities that let it take the place of both wine and butter in cooking. Darker misos have the layered flavors you get when cooking with wine. Miso does not taste like butter, but mashed into potatoes, carrots, and other root vegetables, a light miso makes them creamy and imparts a satisfying richness, without fat. Miso also adds a delicate glaze to carrots and pearl onions. A tiny bit of miso, no more than a teaspoon, adds winelike notes in fruit desserts such as apple cobbler.

When cooking with miso, keep in mind that the paler ones taste sweeter and less salty, while darker misos are saltier and more intense. For example, sweet white miso, almost ivory in color, contains only 5.5 percent salt, while chocolate-dark Hatcho miso contains 10.5 percent.

When buying miso, it helps to know that among all those tubs and jars, there are three major families of miso and more than a dozen varieties. The chart on page 19 gives an overview of them.

The kind of grain used determines the family a miso belongs to. Rice (komé) miso is made with rice and soybeans. Barley (mugi) miso combines barley and soy. Hatcho miso contains only soybeans.

Often, the name of a miso relates to the prefecture or town where it was first made, as in Sendai or Hatcho miso. The amount of time it has fermented is also a factor in defining what variety it is.

Rice miso is most common. In Japan, 80 percent of miso varieties are made with rice. The one you see most often is red (aka) miso. It is made using white rice. Aged for six to twelve months, it is salty and a bit tart. Rice misos range in color from pale reddish to dark brown, and in texture from moist and soft to dry and firm.

Brown rice is another popular variety in the rice family. Made with whole-grain brown rice, it is usually fermented for up to eighteen months. It tends to have some texture because

Salt and Miso

Salt is an important ingredient in miso. It slows down the rate of fermentation, so the yeasts and bacteria have enough time to do their work. One tablespoon of Hatcho miso contains 750 milligrams of sodium, while the same amount of table salt contains over 7,000 milligrams of sodium. In fact, miso contains little enough sodium that I usually find myself adding a bit of salt to finished dishes made with miso, because they still need the lift that only salt can give.

Certainly, people who must restrict their sodium intake should not cook with miso. If sodium is not a problem, remember that miso also contains beneficial enzymes and other micronutrients.

COMMON KINDS OF MISO

Made with	English Name Variety	Japanese Name(s)	Description	Flavor	Aging Time	% Total Protein	% Salt
Soy only	Hatcho miso	Hatcho miso	Chocolate brown Dry, dense	Mellow, slightly tart	1 to 3 years	21.0	10.6
Soy and barley	Barley miso	Mugi miso	Dark reddish brown Nubbly	Rich, salty earthy	1 to 3 years	12.8	13.0
Soy and barley	Mellow barley miso	Mugi miso	Yellowish to russet brown Nubbly	Rich, subtly sweet	10 to 20 days	11.1	10.0
Soy and rice	Red rice miso, brown rice miso	Aka, genmai, Sendai miso	Pale red brown to russet Moist	Rich, deep, salty tangy	6 to 12 months	13.5	13.0
Soy and rice	Mellow red miso	Aka miso	Yellowish red	Deep, semi-sweet	3 to 6 months	11.2	13.0
Soy and rice	Mellow beige	Tanshoku miso	Tan to yellow	Light, semi-sweet	5 to 20 days	13.0	7.0
Soy and rice	Mellow white	Shiro-koji miso	Light beige Moist, velvety	Rich, mellow	4 weeks	12.3	9.1
Soy and rice	Sweet white	Shiro, saikyo, Sendai miso	Ivory to yellowish white, Velvety	Light, rich, winey	1 to 4 weeks	11.1	5.5
Soy and rice	Light yellow	Sinshu, Akita miso	Light yellow Smooth, creamy	Tart and salty	1 to 2 years	19.6	12.5

Adapted from *The Book of Miso* by William Shurtleff and Akiko Aoyagi (Ten Speed Press)

of the bran from the unpolished rice. I particularly recommend the Sweet Tasting Brown Rice Miso from South River Miso Company.

Other rice-and-soy varieties range from beige to almost ivory, including mellow beige, which is actually somewhat sweet, and sweet white, reminiscent of fruity white wine. These are called quick misos because they ferment for only five to twenty-eight days. This brief fermentation leaves more of the natural sugar in the beans and rice. Their lighter flavors go especially well in dips, dressings, and dishes made with white beans. Try mashing a teaspoon of any of these pale misos into a hot baked potato; it makes the potato creamy as well as delicious.

More rustic barley miso is rich-tasting and earthy. It is aged for one to three years, except for quick mellow mugi miso, which is made in just ten to twenty days. Barley misos go well in chili and other red bean or lentil dishes. I also like it for flavoring gravy, though the small bits of barley in it mean you may want to strain the gravy before serving.

I am particularly fond of Hatcho miso's dry, astringent flavor. This is the miso reminicent of coffee and cocoa beans. It also contains 21 percent protein, nearly double that of most other forms of miso.

Most miso is made by first innoculating rice or barley with mold spores, making *koji*.

A Venerable Age

The age of a miso is determined by the number of calendar years it has been left to ferment. Hence, Hatcho miso set to ferment in autumn of 2000 and packaged in the spring of 2002 would be considered "three-year miso," although it may have spent only sixteen to eighteen months fermenting. Probably, this way of marking the age of a miso derives from the Asian practice of adding a year to a person's age each New Year.

A more ancient way of setting its age is by counting the summers it has seen. This custom relates to the fermentation process. The bacteria and enzymes in miso are active only during the hot summer months. During the chill of winter, miso goes dormant. (This is important. The long rest during months of cold weather help kill off any bacteria and enzymes not beneficial to miso.) Based on this alternation of active fermentation and dormancy, a one-year miso could be as young as six months or it could be as old as fourteen months.

Miso and Health

With so much focus on the benefits of eating soy protein, which miso helps to augment when added to dishes, forgetting its other virtues is easy. The enzymes in miso, produced by yeasts, lactobacillus, and other microorganisms, perform a function similar to those in yogurt. They can aid in digestion.

In holistic circles, miso is valued as an alkalizer, supposedly counterbalancing the body's tendency to acidity, and thereby increasing resistance to disease. Some people also feel it cleanses toxins from the system, including everything from nicotine to radiation.

To benefit from these aspects, miso must be unpasteurized. When you cook with it, the food must not be allowed to boil, at which point the bacteria will be killed and enzymes inactivated.

This cultured grain is, in turn, used to innoculate soybeans, starting the process of fermentation. For Hatcho miso, a part of the soybeans are cultured instead.

Today, true Hatcho miso, dense and dry enough to cut with a knife, is made by only two Japanese companies. Both are located on a riverbank in a town near Nagoya, in central Japan, on Eight Street, or *Hat-Cho*. Hatcho miso is considered very yang, or warming, in macrobiotic terms. For this reason, Japanese expeditions have carried it to sustain them and fortify them against the cold on six forays to the South Pole.

Until you have some experience with miso, I recommend buying it in a natural food store, where the miso is usually good and naturally made. The products they carry will have English names, which are often descriptive, like mellow white miso. In Asian stores, where there is usually little or no English on the label, you can buy miso by color—light, medium, or dark—but you have no way of knowing if it contains preservatives, bleach, or additives like riboflavin, used for coloring. On the other hand, miso clearly labeled as organic is being sold in a growing number of Asian markets.

Miso sold on the shelf is usually pasteurized. Hatcho miso is the one exception, because it contains enough salt and too little moisture to spoil.

For all other miso, including refrigerated packages, check the label to see if it has been pasteurized. This is done to commercially made miso in order to kill the live bacteria so they stop giving off gases that could eventually make the package explode. Unfortunately, this high heat process also inactivates the enzymes left by the bacteria.

Live miso must be kept refrigerated. If it is in a pouch or plastic tub, you can transfer it to a glass jar with tight-fitting lid. Stored this way, miso keeps for at least a year. When you need some miso, use a clean spoon to dip out the amount you want. This avoids introducing bacteria that can contaminate the miso and make it spoil. Most likely, though, refrigerated miso will fade in flavor long before it spoils.

Pasta

I have found two brands, so far, of dry semolina pasta made with enough soy flour to provide 6.25 grams of soy protein in a serving. One is Eddie's, the other is sold at Trader Joe's. They are like any good semolina pasta, though the one from Eddie's has a "bite" more like imported Italian dry pasta. Both come in several shapes. You could not find a nicer way to eat soy.

Protein Powder, Baking Mix, and Flour

I am a pushover for warm muffins in the morning. Later in the day, homemade cakes, pies, and good bread are equally enticing. *Good* is the essential word. "Good, considering it is healthy," won't do. Working with soy protein powder, soy baking mix, and soy flour, I have arrived at a great result in sweet and savory baking, including pizza dough and breads rich in soy protein. Making the right choice among these three forms of soy, then using them in the right proportions is key. Once you get it right, as you will with these recipes, you can successfully add soy to your own favorite muffins, scones, and pancakes, as well as cakes, cookies, pizzas, and yeast breads.

Protein Powder

Soy protein powder is mostly soy protein isolate. A fluffy, beige powder, it is almost tasteless and 90 percent soy protein. Generally used for making drinks, one portion can pack 25 grams of soy protein into a delicious smoothie.

The Health Benefits of Soy Protein Powder

Soy protein powders are easily 90 percent isolated soy protein. One serving, around 1 ounce for most brands, is enough to add 20 to 25 grams of soy protein to a smoothie. It provides 43 to 100 milligrams of isoflavones. Some also contain calcium.

Since a serving of protein powder provides the entire 25 grams of soy protein that may reduce the risk of heart disease, and probably enough isoflavones to ameliorate symptoms of menopause and to help avoid osteoporosis, why not just use a scoop a day?

No one yet knows if the benefits of using this "silver bullet" approach will turn out to differ from those of eating whole soyfoods. It is your call whether you want high-tech efficiency or the natural benefits soy-eating cultures have enjoyed for centuries, just from whole soyfoods.

For baking, avoid powdered soy drink mixes. Flavored, sweetened, and containing texturizers, including guar and other gums, sweeteners, cellulose, rice flour, or other ingredients, they are best used in recipes created by the manufacturers. Lecithin, bromelain or papain (both enzymes), and isoflavone concentrate do not affect baking results.

If you rub a bit of soy protein powder between your fingertips you will notice a slight grittiness. For most baking, the finer the texture the better. Iso-Rich Soy Concentrate Powder from Jarrow Formulas, Inc. is particularly fine. I also use the soy protein powder Whole Foods sells in canisters and in bulk, and the one from Trader Joe's. They both produce good results.

Soy protein powder is good to use in cookies, muffins, and cakes.

Baking Mix

Soy Baking Mix, sold at GNC stores, is a boon for bakers. It produces excellent results in recipes where soy flour and protein powder is not as good. This mix looks similar to protein powder but has a finer texture. (Think of it as the cake flour of soy baking.) It contains soy protein isolate, soy flour, wheat bran, and a number of other ingredients.

Soy Baking Mix is particularly good for light cakes, brownies, and more refined cookies, as well as pancakes and some muffins.

Flour

Soy flour is made from soybeans that have been dried, hulled and split, and finely ground. It is gritty and has a pronounced flavor. It is good for some baking, particularly breads, crackers, and pizza.

Soy flour contains no gluten. It comes in full-fat (4.5 grams per ¼ cup) and de-fatted versions. Arrowhead Mills and Bob's Red Mill soy flours are most commonly found in natural food stores and some supermarkets. Both are full-fat soy flour. De-fatted soy flour is much harder to find. It can be ordered from The Baker's Catalogue (see page 339).

Because of the oil in it, full-fat soy flour is best stored in the refrigerator or freezer.

Canned and Dried Soybeans

The yellow and black soybeans sold canned and dried taste entirely different from edamame. The Japanese call them *daizu,* meaning "powerful beans." These whole soybeans, canned or dried, were off my list of edible soyfoods until the black ones came along. Their texture, somewhere between that of velvety black turtle beans and the hard slipperiness of yellow soybeans, is good in chili, stews, and chunky soups. After Eden Foods came out with canned black soybeans, I also found them dried, to cook from scratch. Shiloh Farms offers them in one-pound bags at natural food stores and you can mail order them from Phipps Country.

Canned black soybeans look more like buffed mahogany, particularly those from Westbrae Naturals, while dried black soybeans hold their color during cooking. But like other dried soybeans, they take a long time to cook, up to 3 hours, after overnight soaking. So consider using a pressure cooker or canned beans.

Recently, I tried canned yellow soybeans, after avoiding them for years. The problem has always been a kind of slimy texture when you chew them. However, well-seasoned, as in Beans and Franks (page 230) or pureed in Southwestern Bean Spread (page 106), they were good. I even included the flavorful gelled bean juice from the can. However, I use only black soybeans in salads and as a vegetable.

Eden Foods and Westbrae Natural offer black soybeans in 15-ounce cans. They are organic, not genetically engineered, and good. Store the unused part of a can, or leftover cooked dried soybeans, as you would any other beans.

Soymilk

Today's soymilk, creamy and smooth, pleasantly rich, and somewhat sweet, is a success story two thousand years in the making. Visit an Asian food store and sample it as it began, the milky liquid squeezed from dried soybeans that have been soaked, ground, and cooked. This soymilk has a pronounced beany flavor, which Asians like, whether drinking soymilk hot in the morning or chilled at other times.

In the soymilk at your supermarket and natural food store, the beany flavor is gone, thanks to technological advances, particularly since 1966, when scientists at Cornell University discovered the enzyme responsible for the beany taste in soymilk. This led to develop-

Nutritional Differences Add Up

If you read the Nutrition Facts panel on containers of soymilk, you will discover significant variations in protein content and a huge difference in the amount of sweetening used. Currently, the protein in an 8-ounce serving of full-fat plain soymilk ranges from 6 grams in Silk Plain to 11 grams in WestSoy SmartPlus. The sugar content varies from 4 grams in Silk Plain to 10 grams in Zendon. Flavored soymilks can contain up to 28 grams of sugar a serving as in Zendon's Chocolate. (Any of these may change as companies refine their formulations.)

More than in tofu, taste matters with soymilk, particularly when it is used on cereal and in smoothies. Differences among the many brands are so noticeable, and preferences so personal, that my tasting panel ranked nine brands among their top two choices for plain soymilk out of eighteen brands sampled. So, with one glass of soymilk a good way to get more than a third of your soy protein when your goal is 25 grams a day, I recommend testing brands on cereal, or however you prefer to consume it. You are sure to find one you will enjoy.

ment of a natural process for manufacturing better-tasting soymilk. Then manufacturers added natural sweeteners and thickeners to make the soy liquid feel like milk in your mouth. Burgeoning soymilk sales prove how effective all this work has been. From 1992 to 2000, sales of soymilk increased roughly 350 percent.

Soymilk is one of the most useful ingredients in the soy pantry. It often replaces cow's milk seamlessly in recipes for savory dishes and desserts, and it is good on breakfast cereal. Using it in cooking is just a matter of choosing the right type of soymilk.

Soymilk comes in regular, low-fat, and fat-free versions, as well as in plain and flavored versions. Low-fat soymilk simply contains more water. This reduces both the fat and the protein per serving.

Soymilk . . . Is It Now Better than Cow?

Soymilk might be better for you than cow's milk and other dairy milks. An 8-ounce glass starts helping you reduce your risk of heart disease, provided it contains at least 6.25 grams of soy protein, as many of the brands available today do. Of course, you still need to exercise, keep your weight under control, and lead a generally healthy lifestyle to benefit fully from what soy offers.

The isoflavones in soymilk are what scientists think may help reduce the risk of cancers in men as well as women. A plant form of estrogen milder than what our bodies produce, isoflavones are also helpful in protecting against osteoporosis. They do this by slowing down the rate at which calcium is drawn from our bones. They also help provide some women with relief from hot flashes and other symptoms of menopause.

Calcium-fortified soymilk provides the same amount of this essential mineral as the other milk, i.e., roughly a third of the USDA's Recommended Daily Value per glass. (Check the label; most but not all soymilk is calcium fortified these days.) In addition, soymilk contains no cholesterol or saturated fat. People who are lactose-intolerant are usually comfortable using soymilk and the other soy dairy products.

If you are used to drinking cow's milk, switching to soymilk may require an adjustment. Start off blending them together in equal parts. Then gradually increase the proportion of soymilk until you are comfortable with the soy.

Fresh and Unrefrigerated—What's the Difference?

Putting soymilk in a milk carton and selling it from the refrigerated dairy case was the turning point for widespread acceptance of soymilk. This refrigerated soymilk seems more appealing, yet in the blind tasting I conducted, the top three choices from most of the panel came in shelf-stable boxes. Since we all assumed before the tasting that milk we saw as "fresh" would taste better, this was quite a surprise. In reality, it is not very different from the soy milk sold in aseptic boxes.

Full-fat soymilk is about equal in fat to reduced-fat cow's milk (2 percent). All soymilk is cholesterol-free. Often, it is enriched to contain the same amount of calcium as cow's milk, along with folate, B_{12}, and other vitamins and minerals. Some soymilk now also contains live cultures, such as acidophilus.

Unsweetened soymilk contains only soybeans and water. When the package says plain, regular, or original, the soymilk contains some kind of sweetener; brown rice syrup, malted barley, and raw cane crystals from sugar cane are most common. There will also be a thickener, probably carrageenan or xanthan gum, and some oil.

Vanilla and chocolate are the most popular soymilk flavors. There is also mocha, chai, coffee, cappuccino, strawberry, and not-nog, with other possibilities to come. These more elaborate flavors make soymilk attractive as a beverage, although more so on cereal, in desserts and other dishes, than to drink by the glass.

For use on cereal and in smoothies, buy the soymilk with the taste and texture you like most, regardless of whether it is refrigerated or shelf-stable. Refrigerated soymilk has a shelf-life of approximately 3 weeks before it is opened. If you have a large family and want to buy in quantity, perhaps when the brand you like is specially priced, aseptically packaged, boxed soymilk has the advantage of not requiring refrigeration until the package is opened. It will keep in the pantry until the expiration date stamped on the carton, up to two years from the time it is produced.

Once they are opened, all soymilks keep for about the same length of time, from 5 to 10 days, depending on how cold your refrigerator is, how often the milk is taken out, and so on.

Soynuts

Soynuts are a great snack that allows you to munch soy anytime, anywhere. At the rate they are showing up everywhere, I fully expect a flight attendant to hand me a bag in midair some day soon.

High in protein and fiber, but also fat, soynuts are dry roasted. They come in flavors, like potato chips, and are combined in trail mix blends. You can also use them to make your own combinations.

Little round whole soynuts are roasted in the hull. The halves have been hulled before roasting. Toss the soynuts on top of salads and eat them out of hand.

Soynut Butter

Jars of roasted soynut butter look like peanut butter. Like peanut butter, many brands are mixed with sweeteners, emulsifiers, and stabilizers. The natural ones, made of just nuts and oil, separate; they must be stirred well. Soynut butters can be chunky or smooth, with or without salt. Some are sweetened with honey.

Soynut butter is fine on sandwiches. For a new twist on peanut butter and jelly, try blending it with a sweet miso and using orange marmalade. You can use it to replace peanut butter in Asian recipes, like peanut sauce, but most brands are more dense and slightly gritty compared to peanut butter. They also have a noticeable soy flavor.

There are many brands, and taste in this product is individual, so go with the one you like best.

Soy Sauce

One of the most familiar and widely used soyfoods, soy sauce can be an appealing, naturally brewed condiment made from soybeans, wheat, sea salt, and koji, a culture containing the same *Aspergillis orzyea* used in making miso. Or it can be a nasty-tasting brew made with hydrolyzed vegetable protein, caramel color, corn syrup, and preservative.

Good-quality soy sauce, rich in amino acids and glutamic acid, a natural flavor enhancer, is fermented in wooden kegs for a year or more. The chemical stuff is cooked up in 24 hours. Besides looking at the ingredients listed on the label, you can tell the good from the bad in soy

The Amazing SoyaCow

Thanks to ProSoya Inc., a food technology company located in Canada, the SoyaCow is helping to meet the global need for high-quality protein, especially in Russia and third-world countries where the land will not support dairy cows or people are too poor to keep them.

The milk from the SoyaCow, like any other soymilk, contains protein as nutritionally complete as that in meat and dairy products. But the beans it uses require less than 10 percent of the land and other natural resources needed to produce meat and dairy foods.

This "cow" is actually a machine weighing about 200 pounds. Small enough to sit on a table in the most cramped kitchen, it takes in whole soybeans, processes them, and gives good-tasting soymilk. In two 8-hour shifts, one of these cows can turn 175 pounds of soybeans into more than 600 quarts of soymilk.

One SoyaCow costs about $3,200 for developing countries (the price is higher for small businesses that might wish to use it here in the U.S.). This patented invention, created by Raj Gupta, ProSoya's president, is part of his effort to help alleviate world hunger.

In the year 2000, about 1,000 SoyaCows were at work in thirty-five countries worldwide, providing needed protein. If you would like to help by contributing a SoyaCow to a third-world country, or by making a contribution toward one, email gupta@prosoy.ca or write to ProSoya Inc., 2–5310 Canotek Road, Ottawa, ON Canada K1J 9N5.

sauce by vigorously shaking the bottle. The foam that forms lasts up to 15 minutes in good quality soy sauce. It dissipates quickly in inferior ones.

The Japanese produce five types of soy sauce, two of them well-known outside Japan. Shoyu is made with soybeans and wheat. It tastes lighter and sweeter than tamari, which is made with just soybeans. Originally, tamari was a by-product of miso making. Earthier and more intense than shoyu, it is useful for people who cannot eat wheat.

Kikkoman, the most popular brand of shoyu, is naturally brewed. The company also makes a reduced-sodium soy sauce.

Mostly the Chinese use light, or thin and dark, or black soy sauce. The stir-fries in this book use the thin kind. Japanese shoyu works fine in its place. Dark soy sauce, which is thicker and sweeter, is used in stews and other hearty dishes. In Chinese markets, you will find other kinds of soy sauces as well, but they are used less often. Stores selling Southeast Asian foods offer still more types, including syrup-thick Indonesian kecap manis.

Sodium content is an issue with soy sauce. One teaspoon contains 333 milligrams of sodium, the same amount of table salt contains 2360 milligrams. If you must restrict your salt intake, avoid soy sauce or make judicious use of those with reduced sodium. Soy sauce does not figure in decisions on soy and health because it is not a rich source of soy protein or the isoflavones that may offer health benefits. Mostly, it is useful in cooking with soy because its meaty and rich savory flavors help make dishes appealing.

Tamari can be added at the beginning, shoyu when dishes are almost done, because the bolder flavors of tamari hold up well during cooking while simmering drives off volatile compounds that give shoyu its complexity.

Because of these compounds, it is preferable to buy smaller bottles of soy sauce more frequently. Store it in a cool place; refrigeration is not necessary.

Tempeh

Tempeh is the soyfood that most naturally resembles meat. It is also the most exotic soyfood. Tempeh was first made in Java, perhaps more than one thousand years ago. The Dutch discovered it there when they colonized Indonesia in the 1600s, and they were the first to describe how it is made. During World War II, many prisoners of war in Indonesia owed their lives to tempeh.

Today, tempeh-making is still a simple process. The beans are partially cooked, the hulls removed, and the split beans are innoculated with *Rhizopus oligosporus* spores. Formed into inch-thick cakes and spread out on trays, the mixture is incubated in a warm, moist place for about 24 hours. When the beans are bound together in a slab by mycelium, threads that form during fermentation, the tempeh is ready to cut and use. This process is a bit like aging cheese, except with tempeh, a benevolent mold transforms the soybeans rather than wheels that started as milk. In fact, tempeh vaguely resembles brie made from soybeans. Freshly made, the supple cake of pale beige beans is enrobed in and interwoven with mycilia, the cottony white threads spun by the *Rhizopus oligosporus* mold that are reminiscent of the downy rind on a fresh brie. However, a cake can also have grayish patches of mold. Since tempeh is a living food, these patches may darken over time.

Making tempeh remains a cottage industry for the most part. Check around and you may find a natural foods restaurant or store making their own tempeh. The process is virtually the same when big companies like White Wave and Lightlife make it. The main difference is that they seal the inoculated beans in plastic bags that hold the 8-ounce cake. After fermenting in the bags, the tempeh is blanched or frozen to retard further fermentation without killing the active enzymes.

The clear presence of edible mold leaves uncooked temepeh with an image problem. This ugly duckling of soyfoods is a great, healthy, interesting food. When I catered parties, nearly everyone enjoyed the tempeh dishes I served, particularly the meat eaters. The fact that tempeh offers as much as 21 grams of soy protein in one serving should add to its appeal, along with the fact that it is naturally fermented and minimally processed.

In savory dishes, temepeh is almost as versatile as tofu. It is good grilled, sautéed, braised, and pan-crisped or fried. It is excellent in stews, salads, curries, chili, pasta sauces, loaves, and pâtés, as well as served as burgers and kebabs.

Croutons made of tempeh are good to keep on hand. They turn any salad into a protein-rich dish.

Some tempeh is made entirely from soybeans. More often, it is made from a combination of soy and one or more grains, frequently brown rice, wild rice, millet, barley, or quinoa. For flavor, other ingredients may also be used, like sea vegetables, sesame seeds, or dehydrated vegetables. Tempeh containing several kinds of grain tastes milder than those made only from soybeans, or soybeans blended with rice. Lightlife's Three Grain Tempeh and White Wave's Five Grain Tempeh are two mild-tasting tempehs.

Soy tempeh contains the most protein per serving of any soyfood, about 21 grams in a 4-ounce serving. Adding grains can reduce this to 12 or 13 grams of protein, not all of it from soy. At about $1.75 for an 8-ounce package that serves two to four people, this high-quality protein is an amazing value.

Soybeans are naturally rich in oil, so one serving of tempeh contains 5 to 10 grams of fat. All of it is unsaturated and cholesterol-free. For me, this fat makes tempeh a sustaining cold-weather food, perfect to enjoy like a thick chop after skiing or in chili on a raw, blustery day.

Tempeh is sold in 8-ounce vacuum-sealed packages. It keeps well in its original package. You can freeze it this way, and it will keep for months. Once opened, any unused portions should be wrapped in plastic and refrigerated. It will keep for 5 days or longer.

Black and even blue mold spots do not mean tempeh is spoiled. Signs of spoilage are reddish mold, sliminess, or the smell of ammonia.

The best tempeh I ever had is made by Tanya Petrovna, who uses it in her Native Foods restaurants in California. It is soft and supple, and has a nutty, mild flavor. You can order it from her (see Sources, page 345).

Tofu

The first time I tasted tofu, in the form of soft, custardy cubes floating in a bowl of steaming soup, I was eight years old. It was 1953, and even at The Great Shanghai, a Cantonese restaurant near Columbia University in New York City whose customers included students of Chinese culture, the most adventurous non-Asians, like my parents, ordered tofu. When the waiter explained that the ivory, delicate-tasting "Jell-O" in my soup was made from the milk of a bean, not a cow, I was enchanted.

Today, tofu is found everywhere, from delis to supermarkets. Most stores offer it in several textures, from fragile, custardlike silken to dense extra firm. Natural food stores have an even greater selection, including various textures in several brands, plus a host of flavorful baked and smoked choices.

Making Tofu

Visit the San Jose Tofu Company (175 E. Jackson Street, San Jose), and you will see a tofu-master making tofu as it has been for nearly two thousand years. Working alone in this small, Spartan tofu shop, he soaks and grinds yellow-beige soybeans, boiling them in a steaming cauldron over an open fire. Then he ladles the hot mash into a long cloth bag, which he suspends from a hook until the white milk drains out. Next he adds the coagulant and vigilantly observes, waiting to stir the curds with a long paddle at just the right moments, until they are precisely the right size for *momen* tofu. Then, moving rapidly, he scoops the creamy curds into handmade, cloth-lined wooden forms. He then sets precisely fitted, weighted covers over the soft, wobbly curds. When they reach the density he wants, in about 30 minutes, he turns the pristine blocks of warm tofu into a huge sink overflowing with cold water. As a customer waits at the small counter at the front of the shop, he cuts one of these ivory blocks into roughly one-pound cubes, and sets one into the plastic box the customer hands over to him, brought to carry home her daily tofu.

What Is Tofu?

Tofu is soymilk coagulated through the addition of mineral salts and the addition of heat. To make custardlike silken tofu (*kinugoshi* in Japanese), the coagulant is blended with the hot soymilk, which is allowed to set like yogurt. This refined form of bean curd got its name from actually being strained through silk, to make it as smooth as possible. In Japan, artisanal tofu shops still produce *kinugoshi* this fine.

For the soft, firm, and extra firm kinds of tofu (called *momen* in Japan), after the coagulant is added, the milk is stirred until it separates into curds and water that is like whey. The curds are poured into large, cloth-lined stainless steel boxes with holes and pressed to extract more water. The amount of water removed determines the firmness of the tofu. This process is so much like making cheese that many producers use stainless-steel boxes modified from cheese-making. Finally, the tofu is cut into blocks, sealed in a tub or plastic pouch, and pasteurized.

Making the Right Choice

At the store you find fresh tofu in water-filled tubs labeled silken, soft, firm, and extra firm, as well as aseptic cartons of tofu, also labeled soft, firm, and extra firm. There is also tofu called enriched, "lite," and fat-free. Which one should you buy? It all depends on how you plan to use the tofu, which means successfully pairing its texture with your recipe.

Silken tofu is generally used for dressings, soups, sauces, smoothies, and anything else that is creamy. It gives cheesecake and other desserts texture as smooth as the finest chef's pastry cream.

Soft tofu is more suited to spreads. It can replace eggs in a quiche or soft cheese in manicotti and other baked pasta dishes.

Firm tofu is best for most stir-fries, stews, sautés, and other savory cooking, including kebabs for grilling. Avoid using it for any kind of puree or spread.

Extra firm is what I call Westernized tofu because non-Asians like its hard, dry texture. It can be used in most dishes where firm tofu works; however, I prefer pressing firm tofu to further compact it (see page 49) because extra firm tofu often has a grainy texture that feels pasty in your mouth.

Confusion comes in because the tofu sold in boxes is always silken tofu; whether it is labeled soft, firm, or extra firm, *all* of it is silken.

The soft tofu sold in boxes is equivalent to the silken tofu sold in tubs from Nasoya, Azumaya, Hinoichi, and other producers. Use it, pureed, in dressings and desserts. The firm boxed tofu is halfway between tofu and a kind of gel. Besides being pureed, it can be sliced or chopped for salads, and firmed to use in hot dishes, either by blanching (see page 49) or baking (see page 50). Extra firm silken tofu can be stir-fried, sliced, and pureed.

I like the refrigerated silken tofu in tubs because of its cleaner, whiter color and fresher taste. It is also easier to get out of the package and to keep when using less than an entire package.

For what is lost in texture, I do not think the calories saved using reduced-fat and fat-free tofu are worth the difference. Mori-Nu's full-fat silken tofu has only 2.5 grams of fat per serving in soft, the same as Nasoya's fresh silken tofu. Mori-Nu extra firm tofu has 1.5 grams of fat in one serving.

There is also enriched tofu, made by adding soy protein isolate to boost the protein and isoflavones content. It is denser and slightly gritty compared to other products, so see how it works for you.

Smoked and Baked Tofu

Comparing these flavorful, almost meaty forms of tofu to a block of basic white is like comparing a barbecued chicken to an uncooked breast. In fact, pieces of this tofu even look like miniature, rectangular roasts.

Commercially made baked and smoked tofu are similar in all but flavor. Both are marinated and then either baked or hot smoked, which firms the tofu even more. Beyond the distinctive flavor imparted by smoking, the main difference is the highly flavored brown "crust" on the outside of the baked tofu.

White Wave, Nasoya, and a host of smaller companies make baked tofu. Each produce it in a number of flavors. If you are on the West Coast, look for smoked and baked tofu from Wildwood Natural Foods and Tofu Life. These two small companies make particularly delicious products. Good as they are, though, nothing beats tofu you bake or smoke yourself. Both are simple to make, as I explain in Techniques.

Using baked or smoked tofu is as easy as slicing or dicing it. Add it to any green salad, stir-fry, and the Salad Handroll (page 185).

Asian Tofu

Visiting an Asian market can feel like entering Ali Baba's cave for an avid cook. For soy, in particular, there is a trove of new forms, especially tofu, each a treasure to be taken home and sampled. There is fried tofu in various shapes and densities, from bubbles light enough to float in soups to bricks meant to be sliced and heated in stews, and ivory sheets of tofu as thin and supple as the pasta used for making lasagne.

Thanks to the burgeoning number of Asian communities around the country, more people than ever can get to an Asian market, perhaps even one of the enormous superstores like the Ranch 99 markets scattered around California. You can wander for hours in them, lost in a world of bakery cases filled with lavender, crème-filled rolled cakes made with taro; tanks of live, two-foot-long geoduck clams; heaps of spicy Thai basil; and many of the soyfoods used in Chinese, Japanese, Korean, and Filipino cooking. (Indonesian tempeh is about the only major soyfood these stores do not carry.)

If you think of tofu as mild and bland, I dare you to try fermented bean curd, ripe as Limburger cheese, which is sold in jars at Asian markets. If, on the other hand, you appreciate tofu's subtle side, then you must sample warm *dofu*. Ethereally delicate, this custardlike fresh tofu, also known as *dofu-fa*, the flower of the tofu, is quintessential comfort food. In Chinatown, tofu shops sell this warm tofu, or you may come across a street vendor ladling this humble specialty out of a deep pot, to be taken home in pint and quart containers, accompanied by salad dressing-size plastic cups of flavoring syrup. In fact, one way of locating a source for this unique bean curd is to look around in midafternoon, when women and school children line up to buy several containers of it at a time and take it home for a sustaining snack. It is also served at some Chinese restaurants, usually as part of the dim sum menu.

I have found this special silken tofu in California's Asian supermarkets, refrigerated, in yogurt-like quart containers, its cup of syrup taped to the top. The best one, made by a Vietnamese company in Orange County comes in a yellow container with red lettering. Reheated in the microwave, it is as good as any I have bought on the street, freshly made. While this tofu is quite perishable, it keeps for about 48 hours, becoming progressively denser and like conventional silken tofu as wheylike water floods out of it.

Chinese Tofu

In general, Chinese tofu is firmer than what you find in Japanese markets. The red-cooked kinds are super dense.

Basic Tofu: These 3-inch square tofu pillows are sold fresh, from a water-filled pail, or packaged in a plastic tub. This is the basic tofu used in Chinese cooking. Its texture is between that of Western-style soft and firm. It can be diced or sliced for stir-frys, added to soups and salads, or squeezed and crumbled to use in Western lasagne or a scramble.

Bean Curd Skin and Noodles: This is a whole family of items. It includes refrigerated fresh, beige tofu sheets folded like dish towels, and the huge, round, dried sheets resembling translucent plastic used in making Bok Choy with Soft Soy Sheets. Some of these sheets are a form of tofu. Others are a skin that forms on the top of hot soymilk. The soft, fresh sheets can be sliced and served with a red pasta sauce or finely cut and used in soup. The dried ones, softened in water, may be wrapped around a mushroom filling to make mock duck. There is also fresh bean curd skin that looks like short, fine noodles. It comes plain and red-cooked. Another choice is dried tofu skin cut in fine shreds, which needs to be rehydrated. These all might be used in a slaw or other salad, but you will have to experiment some to make them work.

Dessert Tofu: This silken tofu is sweetened and flavored. Dessert tofu comes in a plastic tub. It should be heated in the microwave before serving. It is lovely served with canned fruit salad.

Fermented Bean Curd (red and white): This cubed bean curd in jars, in brine or chile-flavored sauce, is a potent, strongly fermented product. It is best left to Asian cooks who know what to do with it.

Fried Tofu: These are puffy, hollow, golden balls and cubes that are light and chewy. They can be added to stir-fries and soups, or cut in half and stuffed, then fried. They are good bathed in the tomato-flavored sauce of Smoky Southwestern Stew (page 213). This tofu is sold in bags, from the refrigerator case.

Pressed Tofu: These 3-inch by ¾-inch slabs of tofu are sold in plastic bags in the refrigerator case. Dense and dry as plaster, it is best left for Asian cooks who know what to do with it.

Red-Cooked Tofu: These dark, mahogany squares come in various sizes, from 3-inch to 1-inch "chips." Simmered in soy sauce seasoned with star anise, they are mostly used in dishes like shredded pork with garlic chives. They can also be diced and added to Western-style bean soups, tossed into fried rice, or very thinly sliced and used in salads. They are sometimes spiced with red pepper. They are sold in a plastic bag, refrigerated.

Red-Cooked Baked Tofu: This tofu is hard to distinguish from the softer-textured red-cooked tofu that is not baked. Hard and dry, it is best used in Asian dishes. It is sold in a plastic bag, refrigerated.

Silken: Packaged in a plastic tub, silken tofu can be pureed to use in Western salad dressings, soups, and desserts.

Tofu Powder: Sold in boxes, like gelatin dessert, tofu powder is a dry mix, like instant powdered milk. It is used to make soft *dofu* at home.

Japanese Tofu

Japanese tofu is softer than what is sold in mainstream stores for Western cooking.

Yakidofu (Broiled Tofu): This dense, firm, grilled tofu sold in a tub has a pleasant baked flavor and dark marks from the grill. It is excellent in Western recipes. Slice and grill, bake, or smoke it. Use it as you would firm tofu.

Momen Cotton Tofu: This is the regular tofu we are used to, though usually softer. It comes in a tub. It is good in Western-style dishes.

Agé (Deep-Fried Tofu): This comes in many forms, including *atsu-agé* (inch-thick cakes or triangles). Boiled briefly to remove some oil, it is pleasant cut into pieces and added to hot soup and stir-fries. It is sold in vacuum-sealed plastic, refrigerated.

Koya Dofu (Freeze-Dried Tofu): Using this snow-dried, dehydrated tofu requires experience. Save learning about it for a trip to Japan. It is not refrigerated.

Aburagé (Fried Tofu Pouches): These are stuffed with rice, as a kind of sushi. They are also sold as long bars, to be sliced, and as a flat sheet of tofu that looks like a rectangular omelet. Cut it into strips, blanch, and add it to broth. Aburagé comes in plastic vacuum-sealed packages, refrigerated.

Ganomodoki: These deep-fried tofu balls and patties contain chopped vegetables. They are blanched and added to stews and casseroles.

Pureed Tofu: This comes in a fat plastic tube, refrigerated and ready to use in any dressing or dessert recipe. Due to its beany taste, I recommend it only in highly flavored dishes.

Kinugoshi (Silken Tofu): This custard-like tofu comes in tubs and in aseptic boxes. Use it like any silken tofu. The fresh *kinugoshi* made by Global Tofu, sold in the New York City area, is perhaps the best commercially made silken tofu I have tasted. Chefs like Todashi Ono at Sono Restaurant use it. The kind with only Japanese on the box is whiter and milder tasting.

Buying and Storing Tofu

As perishable as chicken or meat, tofu should be handled similarly. Boxed tofu does not need to be refrigerated. Only buy all other tofu where it has been kept properly refrigerated. The

To this day, we do not know who actually discovered the miracle of transforming soymilk into something more solid, enduring, and useful. Speculation is that bean curd may have been created around 164 B.C. by Lieu An, a Chinese scholar interested in alchemy and Taoist meditation. Possibly he drew on cheese-making techniques known from India and Mongolia. It is also possible that he accidentally added sea salt to a cooking pot of ground dried soybeans and water, causing the thick soup to coagulate into curds, then realized that these curds could be drained and pressed into firm cakes. At any rate, the first concrete evidence of tofu is a kitchen scene found incised into a mural in a Han tomb in northern China. Dating from about A.D. 220, it clearly depicts the preparation of both soymilk and tofu.

Domingo Ferruindez de Navarrete, a Dominican missionary in China, in *A Collection of Voyages and Travels*, published in 1665, was the first Westerner to specifically mention tofu. He wrote: "I will here . . . mention the most usual, common and cheap sort of food all China abounds in, and which all men in that empire eat, from the emperor to the meanest Chinese, the emperor and great men as a dainty, the common sort as necessary sustenance. It is call'd teufu . . . They . . . make great cakes of it like cheeses. All the mass is as white as the very snow. It is eaten raw, but generally boil'd and dressed with herbs, fish, and other things. Alone it is insipid, but very good so dressed and excellent fry'd in butter. They have it also dry'd and smok'd, and mix'd with caraway-seeds, which is best of all."

one exception I make to this rule is in Chinatown, where a number of tofu shops sell tofu that is rarely more than 24 hours old, and is kept chilled in fresh water.

Get the tofu home and refrigerate it promptly, as you would dairy or meat products. When handling tofu, take care to avoid cross-contamination if you also cook fish, poultry, or meat. I keep a separate, small cutting board just for cutting tofu and other soyfoods.

When draining, pressing, or marinating tofu, do not let it sit out more than an hour. Making room for it in the refrigerator may seem like a nuisance, but it is better than practicing poor culinary hygiene.

Bean There . . .

The term "bean curd" was first used by Emil V. Bretschneider, writing in the *Chinese Recorder and Missionary Journal*, in 1870.

In 1965, when the Library of Congress tried to change its subject heading from "Bean Curd" to "Tofu," disputes over how to write this Japanese word in Roman letters were resolved by staying with bean curd, the common term at the time.

In 1985, the Library of Congress finally changed its subject heading to "Tofu," virtually ensuring it as the official name.

What's in a Package?

Have you noticed that a package of tofu can vary from 8 to 19 ounces? Tubs and refrigerated vacuum pouches contain 14 to 16 ounces of tofu, while aseptic boxes contain 12 or 12.3 ounces. Differences in weight often occur even with the same manufacturer. Nasoya, for example, packs 19 ounces in their tubs of silken tofu; 15 ounces in the tubs of soft, firm, and extra firm tofu; and 14 ounces in their tubs of enriched firm tofu.

To eliminate confusion, the recipes in this book give the amount of tofu needed in ounces or in cups. Fortunately, tofu is kind to the cook. Do not give another thought to the differences among 15-, 16-, and 19-ounce packages; unless the recipe indicates the precise amount, a few ounces won't make a difference to the final dish.

Packages of smoked or baked tofu usually contain two or four squares. The packages range in weight from 6 to 12 ounces. This product keeps well, especially before its vacuum-sealed plastic pouch is opened, so when it is on special, stock up. (Freezing will make it spongy and quite chewy, which is nice in a stew or soup.)

Once opened, unless it is in a resealable package, smoked or baked tofu should be transferred to a plastic bag or small, tightly sealed container. Stored this way, it will keep for 3 to 4 days.

Yuba

Besides soymilk, plain tofu, and miso, Asians use a variety of other soyfoods. Most of them are sold only at Asian food stores. For one of the most popular, the Chinese and Japanese heat soymilk, then lift off the thin skin that forms on top of the steaming liquid. The Japanese call the slightly rubbery sheet of soy *yuba*. Fresh, it can be cut into noodlelike strips. Frozen or dried, then moistened to reconstitute it, in Chinese cooking it is wrapped like phyllo around a mushroom filling, then simmered in a broth with soy sauce and star anise, making chewy mock duck.

Techniques

If a recipe calls for an ingredient from an animal that moos, bleats, baahs, oinks, or cackles, there is probably a way to use soy in its place. Because of the quirky particularity of soyfoods, doing this successfully involves selecting the right soyfood and using it in the best way for the recipe. Recipes created for soy are the best way to start. Then, as you get good results, you will enjoy the same success slipping soy into your own favorite recipes. Here are tips for cooking with soyfoods that require some specialized techniques or understanding.

Cooking with Dairy Foods

Sour Cream

In cooked dishes, add this non-dairy product toward the end and avoid boiling it. Though it's flavor is less tangy than that of dairy sour cream, muffins, cakes, and cookies made with it can be quite good.

Yogurt

Plain soy yogurt can be used in salad dressings and dips. It is also good in Indian raita. It does not work well in hot dishes; it loses its body and turns liquid because the natural gums and starches used to thicken it do not stand up to heat. Plain soy yogurt is less tart than dairy yogurt, so it works more successfully in some savory dishes than others.

When using this yogurt in salad dressings, draining improves its texture. Use a yogurt cheesemaker or line a strainer with a sheet of paper toweling. Add the yogurt and set in the refrigerator for at least 2 hours, and up to 24 hours. Dressings made with soy yogurt should be used soon after they are made, as they thin out more quickly than with dairy yogurt.

Cooking with Edamame

Everyone loves sucking edamame from the pod, and you will probably serve them most often boiled in their shells. For snacking, both the Chinese and Japanese boil them in salted water.

(Edamame were originally cooked in sea water, according to Elizabeth Andoh, an American writer living in Tokyo.)

To eat edamame from the pod, bite on one end of it and press the other end with your fingers, squeezing the plump beans right into your mouth. It is more like snacking on popcorn than eating a protein- and fiber-rich vegetable.

If you grow or buy fresh edamame, it is necessary to remove their fuzzy coat before cooking them. The best way to do this is in a *suribachi*, a Japanese mortar with flared sides.

Place a handful of edamame in the *suribachi* and sprinkle them liberally with kosher salt. Using your hands, not the pestle, which would bruise the delicate beans inside the pods, rub the edamame against the grooved surface until most of the fuzz has been removed.

If you do not own a *suribachi*, place about ½ cup of edamame in a plastic bag. Add 1 tablespoon kosher salt. Rub the pods vigorously in the bag, and then rinse them in a bowl of lukewarm water, scrubbing them with a vegetable brush. Rinse again.

To enjoy edamame that taste as good as those served in Japanese restaurants, do *not* follow the cooking instructions on bags of the frozen beans. They produce bland, flat-tasting beans.

To cook 1 pound of fresh or frozen edamame in the pod, bring 4 quarts of water to a boil. Add 2 tablespoons kosher salt. Add the edamame and cook 5 minutes. The beans will still be slightly crunchy but just right when cooled. Drain the beans. Spread the hot pods out on a baking pan or cookie sheet in one layer. Cool by fanning them vigorously with a sheet of cardboard, or set them near an electric fan or air conditioner until they are room temperature, 4 to 5 minutes. *Never* rinse the pods under cold water to cool them after cooking. This makes the beans taste watery and it washes off the salt.

Frozen shelled edamame should be added to dishes close to the end of the cooking, allowing about 5 minutes for the beans to defrost and cook. This also keeps their texture firm. If you are using them alone, add to boiling salted water, cook for 5 minutes, and drain.

Like lima beans and favas, edamame have a skin holding together the two cotyledons inside each bean. Some chefs pop the cooked beans out of this skin if they are going to puree them. Fortunately, few dishes require this refinement. If one does, see if you can get children to do the work, or settle down in front of the television to do it.

Cooking with Meat Alternatives

Soy Crumbles

Soy crumbles are much improved when you enrich their flavor. This process takes about the same amount of time as browning ground meat. It infuses them with great taste that is easily suited to the dish they will go into.

Enriched Soy Crumbles

Makes 3 cups

2 teaspoons canola or olive oil

½ cup finely chopped onion

½ teaspoon salt

1 garlic clove, minced

12 ounces refrigerated soy crumbles (1 package) or 2 cups frozen

1 cup mushroom broth or beef broth or ½ cup red or white wine, or beer

1. Heat the oil over medium-high heat in a skillet. Add the onion, sprinkle with the salt, and sauté until the onion softens, about 4 minutes. Add the garlic. Cook, stirring, until the onion is translucent, about 1 minute more.

2. Mix in the soy crumbles. Add the liquid. Cook until most of the liquid has boiled off and the soy mixture is almost dry, 8 to 10 minutes. Use immediately, or cool and refrigerate in a tightly sealed container for 2 to 3 days. This mixture can also be frozen.

Frozen Soymeat

To use frozen soymeat in your own recipes, you may need to do some adapting. For a curry or salad, sear the defrosted pieces until brown and crisp, using oil or cooking spray. For fajitas, pan-grill them, as the intense heat of a real fire dries them out. In stews or paella, they go in near the end so as not to turn mushy.

Most recipes have you rehydrate TSP with water. I use only broth or a marinade, or add the soy to a moist dish while it is cooking, so it soaks up the flavorful juices. Despite what other recipes may recommend, do not cook this soy protein a long time; it will turn mushy.

Cooking with Miso

The main technique for cooking with miso is creaming, blending it completely with a bit of liquid. This step is essential before adding miso to any large quantity of liquid, otherwise it may not dissolve. In hot liquids, it will ball up, hardly dissolving at all.

To cream miso, place it in a small bowl. A custard cup is good for working with 1 or 2 tablespoons of miso. Add 1 or more tablespoons of liquid from your recipe. This could be dipped from the pot, when you are making soup or a stew, or use the vinegar in a salad dressing. Only skip this step, adding the miso along with the other ingredients, if you are using a blender or food processor to make a dressing, soup, or sauce.

If you enjoy cooking Japanese food, you may have a *suribachi*. This slant-sided bowl lined with concentric ridges is where Japanese cooks cream miso, grinding it against the ridges to break up any bits in it.

As chefs are discovering, miso has affinity for certain Western ingredients. It goes particularly well with tomatoes, root vegetables, winter squashes, and various kinds of fish, including salmon, cod, and Chilean sea bass.

Americans, using the some-is-good, more-is-better principle, often overdo the amount of miso added to dishes. My general rule of thumb is not more than 1 tablespoon per serving in a dish, although you should rarely add more than ¼ cup miso to any dish, unless it serves eight or more.

Miso is usually added to a dish at the last minute. Whether in a hot stew or cold dip, the compounds that are part of miso's distinctive flavor are as volatile as those in wine. They evaporate after a few hours and are driven off during long cooking, just as with fresh herbs. This still leaves the body of flavor, but some top notes are gone. As all rules have exceptions, in Japanese and other Asian cooking, many dishes using miso call for boiling it. Follow the recipe, or add the miso later, as you prefer.

To "refresh" a dip or other miso dish, before serving leftovers, blend in a bit more miso, to bring back the lost volatile flavors.

Baking with Soy Flour, Protein Powder, and Baking Mix

Bread and pizza doughs made with soy flour are tackier than those made with wheat flour, even sticky. And the more you work them, the stickier they get.

Soy flour colors more quickly than wheat flour, so expect a darker color in the finished product. Some items, like Lemon Loaf (page 67), will be quite dark without being at all burned.

To avoid burning, particularly when the batter or dough is moist and needs time, use air-cushioned baking pans and cookie sheets. Definitely use light-colored pans.

To convert your own recipes, one or two tries will probably show which kind of product to use, and how much of it can replace part of the wheat flour. Statements in some cookbooks that you can use up to 50 percent soy flour do not tell the whole story.

As a general rule, 2 tablespoons of soy flour, protein powder, or baking mix can replace an equal amount of wheat flour without noticeable effect. Beyond that, the texture may get denser and you may need to adjust the amount of liquid, as well as other ingredients.

Soy baked goods come out incredibly moist. For muffins and scones, this means they are still good the next day. Quick breads, like the Lemon Loaf, and cookies will keep for days.

I like most soy baked items when they are fully cool, and even the next day, as their texture settles down. When they cool, soy muffins and cakes have a nice contrast between a denser outside and tender, moist center.

If you do not have an air-cushioned cookie sheet, using two regular ones stacked one on top of the other produces similar results.

Not all soy baked goods freeze well. Muffins and quick breads may be soggy when defrosted. But fresh items will keep for as long as 5 days in a dry place, wrapped in foil or plastic wrap.

Cooking with Soymilk

Unsweetened soymilk is useful in cooking. Certainly, in soups and other savory dishes, sweetening is unnecessary, even undesirable. In desserts, it's best that you control the sweetness yourself. The thickeners in many soymilks may also create problems. Still, there are exceptions: sweetened and flavored soymilk is perfect for Espresso Panna Cotta and its Pistachio Sauce.

Color is another variable in soymilk. Products range in color from an ivory white to beige. For drinking and on cereal, color may not matter, but in cooking, it can affect how a finished dish looks. A broccoli soup or cream pie made using a beige milk is not appealing.

If your favorite soymilk brand is more tan than cream colored, you might try a different kind when making a recipe.

Cooking with Tempeh

The main consideration in cooking with tempeh is complementing its definite flavor and particular texture with the other elements in a dish. For example, tempeh croutons are good on a green salad or in a dense green pea soup, but I would not add them to a thin, mild broth.

An 8-ounce cake of tempeh can be cut into burger- or chop-size 4-ounce slabs. It can also be sliced, cubed, or chopped, depending on how you plan to use it. When finely chopped, it tends to crumble.

Tempeh needs to be cooked. In fact, some cooks steam it before they start with the method called for in a recipe. (This softens the tempeh and makes it milder tasting, but I find it unnecessary.) I like to treat it like meat. Often, I marinate it first. Then, I usually sauté, sear, or brown it before taking the next step.

Sealing the surface of tempeh gives it an appealing crusty quality. It also adds attractive color and brings out the mushroom-yeasty flavor of tempeh in a nice way.

Although it is dense, when tempeh is baked in a marinade, as with tofu, it soaks up the flavor all the way through. You can then grill or cook it in any way you like. I particularly like using Spicy Tofu Marinade (see page 53) and making Lemon Grill Tempeh (see page 249), which uses a tangy lemon and garlic marinade.

Smoking Tempeh

Smoked tempeh is magnificent. It is not made commercially, so you will have to smoke your own. Use the same method as for smoking tofu (see page 53). Smoked tempeh keeps for weeks in the refrigerator, months in the freezer. I grill or pan-sear it for burgers, add it to stews, and crisp it to use like bacon bits on salads (see page 181).

Cooking with Tofu

I think many people who dislike tofu would change their minds if they viewed it as an ingredient rather than a food to just slice and eat or add to a dish without some preliminary preparation. This may seem like heresy. "Isn't tofu an ultimate convenience food?" you ask.

When it is already marinated, baked, or smoked, yes. Otherwise, think of plain tofu as the meatless white meat, or, like James Terman, vice-president of marketing at White Wave, Inc., view a block of tofu "as a 5-pound bag of flour." In other words, treat it like an unfinished, "raw" food, like a chicken breast.

Just a little culinary attention removes tofu's raw, mushy, and crumbly qualities, making it far more appealing. It eagerly accepts flavoring when the right technique is used. Changing its texture before adding it to a recipe is simple, too.

There are more than a dozen ways to improve tofu's texture. Some involve cooking; nearly a half-dozen do not. Those that do often improve its flavor at the same time.

Many ways of altering tofu involve drawing off some of its moisture. Compacting it, as in pressing out water, makes tofu nicely chewy and smooth. Heating it, to evaporate out water, firms it as well, while retaining its custardlike texture. The heating also brings out a pleasantly

---

Measuring Tofu

Since packages of tofu can contain 8, 12, 14, 16 ounces or more, how do you get the right amount for your recipe?

To measure soft, firm, or extra firm tofu, cut the block into pieces equal to the amount your recipe calls for. Most often, this will be one-half or a quarter of a package. If not, just eyeball the block to measure the amount to cut off. Being off by an ounce or so will not affect most recipes.

For silken tofu, the firm and extra firm textures sold in a box can be slipped out and cut, too. Spoon softer silken tofu into a measuring cup, using the kind for measuring dry ingredients. Since this tofu has the same volume before and after it is pureed, measure it either way.

Should you want to measure silken tofu by ounces, a tablespoon equals ½ ounce, a quarter cup equals 2 ounces, and a cup is 8 ounces. This holds for pureed silken tofu, too.

sweet quality. Some of these techniques are used in combination with others, such as pressing and marinating. Some are suited to one or more particular types of tofu. The thing to do is try each technique once. You will probably prefer a couple of them, and proceed to ignore the rest.

Draining

Removing some of the water from silken and soft tofu produces rich-textured desserts and dips. It makes soft tofu more firm and even-textured, though this method leaves it less chewy than pressing (see page 49).

For silken tofu, first pour off any water from the surface of the bean curd. Then, jiggle it by tilting the open container around; this makes sure chunks do not stay behind when you invert the container. (This is not necessary for soft tofu.) Hold a large, fine-mesh strainer in one hand. With your other hand, invert the tub over the strainer, so the tofu drops into it.

Set the strainer over a bowl. Place it in the refrigerator for 1 to 2 hours, until 3 to 4 tablespoons of liquid accumulates in the bowl. Draining silken tofu longer than this produces a puree that is faintly grainy and "oily" in the mouth.

Silken tofu should be pureed immediately once it has been drained. It can then be stored for up to 48 hours before using. Soft tofu will keep several days after draining. Covered with water in a container, it retains its firmer texture.

Squeezing

Squeezing small amounts of tofu in your hand gives it a texture like cottage cheese or scrambled eggs. Use this technique on soft tofu before scrambling it, and in recipes where the tofu is used like ricotta cheese as in Eggplant Manicotti (page 223) or as a binder in Crab Cakes (page 280).

To squeeze tofu, break or cut a 16-ounce block into about 16 pieces. Gently squeeze one piece of the tofu at a time in your fist, holding your hand over the sink or a bowl. (Depending on the size of your hand, you may be able to manage a larger amount.) For scrambled tofu, squeeze out about a third of the water. Crumble the tofu into a bowl, making it resemble large-curd cottage cheese. To make it like ricotta cheese, squeeze out about half the moisture, using enough pressure that some of the tofu comes out on the sides of your hand. It should resemble small-curd cottage cheese. Use immediately.

Pressing

Pressing makes soft, firm, and extra firm tofu appealingly chewy and smooth. This mechanical compacting eliminates the crumbliness you may dislike, turning slabs of bean curd into springy cutlets and steaks. I press tofu before marinating and grilling it or cutting it up to use in stir-fries, salads, and stews.

Many people wrap tofu in paper towels when pressing it. I find this wasteful, since even several layers of towels do not absorb enough of the moisture. (Do blot tofu with paper towels before frying it; this helps to minimize spattering.)

To press tofu, stand a block of it on its side, on a clean cutting board, setting it at roughly a 45-degree angle leading away from you. Slice the tofu vertically into two equal, inch-thick slabs.

Lay a piece of plastic wrap or foil on a cutting board to cover it. This prevents the tofu from picking up possible bacteria or the taste of other foods.

Arrange the two pieces of tofu, long sides together, in the center of the board. Cover them with a piece of wrap or foil. Lay another cutting board on top of the tofu, centering it. Weight the tofu until its sides curve slightly—two or three large cans of tomatoes work well. (I use two cast-iron skillets, one inside the other, or one skillet with cans set inside it.) Arrange the weight evenly or the pressed slabs will be wedge-shaped. Check after 10 minutes or so to make sure the weight has stayed evenly balanced. Press the tofu for 30 to 60 minutes.

To let the drained water run into the sink, position one edge of the cutting board at the edge of the sink. Slip a mayonnaise jar cap or other small object under the opposite side, creating a gentle slope. If you do not have two cutting boards, or if you want to catch the water without pressing the tofu near the sink, use a platter large enough to hold both pieces of tofu, in one layer, plus a cutting board set over them.

Pressed tofu will keep, in a tub of water, tightly covered, in the refrigerator and remain compressed. Depending on its freshness, if you change the water every day, it can keep for 3 to 4 days.

Blanching

This rapid method gives silken, soft, and firm tofu a fresh, slightly sweet taste. It also firms the texture. I recommend it for tofu to be used in dips, dressings, soups, stews, sautés, and casseroles. Blanch tofu shortly before you will use it.

To blanch up to 19 ounces of tofu, boil 6 cups of water in a pan. Add 1 teaspoon salt. Take the pan off the heat. Add sliced or cubed tofu. Let it sit for 3 to 5 minutes, less time for silken, more for firm tofu. Gently drain the tofu into a colander or scoop it out with a strainer. If desired, put the tofu in a bowl of cold water to cool it. Drain on paper towels. To blanch more than 19 ounces of tofu, increase the amount of water and salt.

Quick-Firming and Pan-Crisping

Faster than pressing, these techniques remove the raw flavor of silken, soft, firm, and extra firm tofu. They add color and more pleasing texture. Quick-firmed and pan-crisped tofu are good in stews, casseroles, and salads.

For quick-firming, set a nonstick skillet over medium-high heat. When the pan is hot, 1 to 2 minutes, add sliced or cubed tofu in one layer, leaving ½ inch between the pieces. Cook until water bubbles around the edges of the tofu and you see steam. Reduce the heat to medium. Cook until the tofu is just lightly colored and all the moisture has evaporated, 4 to 5 minutes, turning it once. (If you like, coat the pan with nonstick cooking spray before heating it, or add 1 teaspoon of oil to the hot pan before the tofu. This bit of fat gives the tofu a richer taste.) This tofu will keep, tightly covered in the refrigerator, for 48 hours.

For pan-crisping, proceed as above, but coat the pan generously with nonstick cooking spray or use 1 tablespoon oil. Cook the tofu until it is golden and slightly crusty, about 4 minutes, before turning it. Do not reduce the heat. Cook until golden on the second side, or all over for cubes, 4 to 8 minutes. Pan-crisping gives tofu a richness and definitely chewy quality.

Oven Firming

Deborah Madison recommends this technique, in addition to cooking tofu in a skillet to firm it. It comes in handy when you need the top of the stove for other cooking. It is also a way of firming a couple of pounds of silken, soft, firm, or extra firm tofu. It both improves the flavor of the tofu and makes it springy.

Preheat the oven to 375°F. Lightly coat a baking sheet with nonstick cooking spray or oil. Arrange sliced or diced tofu on the baking sheet in one layer. Bake until the tofu releases water, about 10 minutes. Drain off the liquid and return the pan to the oven. Continue baking until the tofu feels nicely firm when pressed with your finger, 10 to 15 minutes.

Freezing

After it is defrosted, frozen extra firm, firm, or soft tofu is like a chewy sponge. It is ready to soak up the flavor in sauces, soups, chili, and pasta dishes because the freezing process draws out most of the water.

Crumbled defrosted tofu is close in texture to grains and chopped meat. Defrosted sliced tofu can be glazed with sauce and baked or added to casseroles.

Some people toss unopened packages of tofu into the freezer. Others freeze tofu uncovered, for at least 24 hours, then wrap it. I open and drain the tofu, then wrap it in plastic wrap and freeze it. These blocks keep for months. They take up less space than the whole package and defrost more quickly, too.

To freeze sliced tofu, arrange the slices in one layer on a baking sheet covered with plastic wrap, leaving ½ inch between slices. Freeze, covered with wrap or foil. Once frozen, store the slices in a plastic bag.

Defrosting tofu in a bowl of lukewarm water gives it a springier texture than defrosting it on a plate in the refrigerator or letting it defrost at room temperature. When it has defrosted, squeeze the tofu gently to eliminate the water remaining in it.

Pureeing

Pureed silken and soft tofu is used in dips, dressings, toppings, and desserts in place of yogurt, sour cream, mayonnaise, or eggs. Sometimes the tofu is drained or blanched before it is pureed.

Place the tofu, drained or directly from the package, in a food processor or blender. Whirl until smooth. For 1 cup or less, a mini food processor or blender works best.

To avoid pureeing small amounts of silken tofu, I generally whip up at least 1 cup, measure what I need, and store the rest in the refrigerator, to use in a day or two.

Pureed tofu will keep, in a tightly closed container in the refrigerator, for up to 48 hours. It thickens when cold. Stirring thins it right out.

What to Do with Half a Package

After opening a tub or box of tofu, if some is left over, store it in water in a sealed container. One way is to almost fill a resealable quart-size, freezer-weight plastic bag with water. Drop in the tofu, and seal the bag. (I use filtered water, for taste and safety.) Set the bag in the refrigerator. Change the water daily. Depending on how recently the tofu was manufactured, it may keep for a week, though the sooner it is used, the less beany it will taste. (Look at the sell-by date on containers of tofu and buy packages with the latest date.)

If you come across a tofu corral, buy one for tofu leftovers. This is what I call the plastic reusable box I bought at the San Jose Tofu Company, in San Jose, California, where customers bring their own containers to take home the freshly made tofu. It has a tight-fitting cover and a liner inside with holes in the bottom so the tofu can drain. It holds a 1-pound block perfectly.

Marinating

Most people say marinating surrounds tofu with flavor but it does not penetrate; Spicy Tofu Marinade (page 53) is an exception. In just a few hours, it gets into a cake of pressed tofu completely. Other marinades can be made to penetrate by adding the magic ingredient of heat. If you heat the marinade before pouring it over the tofu, then bake and cool the bean curd in the marinade, one cut will show that the marinade has penetrated. The heat also firms the tofu nicely.

When using your own marinade, make sure it is not too thick. If it is a barbecue sauce, thin it down to the texture of canned tomato sauce or even to that of a vinaigrette, by adding more liquid, including some oil. The only seasoning paste or rub I have used that penetrates into tofu is that in Herb-Roasted Tofu Cutlets (page 240). Others merely coat and flavor it on the outside.

Marinated tofu can keep up to 3 days in the refrigerator.

Spicy Tofu Marinade

This is one of the few marinades which perks up tofu without using heat in the marinating process. Chef Sandy Sonnenfelt of The Pasta Shop in Oakland, California, uses it for making smoked and baked sliced tofu. I also like it for marinating tempeh, then smoking it. This tofu is good in any dish where you want a kick.

Makes 16 ounces

½ cup soy sauce

¼ cup olive oil

1 tablespoon dry sherry

1 tablespoon honey

2 teaspoons dry mustard

1 teaspoon onion powder

1 teaspoon hot red pepper flakes

1 teaspoon ground cumin

1 teaspoon ground coriander

1 tablespoon freshly ground black pepper

1 teaspoon Szechuan peppercorns (not toasted)

4 whole garlic cloves, crushed

16 ounces firm or extra firm tofu, pressed (see page 49)

1. Mix all the ingredients except the tofu with 1 cup water.

2. Place the tofu in a 1-quart size, freezer-weight plastic bag along with the marinade. Marinate in the refrigerator overnight, or for 3 hours at room temperature.

Smoking Tofu

Making smoked tofu is like baking your own bread. You can buy good commercially made ones but with home made smoked tofu, you can taste the fire and the freshness.

When I started making smoked tofu, I used a wok. The cleanup was a mess, even though I lined the wok with aluminum foil. Even after sealing the edges with foil, the process smoked the house along with the tofu. And the tofu came out too acrid unless I used split-second timing.

Next, I tried a Camerons Stovetop Smoker. This metal box produced good results and more easily. But I still did not like the cleanup. Despite its tight-fitting lid, it too leaked enough smoke to make the house smell strongly. If you have good ventilation or really like the fragrance of smoked foods, consider buying this smoker, which is sold in cookware stores and on culinary websites.

Finally, I discovered foil smoker bags. They are a cook's dream. All you do is heat the oven, put the food on a plate, slip the plate into the mylar bag, and pop the whole thing in the oven. The double-walled bag can hold up to 2 pounds of tofu. Tiny holes in the inner layer let the smoke coming from saw dust sandwiched between the layers circulate around the food, while the impermeable outside layer keeps it inside the bag. Made in Finland, these bags are sold at Trader Joe's (see page 348), Hay Day Markets, and other stores. You can also order them from Cystern Inc., the importer (see page 350).

smoker bag method

Bag-Smoked Tofu

Makes 1 to 2 pounds

1 foil smoker bag for light smoke (see above)

1 to 2 pounds (2 to 4 slabs) pressed firm or extra firm tofu, marinated in Spicy Tofu Marinade (page 53)

1. Following instructions on the smoker bag, set the oven rack to the lowest position. Preheat the oven to 475°F.

2. Place the slabs of tofu on an oven-proof plate or in a shallow baking dish in 1 layer. Place the plate inside the smoker bag, making sure the side with the wood chips and vent holes is on the bottom. (Bags are marked "This side down.") Fold the open edge over a half inch. Repeat 1 to 2 to times, making a tight seal. Set the bag on the rack in the oven.

3. Bake 8 to 10 minutes, depending on how much smoke flavor you want. Carefully remove the smoker bag from the oven and set it on a baking rack for 5 minutes. Wearing oven potholder mits, carefully unroll the sealed edge of the bag and remove the plate. Cool the tofu on the plate to room temperature.

stovetop smoker method Follow the excellent instructions that come with the smoker box. Use mild-flavored wood chips, such as alder, apple, cherry, or maple. Smoke the tofu for 10 to 12 minutes after the first wisps of smoke appear and the smoker is sealed. It will take some experimenting to find the level of smokiness you prefer.

Deep-Frying

Americans have a love-hate relationship with fried foods. When fried tofu is added to a casserole, it does not necessarily result in a dish overly high in either fat or calories. The tofu is beautifully chewy and has a lovely brown color.

Asians buy tofu already fried. You can make it up to a day before using it, though its texture is firmer once it has been refrigerated.

Before frying tofu, it is essential to remove as much water as possible in order to minimize spattering. Blot pressed tofu well with paper towels just before adding it to the hot oil. If you use unpressed tofu, wear long sleeves and an oven mitt, as it does spit. Dredging tofu in flour before frying reduces the spattering.

To deep-fry tofu, add enough oil to a heavy skillet to cover the tofu. Heat to 375°F. Add the tofu, a few pieces at a time. Cook until golden brown, 2 to 4 minutes depending on the size of the pieces, turning the tofu once. Remove with a slotted spoon and drain on brown paper or paper towels. Soft and firm tofu are the best choices for deep-frying. Firm silken tofu that has been frozen and defrosted can also be fried.

SOY PROTEIN AND FAT IN SELECTED SOYFOODS

This shows the amounts of soy protein and fat in many familiar soyfoods. It shows how much they vary for some groups of soyfoods. This information is based on the Nutrition Facts panel found on packages and, in some cases, on information from the manufacturer.

Product	Soy protein grams/serving	Fat grams/ serving	Saturated fat grams/serving
SOYMILK			
REFRIGERATED	5–11 g	3–4.5 g	0–1 g
SHELF STABLE			
Unsweetened	6–9 g	3.5–5 g	0–1 g
Plain (also called Original and Creamy)	5–11 g	2.5–5 g	0–1 g
Enriched (contains calcium)	5–10 g	3–5 g	0–5 g
Lite or Low-Fat	3–8 g	2–3 g	0–1 g
Non-fat	3–8 g	0 g	0 g
DRY SOYMILK	7 g	3 g	0 g
EDAMAME			
FROZEN	9–10 g	2.5–5 g	0–1 g
REFRIGERATED	10 g	5 g	1 g
DAIRY PRODUCTS			
SOY CHEESES			
BLOCKS		3–5 g	0 g
SLICES		2–5 g	0 g
CREAM CHEESE	1–3 g	8–9 g	1–2 g
GRATED PARMESAN	2 g	.5 g	0 g
SOY CREAM CHEESE	1–3 g	8–9 g	1–2 g
SOUR CREAM	1 g	5 g	2 g
CULTURED SOY YOGURT	4–5 g	2–4 g	0 g
SOY FROZEN DESSERTS	1–3 g	4–15 g	0–3 g
TOFU			
SILKEN			
Soft	4–7 g	2.5 g	0–.5 g
Firm	6 g	2.5 g	.5 g

Product	Soy protein grams/serving	Fat grams/ serving	Saturated fat grams/serving
TOFU (*continued*)			
Extra Firm	6 g	1.5 g	0 g
Fat Reduced Extra Firm	6 g	.5 g	0 g
Fat-Free		0 g	0 g
SOFT	7 g	3.5 g	0 g
FIRM	9–16 g	4–6 g	0–1 g
ENRICHED FIRM	7 g	1.5 g	0 g
EXTRA FIRM	7–10 g	5–6 g	.5–1 g
BAKED	13–18 g	5–8 g	1 g
SMOKED	11–18 g	5–6 g	1 g
TEMPEH			
SOY	23 g	8 g	1 g
WILD RICE	19 g	7 g	1 g
THREE-GRAIN	20 g	7 g	1 g
FIVE-GRAIN	12 g	4 g	.5 g
SOYMEATS			
SOY CRUMBLES	10–12 g	0 g	0 g
SOYRIZO SAUSAGE	7 g	9 g	0 g
VEAT FROZEN SOYMEAT	8–12 g	2.5–4 g	0 g
TEXTURED SOY PROTEIN	9–12 g	0 g	0 g
SOYBEANS			
CANNED, YELLOW AND BLACK	12–13 g	6–7 g	1 g
DRIED, YELLOW AND BLACK	12–15 g	8 g	1 g
SOYNUTS	11–14 g	4–7 g	1 g
SOYNUT BUTTER	6–10 g	7–14 g	1.5–2 g
SOY FLOUR			
REGULAR	8 g	4.5 g	1 g
DEFATTED			
SOY BAKING MIX	15 g	6 g	1 g
MISO	1–3 g	0 g	0 g
SOY PASTA	6.4 g	1.5 g	0 g
SOY PROTEIN POWDER	25 g	0–2 g	0 g

breakfast

Whatever your morning routine, soyfoods make it easy to have a good breakfast in just seconds. They offer protein equal in amount to eggs, sausages, and milk, but without the cholesterol. For a quick, nutritional breakfast, spoon up some creamy soy yogurt, pour soymilk to use over cereal, or whip up a soy smoothie in any color of the rainbow, using your favorite fruits.

When you sit down to a more leisurely breakfast, scramble up some tofu, alone or combined with eggs, or sip a soy cappuccino while reading the paper. With more time on the weekend, use soy in Stuffed French Toast (page 73) or blend it into featherlight pancakes.

In one thick shake at breakfast, you can consume the entire 25 grams of soy protein per day that can help reduce the risk of heart disease. You'll also get 30 to 60 milligrams of isoflavones. On the other hand, there is no need to make consuming all this soy a morning obligation. Feel free to start the day with Cinnamon Toast (page 59) and add soy to your meals as you go through the day.

Cinnamon Toast

Makes 1 slice

According to Elizabeth Andoh, an American living in Tokyo and author of several cookbooks, the Japanese love cinnamon toast as much as we do, but their topping combines *kinako*, roasted soybeans ground to a fine powder, with brown sugar and cinnamon. The Japanese sprinkle it on warm buttered toast or over vanilla ice cream; I also like it sprinkled over hot cereal. Multiply the recipe and keep a shaker of this topping handy.

1. Combine the kinako, sugar, and cinnamon in a small bowl.

2. Toast the bread.

3. Butter the warm toast. Sprinkle the kinako mixture over the toast. It will melt somewhat into the warm, buttered toast. Serve hot.

NOTES: Made of roasted soybean powder, kinako is sold in Japanese food stores. You can also order it from ethnicgrocer.com. It will keep for months, stored in a jar in the refrigerator.

I recommend Spectrum Spread and Earth Balance. Both are dairy- and cholesterol-free stand-ins for butter. They are also trans-fat-free margarine and nonhydrogenated.

1 teaspoon kinako (see Notes)

½ teaspoon packed brown sugar

⅛ teaspoon ground cinnamon

1 slice white or light whole wheat bread

1 teaspoon unsalted butter or nonhydrogenated margarine (see Notes)

PER SLICE: Calories 146 • Soy Protein 3.3 g • Total Protein 6.4 g • Carbohydrates 16.9 g • Fat 6.4 g • Saturated Fat 0.7 g • Cholesterol 0 mg • Fiber 0.8 g • Sodium 122.2 mg

2½ cups old-fashioned
    rolled oats (see Note)

½ cup soy protein powder

¾ cup (3 ounces) blanched
    almonds, chopped

2 tablespoons flax seed,
    optional

1 teaspoon ground
    cinnamon

3 tablespoons canola oil

¼ cup wildflower honey

¼ cup ginger marmalade

1 teaspoon vanilla extract

½ cup dried cranberries

½ cup chopped dates

Cranberry-Ginger Granola

Good granola is wholesome and homey and offers some unexpected taste. Here a touch of ginger adds the unusual note. Crisp and chunky, this granola with soy protein powder is as good for afternoon snacking as it is for breakfast.

1. Preheat the oven to 325°F. Cover a baking sheet with aluminum foil.

2. Combine the oats, protein powder, almonds, flax seed, and cinnamon in a large bowl.

3. Heat the oil, honey, and marmalade in a saucepan over medium heat, stirring until the marmalade dissolves and the mixture is warm, 2 to 3 minutes. Stir in the vanilla.

4. Pour the warm liquid over the oat mixture. Add the cranberries and dates. Stir with a rubber spatula, turning the mixture and scraping the bowl, until the oats are evenly coated with the protein powder and the mixture is evenly moist. It will be a combination of small clumps and loose oats.

5. Spread the granola in an even layer over the baking sheet. Bake for about 20 minutes, removing the pan every 5 minutes to stir and turn the granola so it dries and colors evenly. When done, it will still feel slightly soft and moist, and it will be a deep, cinnamon brown, with many of the clumps broken up.

6. Cool the granola on the baking sheet. When it reaches room temperature, it will be crisp. Break up the granola, leaving some clusters if you wish. Store in an airtight container for up to 2 weeks.

NOTE: Use only thickly cut, old-fashioned rolled oats.

PER ¼ CUP: Calories 130 • Soy Protein 4.0 g • Total Protein 6.3 g • Carbohydrates 16.6 g • Fat 4.8 g • Saturated Fat 0.4 g • Cholesterol 0 mg • Fiber 1.9 g • Sodium 33.1 mg

Maple Yogurt Sprinkles

Makes 2 cups

Stirring this maple-flavored crunch into a cup of yogurt makes it like the kind sold with crisp mix-ins. Naturally sweetened, this textured soy protein keeps for weeks.

1 cup rice-size textured soy protein (TSP) bits
⅓ cup apple juice
½ cup pure maple syrup

1. Preheat the oven to 350°F. Cover an air-cushioned baking sheet with aluminum foil and coat with nonstick cooking spray. If you don't have an air-cushioned sheet, use two baking sheets, set on top of each other.

2. Shake the textured soy protein in a sieve over the sink to get rid of any fine dust. Place the bits in a bowl and pour the apple juice over them. Mix with a fork until the textured soy protein is moistened. Let the mixture sit until the largest bits have no hard spots in the center when squeezed between your fingers, about 10 minutes. Mix in the maple syrup until the textured soy protein bits are completely and evenly coated.

3. Spread out the coated textured soy protein in an even layer about 12 × 6 inches, using a rubber spatula, keeping the edges as thick as the center of the mass.

4. Bake the textured soy protein for 5 minutes. Remove the pan from the oven. Stir, then respread the layer, taking care not to let it get too thin at the edges or it will burn. Repeat this procedure of baking and stirring twice more, until the textured soy protein is the color of dried apricots, and the pieces are chewy but not hard, about 15 minutes in all.

5. Stir the maple sprinkles once more, and spread them out to cover the whole pan. Set the pan on a rack to cool. The sprinkles will become crisper as they cool. These will keep for 2 to 3 weeks, stored in an airtight container. They may become more chewy over time.

PER 2 TABLESPOONS: Calories 20 • Soy Protein 1.6 g • Total Protein 1.6 g • Carbohydrates 4.0 g • Fat 0 g • Saturated Fat 0 g • Cholesterol 0 mg • Fiber 0.5 g • Sodium 0.8 mg

Serves 4

2 cups unsweetened
soymilk

2 cups old-fashioned
rolled oats

1 teaspoon salt

1 medium apple, peeled
and shredded
(see Notes)

½ cup dried currants

½ cup vanilla soy yogurt

Freshly grated nutmeg

Oatmeal Porridge

I loved my mother's nutty-tasting oatmeal so much that it was only after I went to a summer camp where the stuff they served was gray paste did I understand why the mention of this hot cereal elicited "ughs" from people. Eventually, in Scotland, I discovered that the dense and chewy porridge eaten there was like my mother's oatmeal. Eating it with a bowl of cold buttermilk on the side, into which I dipped each spoonful of the steaming porridge, was heaven. For a similar sensual combination, I dollop soy yogurt, which has a tang similar to that of buttermilk, on the oatmeal just before serving.

1. Combine the soymilk and 1 cup water in a large saucepan. Heat over high heat until the liquid is just bubbling around the edge. Stir in the oats and salt. Reduce the heat so the milk is just foaming. Cook until the oats are tender but still chewy, about 12 minutes, stirring 3 to 4 times as the porridge thickens and becomes creamy.

2. Remove the pot from the heat. Stir in the apple and currants.

3. Divide the porridge among four bowls. Top each serving with 2 tablespoons of the yogurt. Garnish with 2 to 3 gratings of nutmeg, and serve immediately.

NOTES: Firm apples, such as Golden Delicious, Fuji, Ginger Gold, and Crispin, grate well and go nicely with the hot porridge.

To avoid pasty oatmeal, never cover the pot.

PER SERVING: Calories 289 • Soy Protein 5.4 g • Total Protein 12.4 g • Carbohydrates 50.7 g • Fat 5.3 g • Saturated Fat 0.5 g • Cholesterol 0 mg • Fiber 8.2 g • Sodium 585.9 mg

Buckwheat Brûlée

Serves 6

The oatmeal brûlée served at the Ritz-Carlton in San Francisco shows how chefs are into dressing up grains for breakfast. Here, kasha (as Russians call this earthy cereal) nestles under the same kind of crackling brown sugar shell. To make the kasha as special as the presentation, I mix it with soy sour cream, pureed tofu, and roasted hazelnuts and serve it in a custard cup or ramekin just like crème brûlée.

¾ cup whole kasha (toasted buckwheat groats)

1½ cups unsweetened soymilk

1 teaspoon ground cinnamon

Pinch of salt

⅓ cup hazelnuts

¼ cup plus 2 tablespoons lightly packed light brown sugar

¼ cup pureed silken tofu

4 tablespoons soy sour cream

1. Preheat the oven to 350°F.

2. Combine the kasha and soymilk with 1 cup water in a deep saucepan over medium heat. Blend in the cinnamon and salt. Bring to a boil, reduce the heat, cover, and simmer until the kasha is cooked, about 20 minutes. Let it sit, covered, for 10 minutes.

3. While the kasha cooks, roast the hazelnuts for 12 to 15 minutes, until they are fragrant, their skins begin to crack, and the nuts are lightly colored. Shake the pan several times to insure they roast evenly. Rub the nuts vigorously into a dish towel. Let the nuts cool, then chop them coarsely.

4. Mix 2 tablespoons of the sugar into the hot kasha, along with the tofu, sour cream, and chopped nuts. The kasha should be creamy.

5. Firmly pack the kasha mixture into six 6-ounce ramekins or custard cups, filling them almost to the top. Smooth the surface with the back of a spoon. Refrigerate, uncovered, until the tops are dry, at least 6 hours.

6. Preheat the broiler. Place the cold cups of kasha on a baking sheet. Place the remaining ¼ cup of sugar in a sieve, and sprinkle it over the top of each cup, making the layer as even as possible. Use the back of a spoon to help force the sugar through the sieve. The kasha should be lightly blanketed by the sugar.

7. One at a time, place the cups of kasha under the broiler for 1 minute, setting the broiler pan as close to the heat as possible. Check after 30 seconds, turning the cup, if necessary, to insure the sugar colors evenly. The melted sugar may look lacy rather than forming a glossy even layer. Serve immediately.

PER SERVING: Calories 190 • Soy Protein 3.1 g • Total Protein 6.4 g • Carbohydrates 26.9 g • Fat 7.4 g • Saturated Fat 0.9 g • Cholesterol 0 mg • Fiber 2.9 g • Sodium 30.1 mg

Protein Plus

In the morning, if you don't start to eat until you are on the move, a muffin, scone, or a square of bread pudding made with soy provides a substantial moveable breakfast.

Soy protein powder lifts the protein content in baked goods. It also adds tenderness to muffins, scones, and quick breads, and helps keep them moist for several days. Most muffins are best when freshly made, but those made with soy protein powder or baking mix can be baked the night before you want to enjoy them. Packing up to 14-plus grams of protein, more than 10 of it soy protein, these baked goods are as nutritious as they are good-tasting.

Ginger Date Scones

These light scones come out of the oven deliciously crisp outside and tender inside. They make a great midmorning or afternoon snack, enjoyed with a nice, hot "cuppa."

1. Preheat the oven to 375°F. Spray an air-cushioned baking sheet with nonstick cooking spray. If you do not have an insulated baking sheet, use two baking sheets, stacked one on top of the other.

2. Whisk together 1 cup of the flour, the protein powder, sugar, baking powder, baking soda, cinnamon, and salt in a bowl, or combine them in a food processor. Work the butter into the dry ingredients, using a fork, or whirl in the processor until they are a light powder that feels silky. Mix in the poppy seeds. If you are using a food processor, turn the mixture into a bowl.

3. Toss the dates with the remaining 2 teaspoons flour. Mix the dates and ginger into the dry ingredients. Mix the vanilla with the buttermilk. Pour ⅔ cup of the liquid into the dry ingredients. Lightly mix, using a rubber spatula, until the dough comes together, is moist, and almost completely combined. Add more buttermilk, 1 tablespoon at a time, if needed.

4. Form the dough into six disks, about 3 inches in diameter and 1 inch thick, patting them gently into shape on the baking sheet. It is fine for the dough to be loosely formed and craggy on the surface. Leave at least 2 inches between the scones.

5. Bake for 25 minutes, or until the scones are well browned. They should feel crusty and almost firm to the touch when lightly pressed in the center.

6. Cool on the baking sheet for 10 minutes. Serve warm, not hot, or at room temperature.

1 cup plus 2 teaspoons all-purpose flour

⅔ cup soy protein powder

¼ cup sugar

1½ teaspoons baking powder

¼ teaspoon baking soda

1 teaspoon ground cinnamon

¼ teaspoon salt

4 tablespoons (½ stick) cold unsalted butter, cut in small pieces

1 tablespoon poppy seeds

⅔ cup pitted and chopped Medjool dates (6 to 8 dates)

3 tablespoons chopped candied or crystallized ginger

1 teaspoon vanilla extract

About ⅔ cup low-fat buttermilk

PER SCONE: Calories 333 • Soy Protein 10.7 g • Total Protein 14.4 g • Carbohydrates 48.8 g • Fat 9.4 g • Saturated Fat 5.6 g • Cholesterol 21.7 mg • Fiber 1.5 g • Sodium 359.5 mg

Makes 12

1 cup oat bran

1 cup all-purpose flour

¾ cup soy baking mix

¾ cup sugar

½ teaspoon salt

1¼ teaspoons baking soda

1 large egg

1 cup low-fat buttermilk

¼ cup canola oil

½ cup boiling water

⅔ cup raisins

Oat Bran Muffins

These muffins, which are light as a cloud when hot, remain nicely moist for several days. This means you can bake them at night, knowing they will be outstanding the next day at breakfast. If any are left, wrap them in foil, and continue to enjoy them for a couple of more mornings.

1. Preheat the oven to 350°F. Coat a 12-cup muffin pan with nonstick cooking spray.

2. Whisk together the oat bran, flour, baking mix, sugar, salt, and baking soda in a bowl. In another bowl, whisk the egg with the buttermilk, oil, and the boiling water to blend.

3. Pour the liquid ingredients over the dry ones, and whisk just until they are combined. The batter will be quite thick. Stir in the raisins. Scoop the batter into the prepared muffin pan, filling each cup about ⅔ full.

4. Bake for 15 to 18 minutes, until the muffin tops feel firm to the touch, and a bamboo skewer inserted in the center comes out clean.

5. Let the muffins sit in the pan on a rack for 5 minutes before tipping them out. Store these muffins in a plastic bag or wrap them individually in foil. Do not freeze, as they turn pasty when defrosted.

PER MUFFIN: Calories 203 • Soy Protein 4.5 g • Total Protein 8.2 g • Carbohydrates 34.4 g • Fat 5.4 g • Saturated Fat 0.6 g • Cholesterol 1.3 mg • Fiber 2.1 g • Sodium 322.7 mg

Lemon Loaf

The texture of this moist loaf reminds me of financiers— the buttery French cakes made with ground almonds. Here there are no nuts, just soy goodness. Top slices of this golden cake with fresh berries, or enjoy a thick slab instead of a morning muffin.

¾ cup all-purpose flour

¾ cup soy protein powder

¾ cup plus ⅓ cup sugar

1 teaspoon baking powder

¼ teaspoon baking soda

Zest and juice of 1 lemon

2 large eggs

½ cup vanilla soymilk

⅓ cup canola oil

½ teaspoon vanilla extract

1. Preheat the oven to 350°F. Coat a metal 8½ × 4½-inch loaf pan with nonstick cooking spray.

2. Whisk together the flour with the soy protein powder, ¾ cup of the sugar, the baking powder, baking soda, and lemon zest in a bowl. In another bowl, whisk the eggs with the soymilk, oil, and vanilla.

3. Whisk the wet ingredients into the dry just until evenly combined. The batter will be thick. Spread it in the prepared pan, smoothing the top.

4. Bake for 40 minutes, or until the loaf is golden brown and feels firm to the touch in the center. A bamboo skewer inserted into the middle of the loaf should come out clean. Set the pan on a cooling rack.

5. Combine the lemon juice with the remaining ⅓ cup sugar in a small saucepan while the loaf is baking. Heat the mixture until the sugar dissolves, 4 to 5 minutes, stirring occasionally.

6. Poke a knife into the hot baked loaf in 6 to 8 places as soon as it comes out of the oven. Pour the hot lemon syrup over the cake. Let the cake sit on a rack for 30 minutes, or until it has soaked up the syrup and cooled completely.

7. Remove the loaf from the pan. Slice and serve. This cake will keep for up to 3 days, wrapped in foil and stored at room temperature.

PER SERVING: Calories 275 • Soy Protein 7.1 g • Total Protein 9.2 g • Carbohydrates 39.5 g • Fat 9.4 g • Saturated Fat 0.7 g • Cholesterol 0 mg • Fiber 0.7 g • Sodium 260.8 mg

Oatmeal and Carrot Breakfast Jumbles

4 tablespoons (½ stick) unsalted butter or margarine

⅓ cup granulated sugar

⅓ cup packed light brown sugar

2 large eggs

1 teaspoon vanilla extract

¾ cup soy baking mix

¾ teaspoon baking soda

½ teaspoon ground cinnamon

1¾ cups old-fashioned rolled oats (not quick-cooking or instant)

2 cups finely shredded carrots

½ cup raisins

½ cup walnuts, chopped

Milk and cookies for breakfast sounds sinful, but when it is soymilk and these wheat-free cookies, you have the benefits of a bowl of raisin-studded oatmeal, including plenty of natural fiber, plus soy.

1. Preheat the oven to 375°F. Coat two insulated cookie sheets with nonstick cooking spray. Or, duplicate the effect of an insulated sheet by stacking two baking sheets together.

2. Cream the butter with the white and brown sugars, using an electric mixer. Add the eggs, beating at high speed until the mixture is beige and almost thick enough to form a ribbon, 2 to 3 minutes. Mix in the vanilla.

3. Using a rubber spatula, mix in the soy baking mix, baking soda, and cinnamon. Stir in the oats, carrots, raisins, and nuts.

4. Drop the cookie batter onto the prepared baking sheets 1½ inches apart, making mounds the size of a large walnut. With your fingers, lightly flatten the top of each cookie.

5. Bake for 15 to 18 minutes, until the cookies are golden brown on top and dark around the edges. They will feel springy.

6. Cool for 1 minute on the baking sheet. Transfer the cookies to a rack and cool completely. These cookies become crisp as they cool. They keep for up to a week in a tightly sealed tin.

PER COOKIE: Calories 156 • Soy Protein 1.9 g • Total Protein 5.7 g • Carbohydrates 21.3 g • Fat 6.0 g • Saturated Fat 1.7 g • Cholesterol 19.4 mg • Fiber 2.6 g • Sodium 92.6 mg

"Bacon" and Egg Scrambler

To be honest, I considered scrambled tofu something only hippies and health nuts would eat until a vegetarian friend recommended scrambling tofu and eggs together. In this combination the sum is greater than either of its parts—the tofu makes the eggs exceptionally light and allows all their flavor to come through. With them I enjoy soy bacon called breakfast strips, choosing from the crisp ones made by Lightlife and Morningstar Farms or tender tempeh-like ones, also from Lightlife Foods Inc.

1. Beat the eggs with the salt and pepper. Mix in the crumbled tofu.

2. Melt the butter in a nonstick skillet over medium-high heat. When it stops bubbling, add the soy bacon. Reduce the heat to medium. Sauté until the chopped breakfast strips are lightly browned, about 2 minutes.

3. Increase the heat to medium-high. Add the egg and tofu mixture to the pan and scramble the eggs until they are cooked as you like them, about 2 minutes for a soft scramble, 2½ minutes for firm, and 3 minutes for dry eggs. Serve immediately.

PER SERVING: Calories 149 • Soy Protein 5.0 g • Total Protein 12.0 g • Carbohydrates 2.9 g • Fat 10.2 g • Saturated Fat 2.5 g • Cholesterol 218.8 mg • Fiber 0.3 g • Sodium 757.9 mg

4 large eggs

1 teaspoon salt

¼ teaspoon freshly ground black pepper

8 ounces soft tofu, pressed (see page 49) and crumbled

1 teaspoon unsalted butter, margarine, or canola oil

4 soy breakfast strips, chopped into ½-inch pieces

Onion and Pepper Scrambler

1 tablespoon canola oil

1 medium onion, chopped

1 large green frying or
   Cubanelle pepper,
   or 1 medium bell
   pepper, chopped

12 ounces soft tofu,
   pressed (see page 49)
   and crumbled

1 teaspoon salt

½ teaspoon reduced-
   sodium soy sauce

Pinch of ground turmeric

On the rare Sunday morning when my father cooked, pepper and eggs was the only dish he knew how to make. Fortunately, they were very good. He lightly browned thin-walled frying peppers with plenty of onions, then added the eggs. I make his specialty with tofu in place of eggs.

1. Heat the oil in a skillet over medium-high heat. Add the onion and pepper and sauté until they soften and start to color, about 8 minutes.

2. Add the crumbled tofu, breaking it up until it resembles scrambled eggs. Mix in the soy sauce, turmeric, and salt, stirring until the tofu is evenly colored. The tofu should cook for about 2 minutes in all. Serve immediately.

PER SERVING: Calories 101 • Soy Protein 7.6 g • Total Protein 8.3 g • Carbohydrates 4.9 g • Fat 6.4 g • Saturated Fat 0.3 g • Cholesterol 0 mg • Fiber 1.2 g • Sodium 608.0 mg

Migas

In Spanish, *migas* means crumbs. This Southwestern egg dish is named for the crushed corn chips Tex-Mex cooks use in place of bread crumbs. Chef and cookbook author Deborah Madison introduced me to this hearty breakfast in Austin, Texas, at Las Manitas, an ultra-casual, un-air conditioned lunchroom-cum-art-gallery frequented by the locals. It is owned by the Perez sisters, whose home-cooking is full of soul and spirit. Their migas will keep you going full tilt until a very late lunch. Here, tofu replaces the scrambled eggs. Feel free to mix and match when making your migas: Use dairy Jack cheese and tofu, eggs and soy cheese, replace the jalapeño and tomatoes with prepared salsa.

1. Heat the oil in a skillet over medium-high heat. Add the onion and sauté for 1 minute. Add the scallions, jalapeño, turmeric, and soy sauce. Stir just to combine. Stir in the crumbled tofu, and cook until it is evenly pale yellow and looks moist, about 1 minute.

2. Mix in the tomatoes, cheese, tortilla chips, and cilantro. Stir until the cheese is melted.

3. Divide among four warm plates and serve immediately.

1 teaspoon canola oil

2 tablespoon finely chopped onion

2 scallions (white and green parts), chopped

1 jalapeño pepper, seeded and minced

1/8 teaspoon ground turmeric

1/4 teaspoon soy sauce

16 ounces firm tofu, pressed (see page 49) and crumbled

2 plum tomatoes, seeded and chopped

1/2 cup (2 ounces) shredded soy Cheddar

3 cups broken tortilla chips

2 tablespoons chopped cilantro

PER SERVING: Calories 252 • Soy Protein 11.9 g • Total Protein 16.3 g • Carbohydrates 18.2 g • Fat 13.5 g • Saturated Fat 2.0 g • Cholesterol 0 mg • Fiber 1.9 g • Sodium 268.5 mg

⅓ cup dried cherries

⅓ cup golden raisins

½ cup apple juice or water

8 slices whole wheat
   bread

1 medium Golden
   Delicious apple, peeled,
   cored, and cut into
   ⅜-inch pieces

3 large eggs

½ cup lightly packed
   brown sugar

3 cups cappuccino
   soymilk or vanilla
   soymilk plus 1
   tablespoon instant
   coffee dissolved in
   2 tablespoons hot water

⅛ teaspoon freshly grated
   nutmeg

Pinch of salt

Cappuccino Bread Pudding

When there is leftover dessert in the refrigerator, I am quite likely to have it for breakfast. This has inspired me to create dessertlike breakfast recipes that include a good serving of protein. Here soymilk, eggs, and whole-grain bread make a nutritious morning meal that feels sinful.

1. Preheat the oven to 350°F. Coat an 8-inch square baking dish with nonstick cooking spray.

2. Soak the cherries and raisins in the apple juice until they are plump, 15 to 20 minutes. Drain.

3. Tear the bread into 1-inch pieces and place in a large bowl. Add the apple and the drained cherries and raisins to the bread.

4. Beat the eggs in a medium bowl, then whisk in the sugar. Mix in the soymilk, nutmeg, and salt. Pour over the bread and fruit. Stir with a fork until the bread is well moistened, and the fruit is evenly distributed. Turn this mixture into the prepared pan.

5. Bake for 45 to 50 minutes, until a bamboo skewer inserted into the center comes out clean.

6. Cool the pudding on a baking rack for 15 minutes. Run a knife around the sides of the pudding to loosen it. Invert a plate over the pan and, holding it in place, flip the two so the pudding drops onto the plate. When it is lukewarm, cut the pudding into six pieces and serve. If you are not serving immediately, cool the pieces completely. They will keep for up to 4 days, wrapped in plastic and refrigerated. They can be frozen. Reheat the pudding in a toaster oven or eat at room temperature.

PER SERVING: Calories 341 • Soy Protein 3.31 g • Total Protein 10.7 g • Carbohydrates 54.9 g • Fat 6.1 g • Saturated Fat 1.6 g • Cholesterol 106.3 mg • Fiber 4.3 g • Sodium 337.5 mg

Stuffed French Toast with Banana Maple Syrup

Delight your inner child with this cozy combination of raisin bread, cream cheese, cinnamon, bananas, and maple syrup. Freezing individual portions to reheat in the toaster oven is a great way to lure resisting youngsters into eating breakfast.

1. Spread each slice of bread with 2 teaspoons of the cream cheese. Spread 1 tablespoon of the apple butter on 4 of the slices. Cover with another bread slice, cheese side down.

2. In a lasagne pan or other large, shallow dish beat the eggs with the soymilk and cinnamon with a fork, until well combined. Add the sandwiches. Soak for 1 minute on each side.

3. Generously coat a nonstick skillet or griddle with nonstick cooking spray and place over medium-high heat. Arrange the soaked bread in one layer, cooking it in two batches, if necessary. When the bread is browned, about 3 minutes, turn and brown the second side, 2 to 3 minutes. Transfer to a warm plate.

4. Generously coat a nonstick skillet with nonstick cooking spray. Place the pan over medium-high heat. Add the walnuts and stir until they are fragrant, 1 to 2 minutes. Mix in the banana and cook until it softens slightly, 2 minutes. Remove the pan from the heat. Stir in the maple syrup. Pour the syrup into a pitcher and keep warm. The syrup will keep for up to 2 days in a tightly sealed container in the refrigerator. Reheat in the microwave before serving.

5. Serve the French toast accompanied by warm syrup.

8 slices cinnamon-raisin bread

⅓ cup soy cream cheese

4 tablespoons apple butter

4 large eggs

½ cup vanilla soymilk

½ teaspoon ground cinnamon

SYRUP

2 tablespoons chopped walnuts

1 firm medium banana, chopped

½ cup pure maple syrup

PER SERVING INCLUDING SYRUP: • Calories 496 • Soy Protein 1.36 g • Total Protein 15.6 g • Carbohydrates 72.3 g • Fat 17.0 g • Saturated Fat 3.4 g • Cholesterol 246.0 mg • Fiber 3.3 g • Sodium 383.7 mg

Cloud-Light Blueberry Pancakes

½ cup all-purpose flour

½ cup soy protein powder
   or soy baking mix

1 teaspoon baking powder

⅛ teaspoon baking soda

Pinch of salt

1 large egg

1 large egg white

2 tablespoons sugar

¾ cup low-fat buttermilk

1 tablespoon canola oil

½ cup fresh or frozen
   blueberries

Oil or butter for the pan

Warm Blueberry Sauce
   (recipe follows)

I used to blend soy flour into pancakes, but using more than a couple of tablespoons made them heavy and added a pronounced soy taste. Then I tried using soy protein powder and soy baking mix, a protein powder specially formulated for baking and pancakes. The result not only packs in plenty of protein, it also makes pancakes so light and tender they almost float.

1. Combine the flour, protein powder, baking powder, baking soda, and salt in a bowl. Whisk together the egg, egg white, sugar, buttermilk, and oil in another bowl.

2. Pour the liquid ingredients into the bowl with the dry ingredients. Add the blueberries and whisk just until the batter is evenly moist. Do not overmix. The batter will be quite thick.

3. Lightly coat a nonstick griddle or heavy skillet with oil. Set it over high heat. When the surface is very hot, reduce the heat to medium. Make 3-inch pancakes, using 2 tablespoons of batter for each, placing them 1 inch apart on the griddle. Cook for 1 minute, until the pancakes are dark on the bottom. Carefully turn the pancakes; they will be soft. If you are using a pan, it may help to tilt it as you slip the pancake turner under each pancake. Cook for 1 minute, or until they have puffed up about ½ inch, and are dark on the other side.

4. Serve hot, passing the blueberry sauce at the table. Cooked pancakes can be held in a warm (200°F) oven for 20 minutes.

PER SERVING WITHOUT SAUCE: Calories 201 • Soy Protein 9.0 g • Total Protein 14.7 g • Carbohydrates 23.5 g • Fat 5.4 g • Saturated Fat 1.0 g • Cholesterol 55.8 mg • Fiber 0.9 g • Sodium 405.0 mg

Warm Blueberry Sauce

Combine the maple syrup, berries, and zest in a saucepan. Bring to a boil over medium heat. Simmer for 2 minutes, until the berries are very soft. Pour the hot syrup into a pitcher and serve.

¾ cup maple syrup

½ cup frozen blueberries

1 teaspoon grated
    orange zest

PER 2 TABLESPOONS: Calories 84 • Soy Protein 0 g • Total Protein 0.1 g • Carbohydrates 21.3 g • Fiber 0.3 g • Fat 1.0 g • Saturated Fat 0.1 g • Cholesterol 0 mg • Sodium 2.8 mg

Lemon Silver Dollar Pancakes

8 ounces extra firm tofu, squeezed (see page 48)

4 large eggs, beaten

6 tablespoons all-purpose flour

3 tablespoons unsalted butter, melted

3 tablespoons canola oil

2 teaspoons grated lemon zest

¼ teaspoon salt

Confectioners' sugar

Tender cottage cheese pancakes were one of my brunch specialties for years, but using soft tofu in place of small-curd cottage cheese works splendidly. A light sprinkling of confectioners' sugar is all the embellishment they need, though I often pass sliced strawberries, too.

1. Mash the tofu in a bowl, using a fork. Add the eggs and beat with the fork. It will be a lumpy, thin batter. Mix in the flour, butter, oil, lemon zest, and salt.

2. Coat a nonstick skillet with nonstick cooking spray and place it over medium-high heat. When a drop of water dances on the surface, make small pancakes, using 2 generous tablespoons of the batter for each. Space the pancakes about 1½ inches apart. Cook until they are lightly colored on the bottom and begin to look dry around the edge, about 1½ minutes. Turn and cook until the other side is lightly colored, about 1 minute. Transfer the pancakes to a warm serving plate.

3. Sprinkle the pancakes lightly with the confectioners' sugar and serve.

PER SERVING: Calories 337 • Soy Protein 5.9 g • Total Protein 13.4 g • Carbohydrates 10.8 g • Fat 27.1 g • Saturated Fat 8.8 g • Cholesterol 235.0 mg • Fiber 0.7 g • Sodium 69.0 mg

Zucchini Frittata

Now that Italian cooking has become more popular than French cuisine, frittatas are as commonplace as quiche. Summer or winter, this one, thickly layered with sliced squash and sparked with the Mediterranean flavors of basil and Parmesan, is equally good served for brunch, supper, or presented on a buffet table.

1. Preheat the broiler.

2. Heat 1 tablespoon of the oil in a skillet that can go under the broiler. Add the zucchini and scallions and sauté until the squash softens but is still firm, about 4 minutes. Set aside in the pan.

3. Whisk the eggs in a bowl. Crumble the tofu into the eggs. Whisk until the eggs and tofu are well combined and the mixture looks creamy. The tofu should be in fine pieces. Mix in the cooked vegetables, basil, mint, cheese, salt, and pepper.

4. Heat the remaining 2 teaspoons oil in the skillet over medium-high heat. When the pan is hot, pour in the egg mixture and reduce the heat to medium. As the eggs set, lift the edges with a fork and tilt the pan so the uncooked egg flows to the outside. Cook until the frittata is golden on the bottom, and set in all but the center, about 6 minutes.

5. Place the frittata under the broiler until the eggs are set in the center and it is puffed, 3 to 4 minutes.

6. Serve hot, warm, or at room temperature.

1 tablespoon plus
    2 teaspoons extra
    virgin olive oil

1 medium zucchini, thinly
    sliced

2 scallions (white and
    green parts), chopped

6 large eggs

8 ounces soft tofu,
    squeezed
    (see page 48)

½ cup chopped basil

2 tablespoons chopped
    mint

2 tablespoons grated
    Parmigiano-Reggiano or
    soy Parmesan

1 teaspoon salt

¼ teaspoon freshly ground
    black pepper

PER SERVING: Calories 151 • Soy Protein 3.4 g • Total Protein 11.0 g • Carbohydrates 3.0 g • Fat 10.8 g • Saturated Fat 2.5 g • Cholesterol 214.1 mg • Fiber 0.7 g • Sodium 417.6 mg

Matzoh Brei

4 large eggs

4 ounces soft tofu, lightly
  squeezed
  (see page 48)

½ teaspoon salt

3 sheets matzoh

2 tablespoons unsalted
  butter or margarine
  (see Note, page 63)

Dark Cherry Sauce (recipe
  follows) or cinnamon
  sugar

Y ou do not have to be Jewish to love matzoh brei. Just
  think of it as a frittata made with matzoh. Any two Jewish
cooks will disagree on how to make matzoh brei. Some
moisten the matzohs with water, but I crumble dry matzohs
directly into the beaten eggs. And I do not scramble them
together as they cook, but rather let the eggs set, making a
pancake. What to serve with matzoh brei is just as hotly
debated. Apple sauce, a sprinkling of confectioners' sugar or
cinnamon sugar, and maple syrup are all good, but I think
Dark Cherry Sauce is best.

1. Beat the eggs in a medium bowl. Crumble the tofu into
the eggs. Add the salt. Beat the eggs and tofu together until
well-combined, using a fork.

2. Break a sheet of matzoh into three strips. Stack the strips
on top of one another. Holding the matzoh over the bowl of
egg mixture, break it into pieces. Some will be about 1-inch
wide and others smaller. Repeat with the remaining matzohs.
Mix until the matzoh is coated with the egg, about 1 minute.

3. Heat the butter in a skillet over medium-high heat. When
the butter stops bubbling, add the matzoh mixture, spreading it in an even layer, and smoothing it with a fork. Cook
until the matzoh brei is set, and the bottom is browned,
about 4 minutes. Invert a dinner plate over the pan and,
holding it in place with your hand, flip the two so the pancake drops onto the plate.

4. Slide the matzoh brei back into the skillet, uncooked side
down. Set the pan back over the heat. Cook until the bottom
is well browned, about 3 minutes, pressing on it occasionally.

5. Slip the matzoh brei onto a plate. Serve hot, topped with Dark Cherry Sauce or sprinkled with cinnamon sugar.

PER SERVING WITHOUT TOPPING: Calories 226 • Soy Protein 2.5 g • Total Protein 11.0 g • Carbohydrates 19.2 g • Fat 11.5 g • Saturated Fat 5.6 g • Cholesterol 227.5 mg • Fiber 0 g • Sodium 298.2 mg

Dark Cherry Sauce

Makes 1½ cups

1. Place the cherries, granulated sugar, brown sugar, and cinnamon in a saucepan. Dissolve the arrowroot powder in 1 tablespoon of water and stir into the cherry mixture. Bring to a boil over medium-high heat, stirring constantly. Reduce the heat and, still stirring constantly, cook until the sauce thickens and is clear, about 5 minutes.

2. Cool slightly before serving. This sauce will keep for up to 4 days, covered in the refrigerator. Reheat in the microwave before serving.

1½ cups frozen dark cherries

¼ cup granulated sugar

¼ cup lightly packed brown sugar

¼ teaspoon ground cinnamon

1 tablespoon arrowroot powder

PER 2 TABLESPOONS: Calories 55 • Soy Protein 0 g • Total Protein 0.4 g • Carbohydrates 14.0 g • Fat .01 g • Saturated Fat 0 g • Cholesterol 0 mg • Fiber 0.3 g • Sodium 1.5 mg

CRÊPES [*Makes 12*]

½ cup unsweetened
  soymilk, plus more as
  needed

½ cup all-purpose flour

½ cup sugar

1 large egg

2 tablespoons canola oil,
  plus more as needed

FILLING

½ cup part-skim-milk
  ricotta, drained

4 ounces soft tofu, lightly
  squeezed
  (see page 48)

2 tablespoons sugar

1 tablespoon orange-
  flavored liqueur or
  orange juice

½ teaspoon vanilla extract

Pinch of salt

2 tablespoons unsalted
  butter or margarine

Blintzes

My mother always gave her recipes a sophisticated twist. Back in the 1950s, she made blintzes using a crêpes suzette recipe. The filling was pot cheese moistened with Grand Marnier. I still use her crêpe recipe, which works beautifully with soymilk. (Unsweetened soymilk ensures the crêpes do not stick to the pan or brown too quickly around the edges.) Tofu blended with drained ricotta replaces my mother's pot cheese filling, but I still use the liqueur. These blintzes taste just like hers, especially when browned in butter.

1. To make the crêpes, combine the ½ cup soymilk, flour, sugar, egg, and 2 tablespoons oil in a bowl. Whisk until the ingredients are blended; some lumps will remain. The batter should have the thickness of heavy cream. It will look satiny and golden beige. Let the batter sit for at least 1 hour, or cover with plastic wrap and refrigerate for up to 24 hours.

2. If the batter has been refrigerated, bring it to room temperature, about 20 minutes. If it has thickened, thin it back to its original texture by mixing in more soymilk, 1 tablespoon at a time.

3. Heat a crêpe pan or small nonstick skillet over medium-high heat. Wipe the pan lightly with 2 to 3 drops of oil. When a drop of water dances when flicked onto the surface, pour in ¼ cup of the batter. Holding it by the handle, tilt the pan, rotating it so the batter covers the bottom of the pan evenly. Cook until the crêpe begins to color at the edges and the bottom is light golden brown, about 2 minutes. Turn and cook until the crêpe is lightly browned in places, about 1 minute. Do not overcook, or the crêpe will dry out. Place the crêpe on a plate. Continue making crêpes until all the batter is used up. (If not using immediately, place a piece of waxed paper

between each crêpe, cover the stack with plastic wrap, and refrigerate for up to a day.) Extra crêpes, wrapped in plastic, then foil, can be frozen up to 1 month.

4. To make the filling, place the cheese in a bowl. Crumble in the tofu. Add the sugar, liqueur, vanilla, and salt. Mash with a fork until the mixture has the texture of small-curd cottage cheese.

5. Place a crêpe, browned side down, on the counter. Spoon about 2 tablespoons of the cheese mixture into the center of the crêpe. Fold up the bottom, then tuck the two sides in. Fold down the top of the blintz, enclosing the filling. Repeat, making 8 filled blintzes. Place the blintzes, folded side down, on a plate. (The blintzes can be made up to 24 hours ahead and refrigerated, covered with plastic wrap.)

6. Melt the butter in a skillet over medium-high heat. Add the blintzes to the pan, folded side down. Heat until they are lightly browned, about 4 minutes. Turn, and brown on the other side, about 3 minutes. Serve hot or warm.

FOR 2 BLINTZES: Calories 199 • Soy Protein 2.3 g • Total Protein 5.7 g • Carbohydrates 23.9 g • Fat 9.0 g • Saturated Fat 2.9 g • Cholesterol 36.7 mg • Fiber 0.7 g • Sodium 68.4 mg

smoothies and drinks

Whether you charge into a workout before breakfast, start the day slowly and have breakfast around lunchtime, or need an afternoon lift to keep from crashing, here are drinks to lift your energy and your spirits. A soy-packed smoothie is the ideal breakfast—quick and easy, nutritious and delicious. Whether you drink cow's milk or are a vegan, follow a carbohydrate-rich diet or one high in protein, there is a soy smoothie for you.

My favorites are made with frozen fruit, tossed in a blender with creamy soymilk and, perhaps, soy yogurt, which adds live cultures as well as flavor and richness. For variety, blend chocolate soymilk with a frozen banana for a lush, dark smoothie. If the wake-up call of a double espresso is essential, you can whiz it with coffee- or mocha-flavored soymilk, making a cappuccino smoothie.

Soy smoothies vary nutritionally, particularly in the amounts of soy protein and isoflavones provided. Those made with soymilk offer 6 to 11 grams of soy protein and from 35 to more than 70 milligrams of isoflavones. If the soymilk you use is fortified, 8 ounces provides as much calcium as a glass of cow's milk.

Using soy yogurt in smoothies increases the protein content by another 5 grams, adds 30 or so milligrams of isoflavones, and may contribute live acidophilus and other beneficial cultures.

Smoothies made with protein powder sometimes have a slightly gritty texture. This form of soy offer is also highly processed. However, one portion of most soy protein powders makes a smoothie with the entire 25 grams of soy protein the American Heart Association recommends. These powders give some smoothies a slightly gritty texture, and they are a highly processed form of soy, but their protein content and convenience cannot be beat.

In my smoothies I use unflavored, unsweetened soy protein powder made from soy protein isolate. Although there are dozens of powdered soy drink mixes on the market, all flavored and ready to blend with milk, fruit juice, soymilk, or water, most of them are heavily sweetened with sugar or artificial sweeteners such as aspartame, and contain thickeners, too. Because of all these other ingredients the powdered mixes provide significantly less soy protein per serving than an equivalent measure of protein powder.

Kiwi Melon Smoothie

1 kiwi, peeled and cut into
8 pieces

1 cup frozen honeydew
melon cubes

One 6-ounce container
kiwi-lemon, lemon, or
key lime soy yogurt

1 cup vanilla soymilk

1 tablespoon frozen apple
juice concentrate

Cubed melon from a salad bar or the sliced melon sold in
packages at most markets is perfect for making this
pale green smoothie. The cut melon saves time and allows
you to select ripe fruit. On a sweltering day, this refreshing
meal-in-a-glass makes a cooling lunch or light supper.

1. Combine the kiwi, melon, yogurt, soymilk, and apple
juice concentrate in a blender. Blend until creamy and
smooth.

2. Divide the smoothie between two tall glasses and serve.

PER SERVING: Calories 143 • Soy Protein 5.3 g • Total Protein 6.5 g • Carbohydrates 23.6 g •
Fat 3.5 g • Saturated Fat 0.3 g • Cholesterol 0 mg • Fiber 1.9 g • Sodium 72.3 mg

HIGH-PROTEIN KIWI-MELON SMOOTHIE: For additional protein, add 1 serving (according to the package directions) soy
protein powder.

PER SERVING: Calories 212 • Soy Protein 18.9 g • Total Protein 20.0 g • Carbohydrates 26.1 g •
Fat 4.5 g • Saturated Fat 0.3 g • Cholesterol 0 mg • Fiber 1.9 g • Sodium 194.0 mg

Frozen Fruit for Smoothies

I keep bags of cut-up fruit in the freezer, including bananas, peeled and cut in
1-inch pieces. Using them not only saves time. It also lets you make smoothies
without using ice cubes. The result is thicker and richer tasting drinks.

Creamy Orange Smoothie

This smoothie combines juice, protein, and a serving of fresh fruit in a tall, revitalizing drink. It also includes as much calcium as a glass of cow's milk. With all this goodness, it still is a treat, particularly if you like creamsicles, the frozen pop made from orange sherbet and vanilla ice cream.

1. Combine the yogurt, melon, soymilk, juice concentrate, and orange oil in a blender. Whirl until completely blended and smooth.

2. Divide the smoothie between two tall glasses and serve.

One 6-ounce container orange soy yogurt

1 cup frozen cubed cantaloupe

½ cup vanilla soymilk

¼ cup frozen orange juice concentrate

3 to 4 drops orange oil or 2 teaspoons grated orange zest

PER SERVING: Calories 156 • Soy Protein 4.1 g • Total Protein 5.7 g • Carbohydrates 24.3 g • Fat 3.2 g • Saturated Fat 0.4 g • Cholesterol 0 mg • Fiber 1.2 g • Sodium 43.2 mg

¼ cup light coconut milk
(see page 273)

1½ cups vanilla soymilk

1 medium banana, cut into
1-inch pieces and
frozen (see box,
page 84)

2 tablespoons apple juice
concentrate

1 portion soy protein
powder

Colada Smoothie

Using coconut milk with reduced fat makes this smoothie creamy while cutting down on fat.

1. Combine the coconut milk, soymilk, banana, apple juice concentrate, and soy protein powder in a blender. Puree until smooth and thick.

2. Divide the smoothie between two tall glasses and serve.

PER SERVING: Calories 206 • Soy Protein 16.4 g • Total Protein 17.4 g • Carbohydrates 27.9 g • Fat 4.9 g • Saturated Fat 1.5 g • Cholesterol 0 mg • Fiber 2.3 g • Sodium 175.9 mg

Cocoa Nutty Smoothie

Serves 1

Chocoholics adore this fudge-rich smoothie, with its perfect balance of cocoa flavor, peanut butter, and sweet banana. When it sits for about twenty minutes, it becomes thick enough to spoon up like chocolate mousse.

1 cup chocolate soymilk

1 small banana, cut into 1-inch pieces and frozen

2 tablespoons smooth natural peanut butter

2 tablespoons cocoa powder

2 ice cubes

1. Combine the soymilk, banana, peanut butter, and cocoa in a blender. Blend until creamy. With the blender running, add the ice cubes and blend until smooth.

2. Pour into a tall glass and serve.

PER SERVING: Calories 410 • Soy Protein 4.8 g • Total Protein 16.1 g • Carbohydrates 50.5 g • Fat 17.8 g • Saturated Fat 4.12 g • Cholesterol 0 mg • Fiber 8.2 g • Sodium 249.6 mg

HIGH-PROTEIN COCOA NUTTY SMOOTHIE: Double the amount of soymilk to 2 cups and add 1 serving (according to the package directions) soy protein powder. This higher-protein version makes 2 servings.

PER SERVING: Calories 319 • Soy Protein 16.9 g • Total Protein 24.5 g • Carbohydrates 37.8 g • Fat 10.2 g • Saturated Fat 2.7 g • Cholesterol 0 mg • Fiber 7.3 g • Sodium 275.8 mg

Cran-Raspberry Smoothie

1 cup unsweetened
    soymilk

2 tablespoons seedless
    raspberry jam

½ cup frozen cranberries

1 small or medium
    banana, cut into 1-inch
    pieces and frozen

2 tablespoons orange juice
    concentrate

½ inch fresh ginger,
    chopped

When writing for a magazine's holiday issue, I have been known to cook Thanksgiving dinner in July. Once, while roasting in the kitchen while the turkey did the same in the oven, I poured myself a frosty glass of cranberry juice and thought, "Why not put cranberries in a smoothie?" Now, I stow a couple of bags of cranberries in the freezer in December so I can whip up this refreshing combo on hot summer days. Along with brisk flavor, it is full of anthocyanins, one of the phytochemicals that may help prevent cancer.

1. Combine the soymilk, jam, cranberries, banana, orange juice concentrate, and ginger in a blender. Puree until smooth and thick.

2. Divide the smoothie between two tall glasses and serve.

PER SERVING: Calories 169 • Soy Protein 4.25 g • Total Protein 5.2 g • Carbohydrates 34.4 g • Fat 2.4 g • Saturated Fat 0.1 g • Cholesterol 0 mg • Fiber 4.0 g • Sodium 11.5 mg

Maple Walnut Smoothie

Maple walnut is one of my favorite ice-cream flavors. This smoothie has the same naturally sweet appeal. Dark maple syrup, often labeled Grade B, has fuller flavor than lighter-colored, milder-tasting, and more costly grades. Look for it at natural food stores and farmers' markets.

1 cup unsweetened soymilk

1 banana, cut into 1-inch pieces

8 walnut halves

2 tablespoons pure maple syrup

2 ice cubes

1. Combine the soymilk, banana, nuts, and maple syrup in a blender. Blend until creamy. With the blender running, add the ice cubes and blend thoroughly.

2. Pour into a tall glass and serve immediately.

PER SERVING: Calories 396 • Soy Protein 8.5 g • Total Protein 12.1 g • Carbohydrates 61.3 g • Fat 14.8 g • Saturated Fat 0.9 g • Cholesterol 0 mg • Fiber 7.9 g • Sodium 96.0 mg

HIGH-PROTEIN MAPLE WALNUT SMOOTHIE: Substitute 1 cup low-fat milk for the soymilk. Combine in a blender with the banana, 10 walnut halves, and maple syrup. Blend until creamy. With the blender running, add 1 portion soy protein powder and 3 ice cubes. Blend thoroughly. This higher-protein version serves two.

PER SERVING: Calories 265 • Soy Protein 12.4 g • Total Protein 19.0 g • Carbohydrates 35.5 g • Fat 8.1 g • Saturated Fat 1.3 g • Cholesterol 7.5 mg • Fiber 2.2 g • Sodium 170.2 mg

Serves 1

3 tablespoons golden
   raisins

¼ cup apple juice

1 cup unsweetened or
   vanilla soymilk

1 small banana, cut into
   1-inch pieces and
   frozen

¼ teaspoon brandy, rum,
   or rum flavoring

Freshly grated nutmeg

Ground cinnamon

Not-Nog Smoothie

The rich, rum-raisin flavor of eggnog makes any morning seem festive. Here, it adds cheer to a thick, dairy-free smoothie. If you can get eggnog-flavored soymilk, by all means use it to give this golden drink a double burst of flavor.

1. Soak the raisins in the apple juice for 10 to 20 minutes to plump them. Drain well.

2. Combine the soymilk, banana, drained raisins, and brandy flavoring in a blender. Add several gratings of the nutmeg and whirl until the smoothie is blended and thick.

3. Pour into a large glass, top with a dash of cinnamon, and serve.

PER SERVING: Calories 378 • Soy Protein 7.0 g • Total Protein 9.0 g • Carbohydrates 62.0 g • Fat 9.2 g • Saturated Fat 0.3 g • Cholesterol 0 mg • Fiber 11.2 g • Sodium 251.0 mg

Avocado Frappé

This lush iced drink is based on the popular Filipino custom of blending avocado with evaporated milk and sugar to make a rich, soft green milk shake with subtle flavor. On a hot day, it is an adventure you can enjoy as a light lunch. It is also restoring at teatime.

1. Combine the avocado, lime juice, sugar, and soymilk in a blender. Blend until creamy. With the blender running, add the ice cubes. Whirl until the drink is smooth and thick.
2. Pour into a tall glass and serve.

½ medium ripe avocado

2 teaspoons fresh lime juice

3 tablespoons palm or light brown sugar

¾ cup unsweetened soymilk

4 ice cubes

PER SERVING: Calories 384 • Soy Protein 6.4 g • Total Protein 8.3 g • Carbohydrates 52.9 g • Fat 18.2 g • Saturated Fat 2.2 g • Cholesterol 0 mg • Fiber 7.3 g • Sodium 30.1 mg

Gazpacho Smoothie

1 cup tomato juice

1 medium tomato, peeled, seeded, and chopped

1 small garlic clove, chopped

1 teaspoon white wine vinegar

Hot pepper sauce

Freshly ground black pepper

3 ice cubes

1 portion soy protein powder

1 teaspoon extra virgin olive oil, optional

Brisk as a bowl of tangy gazpacho and nourishing as a smoothie, this icy, vibrant drink is perfect in summer or winter as a light meal. I use Muir Glen's organic tomato juice, but try a tomato-vegetable blend if you wish. If you include the olive oil, choose one from Tuscany or Puglia that is fruity and strong.

1. Combine the juice, tomato, garlic, vinegar, and hot pepper sauce and black pepper to taste in a blender. Add the ice cubes and the protein powder. Whirl until the ice no longer rattles in the container. Add the oil, if using, and whirl to blend.

2. Pour into a tall glass and serve immediately.

PER SERVING: Calories 249 • Soy Protein 25.0 g • Total Protein 32.1 g • Carbohydrates 22.1 g • Fat 5.2 g • Saturated Fat 0.6 g • Cholesterol 0 mg • Fiber 4.0 g • Sodium 741.0 mg

Date Shake

Southern Californians have long enjoyed thick date shakes. Now, it is time for the rest of us to discover this lotus-land milk shake, too, with this dairy-free version. The secret to turning fiber-rich dates into a smooth shake is to start with moist, soft Medjool dates and blend them with hot water before adding the other ingredients. A touch of instant espresso powder adds an interesting note.

1. Combine the dates and boiling water in a blender and puree.

2. Add the frozen dessert, soymilk, instant coffee, if using, and ice cubes. Whirl until the ice is blended.

3. Pour into two tall glasses and serve immediately.

½ cup chopped, pitted Medjool dates (4 to 6 dates)

½ cup boiling water

1 cup vanilla soy frozen dessert

1 cup unsweetened soymilk

¼ teaspoon instant espresso coffee powder, optional

4 ice cubes

PER SERVING: Calories 367 • Soy Protein 6.5 g • Total Protein 7.4 g • Carbohydrates 56.2 g • Fat 13.5 g • Saturated Fat 1.6 g • Cholesterol 0 mg • Fiber 5.3 g • Sodium 91.3 mg

1 cup unsweetened
soymilk

One 6-ounce container
lemon soy yogurt

½ cup lemon sorbet

Juice of ½ lemon

1 tablespoon chopped
lemon rind and pulp
from the squeezed
lemon (see Note)

1 or 2 ice cubes

Lemon Frullato

Tell friends you discovered this tart-sweet lemon refresher at a little bar in Portofino, where they made it with the local lemons. Do not tell them it contains nearly 7 grams of soy protein because they will not believe you. Since part of the lemon rind goes into this drink, I recommend that it be organic. Use a top-quality, intensely flavored sorbet. On a very hot day, you might whip up this frullato for breakfast or have it in place of your afternoon iced tea.

1. Combine the soymilk, yogurt, sorbet, lemon juice, rind with pulp, and ice cubes in a blender. Whirl until the ice is blended.

2. Pour into two tall glasses and serve.

NOTE: After squeezing the juice from the lemon, cut it into four pieces. Chop one and discard the rest. This will give you the right amount of whole rind and pulp.

PER SERVING: Calories 145 • Soy Protein 6.9 g • Total Protein 7.1 g • Carbohydrates 21.7 g • Fat 4.3 g • Saturated Fat 0.3 g • Cholesterol 0 mg • Fiber 2.9 g • Sodium 71.3 mg

Morning Miso

I am partial to savory breakfasts, especially the Japanese habit of drinking miso soup in the morning. It gives you a stimulating wake-up call without your having to resort to caffeine. Hatcho miso provides depth reminscent of good, brewed coffee, and ginger gives it an extra zing. In addition, red lentils add more protein to this fortifying hot drink, which you can sip from a mug morning, noon, or night.

1. Combine the broth, lentils, onion, ginger, paprika, and turmeric in a deep saucepan. Bring the soup to a boil, reduce the heat, and simmer, uncovered, until the lentils are soft, 20 to 25 minutes. Let it sit for 10 minutes to cool slightly.

2. Puree the soup in a blender. Add the miso and whirl to blend.

3. Season the soup to taste with salt and pepper. Pour into mugs and serve hot. If you reheat the soup, take care not to let it boil, as this kills the live enzymes in the miso.

4 cups vegetable broth

½ cup red lentils, rinsed and drained

1 medium onion, chopped

2 teaspoons chopped peeled fresh ginger

½ teaspoon sweet paprika

½ teaspoon turmeric

3 tablespoons Hatcho or barley miso

Salt and freshly ground black pepper

PER SERVING: Calories 127 • Soy Protein 2.3 g • Total Protein 8.2 g • Carbohydrates 19.6 g • Fat 1.2 g • Saturated Fat 0 g • Cholesterol 0 mg • Fiber 4 g • Sodium 1217.7 mg

4 cardamom pods

4-inch cinnamon stick

4 cloves

1 vanilla bean

1 inch fresh ginger, peeled

4 teaspoons black tea or
    4 tea bags

2 cups plain soymilk

2 tablespoons honey

2 tablespoons sugar

Supercharged Chai

Chai should be hot, sweet, and spicy. Its preparation is rooted in the Ayurvedic tradition of India, a practice in which food is used to help create balance and promote well-being. Well made, its bracing astringency, stimulating spices, and creamy milk are energizing and sustaining. I also like it chilled. Refrigerated soymilks are the best choice; they make a richer, smoother chai.

1. Combine the cardamom, cinnamon, cloves, and vanilla bean in a saucepan. Add 2 cups water. Grate the ginger over the pot, using a rasp or fine grater. (This assures you will catch all the juice from the ginger.) Bring to a boil over medium-high heat, reduce the heat, and boil gently for 3 minutes. Cover the pot and remove it from the heat. Steep the spices for 10 minutes.

2. Return the pot to medium-high heat and bring back to a boil, uncovered. Add the tea and soymilk. When the pot is about to boil again, stir in the honey and sugar.

3. Strain the chai and pour it into mugs to serve.

PER SERVING: Calories 108 • Soy Protein 4.5 g • Total Protein 5.3 g • Carbohydrates 18.1 g • Fat 2.4 g • Saturated Fat 0 g • Cholesterol 0 mg • Fiber 2.1 g • Sodium 2.5 mg

Heavenly Haute
Hot Chocolate

Serves 4

When Jeffrey Steingarten, *Vogue* magazine's food writer, claimed to have created the perfect cup of hot chocolate, using a recipe from Pierre Hermé, the Parisian pastry chef extraordinaire, I had to see how his distinctive method worked in a dairy-free version. Frothy yet full-bodied, sweet with a slight bitter note, silken as fine chocolate, yet with the sharpness of cocoa, the result is astonishing. Ideally, making this *chocolat chaud* requires an immersion blender, the blending of Scharffen Berger and Valrhona or Lindt chocolates, and the following technique. However, using a traditional blender and any top-quality dark chocolate, including Callebaut or El Rey, is still sure to transport you. When cooled, it will keep for up to three days, covered and refrigerated. This means chocoholics can reheat a fix in minutes.

2 cups plain or vanilla soymilk

¼ cup sugar

3½ ounces dark chocolate, chopped

3½ tablespoons Dutch-processed cocoa powder

¼ to ¾ teaspoon vanilla extract

1. Combine the soymilk, sugar, and ¼ cup water in a saucepan. Cook over medium-high heat until the sugar dissolves and the milk is almost boiling, 4 to 5 minutes. Add the chocolate, cocoa, and ¼ teaspoon of the vanilla. Whisk to blend. Bring the mixture to a boil and remove the saucepan from the heat. Add the remaining ½ teaspoon vanilla, if desired.

2. Froth the hot chocolate using an immersion blender. If you are using a traditional blender, carefully whip the hot liquid on high speed until it is frothy.

3. Serve immediately, or cool, then refrigerate, covered. Reheat, froth, and serve.

PER SERVING: Calories 221 • Soy Protein 4.5 g • Total Protein 6.7 g • Carbohydrates 33.8 g • Fat 9.2 g • Saturated Fat 3.7 g • Cholesterol 0 mg • Fiber 3.5 g • Sodium 75.0 mg

dips and starters

Onion dip and other retro favorites are more nutritionally friendly when made with soy sour cream, while guacamole takes on new interest with edamame blended in. So does My Mother's Vegetarian Chopped Liver (page 111), while miso slips as naturally as mayonnaise into cholesterol-free Deviled Eggs (page 110). Soynuts add the perfect crunch to some unexpected munchies to accompany drinks, while Fried Tofu Sticks (page 117) let you enjoy pleasure akin to that of eating crisp-crusted mozzarella, with only a fraction of the fat and cholesterol.

Broccoli and Mustard Dip

Roasted garlic plus plenty of Dijon mustard give this dip big, bold flavor. Steaming the broccoli brings out its taste and makes the dip bright green. Serve it surrounded by carrot sticks, celery sticks, and strips of sweet red bell pepper. Munching them with the dip, in no time, you will discover you have enjoyed eating a full serving of vegetables, or more.

1. Steam the broccoli until it is tender, about 5 minutes.

2. When the broccoli is cool enough to handle, squeeze it gently to extract most of the cooking water. Place the broccoli in the bowl of a food processor and pulse 4 to 5 times to chop. Add the tofu, garlic, mustard, soy sour cream, oregano, and lemon juice. Process until well blended. Season to taste with salt and pepper.

3. Pour the dip into a serving bowl or plastic container. Cover and refrigerate for at least 1 hour, up to overnight, to let the flavors develop. Serve chilled. (This dip will keep for up to 3 days, tightly covered and refrigerated.)

4 cups (about 8 ounces) broccoli florets

½ cup (4 ounces) silken tofu

4 cloves Roasted Garlic (recipe follows), coarsely chopped

¼ cup Dijon mustard

2 tablespoons soy sour cream

1 tablespoon fresh oregano, chopped, or 1 teaspoon dried

2 teaspoons fresh lemon juice

Salt and freshly ground black pepper

PER 2 TABLESPOONS: Calories 22 • Soy Protein 0.4 g • Total Protein 1.4 g • Carbohydrates 2.0 g • Fat 1.2 g • Saturated Fat 0.2 g • Cholesterol 0 mg • Fiber 0.5 g • Sodium 203.0 mg

SPINACH AND MUSTARD DIP: Use a 10-ounce package frozen spinach, defrosted and squeezed dry, in place of the broccoli.

PER 2 TABLESPOONS: Calories 21 • Soy Protein 0.4 g • Total Protein 1.4 g • Carbohydrates 1.9 g • Fat 1.2 g • Saturated Fat 0.2 g • Cholesterol 0 mg • Fiber 0.5 g • Sodium 208.0 mg

Makes 1 head

1 head garlic
½ teaspoon olive oil
⅛ teaspoon salt

Roasted Garlic

This creamy, gentle garlic is so delicious blended into salad dressings, soups, stews, and pasta sauces that you will always want to have it on hand. This is easy if you make two heads at a time. Roasted garlic will keep for up to 5 days, covered and refrigerated.

1. Preheat the oven to 400°F.

2. Break the garlic apart into cloves. Rub the cloves with the oil. Place them in the center of a large square of aluminum foil. Sprinkle with the salt. Seal the garlic in the foil by bringing up the four corners over the garlic, then crumpling the foil together.

3. Bake the garlic in the center of the oven for 45 to 60 minutes, depending on the size of the cloves, until they are soft when pressed with your fingers in an oven mitt.

4. To use, snip the bottom off each clove and squeeze out the garlic by pressing from the top with your fingers.

NOTE: Another method for roasting garlic is to slice off the top of a whole head, cutting it crosswise 1 inch below the tip. Oil and roast the entire head, wrapped in foil, for 45 to 60 minutes. It looks like a giant flower. To use, squeeze the head until the individual cloves pop out.

Garden Dip with Herbs

Makes 2 cups

This dip is a gift for dairy lovers. It evolved from a recipe that appeared in *Vogue* magazine in the 1970s. Called *coeur du jardin*, it was a savory version of *coeur à la crème*, the French dessert that blends cream cheese and crème fraîche. Here, soy cream cheese and tofu duplicate the silken luxury of these rich ingredients. The fresh herbs turn this dip a delicate spring green. A touch of garlic adds an earthy note. This dip is best made 8 hours before you serve it.

About 16 ounces silken tofu, drained (see page 48)

½ cup soy cream cheese

1 cup chopped flat-leaf parsley

½ cup chopped dill

⅓ cup snipped chives

⅓ cup chopped basil

1 teaspoon fresh lemon juice

1 garlic clove, chopped

Pinch of cayenne

1 teaspoon salt

Freshly ground black pepper

1. Combine the drained tofu and cream cheese in a food processor and blend. Add the parsley, dill, chives, basil, lemon juice, garlic, cayenne, and salt. Process to blend well. Season generously with pepper.

2. Pack the dip into a container. Cover tightly and refrigerate for at least 2 hours to allow the flavors to meld. Serve chilled. (This dip will keep for up to 3 days, refrigerated.)

PER 2 TABLESPOONS: Calories 41 • Soy Protein 2.1 g • Total Protein 2.3 g • Carbohydrates 1.5 g • Fat 2.8 g • Saturated Fat 0.5 g • Cholesterol 0 mg • Fiber 0.1 g • Sodium 157.2 mg

1 cup Onion Marmalade
(recipe follows)

½ cup (4 ounces) silken
tofu

½ cup soy sour cream

1 teaspoon fresh lemon
juice

Freshly ground black
pepper

Natural Onion Dip

This version of the classic onion dip contains a fraction of the sodium in the regular version made with soup mix. Plus you get all the good phytochemicals found in alliums.

1. Combine the marmalade, tofu, sour cream, and lemon juice in a food processor and puree. Season to taste with pepper.

2. Transfer the dip to a bowl, cover with plastic wrap, and refrigerate for at least 2 hours, to allow the flavors to meld and the dip to set up. Serve chilled. (This dip will keep for up to 4 days, covered and refrigerated.)

PER 2 TABLESPOONS: Calories 28 • Soy Protein 0.6 g • Total Protein 0.9 g • Carbohydrates 1.6 g • Fat 2.1 g • Saturated Fat 0.8 g • Cholesterol 0.9 mg • Fiber 0.2 g • Sodium 34.6 mg

Onion Marmalade

Makes 1½ cups

This highly flavored condiment adds the same taste as you get from dehydrated soup mix, but in a wholesome way, with drastically less sodium. The Spanish onions have a pleasant sweetness. If you use regular yellow onions, sprinkle ½ teaspoon sugar over the onions just before adding the broth. The finished condiment keeps for weeks. Use it to add flavor to dips, gravies, and sauces, and as a topping on pizza and focaccia.

2 large Spanish onions

1 tablespoon olive oil

1 tablespoon unsalted butter or olive oil

1 cup defatted beef broth or 1 tablespoon vegetable broth powder dissolved in 1 cup warm water

Freshly ground black pepper

1. Thinly slice the onions, then chop them.

2. Heat the oil and butter in a large Dutch oven over medium-high heat. Stir in the onions until they are coated. Cook, stirring often, until the onions are translucent and look moist, 10 to 12 minutes. Tightly cover and reduce the heat to medium-low. Cook until the onions are soft and very wet, but not colored, stirring them 2 or 3 times, about 30 minutes.

3. Add the broth and bring the liquid to a boil. Reduce the heat, cover, and cook the onions gently until they are very soft. Uncover the pot and increase the heat to medium-high. Cook until the onions have caramelized to a golden brown and are almost dry, stirring often and scraping up any bits sticking to the pot, 10 to 15 minutes.

4. Transfer to a container and cool to room temperature. Cover tightly and refrigerate. This marmalade keeps for up to 4 weeks.

PER 2 TABLESPOONS: Calories 35 • Soy Protein 0 g • Total Protein 0.9 g • Carbohydrates 3.5 g • Fat 2.8 g • Saturated Fat 0.8 g • Cholesterol 2.5 mg • Fiber 0.7 g • Sodium 14.5 mg

1 envelope onion soup mix

1 cup soy sour cream

2 teaspoons fresh lemon
juice

Freshly ground black
pepper

Quick Onion Dip

Everyone knows this irresistable dip when made with real sour cream is a killer, nutritionally speaking. Here, soy sour cream keeps the taste we love while eliminating all the cholesterol and lactose of dairy sour cream.

1. Combine the soup mix, sour cream, and lemon juice in a bowl. Season to taste with pepper.

2. Cover with plastic wrap and refrigerate for at least 1 hour, to allow the flavors to develop and the dip to set up. Serve chilled. (This dip will keep for up to 4 days, covered and refrigerated.)

PER 2 TABLESPOONS: Calories 31 • Soy Protein 0.4 g • Total Protein 0.4 g • Carbohydrates 1.1 g • Fat 2.2 g • Saturated Fat 0.9 g • Cholesterol 0 mg • Fiber 0.1 g • Sodium 271.1 mg

Edamole

It almost seems like cheating to slip edamame into guacamole because they disappear so completely, but that little bit of soy added here and there adds up at the end of the day. Serve with regular or baked corn chips.

¼ cup lightly packed cilantro leaves

½ cup frozen shelled edamame

1 medium ripe avocado

1 garlic clove, finely chopped

1 tablespoon fresh lime juice

½ teaspoon salt

Freshly ground black pepper

1. Bring a medium pot of water to a boil. Fill a medium bowl with ice and cold water. Place the cilantro in a sieve and hold the sieve in the boiling water for 1 minute to wilt the cilantro. Immediately transfer the cilantro to the bowl of ice water to stop the cooking and keep it bright green. Squeeze out the water and coarsely chop the cilantro. Add the cilantro to the bowl of a food processor.

2. Boil the edamame in the same pot for 5 minutes. Drain them, and chill them in the bowl of ice water. Drain the beans and add to the food processor. Scoop the avocado out of its peel and add it to the food processor, along with the garlic, lime juice, and salt. Puree, stopping occasionally to scrape down the sides of the bowl. If the mixture is too thick to start flowing in the food processor, add 1 or 2 tablespoons water and continue processing. Season to taste with pepper. This dip keeps 1 day, covered and refrigerated.

PER 2 TABLESPOONS: Calories 32 • Soy Protein 2.8 g • Total Protein 3.4 g • Carbohydrates 5.9 g • Fat 5.3 g • Saturated Fat 0.2 g • Cholesterol 0 mg • Fiber 4.0 g • Sodium 123.5 mg

Southwestern Bean Spread

One 15-ounce can yellow
    soybeans, rinsed and
    drained

1 large garlic clove,
    chopped

3 tablespoons tomato
    paste

2 tablespoons distilled
    white vinegar

1 tablespoon canola oil

¼ cup cilantro leaves

1 teaspoon sugar

1 teaspoon ground cumin

1 teaspoon dried oregano

½ teaspoon onion powder

¼ teaspoon ground
    chipotle chile powder

1 teaspoon salt

Freshly ground black
    pepper

The velvety texture and zesty taste of this spread make it hard to believe it is made from canned soybeans. How I discovered the recipe is an amusing story. When I asked the friend who first served me the dip how to make it, he handed me the jar it came in. Back home, I read the ingredients, and was able to duplicate its smoky, spicy flavor. Enjoy it with tortilla chips and celery sticks. It also works nicely as a sandwich spread, in place of mustard, and heated, as part of Nachitos (page 120).

1. Combine the beans, garlic, tomato paste, vinegar, oil, cilantro, sugar, cumin, oregano, onion powder, chipotle powder, and salt in a food processor. Process until they are well blended, stopping 2 or 3 times to scrape down the sides of the bowl. Season with pepper to taste.

2. Serve immediately. (The spread will keep for up to 4 days, covered and refrigerated.)

PER 2 TABLESPOONS: Calories 82 • Soy Protein 6.8 g • Total Protein 7.0 g • Carbohydrates 5.5 g • Fat 3.7 g • Saturated Fat 0.1 g • Cholesterol 0 mg • Fiber 0.5 g • Sodium 185.0 mg

Goat Cheese Spread

Makes 1¼ cups

Blending fresh goat cheese, such as Montrachet, with tofu and soy cream cheese turns the cheese into an earthy, creamy spread. Besides serving it on bread, I add a dollop to hot soups. Place a couple of generous spoonsful in the bottom of the salad bowl and blend with the olive oil and vinegar, making a lovely, creamy dressing for a green salad. A spoonful is delicious mashed into a baked potato as well.

5 to 6 ounces soft mild goat cheese

¼ cup plus 2 tablespoons (3 ounces) silken tofu

2 tablespoons soy cream cheese

4 to 5 cloves Caramelized Garlic (recipe follows) or Roasted Garlic (page 100)

1 teaspoon fresh lemon juice

Salt and freshly ground black pepper

1. Combine the cheese, tofu, cream cheese, garlic, and lemon juice in a food processor. Blend well. Season to taste with salt and pepper.

2. Transfer to a bowl. Cover the spread with plastic wrap and refrigerate for 1 to 4 hours, to allow the flavors to meld. Let sit at room temperature for 20 minutes before serving.

PER 2 TABLESPOONS, INCLUDING WALNUTS: Calories 73 • Soy Protein 0.5 g • Total Protein 3.8 g • Carbohydrates 1.0 g • Fat 6.0 g • Saturated Fat 2.9 g • Cholesterol 7.8 mg • Fiber 0 g • Sodium 76.8 mg

Caramelized Garlic

This cooking method intensifies the sweetness of garlic more than roasting does, along with leaving it soft.

Makes about 12 cloves

1 tablespoon extra virgin olive oil
1 medium head garlic, cloves separated and peeled

Heat the oil with 2 tablespoons water in a small, covered saucepan. Add the garlic. Cover and cook for 4 minutes over medium heat. Turn the cloves. Cook, uncovered, turning the cloves until they are deep brown on all sides, 8 to 10 minutes. Caramelized garlic will keep for up to 3 days, in a tightly covered container and refrigerated.

Goat Cheese Crostini

Four ½-inch slices whole wheat Italian or other whole wheat bread

½ cup Goat Cheese Spread (page 107)

4 teaspoons chopped walnuts

2 to 3 teaspoons snipped chives

These simple open-faced cheese sandwiches are a country-style treat that can turn a bowl of soup into a memorable lunch or dinner. Or serve them with a plate of sun-ripened sliced tomatoes or a big mixed green salad. They are even special enough to accompany a glass of wine for a relaxing and sustaining break. Wrapped in waxed paper, they travel well for lunch. Though any toasted whole wheat bread will do, using a crusty Italian loaf makes heartier crostini. Since walnuts and cheese are a fine combination, sometimes I sprinkle the crostini with a teaspoon of chopped nuts, adding snipped chives for color.

1. Preheat the oven to 400°F. Set the rack in the center of the oven.

2. Arrange the bread slices in one layer on the rack. Toast until the bread is crisp, about 8 minutes.

3. Spread 2 tablespoons Goat Cheese Spread on each toasted bread slice and sprinkle with nuts and chives. Serve at once, or cover with foil and refrigerate up to 4 hours.

PER CROSTINO: Calories 160 • Soy Protein 0.5 g • Total Protein 7.1 g • Carbohydrates 15.8 g • Fat 8.2 g • Saturated Fat 3.1 g • Cholesterol 7.8 mg • Fiber 2.2 g • Sodium 244.6 mg

Caponata

Edamame blend seamlessly into this sweet and savory antipasto. The vinegar and sugar, when heated together in classic Sicilian fashion, distribute their flavors more evenly into cooked vegetables. Use a good-quality imported tomato sauce and salted capers. Caponata is a good dish for parties because it can be made ahead and it is easily multiplied. For a light main course, serve canned tuna on a bed of caponata garnished with chopped parsley.

1. Place the capers in a small bowl, cover with water, and soak for 20 minutes. Drain, rinse well, and drain again. Chop the capers and set them aside.

2. Heat the oil in a large skillet over medium-high heat. Add the onion and sauté until it is lightly browned, about 8 minutes. Mix in the eggplant. Cook until the eggplant is soft and lightly browned, about 15 minutes, stirring occasionally. Add the celery, edamame, tomato sauce, and ½ cup water. Cook until the eggplant is very soft, about 5 minutes. Mix in the olives, capers, and pine nuts. Season to taste with salt and pepper. Remove the pan from the heat.

3. Heat the vinegar and sugar in a small saucepan over medium heat until the sugar dissolves, about 2 minutes. Pour the warm liquid over the caponata. Set the caponata back over medium heat and cook until all the liquid is absorbed, 1 to 2 minutes.

4. Let the caponata rest at room temperature for at least 2 hours, or refrigerate up to overnight, before serving, to allow the flavors to meld. Serve at room temperature. (The caponata will keep for up to 1 week, tightly covered and refrigerated.)

PER SERVING: Calories 207 • Soy Protein 3.7 g • Total Protein 5.6 g • Carbohydrates 19.3 g • Fat 12.7 g • Saturated Fat 1.7 g • Cholesterol 0 mg • Fiber 4.5 g • Sodium 210.7 mg

Ingredients

- 2 tablespoons capers, preferably salt-cured
- ¼ cup extra virgin olive oil
- 1 medium onion, diced
- 1 large (1½-pound) eggplant, peeled and cut into ½-inch cubes
- 1 garlic clove, minced
- 1 large celery rib, cut into ½-inch slices
- ⅔ cup frozen shelled edamame
- ½ cup tomato sauce
- 6 Sicilian green olives, pitted and chopped
- 1 tablespoon pine nuts
- Salt and freshly ground black pepper
- ¼ cup red wine vinegar
- 3 tablespoons sugar

Deviled Eggs

6 large eggs, hard-cooked

1 cup cooked or canned
  chickpeas, drained

4 tablespoons mellow
  white miso

1 teaspoon yellow mustard

1 tablespoon mayonnaise

2 tablespoons minced red
  onion

1 tablespoon chopped flat-
  leaf parsley

Salt and freshly ground
  black pepper

Paprika, for garnish

I f you love deviled eggs, you will relish the creamy chickpea and miso yolks in these tangy, nearly cholesterol-free eggs. This mixture is so good you can also enjoy it spread on warm toast.

1. Peel the eggs and cut each in half lengthwise. Set the yolks aside for another use.

2. Pulse the chickpeas in a food processor until they are coarsely chopped. Add the miso, mustard, and mayonnaise. Process until the mixture is pureed but still has a pleasantly grainy texture, stopping occasionally to scrape down the sides of the bowl. Add the red onion and parsley and pulse to blend. Season to taste with salt and pepper.

3. Roll 1 tablespoon of the filling into a ball the size of an egg yolk. Set it into one of the egg white halves. Repeat, replacing the yolks in all the eggs.

4. Just before serving, sprinkle lightly with paprika. (These deviled eggs will keep for up to 4 hours, covered with plastic wrap and refrigerated. The filling will keep for up to 8 hours, covered and refrigerated. Stuff the eggs just before serving.)

PER STUFFED EGG-HALF: Calories 53 • Soy Protein 0.7 g • Total Protein 3.4 g • Carbohydrates 5.4 g • Fat 1.5 g • Saturated Fat 0.2 g • Cholesterol 0.6 mg • Fiber 1.4 g • Sodium 287.2 mg

My Mother's Vegetarian Chopped Liver

1 cup frozen shelled
   edamame

1 tablespoon canola oil

1½ cups chopped onions

1 teaspoon salt

½ cup drained canned
   baby sweet peas

¼ cup chopped pecans

Salt and freshly ground
   black pepper

Serving chopped liver is a tradition among Jews of Eastern European descent, particularly as part of the weekly Sabbath dinner and on holidays. This meatless version pleases everyone, though, including people who do not care for liver. My mother's version uses canned baby peas in place of the green beans most recipes call for. When I gave her some edamame, she used them instead. Now, she skips the peas entirely, while I prefer combining them with some edamame. Spread this vegetarian chopped liver on crackers or scoop it onto individual salad plates, surrounded by green bell pepper rings and accompanied by matzohs or your favorite crackers.

1. Add the edamame to a pot of boiling salted water and cook until they are very tender about 8 minutes. Drain the beans and place them in the bowl of a food processor.

2. Heat the oil in a skillet over medium-high heat. Add the onions, stirring to coat them with the oil. Sprinkle on the salt and sauté the onions until they are browned, about 8 minutes. Transfer the onions to the food processor.

3. Add the peas and pecans to the food processor and pulse until the mixture has the texture of chopped liver. It should be dense, but spreadable. Season to taste with salt and pepper.

4. Serve immediately, or, if chilled, let sit 20 minutes at room temperature before serving. (The vegetarian chopped liver will keep for up to 3 days, tightly covered and refrigerated.)

PER SERVING: Calories 140 • Soy Protein 5.6 g • Total Protein 7.1 g • Carbohydrates 10.6 g • Fat 8.5 g • Saturated Fat 1 g • Cholesterol 0 mg • Fiber 3.3 g • Sodium 356.9 mg

1 tablespoon canola oil

1 medium shallot, finely
    chopped

1 medium leek (white part
    only), chopped

2 teaspoons curry powder

2 medium carrots, cut into
    ½-inch slices

¾ cup red lentils, rinsed

1 teaspoon dried thyme

3 to 4 whole dried
    California apricots

2 to 2½ cups vegetable
    broth

4 ounces soft tofu, diced

2 tablespoons mellow
    white miso

Salt and freshly ground
    black pepper

Carrot and Red Lentil Pâté

Tart dried apricots contrast nicely with the carrots, curry, and thyme in this golden pâté. Their acid edge also complements the miso in this spreadable hors d'oeuvre. Serve it scooped onto a bed of shredded romaine lettuce, accompanied by Curry Flatbread (page 143). For finger food, nestle a tablespoon of the pâté in the base of an endive leaf and garnish with a sliver of Granny Smith apple.

1. Heat the oil in a saucepan over medium-high heat. Add the shallot and leek and sauté until softened, 4 to 5 minutes. Stir in the curry powder and cook for 1 minute.

2. Add the carrots, lentils, thyme, apricots, and 2 cups of the vegetable broth. Bring to a boil, reduce the heat, cover, and simmer until the lentils and carrots are very soft, 20 to 25 minutes, adding more broth after 10 minutes, if the lentils appear dry on top. Let it sit, uncovered, for 10 minutes to cool slightly.

3. Transfer the lentil mixture to a blender and puree. Add the tofu and puree, scraping down the sides of the container with a rubber spatula as needed. Blend in the miso. Season to taste with salt and pepper.

4. Serve at room temperature or slightly chilled.

PER ¼ CUP: Calories 84 • Soy Protein 1.3 g • Total Protein 4.7 g • Carbohydrates 12.4 g • Fat 1.8 g • Saturated Fat 0.1 g • Cholesterol 0 mg • Fiber 2.7 g • Sodium 271.3 mg

Smoked Tempeh Pâté with Walnuts

Makes 1 cup

Together, tempeh and walnuts make a dense spread remarkably like a meat pâté. The popularity of the tempeh spread at Angelica Kitchen, a vegan restaurant in New York City, which even my meat-eating friends enjoy, is proof of this. I use smoked tempeh (see page 114), which adds spectacular depth to my version, though it is also good if you skip the smoking and simply bake the tempeh in Spicy Tofu Marinade (page 53). Spread this pâté on pumpernickel bread.

1 tablespoon extra virgin olive oil

1 medium onion, chopped

1 large garlic clove, chopped

4 ounces (1 piece) smoked tempeh made with soy tempeh (see page 114)

¼ cup walnuts

¼ cup chopped dill

1 tablespoon fresh lemon juice

Salt and freshly ground black pepper

1. Heat the oil in a skillet over medium-high heat. Add the onion and garlic and sauté until the onion is very soft, but not colored, about 5 minutes.

2. Transfer the onion mixture to a food processor. Crumble or coarsely chop the tempeh and add it to the processor. Pulse until the mixture is combined but still has some texture. Add the nuts, dill, and lemon juice. Process until the mixture is like a spreadable pâté. Season to taste with salt and pepper.

3. Serve at once, or let sit at room temperature for 20 minutes if chilled. (This spread will keep for up to 3 days, covered and refrigerated.)

PER 2 TABLESPOONS: Calories 82 • Soy Protein 3.1 g • Total Protein 4.0 g • Carbohydrates 3.0 g • Fat 6.2 g • Saturated Fat 0.8 g • Cholesterol 0 mg • Fiber 1.6 g • Sodium 123.4 mg

Smoked Tempeh

This recipe started when I had Spicy Tofu Marinade (page 53) left over and decided to try it with tempeh. The result was tender and buttery, with a spicy backnote. I like it best in Smoked Tempeh Pâté with Walnuts (page 113) or chopped, pan-crisped (see page 181), and sprinkled over a Spinach Salad (page 155). It is also good sautéed and broken up, then simmered in a light tomato sauce to use over pasta. When smoking, remember to keep the flavor light so it does not overpower the other ingredients in the dish.

Makes 8 ounces, in 2 pieces

Smoker Bag Method

Using a bag labeled "light smoke," bake marinated tempeh for 20 minutes. Take the bag out of the oven and let it sit, sealed, for 5 minutes. Open, and remove the tempeh. Discard the bag.

Stovetop Smoker Method

Follow the instructions accompanying the smoker box. Using mild-flavored wood chips such as alder, apple, cherry, or maple, smoke the tempeh for about 10 minutes once the first wisps of smoke appear and the smoker is sealed. (It may take some experimenting to find the level of smoked flavor you enjoy.)

Chestnut Pâté

A guest at a party I catered called me three years later to cater her wedding because she remembered this pâté. That's how much she loved its coarse, meaty texture—and she was not a vegetarian. Serve it on thinly sliced black bread spread with Dijon mustard and topped with tiny cornichons. Vegetarians also enjoy it served hot as a main course, accompanied by Rich Mushroom Gravy (page 239). Using sharp Cheddar is important; a milder cheese or soy cheese makes an overly bland pâté. This pâté freezes well. It is best defrosted slowly in the refrigerator before slicing.

1. Preheat the oven to 400°F. Lightly coat a 9 × 5-inch loaf pan with nonstick cooking spray.

2. Combine the walnuts and cashews in a food processor and pulse to chop finely. Transfer the nuts to a large bowl.

3. Combine the onion and celery in the food processor, chop finely, and set them aside. Finely chop the mushrooms in the food processor and set them aside.

4. Heat 2 tablespoons of the butter in a skillet over medium-high heat. Add the onion and celery, and sauté until the vegetables are soft, about 7 minutes. Add the mushrooms and cook until they give up their liquid. Continue cooking until the vegetables are very soft, about 15 minutes, stirring occasionally. Add them to the bowl with the nuts. Melt the remaining 1 tablespoon butter in the pan. Add the tempeh and sauté until it is golden brown, about 5 minutes, stirring occasionally. Add it to the bowl with the nuts and cooked vegetables.

5. Chop the chestnuts in the food processor. Add them to the bowl with the nuts and vegetables along with the shredded cheese, egg, paprika, thyme, salt, and pepper. Mix until the pâté is well combined.

- 1½ cups walnuts
- 1½ cups roasted cashews
- 1 large onion, coarsely chopped
- 1 celery rib, cut into 1-inch pieces
- 8 ounces mushrooms, stemmed
- 3 tablespoons butter
- 4 ounces (½ package) three- or five-grain (see page 31) mild flavored tempeh, finely chopped
- 2 cups cooked chestnuts
- 1 cup shredded sharp Cheddar cheese
- 1 large egg, lightly beaten
- 1 tablespoon sweet paprika
- 1 teaspoon dried thyme
- 1 teaspoon salt
- ½ teaspoon freshly ground black pepper

6. Pack the mixture into the prepared pan. Rap the pan firmly on the counter to eliminate any air pockets. Place the pan in the center of a large piece of heavy-duty aluminum foil. Bring the sides of the foil up over the center of the pan. Roll the edges together, making a tight seal. Roll the ends under to seal them.

7. Bake the pâté for 45 to 50 minutes, or until it feels firm in the center when pressed lightly. Unwrap the pâté and cool it completely on a wire rack. It will crumble if unmolded while still warm.

8. Cut the pâté into slices and serve.

PER SERVING: Calories 164 • Soy Protein 1.0 g • Total Protein 5.7 g • Carbohydrates 13.0 g • Fat 10.9 g • Saturated Fat 3.5 g • Cholesterol 21.2 mg • Fiber 2.4 g • Sodium 143.5 mg

Prepared Chestnuts

The roasted, peeled chestnuts vacuum-packed in jars and plastic pouches are much better than the watery ones sold in cans. Of course, fresh chestnuts are good too, but not worth the work if you can get the vacuum-packed ones.

Fried Tofu Sticks

Fried creamy mozzarella sticks are always popular. Using tofu in place of cheese produces a remarkable, leaner look-alike. Golden and crunchy outside, they melt inside if you use soft tofu. Using firm tofu transforms them into a dead-ringer for chicken nuggets.

½ cup dried bread crumbs

1 teaspoon dried oregano

½ teaspoon dried thyme

1 teaspoon salt

¼ teaspoon freshly ground black pepper

16 ounces soft or firm tofu

1½ cups canola oil

½ cup olive oil

2 large eggs, beaten

Honey Mustard (page 179)

1. Toast the bread crumbs in a dry skillet over medium heat, stirring often until they are golden brown, about 5 minutes. Transfer to a bowl and let cool to room temperature, about 20 minutes. Mix in the oregano, thyme, salt, and pepper.

2. Cut the block of tofu horizontally in half. Then cut it in half the long way. Make 5 cuts perpendicular to the long cut, creating 24 pieces. Cover a sheet pan with paper towels. Place the tofu in one layer on the towels. Blot the tofu, pressing it gently with additional towels to remove excess moisture.

3. Heat the oil in a deep skillet to 375°F. Cover a second baking sheet with more paper towels. Place the beaten eggs in a wide, shallow dish.

4. Dip the tofu in the egg. Dredge the pieces in the bread crumb mixture until completely coated. Slip the breaded tofu into the hot oil, 3 or 4 pieces at a time. Fry until golden brown, 2 to 3 minutes. Turn and brown on the other side, 1 to 2 minutes. Remove from the pan using a slotted spoon. Drain on paper towels.

5. Serve immediately, accompanied by the mustard for dipping. Or, let the sticks cool and arrange them in a single layer on a baking sheet. Cover with foil and refrigerate for up to 4 hours. Before serving, recrisp by baking in a 350°F oven for about 12 minutes.

PER STICK: Calories 48 • Soy Protein 1.7 g • Total Protein 2.5 g • Carbohydrates 2.1 g • Fat 3.5 g • Saturated Fat 0.3 g • Cholesterol 17.7 mg • Fiber 0.1 g • Sodium 181.4 mg

Shrimp Balls with Dipping Sauce

8 ounces shrimp, peeled and deveined

6 ounces firm tofu, squeezed and crumbled (see page 48)

3 to 4 whole canned water chestnuts, chopped

1 teaspoon minced peeled fresh ginger

1 scallion (white and green parts), finely chopped

½ teaspoon sugar

1 large egg white, beaten until frothy

½ teaspoon salt

¼ teaspoon freshly ground white or black pepper

2 or 3 napa cabbage leaves

½ cup cornstarch

SOY DIPPING SAUCE

2 tablespoons thin soy sauce

1 tablespoon hoisin sauce

1½ teaspoons Chinese red vinegar

1 tablespoon finely shredded peeled fresh ginger

½ teaspoon grated orange zest

Rosy, sweet-tasting shrimp balls are perfect as an hors d'oeuvre or part of a dim sum spread. Pairing tofu with shellfish is a Chinese culinary tradition.

1. Pulse the shrimp in a food processor, taking care it does not become a paste. Transfer the shrimp to a bowl.

2. Add the tofu, water chestnuts, ginger, scallion, sugar, egg white, salt, and pepper to the bowl. Mix with a rubber spatula until well blended.

3. Fill a wok or large pot with steamer insert, with 3 to 4 inches of water. Line the bottom of a bamboo steamer or pot insert with the cabbage leaves, cutting them to fit and leaving a 1-inch border around the edge of the steamer. Set aside.

4. Spread the cornstarch on a plate. With wet hands, make 1-inch-thick balls of the shrimp mixture. Roll them in the cornstarch to coat them lightly. Place the shrimp balls in the steamer, leaving at least ½ inch between them. (You will probably have to cook the shrimp balls in 2 or 3 batches.)

5. Cover the steamer and set it over the pot. Steam until the shrimp balls are cooked through, about 5 minutes. Repeat to cook the second batch, if necessary. Arrange the shrimp balls on a serving plate, covering them with a paper towel to keep them warm until you are ready to serve.

6. Reserve 1 tablespoon of the cooking liquid from the pot under the steamer and discard the rest.

7. To make the sauce, combine the soy sauce, hoisin sauce, vinegar, ginger, orange zest, and the reserved tablespoon of cooking liquid from the steamed shrimp balls. Mix well.

8. Serve the shrimp balls warm, passing the sauce on the side.

PER SHRIMP BALL, WITHOUT SAUCE: Calories 25 • Soy Protein 0.6 g • Total Protein 2.2 g • Carbohydrates 3.0 g • Fat .5 g • Saturated Fat 0 g • Cholesterol 13.5 mg • Fiber 0 g • Sodium 25.5 mg

Sweet-and-Sour Meatballs

Soy crumbles paired with lean ground turkey become virtually invisible, yet they substantially reduce the fat and cholesterol in this golden oldie. Baking the meatballs saves work and reduces the fat content even further.

1. Preheat the oven to 375°F. Line a baking sheet with aluminum foil, and coat it with nonstick cooking spray.

2. Heat the oil over medium-high heat in a medium skillet. Add the 2 tablespoons onion and sauté until the onion is translucent, 2 to 3 minutes. Mix in the soy crumbles, and add the broth. Cook until the liquid has boiled off and the soy mixture is almost dry, 8 to 10 minutes. Let it cool for 5 minutes.

3. Combine the turkey with the enriched crumbles, the remaining ¼ cup onion, garlic, salt, and pepper in a bowl. Form the mixture into 1-inch balls and set them about 1 inch apart on the baking sheet.

4. Bake the meatballs for about 12 minutes, or until they are lightly browned and firm to the touch.

5. To make the sauce, combine the chili sauce, ketchup, grape jelly, chili powder, and ginger in a deep saucepan. Gradually bring to a boil over medium heat, stirring occasionally. Add the meatballs and simmer until the sauce thickens and coats the meatballs, about 5 minutes. Transfer the meatballs and sauce to a serving dish. (Or, cool the meatballs and sauce and refrigerate for up to 2 days in a tightly covered container, or freeze. Defrost in the refrigerator. Reheat, covered, on top of the stove or in a 350°F oven for about 20 minutes.)

PER MEATBALL WITH SAUCE: Calories 35 • Soy Protein 0.7 g • Total Protein 2.0 g • Carbohydrates 5.9 g • Fat 0.6 g • Saturated Fat 0.2 g • Cholesterol 4.9 mg • Fiber 0.2 g • Sodium 102.9 mg

1 teaspoon canola oil

¼ cup plus 2 tablespoons finely chopped onion

6 ounces (½ package) refrigerated soy crumbles, or 1 cup frozen

½ cup chicken or vegetarian chicken broth

½ pound lean ground turkey (7 percent fat)

1 large garlic clove, minced

1 teaspoon salt

¼ teaspoon freshly ground black pepper

SWEET-AND-SOUR SAUCE

⅓ cup chili sauce

⅓ cup ketchup

⅔ cup grape jelly

½ teaspoon chili powder

½ teaspoon ground ginger

6 baked corn chips

2 tablespoons
Southwestern Bean
Spread (page 106)

1 tablespoon chopped
seeded tomato

1 tablespoon finely
chopped sweet onion

12 thin slices (½ ounce)
smoked Gouda or soy
Cheddar, cut into 1-inch
squares

Nachitos

These neat nachos are the ideal hot hors d'oeuvre before a Tex-Mex dinner. A platter of them makes a good snack to enjoy in front of the TV. I also serve them with Tortilla Soup with Black Soybeans (page 129). I prefer making them with smoked soy cheese, but if heat is your thing, Soya Kaas's Tex-Mex cheese is good, too.

1. Preheat the oven to 350°F (see Note).

2. Arrange the chips on a baking sheet. Top each chip with a teaspoon of the bean dip, ½ teaspoon of the tomato, and ½ teaspoon of the onion. Top each Nachito with two pieces of the cheese.

3. Bake the chips until the cheese melts, 3 to 5 minutes. Serve immediately.

NOTE: If using a microwave, place the nachitos on a plate and heat them until the cheese melts.

Calories 103 • Soy Protein 2.7 g • Total Protein 4.8 g • Carbohydrates 16.6 g • Fat 2.7 g • Saturated Fat 0.1 g • Cholesterol 0 mg • Fiber 3.5 g • Sodium 256.4 mg

Chinese Spiced Nuts

Makes 3½ cups

Star anise and cassia cinnamon give Chinese five-spice powder a hauntingly appealing sweet flavor. A modest amount seasons the crunchy, soy protein-coated pecans in this distinctive nut and fruit mix. They are a perfect counterpoint to the dry-roasted flavor of the soynuts.

1. Preheat the oven to 325°F. Cover a baking sheet with aluminum foil and coat it lightly with nonstick cooking spray.

2. Combine the pecans, protein powder, and five-spice powder in a bowl.

3. Whisk the egg white in a small saucepan until it is frothy. Whisk in the brown sugar until it dissolves. Gently heat the mixture over medium-low heat until it is warm, 2 to 3 minutes, stirring constantly and taking care not to let the egg white cook. It should be a syrupy liquid.

4. Pour the warm liquid over the pecan and soy powder mixture. Stir with a rubber spatula, turning the mixture and scraping the bowl until the nuts are evenly coated and moist. The coating will be clumpy on the nuts.

5. Spread the nuts in an even layer on the baking sheet. Bake for 20 to 30 minutes, or until the nuts are a deep cinnamon brown, and many of the clumps have broken up. They may not be completely crisp.

6. Cool the nuts on the baking sheet. When they reach room temperature, they will be crisp. Break up the nuts, if necessary, and mix with the soynuts, cashews, and sour cherries. (The mix will keep for 1 week, stored at room temperature in a tightly closed container.)

Ingredients

- 1½ cups pecan halves
- ⅓ cup soy protein powder
- ½ teaspoon Chinese five-spice powder
- 1 large egg white
- ¼ cup dark brown sugar
- ½ cup salted roasted whole soynuts
- ½ cup salted roasted cashew pieces
- ½ cup dried sour cherries

PER ¼ CUP: Calories 135 • Soy Protein 4.9 g • Total Protein 6.4 g • Carbohydrates 9.1 g • Fat 8.9 g • Saturated Fat 1.0 g • Cholesterol 0 mg • Fiber 2.0 g • Sodium 61.3 mg

2 large egg whites

1 tablespoon finely chopped garlic

1 tablespoon chili powder, preferably without dehydrated garlic

1 tablespoon Worcestershire sauce

2 teaspoons soy sauce

1 teaspoon dried oregano

1 teaspoon hot red pepper flakes

1 teaspoon salt

2 cups (6 ounces) hulled whole soynuts

Hot Chili Soynuts

Many bar nibbles rely on the seduction of salt to keep your hand in motion. With these mildly spicy soynuts, well-rounded heat is the drive. Besides sufficient chile to make your mouth tingle, the garlic, oregano, and cumin in the chili powder make these nuts a perfect accompaniment to cold beer or a frosty margarita. Their substantial nutrition makes them a good afternoon snack, too.

1. Combine the egg whites, garlic, chili powder, Worcestershire sauce, soy sauce, oregano, pepper flakes, and salt in a blender. Whirl until the garlic is pureed.

2. Preheat the oven to 250°F. While the oven heats, place the nuts in a large bowl. Pour the spiced egg white mixture over the nuts, stirring to coat them. Set aside for 10 to 15 minutes.

3. Spread the nuts in an even layer on a nonstick baking sheet or a baking sheet coated with nonstick cooking spray.

4. Bake the nuts for 5 minutes, remove the pan from the oven, and stir the nuts, to prevent them from clumping. Redistribute them evenly on the baking sheet and return the pan to the oven. Repeat this three more times, baking the nuts until they are almost crisp, 20 minutes in all.

5. Cool the nuts on the baking sheet. They will not be crisp until they are completely cool. Break up any clumps. (The seasoned soynuts will keep for 1 week, stored at room temperature in an airtight container.)

PER ¼ CUP: Calories 144 • Soy Protein 10.1 g • Total Protein 11.3 g • Carbohydrates 10.6 g • Fat 7.2 g • Saturated Fat 1.0 g • Cholesterol 0 mg • Fibers 5.1 g • Sodium 520.4 mg

soups and breads

Soup served with a thick slab of good bread always makes a satisfying meal for me. Inspired by the possibilities of including nine forms of soy in soups and in home-baked savories that complement them, I have found new ways of pairing these eternally perfect partners in Roasted Tomato Bisque to sip from a mug with focaccia; miso-rich Mediterranean Lentil Soup, accompanied by a thick slice of Goat Cheese Crostini; Asian-accented Thai Sweet Potato Soup with wafer-thin Curry Flatbread; and Tortilla Soup with Black Soybeans plus Nachitos. Creamy pesto, spread on store-bought Italian semolina bread, is perfect with a bowl of Minestrone containing sweet edamame. Of course, there is also nurturing Miso Soup with Tofu and Wakame.

1 small packet dried
   wakame (see Note)

4 cups Vegetable Dashi
   (page 125)

4 tablespoons miso,
   preferably 3
   tablespoons red and
   1 tablespoon mellow
   white miso

4 ounces silken tofu, in
   one piece

Miso Soup with Tofu and Wakame

The former owner of Fuji, the oldest Japanese restaurant in New York City, taught me to make this miso soup. According to her, the secret is using two kinds of miso, one light and one medium or dark. I favor a larger amount of the light miso during warm weather because it is less intense and warming than the darker varieties. This particular recipe calls for a vegetarian dashi, or lightly flavored broth.

1. Place the dried wakame in a bowl. Cover it generously with cold water and set aside.

2. Place the dashi in a saucepan. Place the miso in a small bowl. Ladle ¼ cup dashi over the miso. Whisk until the miso is blended with the liquid, or cream them together using the back of a spoon. Add the dissolved miso to the dashi.

3. Holding the tofu in the palm of one hand, with a knife in the other hand cut it horizontally in 2 or 3 slices. Then cut the tofu crosswise and vertically, making ½-inch cubes. Gently drop the tofu into the soup. Heat the soup over medium-high heat until it is steaming. Do not let it boil.

4. Divide the soup and tofu among four soup bowls. Drain the wakame. Squeeze it to remove as much water as possible. Add about 1 tablespoon of the wakame to each bowl of soup. Serve hot.

NOTE: Wakame is a flat ribbonlike sea vegetable. You can buy it at Asian food stores. It is more tender and mild-tasting than varieties sold at natural food stores.

PER SERVING: Calories 223 • Soy Protein 5.7 g • Total Protein 11.0 g • Carbohydrates 45.0 g • Fat 2.5 g • Saturated Fat 0.1 g • Cholesterol 0 mg • Fiber 7.6 g • Sodium 2049.2 mg

Vegetable Dashi

Dashi is the light, smoky tasting broth fundamental in Japanese cooking for making miso soup and many other dishes. Usually, it is made using kombu, or kelp, a variety of sea vegetable and flakes of finely shaved bonito, *katsuo-bushi*. The fish gives the dashi its smoky quality. Shiitake mushrooms, which are the same as Chinese dried black mushrooms, have a different flavor, but used in place of the fish, they give the dashi the same kind of subtle depth. Mirin is a syrupy sweet rice wine used often in Japanese cooking as a seasoning. Like the mushrooms, mirin is sold at Asian food stores, although I prefer to buy it in natural food stores because their mirin is naturally fermented and contains no additives.

5 dried medium-size shiitake or black Chinese mushrooms

1 leek (green part only), thoroughly washed

1 medium onion, quartered

¾ inch fresh ginger, peeled and cut into 2 slices

1 small parsnip, peeled

1 tablespoon tamari

½ teaspoon mirin

1. Combine the mushrooms, leek greens, onion, ginger, and whole parsnip in a deep pot. Add 6 cups cold water. Bring the liquid to a boil, reduce the heat, and simmer, uncovered, until it is reduced to 4 cups, about 30 minutes.

2. Strain the hot liquid, discarding the vegetables. Mix in the tamari and mirin.

3. Use at once. (This stock keeps for 2 to 3 days, tightly covered, in the refrigerator. Do not boil when reheating.)

PER CUP: Calories 53 • Soy Protein 0.5 g • Total Protein 1.9 g • Carbohydrates 12.8 g • Fat 0.2 g • Saturated Fat 0 g • Cholesterol 0 mg • Fiber 0 g • Sodium 298.7 mg

2 large Spanish onions, coarsely chopped

2 celery ribs, cut into 2-inch pieces

1 medium kohlrabi, peeled and halved

1 small celery root, peeled and cut into 2-inch pieces

1 small parsnip, peeled and halved

1½ inches fresh ginger, cut into 4 slices

2 teaspoons tamari

Three-quarters of a 12-ounce box firm silken tofu, cut in ½-inch cubes (about 1 cup)

¼ cup finely chopped scallion (green part only)

Ginger Consommé with Silken Tofu

A fine consommé is both elegant and soothing. Rather than taking its flavor from meat, this clear broth extracts its aromatic intensity from an assortment of winter vegetables, including celery root and kohlrabi. Traditional consommé is often enriched with a dash of sherry; this one is enhanced with a touch of tamari and ginger. Besides serving it at dinner parties, enjoy this restorative whenever a bleak winter day gets you down.

1. Combine the onions, celery, kohlrabi, celery root, parsnip, and ginger in a deep saucepan. Add 8 cups water. Bring to a boil and simmer for 25 minutes. Remove from the heat, and let it steep for 30 minutes. Strain through a sieve. Discard the solids.

2. Add the tamari to the broth. If you are serving immediately, ladle the hot broth into soup bowls, add a quarter of the tofu to each bowl, and garnish with the scallions. (Or, refrigerate the soup, covered, for up to 2 days, then reheat and serve with the tofu and scallions.)

PER SERVING: Calories 125 • Soy Protein 3.5 g • Total Protein 6.6 g • Carbohydrates 22.5 g • Fat 1.6 g • Saturated Fat 0.1 g • Cholesterol 0 mg • Fiber 0 g • Sodium 285.1 mg

Thai Sweet Potato Soup

This silky cream soup contains just enough heat to stimulate your appetite. Following a technique I learned from Nancie McDermott, author of *Real Thai*, I use some of the coconut milk in this soup in place of oil for sautéing its aromatic ingredients. If you cannot get an Asian hot pepper, a serrano chile works nicely. Accompanied by sheets of Curry Flatbread (page 143), this soup is the ideal prelude to Herb-Roasted Tofu Cutlets with Fresh Mango Salsa (page 240).

1 cup plus 3 tablespoons light coconut milk

1 cup chopped onion

½ teaspoon salt

1 garlic clove, chopped

1 green chile, seeded and chopped

2 teaspoons finely chopped ginger

½ teaspoon red Thai curry paste (see Note)

1 large sweet potato, peeled and cut into 1-inch pieces

2 cups unsweetened soymilk

½ cup cilantro leaves

Juice of 1 lime

Salt and freshly ground black pepper

1. Heat 3 tablespoons coconut milk in a small Dutch oven or large heavy saucepan over medium-high heat. Stir in the onion and salt. Cook, stirring occasionally, until the onion is soft, about 5 minutes. Mix in the garlic, chile, and ginger. Cook for 1 minute. Mix in the chili paste, and cook for 1 minute.

2. Add the sweet potato, the remaining 1 cup coconut milk, the soymilk, and cilantro. Bring to a boil, reduce the heat, and simmer, covered, until the potato is very soft, about 20 minutes. When the soup is slightly cooled, puree it in a blender. If necessary, do this in two batches. Blend in the lime juice.

3. Season to taste with salt and pepper, and serve.

NOTE: Thai cooks often buy curry paste rather than going through the laborious process of making it from scratch. Many supermarkets and natural food stores carry the excellent Thai Kitchen line, which includes a Red Curry Paste.

PER SERVING: Calories 203 • Soy Protein 4.5 g • Total Protein 7.2 g • Carbohydrates 25.8 g • Fat 8.6 g • Saturated Fat 3.7 g • Cholesterol 0 mg • Fiber 5.4 g • Sodium 279.7 mg

Serves 6

1 tablespoon extra virgin
    olive oil

1 medium onion, chopped

1 carrot, chopped

One 14½-ounce can
    vegetable broth plus
    2 cups water, or 4 cups
    water

¼ pound red-skinned new
    potatoes, cut into
    1-inch pieces (about
    1 cup)

1 cup canned plum
    tomatoes, seeded, with
    their liquid

1 cup frozen shelled
    edamame

1 medium zucchini,
    chopped

½ cup green beans, cut in
    1-inch pieces

3 large leaves Swiss chard
    (green part only), cut
    crosswise in ½-inch
    strips

⅛ teaspoon hot red
    pepper flakes, optional

½ cup ditalini, spaghetti
    broken into ½-inch
    lengths, or small shells

Salt and freshly ground
    black pepper

Minestrone

Edamame show their versatility in this Italian favorite. The combination of soy and pasta provides a hearty meal complete with protein plus a good amount of fiber. Although nothing equals genuine Parmigiano-Reggiano, if you avoid dairy products, you can sprinkle this soup with grated soy Parmesan. To make a meal, have a chunk of Pesto Herb Bread (page 140) with this.

1. Heat the olive oil in a medium Dutch oven over medium-high heat. Add the onion and carrot and sauté until the onion is soft, 6 to 8 minutes. Pour in the vegetable broth, if using, and the water. Add the potatoes and bring the soup to a boil. Reduce the heat, and simmer until the potatoes are al dente, 8 minutes.

2. Add the tomatoes, edamame, zucchini, green beans, chard, and red pepper flakes, if using. Increase the heat to medium-high and stir in the pasta. When the soup returns to a simmer, cook until the pasta is done, about 15 minutes.

3. Season to taste with salt and pepper and serve.

PER SERVING: Calories 163 • Soy Protein 5.6 g • Total Protein 9.0 g • Carbohydrates 21.3 g • Fat 5.8 g • Saturated Fat 0.7 g • Cholesterol 0 mg • Fiber 3.6 g • Sodium 387.7 mg

Tortilla Soup with Black Soybeans

Think of this as chicken soup with Latin soul. Along with a chile-fired glow, it provides good servings of grain and fresh vegetables, protein and fiber. Though home-fried tortilla strips taste best, I sometimes settle for a handful of chips pulled from a bag, which can be baked and low-fat. This soup travels well in a wide-mouth insulated container, accompanied by a plastic bag of tortilla strips. Add some Nachitos (page 120), and you have the equivalent of soup and sandwich.

1. If using tortillas, cut them in half. Stack two of the halves. Cut them crosswise into ½-inch strips. Repeat with the second tortilla.

2. Heat the corn oil in a small skillet over medium-high heat. Fry the tortilla strips until crisp, about 1 minute, turning them as needed. Drain on paper towels and set aside. Disregard these steps if using tortilla chips.

3. Heat the canola oil in a large saucepan over medium-high heat. Add the onion, jalapeño, and garlic and sauté until the onion is slightly soft, about 2 minutes. Add the chicken broth, oregano, zucchini, soybeans, and tomato. Cook until the squash is almost soft, about 3 minutes. Mix in the lime juice.

4. Ladle the soup into bowls and top each bowl with a quarter of the cheese and cilantro, if using. Add the tortilla strips or chips, and serve.

2 corn tortillas, or 2 cups tortilla chips, slightly crushed

2 tablespoons corn oil

2 tablespoons canola oil

1 large onion, chopped

1 jalapeño pepper, seeded and chopped

1 garlic clove, minced

3 cups chicken or vegetarian chicken broth

½ teaspoon dried oregano

1 small zucchini, cut into ½-inch slices

1 cup cooked or canned black soybeans, rinsed and drained

1 large tomato, seeded and chopped

2 tablespoons fresh lime juice

4 tablespoons shredded soy cheese, either with jalapeño or Jack-flavor

4 teaspoons chopped cilantro, optional

PER SERVING: Calories 255 • Soy Protein 4.9 g • Total Protein 9.4 g • Carbohydrates 20.1 g • Fat 17 g • Saturated Fat 2 g • Cholesterol 0 mg • Fiber 4.9 g • Sodium 622.9 mg

Mediterranean Lentil Soup

2 tablespoons extra virgin olive oil

1 medium onion, chopped

1 small garlic clove, finely chopped

1 cup green lentils, rinsed

2 cups ¾-inch eggplant cubes

4 cups mushroom broth

½ teaspoon ground cinnamon

½ cup flat-leaf parsley, chopped

3 large plum tomatoes, seeded and chopped

2 tablespoons brown rice miso

Made with green lentils, this meatless soup gets its intense flavor from a combination of miso and the mushroom broth sold at natural food stores and supermarkets. Light enough to enjoy in the summer, it has a warm note of cinnamon that goes well on a cold winter afternoon. Accompany this soup with Goat Cheese Crostini (page 108).

1. Heat the oil in a deep saucepan over medium-high heat. Add the onion and sauté until it is soft, about 4 minutes. Mix in the garlic and cook for 1 minute.

2. Add the lentils, eggplant, broth, cinnamon, and parsley. Bring the soup to a boil, reduce the heat, and simmer, partially covered, for 20 minutes. Add the tomatoes, and cook until the lentils are soft, 10 minutes. Remove the soup from the heat.

3. Dissolve the miso in 2 tablespoons water. Mix into the soup and serve. When reheating leftovers, take care not to let the soup boil.

PER SERVING: Calories 138 • Soy Protein 0.5 g • Total Protein 7.7 g • Carbohydrates 18.8 g • Fat 3.6 g • Saturated Fat 0.5 g • Cholesterol 0 mg • Fiber 4.7 g • Sodium 244.8 mg

Lion's Head Soup

Usually, lion's heads refer to big pork meatballs. But there are no meatballs in this Chinese soup, because when I tried to use tofu in place of the pork, my meatless meatballs disintegrated during cooking. Since I had guests waiting to eat, I decided to ladle out the resulting chunky soup. Guests raved over its warming Asian flavors and loved the combination of tender cabbage with crisp water chestnuts. I surrendered to the kitchen gods and kept this recipe as is.

1. Soak the mushrooms in warm water to cover until they are soft, about 20 minutes. Drain the liquid and reserve it for another use. Discard the stems and cut the mushroom caps into thin strips. Set aside.

2. Combine the soy sauce, sherry, and cornstarch in a small bowl. Stir in the sesame oil. Set aside.

3. Heat the peanut oil in a Dutch oven over medium-high heat. Add the shallot and ginger, and stir-fry for 30 seconds. Add the cabbage, stirring to coat it with the oil. Mix in the carrot and scallions. Stir-fry until the vegetables are wilted, 3 to 4 minutes. Add the water chestnuts, mushrooms, and tofu.

4. Add 4 cups water. Add the vegetable broth powder and bring the soup to a boil. Simmer until the cabbage is tender, about 10 minutes.

5. Restir the soy sauce and cornstarch mixture. Blend it into the soup. Cook until the soup thickens, 2 to 3 minutes, stirring constantly.

6. Serve immediately.

4 large dried Chinese black or shiitake mushrooms

1 tablespoon dark Chinese soy sauce or Japanese soy sauce

2 tablespoons dry sherry

2 tablespoons cornstarch

¼ teaspoon roasted sesame oil

2 tablespoons peanut oil

1 tablespoon minced shallot

1 inch fresh ginger, finely chopped

12 ounces napa cabbage, cut crosswise into ½-inch strips

1 small carrot, shredded

1 to 2 scallions (white and green parts), sliced

6 whole canned water chestnuts, chopped

8 ounces firm tofu, squeezed (see page 48) and crumbled

1 tablespoon vegetable broth powder or 2 vegetable bouillon cubes

PER SERVING: Calories 121 • Soy Protein 4.0 g • Total Protein 5.4 g • Carbohydrates 10.5 g • Fat 6.6 g • Saturated Fat 1.0 g • Cholesterol 0 mg • Fiber 2.9 g • Sodium 316.0 mg

Mug Soups

These are soups to sip while juggling deadlines, carpooling, and life. They are sustaining meals you can drink right from a cup. When I am in a time crunch, I rely on them for lunch and sometimes dinner, too. Some are served hot, others refreshingly chilled. All are substantial enough to keep you going and going and going. And did I mention that most of them are low-fat?

Making these soups is as efficient as consuming them. First thing in the morning, tossing all their ingredients into a pot takes about 10 minutes. While you shower and dress, they cook, untended. Finally, you puree them using an immersion blender. (If you do not have one of these magic wands, also known as a stick blender, I highly recommend them. They save time by letting you cook and puree soups and sauces right in the pot.) Every time you drink a mug of one of these soups, you get a serving of vegetables and several grams of soy protein.

Roasted Tomato Bisque

Adding soymilk at the end brings together all the other flavors in this robust chilled soup and illustrates how well soymilk can stand in for dairy milk in savory cooking. If you do not want to make Roasted Vegetable Stock there are prepared vegetable broths you can buy. Serve with focaccia or crisp Curry Flatbread (page 143).

1. Preheat the oven to 450°F.

2. Arrange the tomatoes and peppers in one layer, cut side down on a baking sheet. Roast until the tomato skins are puffed and lightly browned, 30 minutes. When the vegetables are cool enough to handle, peel away their skins. Scrape the vegetables into a bowl and set aside.

3. Heat the oil over medium-high heat in a saucepan. Add the onion and garlic and sauté until the onion softens, 4 to 5 minutes. Stir in the cumin and cayenne and add the tomatoes and peppers. Pour in the vegetable stock. Bring the soup to a boil, reduce the heat, and simmer, covered, until the vegetables are very soft, 30 minutes.

4. Place an immersion blender in the pot and puree, or transfer the soup to a blender or food processor and puree. Blend in the tomato paste. Set the soup aside to cool to room temperature, about 30 minutes.

5. Using an immersion blender or food processor, gradually blend in the soymilk. Season to taste with salt and pepper. Pour the soup into a covered container and chill for 2 hours or overnight.

6. Just before serving, squeeze in the lime juice.

1½ pounds plum tomatoes, halved lengthwise

1 large red bell pepper, seeded and cut into quarters

2 teaspoons extra virgin olive oil

½ cup chopped onion

1 garlic clove, chopped

1 teaspoon ground cumin

⅛ teaspoon cayenne

3 cups Roasted Vegetable Stock (recipe follows) or one 14½-ounce can vegetable broth plus 1 cup water

2 tablespoons tomato paste

1 cup unsweetened soymilk

Salt and freshly ground black pepper

Juice of 1 lime

PER SERVING: Calories 224 • Soy Protein 2.3 g • Total Protein 6.8 g • Carbohydrates 29.9 g • Fat 10.5 g • Saturated Fat 0.8 g • Cholesterol 0 mg • Fiber 7.1 g • Sodium 164.1 mg

Roasted Vegetable Stock

2 carrots, coarsely chopped

2 medium leeks (green and white parts), coarsely chopped

1 large onion, coarsely chopped

1 white turnip, coarsely chopped

1 medium zucchini, coarsely chopped

1 cup coarsely chopped celery root

2 tablespoons canola oil

2 bay leaves

10 parsley stems

For convenience, I do use commercially made vegetable broth on occasion. However, few of them are good, in my opinion. If not overloaded with carrot, garlic, or some other overwhelming flavor, they have a color that lacks appeal and affects the look of some soups. Rather than throw a good soup off balance by using them, I try to keep some of this stock in the freezer.

1. Preheat the oven to 425°F.

2. Heap the carrots, leeks, onion, turnip, zucchini, and celery root on a baking sheet. Drizzle with the oil, then toss and rub the vegetables with your hands to coat with the oil. Spread out the vegetables in an even layer.

3. Roast the vegetables for about 55 minutes, or until well browned. Stir the vegetables two or three times while they are cooking, to prevent them from burning in places.

4. Place the roasted vegetables in a stockpot. Add 3 quarts cold water. Bring the liquid to a boil, reduce the heat, and simmer gently for 2 hours. Strain the stock, pressing on the vegetables. Discard the solids.

5. Use immediately or cool the stock, uncovered. Pour the stock into containers, cover, and refrigerate or freeze.

PER CUP: Calories 93 • Soy Protein 0 g • Total Protein 1.7 g • Carbohydrates 11.6 g • Fat 4.9 g • Saturated Fat 0.3 g • Cholesterol 0 mg • Fiber 2.5 g • Sodium 51.4 mg

Broccoli Velvet

Using leeks and onions together gives extra depth to soups, stews, and other dishes. A jalapeño pepper also brings a touch of heat.

1. Combine the broccoli, onion, leek, jalapeño, thyme, and salt in a saucepan. Add 2 cups water. Bring to a boil, cover, reduce the heat, and simmer until the vegetables are very soft, 20 to 25 minutes. Let the soup sit, uncovered, for 10 minutes.

2. Puree the soup in the pot with an immersion blender or transfer to a blender and puree. Add the soymilk and whirl to blend. Blend in the lime juice. Season to taste with salt and pepper.

3. If you are using a blender, return the soup to the saucepan. Reheat gently, if desired, and serve.

2 cups broccoli florets and peeled stems

¾ cup coarsely chopped onion

1 medium leek (white part only), chopped

1 small jalapeño pepper, seeded and chopped

1 teaspoon dried thyme

1 teaspoon salt

1 cup unsweetened soymilk

2 teaspoons fresh lime juice

Salt and freshly ground black pepper

PER SERVING: Calories 55 • Soy Protein 2.3 g • Total Protein 3.9 g • Carbohydrates 9.2 g • Fat 1.4 g • Saturated Fat 0 g • Cholesterol 0 mg • Fiber 2.9 g • Sodium 488.1 mg

Tangy Carrot Soup

3 medium carrots, sliced, or 2½ cups miniature carrots

1 medium onion, chopped

1 garlic clove, chopped

Pinch of cayenne pepper

2 tablespoons frozen orange juice concentrate

½ cup silken tofu

1 tablespoon sweet white miso

⅓ cup lightly packed cilantro leaves

Salt and freshly ground black pepper

A blend of miso and tofu gives this cholesterol-free soup the richness of a creamy bisque, while one serving has less than 1 calorie of fat. When pressed for time, I use the small carrots sold prewashed in plastic bags. Already peeled, they can be cut in half and tossed right into the pot.

1. Place the carrots, onion, garlic, and cayenne pepper in a deep saucepan and add 2 cups water. Bring the liquid to a boil, cover, reduce the heat, and simmer until the vegetables are soft, 20 to 25 minutes.

2. Puree the soup, using an immersion blender or a blender. If you are using a blender, you may want to puree the soup in two batches. Add the orange juice concentrate and tofu to the blended soup. Cream the miso in ¼ cup lukewarm water. Add to the soup, together with the cilantro. Blend the soup again. Season to taste with salt and pepper and serve.

PER SERVING: Calories 79 • Soy Protein 2.7 g • Total Protein 4.1 g • Carbohydrates 14.4 g • Fat 0.6 g • Saturated Fat 0 g • Cholesterol 0 mg • Fiber 2.7 g • Sodium 206.6 mg

Green Gazpacho

For this green gazpacho, tart tomatillos and tangy yogurt replace the more traditional vinegar. Like most gazpachos, it tastes best twelve to twenty-four hours after it is made, when the flavors have had a chance to fall in love and harmoniously marry.

1. Coarsely chop half the cucumber, and transfer to a blender. Finely chop the rest, transfer to a small bowl, cover, and refrigerate.

2. Coarsely chop half the green pepper and add to the blender. Finely chop the rest, transfer to a small bowl, cover, and refrigerate.

3. Add the lime juice to the blender and whirl until the vegetables are chopped, starting on a low speed, then increasing to a higher one. Add the tomatillos, scallions, cilantro, and garlic, and blend. Add the bread and yogurt and blend. With the motor running, drizzle in the olive oil. There will be about 3 cups of intensely green soup. Season to taste with salt and pepper.

4. Refrigerate the gazpacho until well chilled, at least 2 hours. Before serving, check the seasoning and adjust as needed. Pour ¾ cup of the soup into individual bowls. Top each serving with 2 tablespoons each of the chilled chopped cucumber and green pepper.

1 large cucumber, peeled and quartered lengthwise

1 large green bell pepper, halved and seeded

Juice of 1 lime

2 small tomatillos, chopped

2 scallions (white and green parts), cut into 1-inch pieces

½ cup packed cilantro leaves

2 large garlic cloves, chopped

1 slice day-old white bread, crust removed

2 cups or two and a half 6-ounce containers plain soy yogurt

1 tablespoon extra virgin olive oil

Salt and freshly ground black pepper

PER SERVING: Calories 93 • Soy Protein 2.5 g • Total Protein 3.8 g • Carbohydrates 9.4 g • Fat 4.9 g • Saturated Fat 0.7 g • Cholesterol 0 mg • Fiber 1.7 g • Sodium 31.4 mg

2 cups chopped, peeled
    butternut squash

1 Granny Smith apple,
    peeled, cored, and
    chopped

1 medium onion, chopped

1 garlic clove, chopped

1 teaspoon curry powder

½ teaspoon ground
    cinnamon

1 cup unsweetened
    soymilk

Salt and freshly ground
    black pepper

Curried Butternut Squash Soup

Tart apple, the glow of cinnamon, and the boldness of curry powder complement the mild-mannered butternut squash in this easy-to-sip soup.

1. Combine the squash, apple, onion, garlic, curry powder, and cinnamon in a saucepan and add 2 cups water. Bring the liquid to a boil over medium-high heat. Cover and simmer until the vegetables and apple are soft, about 25 minutes.

2. Puree the soup, using an immersion blender or a blender. If you are using a blender, you may want to puree half of the solids and liquid first, then add the rest. Blend in the soymilk.

3. Season the soup to taste with salt and pepper and serve.

PER SERVING: Calories 89.1 • Soy Protein 2.2 g • Total Protein 3.6 g • Carbohydrates 18.5 g • Fat 1.2 g • Saturated Fat 0 g • Cholesterol 0 mg • Fiber 5.0 g • Sodium 4.6 mg

Mushroom and Miso "Cappuccino"

This intense puree of shiitake and white mushrooms demonstrates another way to enjoy miso in soups. The mushrooms contribute flavor and a creamy consistency to this lush soup. Sipped from a cup, it is like a savory cappuccino.

1½ cups chopped onions

1 large garlic clove, sliced

4 ounces white mushrooms, stemmed and sliced

2 ounces fresh shiitake mushrooms, stemmed and sliced

1 teaspoon dried oregano

2 tablespoons barley miso

1. Combine the onions, garlic, white mushrooms, and shiitakes in a large saucepan and add 4 cups water. Cover and bring to a boil. Reduce the heat and simmer for 20 minutes. Uncover and let the soup sit for 10 minutes.

2. Add the oregano. Puree the soup in the pot with an immersion blender, or transfer the soup to a blender and puree. Return the soup to the saucepan.

3. Cream the miso with 2 to 3 tablespoons of the pureed soup in a small bowl, using the back of a spoon. Add the dissolved miso to the soup and whisk to blend thoroughly.

4. Serve immediately, or reheat and serve, taking care not to let the soup boil.

PER SERVING: Calories 61 • Soy Protein 1.5 g • Total Protein 3.5 g • Carbohydrates 10.2 g • Fat 1.4 g • Saturated Fat 0 g • Cholesterol 0 mg • Fiber 1.7 g • Sodium 471.3 mg

One 16-ounce loaf
semolina or other Italian
bread
Herb Pesto (recipe follows)

Pesto Herb Bread

While visiting a convent in Polizzi-Generosa, the mountains of Sicily, I had some toasted bread that I will always remember. It was a loaf of sturdy golden semolina, slit and spread with olive oil and a paste of fresh herbs. Wrapped in foil, the bread was slipped into the oven until it was hot, the crust quite crisp and the herbs aromatic. If you cannot get semolina bread, use another dense country-style bread. Besides soup, this bread goes well with Eggplant Manicotti (page 223).

1. Preheat the oven to 350°F.

2. Cut the bread diagonally into 1-inch slices, taking care not to cut all the way through. The slices should remain attached at the bottom and the loaf intact.

3. Spread enough pesto on one side of each slice to coat it generously, gently pulling the bread open so you can reach in with a knife to spread the pesto over the entire slice. Place the bread in the center of a large piece of foil. Bring up the two long sides and fold them over to seal the bread. Roll up the ends.

4. Bake the bread for 20 minutes, or until it is hot all the way through and the crust is crisp.

5. Open the foil. Either let everyone pull apart the slices, or do this before serving. (Slices can be wrapped in foil and reheated later, if this is done the same day the bread is first assembled.)

PER SLICE: Calories 174 • Soy Protein 0.6 g • Total Protein 4.4 g. Carbohydrates 20.8 g • Fat 7.7 g • Saturated Fat 1.1 g • Cholesterol 0 mg • Fiber 1.5 g • Sodium 377.6 mg

Herb Pesto

To make the pesto, combine the basil, walnuts, and garlic in a food processor, and pulse 5 to 6 times, until they are chopped. Whirl in the miso. With the motor running, drizzle in the olive oil. Season to taste with salt and lots of pepper. Make this dressing the day it will be used, up to 8 hours ahead. Cover and refrigerate if you are not using it immediately.

2 cups packed basil leaves

¼ cup walnuts

2 garlic cloves

2 tablespoons mellow white miso

¼ cup extra virgin olive oil

Salt and freshly ground black pepper

Southwestern Corn Muffins

¾ cup stone-ground
   yellow cornmeal
   (see Note)

¾ cup all-purpose flour

½ cup soy protein powder

2 teaspoons baking
   powder

½ teaspoon baking soda

¼ teaspoon salt

1 cup low-fat buttermilk

½ cup sugar

1 large egg

¼ cup canola oil

½ cup canned corn,
   drained, or defrosted
   frozen corn, blotted dry
   with paper towels

¾ cup finely chopped
   jalapeño soy cheese

½ cup chopped cilantro

particularly love the way these muffins contrast the heat of chiles with creamy cheese and sweet corn. Soy keeps these muffins moist after they have cooled to room temperature. They are perfect to take along on a picnic, to bring to a potluck chili supper, or to accompany Tortilla Soup with Black Soybeans (page 129).

1. Preheat the oven to 400°F. Coat a 12-cup muffin pan with nonstick cooking spray.

2. Whisk together the cornmeal, flour, protein powder, baking powder, baking soda, and salt in one bowl. In another bowl, whisk together the buttermilk, sugar, egg, and oil.

3. Add all the dry ingredients to the bowl of wet ingredients at once. Whisk just until the batter is almost completely combined. A few lumps will not matter. Mix in the corn, cheese, and cilantro with a wooden spoon. The batter will be very thick.

4. Scoop the batter into the prepared muffin pan, filling the cups three-quarters full.

5. Bake for 15 to 20 minutes, or until the muffins are golden brown on the sides and around the top, and they feel firm to the touch. A bamboo skewer inserted into the center of a muffin should come out clean.

6. Let the muffins sit in the pan on a rack for 5 minutes, and then tip them out. Serve warm or at room temperature.

NOTE: Using stone-ground cornmeal ensures that you get the germ of the grain and muffins with a tender crumb.

PER MUFFIN: Calories 178 • Soy Protein 3.3 g • Total Protein 7.0 g • Carbohydrates 24.2 g • Fat 6.5 g • Saturated Fat 0.6 g • Cholesterol 1.3 mg • Fiber 1.2 g • Sodium 322.4 mg

Curry Flatbread

Rolling out the dough as thinly as possible is essential to this crisp flat bread. Using a pasta machine is ideal. Rolling the dough by hand produces a thicker but equally appealing cracker. It also gives you a good workout! If possible, use a pizza stone. If you do not have one, using a light-colored baking sheet is important to help avoid burning.

1. Combine the flour, semolina flour, soy flour, curry powder, salt, and pepper in a large bowl. Make a well in the center and pour in ½ cup water. Using a fork, and working around the edge of the liquid, combine the ingredients to make a dough. When it is crumbly, start working the dough together to form a ball. If necessary, add more water, 1 teaspoon at a time. The dough will be fairly stiff.

2. Knead the dough until it is smooth, 2 to 3 minutes. It will be tough and hard in comparison to bread or pasta dough and may feel a bit grainy. Wrap the dough in plastic wrap and refrigerate for at least 1 hour, up to overnight.

3. If you are using a pizza stone, place it in the oven. Preheat the oven to 450°F.

4. Tear off a piece of dough the size of a walnut. Wrap the rest of the dough in plastic wrap and place in the refrigerator. Press the piece of dough into a 2½ × 1-inch oval.

5. **With a pasta machine:** Set the rollers at the widest setting and pass the dough through. Turn the dough 90°. Set the rollers at the next setting. Pass the dough through again. Repeat until the dough is too wide to turn, raising the setting each time you pass the dough through. When the strip of dough is about 10 inches long, cut it crosswise into 2 pieces. Keep rolling each piece until it has passed through at the highest setting. It should be almost thin enough to see through; do not worry if there are some holes.

¾ cup all-purpose flour

¾ cup semolina flour

½ cup soy flour

1 tablespoon curry powder

1 teaspoon salt

¼ teaspoon freshly ground black pepper

TOPPING

Extra virgin olive oil

Kosher salt

By hand: Place the dough on a lightly floured board and, working from the center, roll it out as thinly as possible, rotating the dough and flipping it over occasionally.

6. Place pieces of rolled out dough on the heated baking stone, or on an ungreased baking sheet. Bake for 2½ to 3 minutes, or until the flatbread is covered in tiny blisters and is mostly light brown, with some golden areas. With a spatula, transfer the flatbread to a rack. Immediately brush it very lightly with a bit of olive oil and sprinkle with salt. Repeat, using up the remaining dough.

7. When cool, stack the pieces of flatbread and serve. (They will keep for up to 3 days, wrapped loosely in foil, in a dry place.)

PER PIECE WITHOUT OIL AND ADDITIONAL SALT: Calories 28 • Soy Protein 0.4 g • Total Protein 1.1 g • Carbohydrates 5.0 g • Fat 0.3 g • Saturated Fat 0.1 g • Cholesterol 0 mg • Fiber 0.4 g • Sodium 52.7 mg

Big Dill Loaf

Makes one 9-inch loaf

(Serves 12)

1 tablespoon active dry
yeast (about 1½
packets) (see Note)

3 tablespoons sugar

About 4⅔ cups bread flour

2 tablespoons canola oil

¼ cup minced shallots

8 ounces soft tofu,
squeezed (see page 48)
and crumbled into
cottage cheese–size
pieces

½ cup chopped dill

2 large eggs, lightly beaten

1 cup soy flour

2 teaspoons salt

This thin-crusted white bread flecked with feathery dill is versatile. Thickly sliced and toasted, it is perfect with Roasted Tomato Bisque. Big Dill Loaf is also outstanding for open-faced and regular sandwiches made with smoked salmon, smoked turkey, or thinly sliced smoked tofu. With any of them, spread on some Honey Mustard (page 179), and add tomato slices. Using soy flour in bread is not unusual; adding tofu is. Here it is crumbled like cottage cheese, a frequent ingredient in dill breads.

1. Dissolve the yeast in 1½ cups warm water (110°F) in a large bowl. Add the sugar, and 1 cup of the bread flour. Mix well, using a wooden spoon. Cover the bowl with a dish towel and set it in a warm, draft-free place until the sponge is light and bubbly, about 30 minutes.

2. Meanwhile, heat the oil in a skillet over medium-high heat. Add the shallots and sauté until they are soft, 3 minutes. Scrape them, along with the oil in the pan, into a mixing bowl. When cooled to room temperature, add the tofu, dill, and eggs. Mix and set aside.

3. Transfer the sponge to the bowl of an electric mixer fitted with a dough hook.

4. Add the tofu-dill mixture, 3 cups of the bread flour, the soy flour, and salt. Knead on medium speed for 3 to 4 minutes, adding flour, ⅓ cup at a time, as needed, until the dough is smooth. The dough will be sticky, but not wet. Alternatively, the dough can be kneaded by hand for 6 to 8 minutes.

5. Place the dough in an oiled bowl, turning to coat it with the oil. Cover with a moist towel and set it to rise in a warm (85°F) dry place until it doubles in size, about 1 hour.

6. Meanwhile, preheat the oven to 400°F. Butter or oil a 9 × 5-inch loaf pan. (Use one that is light-colored. Soy darkens

quickly because of the sugar in it, and the bread burns in a black metal pan.)

7. Punch the dough down. Form it into a loaf and put it in the prepared pan. Cover and let it rise until the loaf is 1 inch above the rim of the pan, about 30 minutes.

8. Bake the bread for 35 to 40 minutes, or until the loaf sounds hollow when tapped and the crust is dark brown.

9. Remove the bread from the pan immediately, and cool it on a rack.

NOTE: The contents in a packet of yeast can vary by up to ⅓ teaspoon. Therefore, I always measure yeast with measuring spoons.

PER SLICE: Calories 228 • Soy Protein 5.3 g • Total Protein 11.0 g • Carbohydrates 33.4 g • Fat 6.3 g • Saturated Fat 0.8 g • Cholesterol 35.4 mg • Fiber 1.8 g • Sodium 328.5 mg

If soy flour simply boosted the protein in breads, it would not be so interesting. But, as commercial bakers have long known, it also makes exceptionally well-crusted loaves that stay fresh longer. See for yourself in colorful Big Dill Loaf or hearty Pumpkin Caraway Bread and you may be inspired to integrate soy flour into your own favorite bread recipes.

Pumpkin Caraway Bread

Makes one 8-inch loaf
(Serves 12)

Thickly cut and toasted, this dense bold loaf is a bread lover's dream. While it is still warm, spread the toasted slices with apple butter in the morning, or with spicy Southwestern Bean Spread (page 106) any time after noon. Caraway seeds make this savory bread a natural companion to a mug of Tangy Carrot Soup (page 136) or Curried Butternut Squash Soup (page 138).

1 tablespoon active dry yeast (about 1½ packets) (see Note)

2 tablespoons unsulphured molasses

About 3½ cups bread flour

1 cup canned pureed pumpkin

2 tablespoons canola oil

2 teaspoons caraway seeds

1 cup soy flour

2 teaspoons salt

1. Dissolve the yeast in ½ cup warm (110°F) water in a bowl. Add the molasses and ½ cup of the bread flour. Mix well, using a wooden spoon. Cover the bowl with a dish towel and set it in a warm, draft-free place until the sponge is light and bubbly, about 30 minutes.

2. Mix the pumpkin, oil, and caraway seeds into the sponge. Transfer the mixture to the bowl of an electric mixer fitted with a dough hook.

3. Add 2½ cups of the bread flour, the soy flour, and salt. Knead on medium speed for 3 minutes, adding more flour, as needed, to keep the dough from sticking to the mixing bowl. Alternatively, the dough can be kneaded by hand for 6 to 8 minutes.

4. Place the dough in an oiled bowl, turning to coat it with the oil. Cover with a moist towel. Set it to rise in a warm (85°F) dry place until it doubles in size, about 1 hour.

5. Meanwhile, preheat the oven to 400°F. Butter or oil an 8½ × 4½-inch loaf pan.

6. Punch the dough down. Form it into a loaf and put it in the prepared pan. Cover and let rise until the loaf is 1 inch above the rim of the pan, about 30 minutes.

7. Bake the bread for 35 to 40 minutes, or until the loaf sounds hollow when tapped. The crust will be dark brown.

8. Remove the bread from the pan immediately, and cool it on a wire rack.

NOTE: The contents in a packet of yeast can vary by up to ⅓ teaspoon. Therefore, I always measure yeast with measuring spoons.

PER SLICE: Calories 190 • Soy Protein 2.4 g • Total Protein 7.2 g • Carbohydrates 32.1 g • Fat 4.2 g • Saturated Fat 0.5 g • Cholesterol 0 mg • Fiber 2.0 g • Sodium 366.4 mg

salads and dressings

Salads are my favorite meal. Every bite, combining crisp, succulent, soft, sharp, and perhaps spicy or sweet ingredients, stimulates my desire for the next gratifying mouthful. Some of my favorites include French Lentil Salad (page 164), Tofu Tabbouleh (page 151), and Gado Gado (page 162) gathered from the salad bar. Everyone knows these popular main-course salads, but the addition of soyfoods makes them innovative and inspiring.

Besides meal-size salads to serve at home, here are salads you can pack up and take anywhere for a portable meal. Just add a fork and they are ready to satisfy you in a brown-bag lunch, to shine at a potluck, or to enjoy on a picnic. These include tangy Mexican Chopped Salad made with zesty Orange-Baked Tofu and Quinoa and Sweet Potato and Smoked Tofu Salad that wins fans every time I serve it.

In an even lighter vein, here are side salads that include retro favorites. Watch everyone flip when you serve the sparkling Lemon Molded Salad and Seven-Layer Salad, updated with edamame, soy cheese, and a thick, creamy dressing.

Serves 8

Caesar Salad with Parmesan Croutons

DRESSING

1 tablespoon mayonnaise

1 tablespoon silken tofu

2 teaspoons Dijon mustard

1 tablespoon fresh lemon juice

2 tablespoons extra virgin olive oil

Salt and freshly ground black pepper

12 romaine lettuce leaves, torn into 1-inch pieces

Double recipe of Parmesan Croutons (page 180)

Croutons made from tempeh turn this crisp, bright salad with its creamy dressing into a sustaining main dish. I think the nutty flavor of the tempeh croutons even goes better with romaine lettuce than the usual croutons. Dijon mustard adds extra zing to the dressing. Depending on your dietary goals, you can make this dressing with cholesterol-free soy mayonnaise or the regular egg-based kind. Both are available in fat-free versions, if that suits you.

1. To make the dressing, combine the mayonnaise, tofu, mustard, lemon juice, and oil in a food processor or blender, and puree. Season to taste with salt and pepper.

2. Place the lettuce in a bowl. Pour the dressing over and toss until the lettuce is evenly coated. Top with the croutons and serve.

PER SERVING WITH CROUTONS: Calories 305 • Soy Protein 9.7 g • Total Protein 18.4 g • Carbohydrates 23.9 g • Fat 16.9 g • Saturated Fat 3.6 g • Cholesterol 9.0 mg • Fiber 5.5 g • Sodium 633.0 mg

Tofu Tabbouleh

Frozen tofu makes an amazing replacement for bulgur in this unexpected version of tabbouleh, with the bits of tofu providing the same "bite" as the wheat. Like Syrian tabbouleh, this recipe emphasizes the greens and goes light on the "grain," or tofu. Serve this tabbouleh as a salad or use it to stuff a pita pocket. Keep a couple of cakes of tofu in the freezer and, using the magic of the food processor, you can put this refreshing dish together at a moment's notice.

1. Coarsely chop the parsley, mint, and scallions in a food processor. Squeeze the water from the tofu and crumble it in with the greens. Pulse until the mixture is finely chopped and transfer it to a large bowl.

2. Combine the onion and tomatoes with the chopped greens. Add the lemon juice and oil and mix well. Season to taste with salt and pepper.

3. Let the salad stand for 1 hour before serving to allow the flavors to meld. Or, cover and refrigerate for up to 24 hours. Serve on a bed of romaine lettuce.

4 cups loosely packed flat-leaf parsley leaves

1 cup loosely packed mint leaves

3 large or 6 small scallions (white and green parts), cut into 1-inch pieces

8 ounces firm tofu, frozen, defrosted, and finely crumbled (see page 51)

½ cup finely chopped red onion

10 large cherry tomatoes, quartered and drained

Juice of 1 large lemon

3 tablespoons extra virgin olive oil

Salt and freshly ground black pepper

Romaine lettuce leaves

PER SERVING: Calories 191 • Soy Protein 4.6 g • Total Protein 7.8 g • Carbohydrates 12.6 g • Fat 13.8 g • Saturated Fat 2.0 g • Cholesterol 0 mg • Fiber 3.6 g • Sodium 46.0 mg

Chinese Un-Chicken Salad

MARINADE

3 tablespoons rice vinegar

1 tablespoon soy sauce

1 tablespoon sugar

1 tablespoon ginger juice, squeezed from finely grated fresh ginger, or ½ teaspoon ground ginger

2 tablespoons peanut oil

7 ounces frozen soymeat fillet (one package), defrosted and cut into ¼-inch slices (see Note)

4 cups napa cabbage (cut crosswise into ½-inch ribbons)

½ large cucumber, peeled, seeded, and cut crosswise into ½-inch crescents

2 ounces snow peas, cut lengthwise into thin strips

One 11-ounce can mandarin orange sections, drained

¼ cup pecans, chopped

So many restaurants and community cookbooks offer a recipe for an Asian chicken salad with a tart-sweet rice vinegar dressing that I felt a good meatless version would be welcome. Chickenlike frozen soymeat made from spun soy fibers lets you create a salad so close to the original that it may take people a while to notice the difference. For a buffet, double or triple this recipe and present it, arranged in colorful layers, in a wide, shallow serving bowl or on a large platter.

1. To make the marinade, combine the vinegar, soy sauce, sugar, ginger juice, and oil in a saucepan. Bring to a boil, cover, and remove the pot from the heat. Stir in the soymeat and set aside.

2. Place the cabbage in a salad bowl. Arrange the cucumber on top of the cabbage.

3. Plunge the snowpeas into a pot of boiling water for 30 seconds. Drain and immediately place in a bowl of ice water to chill them. Drain well. Arrange the snow peas in a ring on top of the other vegetables.

4. Heap the soymeat and marinade in the center of the bowl. Top with the orange sections and pecans. Toss well before serving. (After tossing, this salad will keep for up to a day, covered and refrigerated.)

NOTE: If you cannot get the fillet, bite-size frozen soymeat can be used.

PER SERVING: Calories 224 • Soy Protein 5.0 g • Total Protein 9.2 g • Carbohydrates 26.4 g • Fat 10.4 g • Saturated Fat 1.4 g • Cholesterol 0 mg • Fiber 4.6 g • Sodium 231.1 mg

Soy Cool Salad with Citrus Dressing

This salad reminds me of the "kitchen sink," a favorite dessert at the old-fashioned ice cream parlor where I misspent time as a teenager. Here, instead of sinful toppings, Chef Tanya Petrovna at the Native Foods restaurants in Los Angeles and Palm Springs, California, piles four kinds of soy—edamame, savory baked tofu, crackling crisp soynuts, and a sparkling soy-sauce dressing—onto a heap of fresh greens. This salad, bursting with energy, makes you feel alive from your taste buds to the tips of your toes.

1. Toast the sesame seeds in a small, dry skillet over medium heat until they pop, 3 to 4 minutes, shaking the pan often. Turn the toasted seeds into a bowl and set aside to cool.

2. Place the salad greens in large shallow bowl. Arrange the cabbage over the greens. Layer the carrots over the cabbage. Place the cucumber in a ring around the carrots. Sprinkle the edamame over the carrots. Arrange the diced tofu over the beans.

3. Pour the dressing over the salad. Sprinkle the toasted sesame seeds and the soynuts over the salad and garnish with the scallions. Present the salad, if possible, before tossing and serving it.

2 tablespoons sesame seeds

2 cups baby salad greens

1 cup finely shredded green cabbage

1 medium carrot, grated

1 medium cucumber, peeled, seeded, and thinly sliced

½ cup frozen shelled edamame, cooked according to package instructions

8 ounces Baked Tofu, cut into 1-inch pieces (recipe follows)

Soy Citrus Dressing (recipe follows)

4 tablespoons roasted unsalted soynuts

½ cup finely chopped scallions (green part only)

PER SERVING, INCLUDING DRESSING: Calories 224 • Soy Protein 20.2 g • Total Protein 26.3 g • Carbohydrates 18.0 g • Fat 15.5 g • Saturated Fat 2.6 g • Cholesterol 0.1 mg • Fiber 7.0 g • Sodium 1067.9 mg

About 8 ounces firm tofu

¼ cup soy sauce

2 tablespoons rice vinegar

1 garlic clove, pressed

2 teaspoons ginger juice,
squeezed from about
2 tablespoons planed or
finely grated fresh
ginger

Baked Marinated Tofu

This flavorful tofu is decidedly milder than the one made with Spicy Tofu Marinade. While its blend of ginger, garlic, and rice vinegar rings a pleasantly familiar Asian note, its savory taste goes well not just in stir-fries but also in grain and vegetable dishes, as well as in Soy Cool Salad (page 153). Double the recipe to make one pound, if you like.

1. Cut the tofu into ½-inch slices. Place the tofu in a shallow, glass or other non-reactive baking dish large enough to hold the slices in one layer.

2. Combine the soy sauce, vinegar, garlic, and ginger juice. Add ¼ cup water. Pour the marinade over the tofu. Set it aside to marinate for 30 minutes at room temperature, or 1 hour in the refrigerator. Bake at 375°F for 15 minutes. Turn the slices. Bake for 10 minutes more. Let the tofu cool in the marinade. This tofu will keep for up to 4 days, tightly covered and refrigerated.

PER 2 OUNCES: Calories 90 • Soy Protein 6.0 g • Total Protein 6.5 g • Carbohydrates 5.0 g • Fat 4.5 g • Saturated Fat 0.5 g • Cholesterol 0 mg • Fiber 0.6 g • Sodium 750 mg

¼ cup rice vinegar

¼ cup soy sauce

1 tablespoon fresh lemon
juice

1 teaspoon roasted
sesame oil

Soy Citrus Dressing

This dressing is best made no more than an hour before it will be used. After that, the lemon juice loses some of its fresh taste.

Combine the ingredients with ¼ cup water in a jar. Cover tightly and shake well.

PER 2 TABLESPOONS: Calories 17 • Soy Protein 0.7 g • Total Protein 0.7 g • Fat 0.8 g • Saturated Fat 0.2 g • Cholesterol 0 mg • Carbohydrates 1.0 g • Fiber 0 g • Sodium 686.6 mg

Spinach Salad with Crisped Tempeh

Crisped tempeh adds the same smoky flavor and crunch to this satisfying salad as you get with bacon in a classic spinach salad. You can stem and wash the spinach a day ahead and store it in a plastic bag. Just be sure to dry it very well. Lightly sautéed Smoked Tempeh (see page 114) or Lemon Grill Tempeh (page 249) are alternatives to the crisped bits when you want to vary the recipe.

1. To make the garlic oil, combine the garlic and oil in a small saucepan over medium heat. Simmer gently but do not boil, until the garlic is soft but not browned, 8 to 10 minutes. Remove from the heat, mix in the oregano, and set aside to steep for 30 minutes. Pour the oil through a fine sieve; there should be about ⅓ cup. Place the garlic on a cutting board. Holding the blade of a large, heavy knife sideways, smear the garlic over the board, chop it to a paste, and set it aside in a small dish.

2. Place the spinach in a large salad bowl, and sprinkle on the scallion. Arrange the mushrooms over the spinach, and the onion rings over the mushrooms.

3. To make the dressing, combine 2 tablespoons of the garlic oil, the vinegar, lemon juice, and garlic paste in the warm pan. Season to taste with salt and pepper.

4. Pour the dressing over the salad. Sprinkle with the Crisped Tempeh and serve immediately.

NOTE: The remaining garlic oil can be kept for another use. It will keep for up to 1 week, covered and refrigerated.

GARLIC OIL

3 garlic cloves, halved lengthwise

½ cup canola oil

1 teaspoon dried oregano

8 cups fresh spinach leaves, stemmed, washed, and dried

1 large scallion (green part only), chopped

2 large white mushrooms, thinly sliced

Four ¼-inch slices red onion, separated into rings

One recipe Crisped Tempeh, made with peanut oil (page 181)

3 tablespoons red wine vinegar

1 teaspoon lemon juice

Salt and freshly ground black pepper

PER SERVING: Calories 347 • Soy Protein 4.4 g • Total Protein 7.0 g • Carbohydrates 10.4 g •
Fat 32.3 g • Saturated Fat 2.6 g • Cholesterol 0 mg • Fiber 3.9 g • Sodium 52.2 mg

Blankit Tunisian Bread Salad

8-inch piece of French
bread, stored overnight
in a plastic bag

1 medium green bell
pepper, roasted,
peeled, and seeded
(see page 177)

3 large plum tomatoes,
seeded and diced

3 slices soy Swiss cheese,
cut into ½-inch squares

One 2-ounce can anchovy
fillets, rinsed and
chopped, optional

¼ cup Sicilian-style green
olives, pitted and
chopped

1 tablespoon capers,
rinsed and chopped

½ cup coarsely chopped
flat-leaf parsley

½ cup chopped mint

2 tablespoons extra virgin
olive oil

1 tablespoon red wine
vinegar

Salt and freshly ground
black pepper

5 cups torn romaine
lettuce leaves

Eating fresh tomatoes and green bell peppers everyday would be a treat if they were like those in Tunisia, where the tomatoes are sweet and tart, succulent and fleshy. And, oh, the peppers! Grown under the hot desert sun, they have the floral, aromatic intensity of fresh chiles, without their heat. Still, using locally available ingredients, this chopped bread-based salad works quite nicely. It reflects the fusion of North African and French cooking. I enjoyed it at a festive lunch served by the Maouia sisters at Dar Maouia, their 17th century home in the old quarter of Tunis.

1. Cut the bread into ½-inch slices. Halve each slice horizontally, then stack and cut the halves into ½-inch pieces. There should be 4 cups.

2. Chop the roasted pepper finely. Combine it with the cubed bread, tomatoes, cheese, anchovies, if using, olives, and capers in a salad bowl. Toss with the parsley and mint. Pour in the oil and vinegar, and toss until the bread is completely moistened; it will reduce in volume. Season to taste with salt and pepper.

3. Arrange the lettuce to make a bed on each of six dinner plates, then mound 2 cups of the salad on each. Serve immediately.

PER SERVING: Calories 236 • Soy Protein 3.0 g • Total Protein 9.5 g • Carbohydrates 23.5 g • Fat 12.9 g • Saturated Fat 1.7 g • Cholesterol 0 mg • Fiber 2.6 g • Sodium 802.8 mg

Sicilian Tuna and Potato Salad

Sicilians love canned tuna packed in flavorful olive oil, including it often in salads and pasta dishes. For them, caponata is a cooked salad as well as a condiment served as an antipasto. Treating it as a salad, I sometimes combine it with canned tuna and diced cooked potatoes; together they make a hearty meal. The edamame in the caponata create a delicious cross-cultural marriage, which is also appropriate, since most of the top-quality tuna caught off the coast of Sicily is shipped to Japan, the land of edamame. This pungent salad goes well alongside Zucchini Frittata (page 77).

3 medium yellow-fleshed
   potatoes, halved

2 cups Caponata
   (page 109)

One 6-ounce can solid
   light tuna in olive oil,
   drained

Freshly ground black
   pepper

1. Place the potatoes in a pot, cover them with cold water, and bring to a boil over high heat. Reduce the heat and cook until the potatoes are tender when pierced with a sharp knife, about 20 minutes from when the water boiled. Drain. When the potatoes are cool enough to handle, peel them. Cut them into 1-inch pieces.

2. Combine the caponata and tuna in a bowl, breaking the tuna into chunks with a fork. Mix in the warm potatoes.

3. Adjust the seasoning to taste, and serve. (Salt will probably not be needed, based on the amount already in the tuna and seasoned caponata.) This salad will keep for up to 24 hours, tightly covered and refrigerated. Bring to room temperature before serving.

PER SERVING: Calories 355 • Soy Protein 3.7 g • Total Protein 13.9 g • Carbohydrates 34.4 g • Fat 18.8 g • Saturated Fat 2.8 g • Cholesterol 15.2 mg • Fiber 5.9 g • Sodium 342.3 mg

Pontormo Salad

DRESSING

1 tablespoon balsamic
vinegar

1 tablespoon red wine
vinegar

1 tablespoon red wine

Salt and freshly ground
black pepper

2 tablespoons extra virgin
olive oil

4 cups baby salad greens

1 teaspoon extra virgin
olive oil

16 ounces soft tofu, lightly
squeezed
(see page 48)

½ teaspoon soy sauce

⅛ teaspoon ground
turmeric

1 teaspoon dried basil

1 teaspoon dried oregano

1 teaspoon dried thyme

Chef Cesar Casella, of the restaurant Beppe in New York City, prepares this warm salad with gently scrambled eggs. Using tofu in their place proves how well a recipe can be translated into soy. I serve this salad as a main course for brunch, along with Roasted Tomato Bisque (page 133). It is such a simple dish to make that I sometimes make up half the recipe for lunch when I am working at home.

1. To make the dressing, whisk together the balsamic and wine vinegars with the wine and salt and pepper to taste in a small bowl. Whisk in the oil and set aside.

2. Arrange 1 cup of the salad greens in the center of four dinner plates and set aside.

3. Heat 1 teaspoon oil in a skillet over medium-high heat. Add the tofu, breaking it up until it resembles scrambled eggs. Mix in the soy sauce, turmeric, basil, oregano, and thyme, stirring until the herbs and seasonings are evenly distributed and the tofu smells fragrant, about 2 minutes.

4. Place a quarter of the scrambled herbed tofu over the greens on the prepared plates, and spoon a quarter of the dressing over each serving of the salad. Serve immediately.

PER SERVING: Calories 165 • Soy Protein 10.1 g • Total Protein 11.0 g • Carbohydrates 5.7 g • Fat 12.1 g • Saturated Fat 1.2 g • Cholesterol 0 mg • Fiber 1.3 g • Sodium 44.8 mg

Quinoa, Sweet Potato, and Smoked Tofu Salad

Serves 6

In summer, this combination of featherlight quinoa, creamy sweet potatoes, and crunchy cool vegetables sparked with fresh mint and lime makes a comfortable one-dish meal. In cool weather, serve this with a mug of Tangy Carrot Soup (page 136).

1. Preheat the oven to 375°F.

2. Roast the sweet potato until it is almost done, but still slightly firm in the center, about 35 minutes. When cool enough to handle, peel it and cut it into ¾-inch cubes. Set aside.

3. Rinse the quinoa in a strainer under cold running water, then drain well. Place the quinoa in a pan over medium-high heat. Cook, stirring constantly, until the grains are dry and separate, and the quinoa smells toasted, about 5 minutes. Add 1¼ cups water, taking care as the liquid will spatter. Cover the quinoa, reduce the heat to medium, and cook until done, about 15 minutes. Let it sit, covered, for 5 minutes. Uncover, and fluff with a fork.

4. Place the warm quinoa in a bowl. Add the sweet potato, tofu, cucumber, bell pepper, parsley, and mint. Toss with a fork to blend. Mix in the lime juice. Season to taste with salt and pepper.

5. Serve at once. (Or store, tightly covered in the refrigerator, for up to 24 hours. If chilled, let the salad sit at room temperature for at least 20 minutes before serving.)

¾ cup quinoa

1 medium sweet potato

4 ounces smoked or baked tofu (see page 34), cut into ¾-inch cubes

¼ cup finely diced cucumber

¼ cup finely diced green bell pepper

¼ cup chopped flat-leaf parsley

3 tablespoons chopped mint

4 teaspoons fresh lime juice

Salt and freshly ground black pepper

PER SERVING: Calories 144 • Soy Protein 4.0 g • Total Protein 8.1 g • Carbohydrates 23.8 g • Fat 2.4 g • Saturated Fat 0.2 g • Cholesterol 0 mg • Fiber 2.5 g • Sodium 79.3 mg

Mexican Chopped Salad

1 green bell pepper, chopped

6 red radishes, cut into ¼-inch cubes

¾ cup jícama, cut into ½-inch cubes

2 tablespoons chopped cilantro

One recipe Orange-Baked Tofu (recipe follows)

4 large romaine lettuce leaves, cut crosswise into ½-inch strips

DRESSING

1 tablespoon fresh lime juice

¼ teaspoon ground cumin

¼ teaspoon ground ancho or New Mexican chile powder

Salt

1 tablespoon extra virgin olive oil

Crisp and colorful, hot and tangy, sweet and succulent all describe this kaleidoscopic salad. I first enjoyed it at Arizona 206 Cafe in New York City, where it was a main-dish salad containing chicken. Here, orange-glazed tofu replaces the chicken. Serve it with your favorite quesadilla or alongside tacos. A double portion serves as a full meal on a hot summer day.

1. Combine the green pepper, radishes, jicama, and cilantro in a bowl. Add the tofu.

2. To make the dressing, combine the lime juice, cumin, chile powder, and salt to taste in a bowl. Beat in the olive oil with a fork. Pour the dressing over the salad and toss to combine.

3. Make a bed of lettuce on each of 4 salad plates or in wide shallow bowls. Heap a quarter of the chopped salad on the lettuce and serve.

PER SERVING: Calories 215 • Soy Protein 11.3 g • Total Protein 12.6 g • Carbohydrates 14.0 g • Fat 12.4 g • Saturated Fat 1.6 g • Cholesterol 0 mg • Fiber 2.0 g • Sodium 569.5 mg

Orange-Baked Tofu

Makes 2 cups (16 ounces)

1. Preheat the oven to 350°F.

2. Cut the tofu into ¾-inch cubes. Arrange the cubes in one layer in a baking dish just large enough to hold them.

3. Boil the orange juice in a stainless steel or other nonreactive saucepan until reduced by a third. Off the heat, mix in the lime juice, soy sauce, orange zest, garlic, and pepper. Stir in the oil. Pour this marinade over the tofu. It will almost cover it.

4. Bake the tofu for 15 minutes, uncovered. Turn the cubes, and bake for another 15 minutes. The tofu will be golden and slightly browned on top.

5. Let the tofu cool completely in the marinade. It will keep in the marinade for up to 4 days, in the refrigerator in a sealed container. With a slotted spoon, remove the tofu from the marinade and pat dry with paper towels. Use in Mexican Chopped Salad or add to other salads.

16 ounces firm or extra firm tofu, pressed into 2 slabs (see page 49)

1 cup orange juice

1 tablespoon fresh lime juice

1 teaspoon soy sauce

2 teaspoons grated orange zest

1 garlic clove, minced

¼ teaspoon freshly ground black pepper

1 tablespoon olive oil

PER ½ CUP: Calories 165 • Soy Protein 11.4 g • Protein 12.0 g • Carbohydrates 10.0 g • Fat 8.7 g • Saturated Fat 1.2 g • Cholesterol 0 mg • Fiber 1.3 g • Sodium 90.2 mg

¾ pound assorted
vegetables, including
broccoli florets; sliced
carrots; cauliflower
florets; mung bean
sprouts; sliced zucchini;
sliced cucumber; sliced
red, yellow, and green
bell peppers; and red
onion rings

3½ to 4 ounces baked tofu
(see page 34), sliced
(see Note)

½ cup Indonesian Peanut
Dressing and Dip
(recipe follows)

2 tablespoons chopped
scallions (white and
green parts)

Salad Bar Gado Gado

The idea for this generous salad came to me while looking at a supermarket salad bar and realizing it could be a convenient source of ingredients. I like to steam the zucchini, broccoli, and carrots, but you may prefer them raw, along with the other vegetables in this simplified Indonesian salad. For backyard picnics, I serve a huge platter of this gado gado like a side salad, omitting the tofu.

1. Steam an assortment of broccoli florets, carrots, cauliflower, bean sprouts, and zucchini, according to your taste.

2. Combine the steamed vegetables, warm or at room temperature, with the cucumber, bell peppers, and onion rings in a salad bowl. Top with the baked tofu. Pour on the dressing and garnish with the scallions.

NOTE: Supermarket and natural food stores sell baked tofu, or you can make it yourself. For a quick family meal, use 3 pounds of vegetables, 16 ounces of tofu, and a double recipe of the dressing.

Calories 398 • Soy Protein 25.2 g • Total Protein 41.6 g • Carbohydrates 31.7 g • Fat 32.6 g • Saturated Fat 8.1 g • Cholesterol 0 mg • Fiber 2.2 g • Sodium 755.2 mg

Indonesian Peanut Dressing and Dip

Makes ¾ cup

Use this dressing on warm noodles as well as on gado gado. It is also thick enough to serve as a dip, perhaps with cucumber sticks and strips of sweet peppers. If you are vegetarian, replace the fish sauce with soy sauce.

1. Combine the tofu, peanut butter, coconut milk, garlic, soy sauce, fish sauce, honey, molasses, lemon juice, and red pepper flakes in a blender. Add the lemon zest, if using. Whirl until the dressing is a smooth puree.

2. Transfer the dressing to a container, cover tightly, and refrigerate for 30 minutes to allow the flavors to mellow. (This dressing will keep for up to 3 days, covered and refrigerated.)

PER 2 TABLESPOONS: Calories 65 • Soy Protein 0.8 g • Total Protein 2.9 g • Carbohydrates 3.1 g • Fat 5.0 g • Saturated Fat 1.1 g • Cholesterol 0 mg • Fiber 0.6 g • Sodium 158.8 mg

⅓ cup silken tofu

3 tablespoons natural smooth peanut butter

2 tablespoons coconut milk

1 garlic clove, chopped

2 teaspoons low-sodium soy sauce

1 teaspoon fish sauce or soy sauce

1 teaspoon honey

1 teaspoon unsulphured (mild) molasses

1 teaspoon fresh lemon juice

¼ teaspoon hot red pepper flakes, or to taste

1 teaspoon minced fresh lemon zest, optional

¾ cup green lentils

1 bay leaf

1 garlic clove, chopped

½ teaspoon dried basil

½ teaspoon dried thyme

8 ounces firm tofu, frozen
and defrosted
(see page 51)

3 plum tomatoes, seeded
and chopped

1 small red onion,
chopped

⅔ cup fresh, canned, or
defrosted corn kernels

½ cup chopped mint

1 tablespoon red wine
vinegar

1 tablespoon fresh lemon
juice

1 tablespoon extra virgin
olive oil

Salt and freshly ground
black pepper

French Lentil Salad

The French, finding sweet corn charmingly exotic, often use it in salads. So adding it to lentils infused with the flavors of bay leaf and thyme, then tossed with tomatoes and fresh mint makes an authentically Gallic combination. The tofu soaks up the sharp dressing, and melds with the lentils, virtually disappearing into the salad. I like it so much that I occasionally omit the corn, then stuff this salad into a pocket pita lined with lettuce. Accompanied by carrot and cucumber sticks, this salad is a complete meal, however you make it.

1. Combine the lentils, bay leaf, garlic, basil, and thyme in a saucepan. Add 2½ cups water and bring to a boil over medium-high heat. Cover, reduce the heat, and simmer until the lentils are cooked, 30 to 40 minutes. Remove from the heat, and discard the bay leaf.

2. Tear the tofu into ½-inch pieces. Mix it into the hot lentils. Add the tomatoes, onion, corn, and mint, along with the vinegar, lemon juice, and oil. Mix to combine and season to taste with salt and pepper.

3. Serve at room temperature. (The salad will keep for up to 2 days, covered and refrigerated.)

PER SERVING: Calories 276 • Soy Protein 5.7 g • Total Protein 15.8 g • Carbohydrates 33.1 g • Fat 10 g • Saturated Fat 1.4 g • Cholesterol 0 mg • Fiber 7.6 g • Sodium 26.7 mg

Salads on the Side

Soy shows up in unexpected, sometimes playful ways in these companionable salads.

Three-Bean Salad

Serves 4

The first time I encountered three-bean salad, it was doused in bottled salad dressing, the green beans were faded and watery, and the other ingredients were no better. Since then, canned beans have improved markedly. So has the quality of frozen vegetables. In fact, since weeks often stretch between the time vegetables are picked and when you buy them, canned and frozen produce sometimes can offer better nutrition and flavor than fresh. Nothing, however, beats making your own dressing. Serve Three-Bean Salad at picnics and barbecues and pack it up for brown-bag lunches.

1. Combine the soybeans, chickpeas, green beans, and onion in a bowl.

2. To make the dressing, whisk the vinegar with the sugar, mustard, and salt until the sugar dissolves. Whisk in the oil.

3. Pour the dressing over the beans and mix to combine. Season to taste with freshly ground black pepper.

4. If possible, let the salad sit for 30 minutes before serving to allow the flavors to meld. (It will keep for up to 3 days, tightly covered and refrigerated. Bring to room temperature before serving.)

1 cup canned black
   soybeans, rinsed and
   drained
One 10½-ounce can
   chickpeas, rinsed and
   drained
1 cup frozen cut green
   beans, defrosted
½ cup finely chopped red
   onion
Freshly ground black
   pepper

DRESSING
2 tablespoons distilled
   white vinegar
2 tablespoons sugar
1 tablespoon coarse
   mustard
½ teaspoon salt
1 teaspoon canola oil

PER SERVING: Calories 181 • Soy Protein 4.5 g • Total Protein 8.7 g • Carbohydrates 28.7 g • Fat 3.6 g • Saturated Fat .0 g • Cholesterol 0 mg • Fiber 8.6 g • Sodium 277.3 mg

Scandinavian Beet Salad

2 medium beets

2 medium celery ribs, coarsely chopped

¼ medium Spanish onion, coarsely chopped (about ¾ cup)

½ medium Fuji apple, peeled, cored, and cut into 1-inch pieces

8 ounces firm tofu, frozen, defrosted, and torn into 1-inch pieces (see page 51)

2 tablespoons low-fat mayonnaise, or soy mayonnaise

2 tablespoons soy sour cream

1 teaspoon yellow mustard

½ teaspoon sugar

1 tablespoon red wine vinegar

Salt and freshly ground black pepper

Scandinavian and Eastern European cooks appreciate beets, using them in dishes like this bright salad. Where they might include chopped herring, I sneak in crumbled frozen tofu. It adds pleasant, nubbly contrast to the silken beets and juicy apple. For a colorful buffet, include this salad alongside Creamy Potato Salad with Green Peas and Cress (page 168) and a big green salad tossed with Lemon Dill Dressing (page 176).

1. Boil the beets until they are easily pierced by a knife, about 40 minutes. Drain. When the beets are cool enough to handle, peel and cut the beets into 1-inch pieces. (This can be done 1 day ahead.)

2. Combine the celery and onion in a food processor. Pulse 6 or 7 times to chop coarsely. Add the beets, apple, and tofu. Pulse until the salad is evenly chopped in ¼-inch pieces. Do not overprocess. Transfer the salad to a bowl.

3. Add the mayonnaise, soy sour cream, mustard, sugar, and vinegar. Mix to blend and season to taste with salt and pepper.

4. Serve at once. If chilled, let sit at room temperature for 20 minutes before serving. (This salad will keep for up to 4 days, tightly covered and refrigerated.)

PER SERVING: Calories 78 • Soy Protein 3.2 g • Total Protein 4.1 g • Carbohydrates 10.5 g • Fat 3 g • Saturated Fat 0.6 g • Cholesterol 0 mg • Fiber 2.1 g • Sodium 123.2 mg

Pasta Salad with Herb Pesto

While working on my first soy cookbook, I found that a mellow, light miso can stand in for the cheese in pesto, with its fermented flavor bringing a tang akin to that of the Parmigiano. A boon for vegans and everyone avoiding dairy foods, it pleases even my Italian friends. To them, combining pasta and potatoes in the same dish is not unusual. Certainly, both are delicious with the pesto. If you can get the semolina pasta enriched with soy flour, this salad will offer enough protein to anchor a meal. I like it accompanied by grilled vegetables.

8 ounces penne

6 medium red-skinned potatoes, peeled and cut into 1-inch pieces

1 cup seeded and ⅜-inch cubed European cucumber

½ cup finely diced red onion

Herb Pesto (page 141), made without the garlic

1. Bring a large pot of salted water to the boil. Stir in the pasta and add the potatoes. When the pasta is al dente, the potatoes will also be cooked. Drain, reserving about ½ cup of cooking water. Place the pasta and potatoes in a large bowl. Add the cucumber and onion.

2. Mix the pesto into the warm pasta and vegetables until they are combined. Add a bit of the cooking water if the pesto is too thick to coat the salad evenly.

3. Serve this salad the day it is made. Do not refrigerate it before serving.

PER SERVING: Calories 284 • Soy Protein 2.2 g • Total Protein 7.3 g • Carbohydrates 40.1 g • Fat 10.2 g • Saturated Fat 1.3 g • Cholesterol 0 mg • Fiber 3.1 g • Sodium 315.6 mg

Serves 8

Creamy Potato Salad with Green Peas and Cress

1¼ pounds small red-skinned new potatoes

½ small green bell pepper, chopped

½ cup frozen green peas, defrosted

2 tablespoons finely chopped shallots

¼ cup chopped fresh dill

½ cup watercress leaves

DRESSING

¼ cup silken tofu

¼ cup soy sour cream

1 tablespoon fresh lemon juice

1 tablespoon red wine vinegar

1 teaspoon wasabi paste

1 teaspoon olive oil

Salt and freshly ground black pepper

Creamy potato salads often owe their appeal to a dressing high in fat, cholesterol, and calories. This combination of new red-skinned potatoes, baby green peas, and watercress is an exception. Its wasabi-spiked, soy-based dressing is low in fat and contains no cholesterol. A generous portion of this salad contains fewer than 100 calories, so you can enjoy seconds comfortably. Serve this salad with a Smoked Turkey and Arugula Wrap (page 184), poached salmon, and all your picnic favorites.

1. Place the potatoes in a pot, cover with cold water, and bring to a boil over high heat. Reduce the heat and cook until the potatoes are tender when pierced with a knife, about 15 minutes from when the water boils. Drain. When the potatoes are cool enough to handle, halve or quarter them, depending on their size, and place them in a bowl.

2. Add the green pepper, peas, shallots, and dill to the potatoes.

3. To make the dressing, combine the tofu, sour cream, lemon juice, vinegar, and wasabi in a blender or food processor and puree. Blend in the oil and season to taste with salt and pepper.

4. Pour the dressing over the potato salad, and toss to blend. Add the watercress and toss until evenly combined. Adjust the seasonings, and serve.

PER SERVING: Calories 91 • Soy Protein 0.6 g • Total Protein 2.9 g • Carbohydrates 16.1 g • Fat 2.1 g • Saturated Fat 0.6 g • Cholesterol 0 mg • Fiber 1.9 g • Sodium 47.4 mg

Warm Potato Salad

Serves 4

Tangy German potato salad is the model for this meatless version. Soy bacon bits nicely replace the expected crumbled bacon. They also provide a pleasant contrast to the creamy baby lima beans. I particularly like this salad with hot dogs made with or without meat, and with Pinto Bean Burgers (page 189).

1. Place the potatoes in a pot, cover with cold water, and bring to a boil over high heat. Reduce the heat and cook until the potatoes are tender when pierced with a knife, about 25 minutes from when the water boils. Remove the potatoes from the pot with a slotted spoon, reserving the cooking water. Cut the potatoes into 1½-inch pieces and place them in a bowl.

2. Add the lima beans to the pot of hot water and cook according to package directions. Drain the limas and add them to the potatoes. Add the onion, celery, and bacon bits to the bowl.

3. To make the dressing, heat the vinegar and sugar in a small pot until the sugar dissolves. Mix in the salt.

4. Pour the dressing over the hot potatoes. Use two wooden spoons to toss the salad. Serve warm.

1½ pounds red-skinned new potatoes
½ cup frozen baby lima beans
½ cup chopped red onion
1 small celery rib, chopped
¼ cup soy bacon bits

DRESSING
¼ cup distilled white vinegar
2 tablespoons sugar
1 teaspoon salt

PER SERVING: Calories 189 • Soy Protein 3.0 g • Total Protein 7.5 g • Carbohydrates 38.8 g • Fat 1.7 g • Saturated Fat 0.1 g • Cholesterol 0 mg • Fiber 4.0 g • Sodium 567.1 mg

Seven-Layer Salad

2 cups shelled frozen or
  fresh edamame

3 cups shredded iceberg
  lettuce

1½ cups shredded carrots

⅔ cup raisins

2 to 3 thin slices red onion,
  separated into rings

1½ cups frozen baby
  green peas, defrosted

1½ cups (6 ounces) soy or
  dairy Gouda, or mild
  Cheddar, cut into
  ¼-inch dice

DRESSING

1 cup pureed silken tofu

½ cup low-fat whipped
  salad dressing

1 teaspoon dry mustard

¼ teaspoon celery seeds

1 tablespoon fresh lemon
  juice

¼ cup (½ ounce) freshly
  grated Parmigiano-
  Reggiano, or soy
  Parmesan cheese

Salt and freshly ground
  black pepper

The inspiration for this recipe comes straight out of my childhood, when my great-aunt Katy often served it. The soy comes from edamame and the invisible blending of tofu into the thick dressing blanketing this retro-style salad. Together, they provide more than the recommended 6.25 grams of soy protein per serving. Use diced cow's milk or soy cheese, as you prefer. Leftovers spooned into a pita pocket make an instant sandwich. I also like them smushed into a big baked potato.

1. Add the edamame to a pot of boiling salted water and cook until they are tender-crisp, about 5 minutes. Drain the beans, and set aside.

2. Arrange the lettuce to cover the bottom of a large clear glass bowl. Layer the edamame, carrots, raisins, onion rings, and peas, one over the other. Complete with a layer of diced cheese.

3. To make the dressing, combine the tofu, whipped dressing, mustard, celery seeds, lemon juice, and cheese in a food processor and puree to make a thick cream. Season to taste with salt and pepper.

4. Spread the dressing over the top of the salad, using a rubber spatula. Bring the dressing out to the edge, making sure it touches the side of the bowl all around, sealing the salad. Cover the bowl with plastic wrap.

5. Refrigerate the salad for at least 4 hours before serving. This allows the dressing to slip down the sides of the bowl. Toss well, and serve. This salad will keep for up to 3 days, tightly covered and refrigerated.

PER SERVING: Calories 225 • Soy Protein 6.6 g • Total Protein 12.6 g • Carbohydrates 19.1 g • Fat 11.6 g • Saturated Fat 4.5 g • Cholesterol 14.3 mg • Fiber 4.0 g • Sodium 225.2 mg

Lemon Molded Salad

Molded gelatin salad. In a twenty-first-century cookbook on healthful soy! Either you are smiling at this idea or you are shocked. Either way you should try this recipe. On a buffet table, it disappears as people scarf it up. I talk trash about sugar myself, but now and then my inner child needs to play with food, and this gelatin mold is a party on a plate. I'll be watching my e-mail for recipes with your variations.

2 packages lemon gelatin dessert (see Note)

1⅓ cups chilled ginger ale

8 ounces firm silken tofu, cut into ⅜-inch cubes

½ cup finely chopped celery

½ cup canned crushed pineapple, well drained

2 teaspoons fresh lemon juice

1. Pour 1⅓ cups boiling water over the gelatin in a metal mixing bowl, following the package directions to dissolve the gelatin.

2. Add the ginger ale, tofu, celery, pineapple, and lemon juice. Set the bowl in a larger bowl filled with ice water. Let it sit, stirring occasionally, until the gelatin has thickened enough to keep the solids evenly mixed.

3. Pour the gelatin mixture into a 6- or 8-cup ring mold. Cover with plastic wrap and refrigerate until the gelatin is firmly set, at least 4 hours, up to overnight.

4. To unmold, just before serving, hold the mold in a bowl of hot tap water for about 30 seconds. Lift it out and vigorously jiggle the mold. Cover the mold with a serving plate. Invert, so the molded salad drops onto the plate. (This salad will keep for up to 3 days, covered and refrigerated.)

NOTE: Vegans can use kosher gelatin dessert powder.

PER SERVING: Calories 94 • Soy Protein 1.2 g • Total Protein 3.3 g • Carbohydrates 20.5 g • Fat 0.3 g • Saturated Fat 0.1 g • Cholesterol 0.5 mg • Fiber 0.4 g • Sodium 82 mg

Serves 10

DRESSING

One 6-ounce container
  lemon soy yogurt,
  drained (see page 48)
¼ cup soy cream cheese
¼ cup low-fat or tofu
  mayonnaise
¼ cup wildflower honey
1 tablespoon orange juice
  concentrate
1 tablespoon fresh lemon
  juice
1 tablespoon grated lime
  zest
Pinch of salt

1 Fuji apple, peeled,
  cored, quartered, and
  sliced crosswise
1 medium banana, sliced
1 cup blueberries
1 cup diced cantaloupe
1 cup green seedless
  grapes
1 navel orange, peeled,
  sliced, and cut into
  1-inch pieces
1 Bosc pear, peeled,
  cored, quartered, and
  sliced crosswise
1 cup halved strawberries
4 teaspoons poppy seeds

Fruit Salad with Citrus-Poppy Seed Dressing

Fruit alone provides all the sweetness in this Southern-style fruit salad. It is a perfect buffet companion to Spinach Salad (page 155) with crisped tempeh, fried chicken, or slices of smoky ham. Though the dressing thins out quickly once tossed with the fruit, the salad and dressing will keep in separate containers for up to 8 hours, covered and refrigerated.

1. To make the dressing, combine the yogurt, cream cheese, mayonnaise, honey, orange juice concentrate, lemon juice, lime zest, and salt in a blender and puree. Use immediately, or place in a covered container and refrigerate for up to 8 hours.

2. Combine the apple, banana, blueberries, melon, grapes, orange, pear, and strawberries in a bowl. Pour the dressing over the fruit and add the poppy seeds. Toss gently, using a wooden spoon, until the fruit is coated with the dressing and the poppy seeds are evenly distributed.

3. Serve within 1 hour of combining the fruit and dressing.

PER SERVING: Calories 144 • Soy Protein 0.7 g • Total Protein 1.7 g • Carbohydrates 24.4 g • Fat 5.6 g • Saturated Fat 1.0 g • Cholesterol 0 mg • Fiber 2.2 g • Sodium 51.0 mg

Raita

Cooling Raita is a yogurt-based fresh salad that lets you cleanse your palate when eating heavily spiced Indian food. It is as refreshing on a hot day as it is served with hot food. A touch of lime juice brightens the overall effect of this dairy-free version.

1. Mix the yogurt in a bowl with the cumin, turmeric, and salt, until the seasonings are evenly distributed and the yogurt has a soft, golden hue. Stir in the mint and lime juice. Mix in the cucumber. Season to taste with pepper. Sprinkle the cilantro over the raita.

2. Serve immediately, or keep the raita refrigerated and serve chilled, within 2 hours.

PER ¼ CUP: Calories 23 • Soy Protein 1.0 g • Total Protein 1.2 g • Carbohydrates 4.1 g • Fat 0.4 g • Saturated Fat 0.1 g • Cholesterol 0 mg • Fiber 0.3 g • Sodium 159.7 mg

¾ cup or one 6-ounce container plain soy yogurt`

½ teaspoon ground cumin

⅛ teaspoon ground turmeric

½ teaspoon salt

1 tablespoon finely chopped mint or ¼ teaspoon dried

2 tablespoons fresh lime juice

1 medium cucumber peeled, halved, seeded, and thinly sliced

Freshly ground black pepper

2 tablespoons finely chopped cilantro

Salad Dressings and Croutons

You can buy bottled salad dressings containing soy but, as with most prepared dressings, their taste does not compare with that of homemade.

Pureed silken tofu is an indispensable ingredient for salad lovers; it lets you make thick, all-natural dressings containing a fraction of the fat found in the bottled kind. One day soon, I hope all stores will carry pureed tofu like the one sold in some Asian markets. Until then, I whip up an entire package of tofu, use the needed amount, and put the rest in the refrigerator, where it keeps for two to three days. Beyond creamy tofu, soy, as miso, adds rousing flavor to salad dressings.

Croutons made with tempeh are also useful. They pack enough soy protein to turn a green salad into a nutritionally balanced meal. I keep them in the freezer, to reheat as needed.

Everybody's Favorite Japanese Salad Dressing

I almost inhale the little salad at Japanese restaurants—the one with a creamy orange dressing smothering iceberg lettuce and a few shredded vegetables. Bottled versions of this dressing can be found but they do not have the fresh taste of this homemade version. Nor can they offer the same soy protein and virtually no fat. You will think that your favorite Japanese restaurant has come to you by filling a bowl with torn-up iceberg lettuce, coarsely chopped red cabbage, some shredded carrot, and a hard tomato wedge. Blanket them with this dense dressing and dive in with chopsticks for a refreshingly ethnic experience at your own table.

1. Combine the carrot, onion, and vegetable broth powder in a small saucepan and add ⅓ cup water. Bring the liquid to a boil and simmer the mixture until the vegetables are soft but not mushy, 3 minutes. Place the vegetables and any liquid in a blender.

2. Add the tofu, scallion, garlic, ginger, miso, vinegar, and oil to the carrot mixture. Blend until the dressing is a smooth puree.

3. Serve immediately. (This dressing will keep for up to 4 days, tightly covered, in the refrigerator.)

1 small carrot, finely shredded

2 tablespoons minced onion

½ teaspoon vegetable broth powder or ½ vegetable bouillon cube

½ cup (4 ounces) silken tofu

1 scallion (white part only), chopped

1 small garlic clove

1 teaspoon grated or minced peeled fresh ginger

2½ tablespoons sweet white miso

2 tablespoons rice vinegar

2 tablespoons canola oil

PER 2 TABLESPOONS: Calories 47 • Soy Protein 1.2 g • Total Protein 1.3 g • Carbohydrates 2.4 g • Fat 3.3 g • Saturated Fat 0.2 g • Cholesterol 0 mg • Fiber 0.4 g • Sodium 131.2 mg

Lemon Dill Dressing

Makes 1 cup

¼ cup fresh lemon juice

⅓ cup silken tofu

¼ cup chopped dill

2 tablespoons Dijon
  mustard

1 small garlic clove,
  chopped

1 teaspoon salt

3 tablespoons canola oil

1 tablespoon extra virgin
  olive oil

Freshly ground black
  pepper

Lemon, dill, and mustard make a harmonious trio, with lemon singing the top note, dill providing a sweet melody, and mustard adding a brassy base line in this pungent dressing. Use it on romaine lettuce and drizzle it over sliced tomatoes. It is also good blended with mayonnaise as a dressing for tuna salad.

1. Combine the lemon juice, tofu, dill, mustard, garlic, and salt in a blender. Process until they are blended. With the motor running, drizzle in the canola and olive oils. Season to taste with pepper.

2. Serve immediately or store for up to 5 days, tightly covered in the refrigerator.

PER 2 TABLESPOONS: Calories 73 • Soy Protein 0.5 g • Total Protein 0.8 g • Carbohydrates 1.4 g • Fat 7.4 g • Saturated Fat 0.6 g • Cholesterol 0 mg • Fiber 0.1 g • Sodium 331.1 mg.

Spanish Roasted Red Pepper Vinaigrette

A little sherry vinegar and the flavor of roasted red pepper make a rosy dressing with the bravura of a vinaigrette and the glow of Mediterranean sunshine.

1. Combine the tofu, roasted pepper, garlic, vinegar, and lemon juice in a blender. Whirl to a fine puree that still has some texture. And add salt and pepper to taste. With the motor running, drizzle in the oil. The dressing will have the consistency of heavy cream.

2. Serve immediately or store up to 3 days in the refrigerator.

PER 2 TABLESPOONS: Calories 93 • Soy Protein 0.5 g • Total Protein 0.7 g • Carbohydrates 1.2 g • Fat 9.6 g • Saturated Fat 1.3 g • Cholesterol 0 mg • Fiber 0.2 g • Sodium 158.0 mg

¼ cup silken tofu

½ medium red bell pepper, roasted, peeled, seeded (see box), and coarsely chopped

1 large garlic clove, chopped

1 tablespoon sherry vinegar

2 teaspoons fresh lemon juice

Salt and freshly ground black pepper

¼ cup extra virgin olive oil

Oven-Roasted Peppers

1. Preheat the oven to 500°F and cover a baking sheet with foil.

2. Place the peppers on the baking sheet. Roast them until their skin feels loose to the touch, 20 to 30 minutes, depending on the size and thickness of the peppers; the peppers will still be somewhat firm. Place the peppers in a bowl and cover with plastic wrap and let sit for 15 to 30 minutes.

3. Pull the skin from the peppers, using your fingers. Hold them over the bowl while you do this, to catch the juices. Pull the peppers in half and discard the stem, seeds, and ribs.

Roasted peppers can be stored 2–3 days, covered with olive oil and tightly covered in the refrigerator.

2 tablespoons tomato
    paste
2 tablespoons finely
    chopped onion
1 tablespoon sweet rice or
    mellow white miso
1 teaspoon sugar
3 tablespoons distilled
    white vinegar
1 tablespoon chopped
    fresh tarragon
    (see Note)
2 tablespoons canola oil

Tangy French-American Dressing

Before Russian and ranch dressings became supermarket staples, Milani's 1890 French Dressing was one of the first commercially bottled choices. I have added tarragon, whose French flavor lends sophisticated presence to the sweet, tomato-edged sharpness we all adored. For an authentic flashback, serve this dressing on a mixed salad of iceberg lettuce, thinly sliced carrots, sliced raw mushrooms, shredded cabbage, unripe tomato wedges, and red onion rings.

1. Combine the tomato paste, onion, miso, sugar, vinegar, and tarragon in a blender. Add the oil, and blend until the dressing is thick and creamy.

2. Serve immediately or store for up to 2 days, tightly covered, in the refrigerator.

NOTE: Use dried tarragon only if it is very fresh. One teaspoon should be sufficient.

PER 2 TABLESPOONS: Calories 60 • Soy Protein 0.3 g • Total Protein 0.6 g • Carbohydrates 3.0 g • Fat 5.1 g • Saturated Fat 0.4 g • Cholesterol 0 mg • Fiber 0.4 g • Sodium 132.6 mg

Honey Mustard

Makes 1½ cups

One taste and your family will insist this versatile condiment is handy at all times. Styled after the honey mustard sauce McDonald's serves with their chicken nuggets, it amazes the most die-hard tofu haters. Serve it with Fried Tofu Sticks (page 117), and use it as a sandwich spread, particularly with cheeses and smoked turkey, on burgers, and with smoked salmon.

¾ cup firm silken tofu

½ cup Dijon mustard

2 tablespoons wildflower honey

2 tablespoons light brown sugar

2 teaspoons fresh lemon juice

2 teaspoons distilled white vinegar

1 tablespoon dry mustard

¼ teaspoon salt

1. Puree the tofu in a food processor. Add the mustard, honey, sugar, lemon juice, vinegar, dry mustard, and salt. Process until well blended. The finished dipping sauce will have the texture of runny mayonnaise.

2. Turn the sauce into a container, cover, and refrigerate until chilled, at least 2 hours. This gives the ingredients time to meld and their flavors to develop. Chilling thickens the sauce to a spreadable texture. Stirring brings it back to the texture of a dip or thick sauce. (This condiment will keep for up to 1 week, tightly covered and refrigerated.)

PER TABLESPOON: Calories 21 • Soy Protein 0.7 g • Total Protein 0.8 g • Carbohydrates 2.7 g • Fat 1 g • Saturated Fat 0 g • Cholesterol 0 mg • Fiber 0 g • Sodium 129 mg

One 8-ounce package
    mild-flavored three- or
    five-grain tempeh
    (see page 31)

1 large egg white

1 to 2 garlic cloves,
    minced

½ cup Italian seasoned
    dried bread crumbs

½ cup grated Parmigiano-
    Reggiano (1 ounce)

¼ teaspoon freshly ground
    black pepper

Parmesan Croutons

Instead of bread, these croutons are made from tempeh. They take advantage of tempeh's yeasty taste, while turning a simply green salad into a complete meal, including soy protein. Baked in the oven, they are made without any added fat. Besides using them in Caesar Salad (page 150), try adding them to your favorite pea soup.

1. Preheat the oven to 375°F.

2. Cut the tempeh into ½-inch strips and cut the strips crosswise into ½-inch cubes. (If desired, trim the rounded edges off the slab of tempeh before cubing to make the croutons more even.)

3. Beat the egg white with the garlic in a wide shallow dish, until foamy. Add the cubed tempeh, tossing to coat evenly. Mix the bread crumbs, cheese, and pepper in a second dish. Transfer the tempeh to the second bowl. Toss to coat the tempeh evenly with the bread crumbs and cheese.

4. Spread the coated tempeh in one layer on a baking sheet. Bake for 15 minutes, or until crisp and lightly browned. Turn the croutons every 5 minutes so they color evenly. Set aside to cool.

PER 1/2 CUP: Calories 198 • Soy Protein 9.5 g • Total Protein 16.3 g • Carbohydrates 20.5 g • Fat 7.0 g • Saturated Fat 2.2 g • Cholesterol 7.2 mg • Fiber 3.5 g • Sodium 543.6 mg.

Crisped Tempeh

Makes 1 cup

created these crisp bits as a substitute for crumbled bacon. They are perfect sprinkled over spinach salad or mashed into a baked potato.

1 tablespoon peanut, extra virgin olive, or canola oil

4 ounces soy tempeh or other, milder flavored kind

1. Chop the tempeh into pieces the size of bacon bits.

2. In a medium skillet, heat the tablespoon of oil over medium-high heat. Mix in the tempeh. Cook, stirring, until the tempeh is browned and crisp, about 10 minutes. Turn into a small bowl. This tempeh keeps in the refrigerator in a tightly sealed container for 3 to 4 days. To recrisp before using, sauté it in a skillet in a teaspoon of oil. These bits can also be frozen and recrisped, using the same method.

wraps, burgers, and savory pies

When a light meal is in order, whether it is lunch to eat at your desk, a homemade burger with personality, or a casual supper with a touch of class, these soy solutions are just right.

Instead of the usual sandwich, soy-filled wraps, with everything rolled up right and tight, are perfect when you need one hand for work and one for lunch. They offer more than just a change from two slices of bread and a filling. Using soy inspires new ideas for what that filling can be.

For a hot light meal, one of the excellent soy-rich burgers you can buy, ready to heat-and-eat, can be a good choice. But sometimes you want a more original Green Bean and Tempeh Burger or a crusty Pinto Bean Burger. Fajitas and tacos made with soymeat are great for a quick light bite; kids and adults all love 'em. For more sophistication, Swiss Chard, Poblano, and Potato Burrito with Baked Tofu, empanada-like Spinach and Mushroom Pies, and French Onion Tart, styled after the quiche-like onion tart of Alsace, in France, are ideal. The rich pastry crust for this tart is one to try with your own favorite quiche recipes.

California "Bacon" and Avocado Wrap

Makes 1

Whether you like your BLT with real bacon or soy bacon, you will appreciate this version. Silky avocado and a kick of barbecue sauce add flavors that enhance the classic trio. You can enjoy the crunch and flavor of bacon, thanks to Lightlife's SmartBacon and Morningstar Farm's Breakfast Strips, or Smokey Tempeh Strips from Lightlife. This sandwich won't get soggy if made in the morning and wrapped in foil to enjoy at lunchtime.

1 pocketless pita bread

1 tablespoon bottled barbecue sauce

1 romaine lettuce leaf

3 thin tomato slices

2 soy bacon strips, cooked according to package directions

2 Hass avocado slices, about ⅛ of an avocado

1 thin slice sweet onion

2 thin slices green bell pepper

1. Preheat the oven to 350°F.

2. Heat the pita bread to make it soft, 3 to 4 minutes.

3. Spread the barbecue sauce over the warm bread. Place the lettuce leaf on a work surface. Press down on it, flattening the spine of the leaf. (If the leaf has a prominent spine, you may want to cut it out.) Place the lettuce on top of the barbecue sauce, covering the pita bread. Arrange the tomato slices in a row down the center of the lettuce leaf. Place the bacon strips along one side of the tomatoes, and the avocado along the other. Separate the onion into rings. Place them on top of the bacon and avocado, along with the green pepper. Fold the two sides of the pita in over the fillings, making a roll.

Calories 287 • Soy Protein 10.7 g • Total Protein 17.7 g • Carbohydrates 45.1 g • Fat 5.0 g • Saturated Fat 0.3 g • Cholesterol 0 mg • Fiber 5.7 g • Sodium 781.7 mg

Smoked Turkey and Arugula Wrap

1 sheet of lavash bread or one 10-inch wheat tortilla (burrito size)

¼ cup Garden Dip with Herbs (page 101) or tofu cream cheese with scallions

3 ounces smoked turkey breast (about 3 thin slices) or sliced smoked tofu

1 tablespoon Honey Mustard (page 179) or commercial sweet mustard

2 or 3 thin slices Granny Smith apple

¼ cup daikon radish, julienned

¼ cup arugula, cut crosswise in fine ribbons

A good wrap offers several textures and flavors in each bite. Here, a tofu-based spread keeps the wrapper soft while adding fresh herbs that complement the smoky turkey, sharp honey mustard, and tart apple. A shower of daikon radish adds crispness, arugula the zing that balances them all. To avoid dough-overload at the ends of this wrap, simply roll it up like a scroll, then cut it into one-inch pieces.

1. Trim the lavash bread to make a rectangle measuring roughly 14 × 12 inches. (If you are using a tortilla, skip this step.) Place the lavash on a work surface, with one of the short ends facing you.

2. Spread the dip over the bread, covering it to within ¼ inch of the edges, all around. Lay the turkey over the spread, covering it. Spread the honey mustard over the turkey. Arrange the apple slices over the mustard. Sprinkle the thin radish strips and the arugula over the sandwich filling.

3. Roll up the wrap from the bottom, working away from you. Gently but firmly pat and compress the filling as you go. Cut the roll diagonally into thirds, and serve. It may be wrapped in plastic and refrigerated for up to 8 hours before serving.

NOTE: If this wrap is not served for several hours, you may want to toss the apple slices with a few drops of fresh lemon juice, to prevent them from discoloring.

Calories 415 • Soy Protein 2.6 g • Total Protein 20.5 g • Carbohydrates 54.7 g • Fat 12.5 g • Saturated Fat 2.3 g • Cholesterol 22.7 mg • Fiber 4.1 g • Sodium 1085.0 mg

Salad Handroll

This is my high-protein, low-carbohydrate, vegetable-packed, single-handed lunch secret. A combination of fresh greens and tofu, wrapped sushi-style in a crisp sheet of delicious nori, it takes mere minutes to make, and it provides several servings of fresh vegetables (though avocado is actually a fruit). A dash of pink ume vinegar adds to the refreshing zest of this handy quick lunch. Tied round with a scallion, a platter of these handrolls makes a nice surprise at a backyard gathering. When presentation is less important, a toothpick or bamboo skewer will also do the job. When lunching at my desk though, I simply roll and eat.

6 scallions (white and green parts)

4 sheets sushi nori

4 large red-leaf lettuce leaves, trimmed of their hard bases

2 cups baby salad greens

½ medium red bell pepper, cut lengthwise into ¼-inch strips

4 ounces baked or smoked tofu, cut into 12 long strips

¼ avocado, cut lengthwise into 4 pieces

4 teaspoons ume vinegar or lemon juice

Freshly ground black pepper

1. Bring 2 to 3 cups water to a boil in a skillet. Boil 2 of the scallions just until they are bright green and the greens are soft, about 1 minute. Immediately plunge the scallions into a bowl of ice water. Drain well. Cut the greens off, discarding the lower, white part of the scallions. Set the long green tops aside. Cut the remaining 4 scallions, separating the white and green parts. Reserve the white part for another use. Trim the greens into 3-inch lengths. Set aside.

2. Lightly toast the nori by holding each sheet along one side and passing it quickly back and forth over the flame of a gas stove until it smells fragrant, about 45 seconds. (Omit this step if you use an electric stove.)

3. Lay the sheet of nori on a work surface, with one corner pointing towards you. Lay a lettuce leaf on the nori, trimming away whatever extends beyond its edges. Cover the lettuce leaf with ½ cup salad greens.

4. Place a quarter of the red pepper strips vertically down the center of the lettuce. Arrange 3 tofu strips alongside the pepper. Add one or two of the 3-inch lengths of scallion, and a piece of the avocado. Sprinkle a teaspoon of the ume vinegar over the filling. Season to taste with pepper.

5. Fold the bottom point of the nori and lettuce leaf up about 2 inches. Working from right to left, roll the nori into a cone, holding the filling in place with your fingers as you do. Make the roll as tight as possible. (If you are left-handed, work from left to right.) Slip one of the blanched scallion greens under the roll and bring its ends up toward you. Tie the scallion, holding the nori in a roll. Tie again, making a knot. Set on a platter. Repeat, making 3 more rolls. Or, skip the scallion tie, hand the prepared salad roll to the person who will eat it, and make the remaining ones.

PER HANDROLL: Calories 84 • Soy Protein 4.0 g • Total Protein 6.0 g • Carbohydrates 6.4 g • Fat 4.3 g • Saturated Fat 0.6 g • Cholesterol 0 mg • Fiber 1.7 g • Sodium 99.6 mg

Fajitas

Where's the beef? You won't miss it in these meatless fajitas, thanks to the new generation of soymeats. These thin strips absorb the pungent marinade and hold their flavor as they are grilled. I particularly like serving these fajitas in the sprouted wheat tortillas from the Alvarado Street Bakery, Sonoma, California.

1. To make the marinade, boil the pineapple juice in a nonreactive pot until it is reduced by one-third. Off the heat, add the tamari, garlic, cumin, pepper, lime juice, and oil.

2. Add the sliced soymeat to the pot and return it to the heat. Bring the marinade to a boil. Cool the meat in the marinade until it comes to room temperature, about 30 minutes. (Removed from the marinade, the soymeat will keep for up to 2 days, tightly covered and refrigerated.)

3. Brush a grill or ridged cast-iron skillet with oil. Heat until very hot.

4. Place the pepper strips in a bowl. Coat them liberally with nonstick cooking spray. Place the onion slices on top of the peppers. Coat them with spray as well. Grill the vegetables until they are tender-crisp, turning them once, about 5 minutes in all. Arrange the vegetables on one side of a serving platter. Set a bowl of the salsa in the center of the platter.

5. Grill the soymeat just until it begins to char, 2 to 3 minutes. Turn and cook until colored on the other side, about 2 minutes. Arrange the soymeat opposite the vegetables on the platter.

6. To eat, arrange a quarter of the soymeat in a line down the center of a tortilla. Top with a quarter of the peppers and onions. Spoon the salsa over the filling, roll, and eat.

MARINADE

1 cup pineapple juice

¼ cup tamari or soy sauce

1 large garlic clove, minced

2 teaspoons ground cumin

¼ teaspoon freshly ground black pepper

Juice of 1 lime

1 tablespoon canola oil

7 ounces frozen soymeat fillet (one package), defrosted and cut crosswise into ½-inch slices

1 large green bell pepper, seeded and cut lengthwise into ½-inch strips

Nonstick cooking spray

½ Spanish onion, cut crosswise into ½-inch slices

Four 8-inch sprouted wheat, whole wheat, or white flour tortillas

¼ cup chipotle salsa

PER SERVING (2 FAJITAS): Calories 312 • Soy Protein 7.9 g • Total Protein 16.8 g • Carbohydrates 55.0 g • Fat 6.5 g • Saturated Fat 0.8 g • Cholesterol 0 mg • Fiber 5.9 g • Sodium 473.0 mg

Green Bean and Tempeh Burgers

1 tablespoon canola oil

⅓ cup finely chopped onion

¼ pound Chinese long beans or green beans, cut into ⅜-inch pieces

2 tablespoons chopped shallots

2 tablespoons snipped chives

4 ounces (½ package) three-grain tempeh, crisped (see page 31)

½ cup cooked wild rice

¾ cup instant potato flakes

Pinch of cayenne pepper

1 teaspoon salt

2 large egg whites

1 teaspoon fresh lemon juice

About 3 tablespoons vegetable or vegetarian chicken broth

City Bakery in Manhattan is one of New York's landmark sweet stops. Chef-owner Maury Rubin also offers a self-service lunch buffet featuring creative gems like a salmon burger studded with crunchy Asian long beans. Here, tempeh produces the same tender, moist texture as the fish. The instant potato flakes I use instead of a bread crumb binder add a velvety quality. Serve with sautéed red cabbage.

1. Heat the oil in a nonstick skillet over medium-high heat. Add the onion, beans, and shallots and sauté until the onion is soft, about 4 minutes. Stir in the chives and cook for 1 minute, stirring occasionally. Turn the cooked vegetables into a bowl.

2. Add the tempeh, wild rice, potato flakes, cayenne, and salt to the vegetables. Whisk the egg whites in a small bowl until they are frothy. Add them to the vegetables. Using a fork, blend the burger mixture until it is evenly moistened. Add the lemon juice and 2 tablespoons of the broth. Work the burger mixture with your fingers until it forms a patty when squeezed together. Add the remaining broth, if necessary.

3. Form five burgers, using ½ cup of the tempeh mixture for each. Wrap each burger in plastic wrap and refrigerate until chilled, at least 1 hour, and up to 24 hours.

4. Coat a grill pan with nonstick cooking spray or brush it lightly with oil. Grill the burgers on both sides until they are firm and heated through, about 15 minutes, turning them once. Serve hot.

PER BURGER: Calories 159 • Soy Protein 4.8 g • Total Protein 9.0 g • Carbohydrates 20.7 g • Fat 5.3 g • Saturated Fat 0.5 g • Cholesterol 0 mg • Fiber 3.8 g • Sodium 539.4 mg

Pinto Bean Burgers with Cumin Mayonnaise

Serves 8

Squash's autumnal flavor, warmed by oregano and cilantro, makes these burgers perfect for fall cookouts and tailgate grilling. These burgers freeze well, so keep a batch in the freezer, ready to throw on the grill if you decide to fire it up on a sunny winter day. Indoor cooks can use a ridged grill pan, as I do, or crisp these burgers in a regular skillet. Serve with Cumin Mayonnaise (recipe follows) and a piping hot bowl of Thai Sweet Potato Soup (page 127).

1. Preheat the oven to 400°F.

2. Toss the cubed squash with 1 tablespoon of the oil on a baking sheet. Bake for about 20 minutes, or until the squash is cooked, turning it 3 to 4 times, so it browns evenly. Set aside.

3. Meanwhile, add 1 cup water to a pot with a steamer insert. Add the tempeh. Cover the pot tightly. Bring the water to a boil. Steam the tempeh for 10 minutes. Set the tempeh aside to cool.

4. Heat the remaining 1 tablespoon of oil in a skillet over medium-high heat. Add the onion and garlic and sauté until they are very soft, about 5 minutes, reducing the heat so they do not color. Mix in the oregano and set aside.

5. Break the toast into 1-inch pieces. Whirl them in a food processor to make bread crumbs. Add the beans, cooked squash, tempeh, walnuts, the onion mixture, cilantro, and cayenne. Pulse until the mixture is coarsely chopped. Do not overprocess, or the burgers will be mushy. Season with salt and pepper to taste. Add the egg white and pulse just to blend.

2 cups peeled and cubed butternut squash (½-inch cubes)

2 tablespoons canola oil

One 8-ounce package soy tempeh, chopped

1 medium onion, finely chopped

1 garlic clove, finely chopped

1 tablespoon chopped fresh oregano or 1 teaspoon dried

2 slices white bread, toasted

2 cups cooked pinto beans or one 15-ounce can, rinsed and drained

⅔ cup finely chopped walnuts

½ cup cilantro leaves

⅛ teaspoon cayenne pepper

Salt and freshly ground black pepper

1 large egg white

8 whole-grain burger buns

Romaine lettuce

1 small green bell pepper, seeded and cut in thin rings

¼ cup mayonnaise

¼ teaspoon ground cumin

2 teaspoons fresh lime
   juice

6. To form the mixture into patties, pack an eighth of the mixture into a dry ½-cup measure, preferably with straight sides. Run the blade of a knife around the inside of the cup. Turn the cup upside down and rap it sharply on the bottom to pop the burger out. Flatten the compacted burger between your palms to the size pattie you like. Repeat with the remaining mixture to make eight patties. They will keep for up to 24 hours, individually wrapped and refrigerated. (The burgers can be frozen as well. Defrost the frozen burgers in the refrigerator before cooking.)

7. To make the mayonnaise, blend the mayonnaise with the cumin and lime juice. Set aside.

8. Brush a grill with the remaining 1 tablespoon oil and preheat to medium-high. Cook the burgers until they are lightly charred on the bottom, about 1½ minutes. Carefully turn them to cook for about 1 minute on the other side. Or, heat the oil in a skillet over medium-high heat. Cook the burgers until they are browned and crisp on both sides, about 5 minutes in all.

9. While the burgers cook, grill or toast the split buns. Place a cooked burger on each bun. Spread the burger generously with the seasoned mayonnaise. Top with some lettuce and two or three rings of the green pepper. Add the top of the bun, and serve.

PER BURGER: Calories 793 • Soy Protein 12.0 grams • Total Protein 32.7 g • Carbohydrates 82.1 g • Fat 40.1 g • Saturated Fat 5.3 g • Cholesterol 7.1 mg • Fiber 17.5 g • Sodium 787.5 mg

Twenty-Minute Tacos

Two of these robust tacos provide nearly all the soy protein experts recommend you should eat in a day to help reduce the risk of heart disease, but no one will think about that once they taste them. Topping them with soy cheese and sour cream may not add much soy benefit, but they keep this a cholesterol-free dish.

1. Heat 1 tablespoon of the oil in a nonstick skillet over medium-high heat. Add ¼ cup of the onion and a third of the garlic and sauté until the onion is soft, 2 to 3 minutes. Mix in the soy crumbles, beer, and broth. Simmer until the liquid has almost evaporated, about 8 minutes. Set the mixture aside. Wipe out the skillet.

2. Heat the remaining 1 tablespoon oil in the pan. Add the remaining ½ cup onion and the rest of the garlic and sauté until the onion is soft, about 4 minutes. Mix in the chili powder, oregano, and jalapeños, stirring until the mixture is fragrant, about 30 seconds. Add the crumble mixture, drained salsa, and cilantro. Season to taste with salt and pepper. Cook for 3 to 4 minutes to meld the flavors.

3. Spoon ¼ cup of the filling into each taco shell. Top with lettuce, salsa, cheese, sliced avocado, sour cream, and chopped scallion, as you wish.

PER 2 TACOS, WITHOUT TOPPINGS: Calories 442 • Soy Protein 19.3 g • Total Protein 24 g • Carbohydrates 47.2 g • Fat 18 g • Saturated Fat 2.1 g • Cholesterol 0 mg • Fiber 9.1 g • Sodium 760.1 mg

2 tablespoons canola oil

¾ cup finely chopped onion

3 garlic cloves, finely chopped

One 12-ounce package refrigerated soy crumbles, or 2 cups frozen

¼ cup dark beer

½ cup beef or vegetable broth

2 teaspoons chili powder

1 teaspoon dried oregano

2 large jalapeño peppers, seeded and finely chopped

⅓ cup salsa, drained

½ cup chopped cilantro

Salt and freshly ground black pepper

8 taco shells

Shredded lettuce

Salsa

Shredded Jack or Tex-Mex soy cheese

Sliced avocado

Soy sour cream

Chopped scallion

Serves 4

Swiss Chard, Poblano, and Potato Burrito with Baked Tofu

3 medium poblano chile peppers, roasted, peeled, and seeded (see page 177)

2 medium boiling potatoes

¾ cup chicken or vegetarian chicken broth

1 tablespoon olive oil

1 medium white onion, cut into ½-inch slices

1 large garlic clove, finely chopped

1 teaspoon dried oregano

1 medium bunch green Swiss chard (12 ounces), stems removed, leaves cut into ½-inch strips

4 ounces baked tofu, cut into ½-inch strips

3 tablespoons soy sour cream

1 teaspoon salt

Freshly ground black pepper

Four 9-inch sprouted wheat or whole wheat tortillas

At Frontera Grill, Rick and Deanne Bayless's Mexican restaurant in Chicago, it is a toss-up whether to have the rajas, strips of roasted fresh poblanos sautéed with browned onions and Swiss chard, then simmered in tangy crema, or to have the chiles with potatoes and onions. I combine them in this earthy burrito. I use thick soy sour cream, eliminating any cholesterol. Snuggled together in a sprouted wheat tortilla, they make a hefty, soul-satisfying burrito.

1. Cut each pepper lengthwise into ½-inch strips and set aside.

2. Cut the potatoes into ½-inch slices. Stack 3 to 4 slices at a time, and cut into matchsticks ½ inch wide. Place the potato in a saucepan with the broth. Cover, bring to a boil, reduce the heat, and cook until the potatoes are cooked through and have absorbed the broth, about 15 minutes. Set aside.

3. Heat the oil in a large nonstick skillet over medium-high heat. Add the onion and sauté until it browns, about 8 minutes. Add the garlic, oregano, the poblano strips, and the chard. Cook, stirring often, until the chard is soft, about 10 minutes. Mix in the potatoes and the tofu. Stir in the sour cream until blended with the vegetables. Season with salt and pepper to taste. Remove the burrito filling from the heat.

4. Heat the tortillas, one at a time, in a dry skillet to soften them, about 1 minute each. Arrange 1 cup of the filling down the center of each tortilla, roll, and serve.

PER SERVING: Calories 256 • Soy Protein 5.5 g • Total Protein 14.0 g • Carbohydrates 49.3 g • Fat 9.4 g • Saturated Fat 2.2 g • Cholesterol 0 mg • Fiber 8.2 g • Sodium 1019.0 mg

Grilled Eggplant, Tofu, and Tomato Stacks

My friend Marie Simmons is brilliant at creating simple dishes packed with flavor. With tofu, she reaches into her Italian background, to treat it like creamy mozzarella, stacking it with fresh tomatoes and eggplant. I follow her lead in this easy recipe.

1. To make the dressing, whisk together the lemon juice, garlic, vinegar, mint, oregano, salt, and pepper in a bowl. Whisk in the olive oil. Set aside.

2. Lightly brush a grill or grill-pan with oil or coat with nonstick spray. Heat until quite hot. Grill the eggplant until it has grill marks, about 3 minutes. Turn, using a broad spatula, and grill the slices on the other side, 5 to 6 minutes in all. Transfer the eggplant slices to a large platter.

3. Halve each piece of tofu crosswise. Grill the tofu until it has grill marks on both sides, turning it once with a broad spatula, 4 to 5 minutes in all. Transfer the tofu to the platter with the eggplant.

4. Add the tomato to the platter with the tofu and eggplant. Pour the dressing over all.

5. Place a slice of the dressed tomato in the center of a dinner plate. Top with a slice of the grilled eggplant, a piece of the tofu, and another eggplant slice. Finish the stack with a slice of tomato. Repeat, making three more stacks. Spoon the dressing remaining on the platter liberally over the stacks. Garnish with a sprig of mint, and serve. Keep for 2 days, tightly covered and refrigerated. Bring to room temperature before serving.

DRESSING

2 teaspoons fresh lemon juice

1 garlic clove, minced

1 tablespoon red wine vinegar

1 tablespoon chopped mint

1 tablespoon chopped oregano

½ teaspoon salt

⅛ teaspoon freshly ground black pepper

3 tablespoons extra virgin olive oil

1 large eggplant (about 1½ pounds), unpeeled, cut crosswise into 8 slices

16 ounces soft tofu, pressed in 2 slabs (see page 49)

2 large tomatoes, each cut into 4 thick slices

4 mint sprigs

PER SERVING: Calories 219 • Soy Protein 10 g • Total Protein 12 g • Carbohydrates 13.7 g • Fat 14.8 g • Saturated Fat 1.5 g • Cholesterol 0 mg • Fiber 4.1 g • Sodium 245 mg

One recipe Savory Tart
Dough (recipe follows)

1 tablespoon unsalted
butter

1 medium Spanish onion,
thinly sliced (about
3 cups)

1 tablespoon soy
bacon bits

2 tablespoons chopped
parsley

2 large eggs

½ cup (4 ounces) silken
tofu

3 tablespoons soy cream
cheese

½ teaspoon salt

⅛ teaspoon freshly ground
black pepper

French Onion and "Bacon" Tart

This version of the traditional Alsatian onion tart, made with bacon and heavy cream, is lighter and vegetarian although just as rich. Since it is best when not refrigerated, I make the tart dough a day or two ahead, then roll it out, make the filling, and bake the tart a couple of hours before serving it. Accompanied by a green salad with Lemon Dill Dressing (page 176), this makes a nice brunch or light supper. Cut into 1-inch wedges, it can be served as an hors d'oeuvre.

1. Preheat the oven to 375°F.

2. Roll out the cold dough between 2 sheets of plastic wrap into a thin 12-inch disk. Pull off the wrap from one side of the dough. Center the unwrapped side over a 9-inch tart pan with a removable bottom. Fit the dough into the pan. Pull away the other sheet of plastic wrap. Fold the overhanging dough into the pan, pressing it to make a thick rim inside the edge of the pan. Set the tart shell in the refrigerator while you make the filling.

3. Heat the butter in a skillet over medium-high heat. Stir in the onions. Reduce the heat, and cook until the onions are soft and golden, about 15 minutes, stirring occasionally.

4. Arrange the onions to cover the bottom of the tart. Sprinkle the bacon bits over the onions. Sprinkle the parsley over the filling.

5. Combine the eggs, tofu, cream cheese, salt, and pepper in a food processor or blender and whirl until they are well combined. Pour this mixture over the onion filling. Spread it with a rubber spatula, if necessary, to cover the filling evenly. Set the filled tart on a baking sheet (do not use an air-cushioned baking sheet).

6. Bake the tart for 25 minutes, or until the crust is golden brown and the filling is puffed and firm to the touch in the center when pressed with your finger.

7. Cool on a rack. Serve at room temperature.

PER SERVING: Calories 264 • Soy Protein 7.4 g • Total Protein 18.1 g • Carbohydrates 17.4 g • Fat 14.0 g • Saturated Fat 8.0 g • Cholesterol 106.0 mg • Fiber 1.4 g • Sodium 412.4 mg

Savory Tart Dough

Makes one 9-inch crust

1. Combine the flour, protein powder, salt, and baking powder in a food processor. Pulse 2 to 3 times, just to blend. Add the butter. Pulse until the butter is completely blended with the dry ingredients, about 20 times. Beat the egg with 1 tablespoon ice water. Add this to the dough mixture. Process until the ingredients form a loose dough.

2. Turn the dough out onto a board. Press it into a smooth 6-inch disk. Wrap it in plastic wrap and refrigerate it for at least 1 hour before using. This dough will keep for up to 2 days, tightly wrapped and refrigerated. Double-wrapped in plastic, it will keep for 1 month, in the freezer.

¾ cup all-purpose flour

½ cup soy protein powder

½ teaspoon salt

¼ teaspoon baking powder

6 tablespoons (¾ stick) chilled unsalted butter, cut into ½-inch pieces

1 large egg

PER SERVING (1/8 OF A TART): Calories 171 • Soy Protein 6.0 g • Total Protein 7.9 g • Carbohydrates 8.3 g • Fat 9.2 g • Saturated Fat 6.2 g • Cholesterol 49.1 mg • Fiber 0.3 g • Sodium 240.1 mg

Spinach and Mushroom Pies

DOUGH

1¼ cups all-purpose flour

1 cup whole wheat flour

½ teaspoon salt

8 tablespoons (1 stick) unsalted butter, chilled, cut into ½-inch pieces

¼ cup nonhydrogenated spread, such as Spectrum Spread, chilled

FILLING

1 tablespoon extra virgin olive oil

1 medium onion, chopped

4 large white mushrooms, stemmed and finely chopped

One 10-ounce package frozen spinach, defrosted and squeezed dry

⅓ cup chopped fresh dill

1 tablespoon sesame salt (see Note)

12 ounces soft tofu, lightly squeezed (see page 48)

2 tablespoons tamari

1 large egg, beaten

When Pat Calhoun, White Wave's CFO, described the spinach pies she and Steve Demos made when they were getting their soyfoods company started, the combination of spinach, dill, and mushrooms she listed for the filling made my mouth water. It cried out for the flavor of a whole wheat crust, which posed an interesting challenge, as whole wheat crusts tend to be hard and dry, or bitter-tasting. This one, though, works perfectly. The filling alone is so good that any leftovers can be simply heated and enjoyed.

1. To make the dough, mix the all-purpose and whole wheat flours and salt in a large bowl. Add the butter and spread. Using a fork, then your fingertips, blend them into the flour until the mixture resembles coarse cornmeal. Sprinkle about ½ cup cold water over the mixture, and work it in until a stiff dough forms. Shape it into a thick disk, wrap it in plastic, and chill for 1 hour or more.

2. Meanwhile, make the filling. Heat the oil in a skillet over medium-high heat. Add the onion and sauté until it is soft, about 4 minutes. Add the mushrooms and cook until they give up their liquid. Continue cooking until the mixture is almost dry, about 12 minutes, reducing the heat if necessary, and stirring occasionally. Mix in the spinach. Add the dill, sesame salt, tofu, and tamari. Stir, breaking up the tofu into small pieces. Cook, stirring occasionally, until the spinach is tender, about 10 minutes. Set the filling aside to cool.

3. Preheat the oven to 350°F.

4. Remove the dough from the refrigerator and let it sit for about 10 minutes. Divide it into eight pieces. Roll out a piece of the dough into a 6-inch circle on a lightly floured surface. Place about ¼ cup of the filling on one side of the dough and

fold the other side over the filling, forming a half moon. Using the tines of a fork, press the dough to seal it. Repeat, making 8 pies in all.

5. Brush the tops of the pies lightly with the beaten egg. Make a small slit in the top of each one and place them on a baking sheet.

6. Bake the pies for about 20 minutes, or until lightly browned.

7. Let the pies cool for 15 minutes on the baking sheet before serving. Or, cool them completely and serve at room temperature.

NOTE: Sesame salt, also called *gomasio*, is sold at natural food stores and Japanese stores. You can also make it by roasting 2 tablespoons hulled sesame seeds in a dry heavy skillet over medium-high heat until they are fragrant and start to pop, about 5 minutes. (Stir often, so they do not burn.) Cool the seeds, then grind them, together with ½ teaspoon sea salt, using a *suribachi* (see page 42) or mortar and pestle.

PER SERVING: PER PIE: Calories 133 • Soy Protein 4.3 g • Total Protein 7.0 g • Carbohydrates 11.3 g • Fat 8.0 g • Saturated Fat 2.4 g • Cholesterol 6.1 mg • Fiber 2.2 g • Sodium 432.8 mg

pizzas and pastas

Pizza connoisseurs will be delighted with these crisp-crusted pies and their delicious toppings. The dough bakes beautifully, whether you like pizza with a thin crust or prefer it more like focaccia. One pie, made with roasted peppers layered over a bold tomato sauce and showered with Parmigiano-Reggiano, shows an unexpected side for creamy tofu. In another pie, a white pizza combining prosciutto and fresh mozzarella, tofu unobtrusively cuts the cholesterol but not the flavor.

Pasta lovers can either use tofu, tempeh, edamame, or other soy in sauces and pasta toppings, or enjoy soy *in* their pasta. Golden, semolina pasta made with soy flour makes the second choice possible. Several brands (see page 339) have the nutty taste and nice bite of imported Italian pasta. They also provide 6.25 grams of soy protein per serving.

Always cook pasta in salted water. Since it is not possible to calculate how much of the salt the pasta absorbs, the sodium content listed in the nutritional analyses of the following recipes does *not* include this amount.

Pizza with Tomatoes, Tofu, and Roasted Red Pepper

Makes one 12-inch pizza

(Serves 4)

Sweet red pepper and tangy tomato complement one another beautifully on this pizza. The real surprise is the tofu. Lightly squeezed and crumbled over the sauce like dollops of drained ricotta, it colors lightly in the oven, coming out like slightly chewy cheese.

1. If you are using a pizza stone, place it in a cold oven. Preheat the oven to 425°F.

2. Roll out the dough on a lightly floured work surface into a 12-inch circle, ¼ inch thick. Sprinkle the pizza peel or an air-cushioned baking sheet with the cornmeal, covering an area slightly larger than the size of the rolled out pizza dough. Transfer the dough to the pizza peel or baking sheet.

3. Spread the tomato sauce over the pizza, using the back of a large spoon and leaving a ½-inch border around the edge. The dough will show through the sauce in places. Sprinkle the tofu over the sauce. Scatter the red pepper strips over the pizza and sprinkle with the cheese.

4. Slide the pizza onto the hot stone, or place it in the oven on the pan. Bake for 20 minutes, or until the crust is golden brown around the edges and on the bottom. Serve hot or warm.

½ recipe Pizza Dough (page 202)

1 tablespoon cornmeal

½ cup Pizza Sauce (page 201) or prepared light tomato sauce

⅓ cup soft tofu, squeezed (see page 48)

½ roasted red bell pepper, cut into ¼-inch strips (see page 177)

2 tablespoons grated Parmigiano-Reggiano or soy Parmesan cheese (¼ ounce)

PER SERVING: Calories 248 • Soy Protein 3.7 g • Total Protein 9.8 g • Carbohydrates 35.8 g • Fat 7.4 g • Saturated Fat 1.4 g • Cholesterol 2.5 mg • Fiber 2.9 g • Sodium 733.0 mg

½ recipe Pizza Dough
(page 202)

4 ounces mozzarella or
part-skim milk
mozzarella, shredded

½ cup soft tofu, squeezed
(see page 48)

1 tablespoon cornmeal

3 to 4 slices prosciutto
(about 1 ounce)

Freshly ground black
pepper

2 tablespoons grated
Parmigiano-Reggiano
cheese or soy
Parmesan (¼ ounce)

White Pizza with Prosciutto

I f I had to pick a favorite pizza topping, it might be this one. It uses three of the best Italian foods: prosciutto, creamy fresh mozzarella, and Parmigiano-Reggiano. Combining the mozzarella with tofu reduces the fat and cholesterol in the topping somewhat and adds soy protein to what is already in the crust.

1. If you are using a pizza stone, place it in the cold oven. Preheat the oven to 425°F.

2. Combine the mozzarella and tofu in a bowl and set aside.

3. Roll out the dough on a lightly floured work surface into a 12-inch circle, ¼ inch thick. Place the dough on a pizza peel or air-cushioned baking sheet sprinkled lightly with cornmeal. Lay the prosciutto over the dough, overlapping the slices slightly. Leave a ¾-inch border of dough around the edge. Cover the prosciutto with the cheese and tofu mixture, spreading and pressing it with the back of a spoon. Some of the meat may show through. Sprinkle the pizza with pepper and grated cheese.

4. Slide the pizza onto the hot stone, or place it in the oven on the pan. Bake for 20 minutes, or until the crust is golden brown around the edges and on the bottom. Serve hot.

PER SERVING: Calories 319 • Soy Protein 4.3 g • Total Protein 18.7 g • Carbohydrates 34.4 g • Fat 11.9 g • Saturated Fat 4.3 g • Cholesterol 23.8 mg • Fiber 2.3 g • Sodium 966.2 mg

Pizza Sauce

Makes 2 cups

make this pizza sauce, which I like to keep somewhat chunky, using canned whole plum tomatoes. One of my favorite brands is Vantia, imported from Italy and sold mainly at Italian food stores. The other is Muir Glen's organic tomatoes. Like Italian cooks, I add a touch of sugar if the tomatoes are very acidic, so their sharpness is not too overwhelming.

1 tablespoon extra virgin olive oil

1 garlic clove, finely chopped

One 28-ounce can plum tomatoes

½ teaspoon sugar, optional

Salt and freshly ground black pepper

1. Heat the oil in a small Dutch oven or large saucepan over medium-high heat. Add the garlic and sauté for 1 minute, taking care not to let it color. Add the tomatoes with their sauce. Chop up the tomatoes in the pan until they are small chunks, using a wooden spoon or potato masher. If the tomatoes are very acidic, stir in the sugar. Bring the sauce to a boil, then reduce the heat so it simmers.

2. As the sauce cooks, stir often, continuing to break up the tomatoes as they soften. Cook until the sauce is thick enough to hold its shape on the spoon, about 30 minutes. Season to taste with salt and pepper.

3. Cool the sauce before using. (This sauce will keep for up to a week, covered and refrigerated.)

PER ¹/₂ CUP: Calories 65.4 • Soy Protein 0 g • Total Protein 1.6 g • Carbohydrates 6.8 g • Fat 3.2 g • Saturated Fat 0.6 g • Cholesterol 0 mg • Fiber 1.6 g • Sodium 361.0 mg

Pizza Dough

Makes enough for two 12-inch pizzas

½ teaspoon sugar

2 teaspoons active dry yeast

2½ cups all-purpose flour

½ cup soy flour

2 tablespoons rye flour

2 teaspoons salt

2 tablespoons extra virgin olive oil

Cornmeal

Pizza lovers will delight in the crisp pies this soy-enriched dough, developed by my colleague Mindy Shreil, produces when thinly rolled out. Left a bit thicker, the edges are more like focaccia.

Containing roughly one-quarter soy flour, this pizza dough behaves differently from others because of soy flour's tendency to hold moisture. Mostly, it becomes stickier during kneading than a conventional dough. Rolling it in a small amount of wheat flour, barely a teaspoon at a time, helps.

Using a pizza stone produces crisp results. If you do not have a stone, use an air-cushioned baking sheet or make a double pan by stacking one regular baking sheet on top of another. This creates an insulating layer of air, giving the same effect as an air-cushioned baking pan. Use only light-colored baking sheets. If these techniques aren't followed, the dough is likely to burn on the bottom before the pizza bakes through.

Set the oven at 425°F for baking this dough, rather than the 500°F or higher use for other pizza dough. (See page 45 on baking with soy for more about this.)

1. If you are using a pizza stone, place it in a cold oven. Preheat the oven to 425°F.

2. Dissolve the sugar in 1 cup warm (110°F) water. Sprinkle the yeast over the water, and set aside until the yeast is foamy, about 10 minutes.

3. Combine 2 cups of the all-purpose flour, the soy and rye flours, and salt in a large bowl. Make a well in the center of the dry ingredients and pour in the yeast mixture. Add the olive oil. Mix the flours and liquid with a fork, working from the center out, to form a moist, shaggy dough. Sprinkle 2 tablespoons of the remaining flour on a work surface and place the dough on it.

4. Start kneading the dough. When it gets sticky, sprinkle on another tablespoon of wheat flour. Roll the dough around, lightly coating it with the flour before starting to knead it again. When the dough gets sticky again, shake it off your hand with a snapping motion. Use a dough scraper if it sticks to the board. Knead the dough for as long as possible before adding more flour, adding less each time and rolling the dough in it before recommencing kneading. (It will probably take only one or two more additions, using about 1 tablespoon of the flour in total.) Knead until the dough is smooth and elastic, 6 to 8 minutes in all.

5. Lightly coat a bowl with a little oil. Form the dough into a 2-inch-thick disk. Turn the dough in the bowl to lightly coat it with the oil. Cover the bowl with a dish towel and set it in a warm place until the dough has doubled in volume, about 30 minutes.

6. Turn the dough onto a lightly floured surface, punch it down, and divide it in half. Shape one half into a ball, wrap it in plastic wrap, and set it aside. Roll out the remaining dough into a 12-inch circle, ¼ inch thick. Sprinkle a pizza peel or an air-cushioned baking sheet with cornmeal, covering an area slightly larger than the size of the rolled-out pizza dough. Transfer the dough to the pizza peel or baking sheet. (You can let this dough rise for 15 minutes before adding a topping, but it is not necessary.)

7. Add the topping of your choice. Transfer the pizza to the hot stone, or place it in the oven on the baking sheet. Bake for 20 minutes, or until the crust is golden brown around the edges and on the bottom. While it is baking, prepare another pizza with the second piece of dough. (This dough will keep for up to 1 day, tightly wrapped and refrigerated, and it can be frozen. Defrost it in the refrigerator before bringing it to room temperature.)

PER ¼ OF A 12-INCH PIZZA: Calories 200 • Soy Protein 1.9 g • Total Protein 6.0 g • Carbohydrates 32.8 g • Fat 4.9 g • Saturated Fat .7 g • Cholesterol 0 mg • Fiber 2.3 g • Sodium 584.2 mg

En-soy Your Favorite Pasta Dishes

Tossing in edamame or tofu adds a useful amount of soy when you are making a favorite pasta sauce. Allow ½ cup edamame per serving. Simmer the frozen beans in the sauce until cooked, about 5 minutes, or boil them in water, then drain and toss the edamame with the hot pasta and sauce.

For tofu, allow 3 ounces of firm or extra firm tofu that has been frozen, defrosted, and crumbled or use 3 ounces quick-firmed tofu (see page 50). Adding tofu works particularly well in marinara and other tomato-based sauces, and in puttanesca and other sharp, chunky sauces.

Spaghetti Bolognese

Serves 6

Butter and cream are used generously in northern Italy. Happily for vegans, this version of the classic meat-and-tomato ragù gives you true Italian flavor. This sauce improves with age, so cook it ahead when you can, and freeze it.

1. To make the sauce, combine the carrot, celery, and onion pieces in a food processor and pulse until they are chopped and slightly moist. On a cutting board, finely chop the tempeh until it has the texture of bits of ground meat.

2. Melt the margarine in a Dutch oven or heavy saucepan over medium-high heat. Add the chopped vegetables and sprinkle with ¼ teaspoon of the salt. Sauté until the vegetables soften, 3 to 4 minutes. Stir in the tempeh.

3. Pour in the white wine and boil until it has almost evaporated, 3 to 4 minutes, stirring occasionally. Add the soymilk and boil until the mixture is soft and moist, about 4 minutes, stirring occasionally.

4. Add the tomatoes, tomato paste, nutmeg, and remaining ¾ teaspoon salt. Break up the tomatoes with a wooden spoon and bring to a gentle boil. Cook the sauce until it thickens, stirring every couple of minutes to help the evaporation. The sauce will seem wet until shortly before it is done, about 20 minutes. Use immediately or cool. The sauce will keep for up to 3 days, covered and refrigerated.

5. Cook the pasta in salted water according to the package directions and heat the sauce, if it has been refrigerated. Drain the pasta and divide it among six serving plates. Spoon the hot sauce over each portion and serve. If desired, pass soy Parmesan at the table.

SAUCE

1 carrot, cut into 1-inch pieces

1 celery rib, cut into 1-inch pieces

1 small onion, cut into 8 pieces

One 8-ounce package soy tempeh

1 tablespoon margarine or olive oil

1 teaspoon salt

½ cup dry white wine

½ cup unsweetened soymilk

One 28-ounce can whole tomatoes with their liquid

2 tablespoons tomato paste

⅛ teaspoon freshly ground nutmeg

Freshly ground black pepper

12 ounces farro, spelt, or whole wheat pasta

Soy Parmesan, optional

PER SERVING: Calories 415 • Soy Protein 8.6 g • Total Protein 21.8 g • Carbohydrates 69.6 g • Fat 5.6 g • Saturated Fat 1.2 g • Cholesterol 0 mg • Fiber 14.2 g • Sodium 592.0 mg

Spaghetti with Asparagus and Lemon

8 ounces medium asparagus spears, cut into 1-inch lengths

8 ounces soy and semolina spaghetti

2 tablespoons unsalted butter

1 tablespoon extra virgin olive oil

Juice of 1 lemon

2 teaspoons lemon zest

Salt and freshly ground black pepper

Freshly grated Parmigiano-Reggiano or soy Parmesan

12 zucchini blossoms, optional

In the spring, when the first asparagus appear, Italians drizzle melted butter over them, then sprinkle on grated Parmigiano-Reggiano. Building on this combination, I add lemon, which complements the nutty browned butter. The soy here is *in* the pasta. Excellent golden durum semolina pasta is available containing 6.25 grams of soy protein. In summer, when zucchini blossoms are available, sauté a dozen of them in the pan after the sauce is done and arrange them over the dish.

1. Cook the asparagus in a pot of boiling water large enough to cook the pasta. When it is tender-crisp, about 4 minutes, transfer the asparagus with a slotted spoon to a bowl of ice water. Do not pour out the cooking water. When the asparagus is cooled, drain well, and set aside.

2. Bring the cooking water back to a boil and add salt. Cook the spaghetti according to package directions until al dente.

3. Meanwhile, melt the butter in a skillet over medium-high heat. When the butter is browned and fragrant, add the oil. All at once, add the lemon juice, lemon zest, and the asparagus, taking care as it may spatter. Mix well. Remove the pan from the heat and season to taste with salt and pepper.

4. Drain the spaghetti and transfer it to a heated serving bowl. Pour the asparagus over the pasta and toss well. If you are using the squash blossoms, add them to the warm pan and set it back over medium-high heat just until they wilt, 2 to 3 minutes. Arrange the blossoms over the asparagus. Serve immediately, accompanied by the grated cheese.

PER SERVING: Calories 257 • Soy Protein 6.7 g • Total Protein 8.7 g • Carbohydrates 45.9 g • Fat 4.4 g • Saturated Fat 0.6 g • Cholesterol 7.5 mg • Fiber 2.3 g • Sodium 9.9 mg

Fusilli with Broccoli, Sun-dried Tomatoes, and Black Soybeans

Garlic lovers will feast on this rustic combination of pasta, sun-dried tomatoes, and soybeans. Cooking the broccoli, then the pasta in the same water lets you serve this dish in about 20 minutes. Leftovers are good served as a pasta salad. Using both soybeans and pasta with soy serves up more than 11 grams soy protein per serving.

1. Cook the broccoli in a pot of boiling water large enough to cook the pasta. When the florets are tender-crisp, about 4 minutes, transfer them with a slotted spoon to a bowl of ice water. Do not pour out the cooking water. When the broccoli is chilled, drain well, and set aside.

2. Bring the cooking water back to a boil and cook the fusilli until it is al dente, following the package directions.

3. While the pasta cooks, heat the oil in a skillet over medium-high heat. Add the garlic and sauté until it is golden, about 3 minutes, and remove it with a slotted spoon to drain on a paper towel. Add the pepper flakes to the pan, if using. Add the broccoli, sun-dried tomatoes, soybeans, and the reserved garlic. Cook until heated through, 2 to 3 minutes.

4. Drain the pasta, leaving some water clinging to it. Add it to the pan with the broccoli, stirring to combine it with the vegetables. Season the pasta to taste with salt and pepper.

5. Serve at once, accompanied by grated cheese.

4 cups (about 8 ounces) broccoli florets

8 ounces soy and semolina fusilli

3 tablespoons extra virgin olive oil

3 large garlic cloves, sliced

⅛ to ¼ teaspoon hot red pepper flakes, optional

12 marinated sun-dried tomato halves, drained and cut into thin strips

1 cup canned black soybeans, rinsed and drained

Salt and freshly ground black pepper

Freshly grated Parmigiano-Reggiano or soy Parmesan

PER SERVING: Calories 381 • Soy Protein 11.1 g • Total Protein 14.3 g • Carbohydrates 52.7 g • Fat 12.9 g • Saturated Fat 1.7 g • Cholesterol 0 mg • Fiber 6.4 g • Sodium 39.5 mg

Baked Spinach Gnocchi

2 tablespoons unsalted
   butter, melted

4 large egg yolks

12 ounces soft tofu,
   squeezed until it is
   almost dry
   (see page 48)

One 10-ounce package
   frozen chopped
   spinach, defrosted and
   squeezed dry

½ cup (1 ounce) freshly
   grated Pecorino or soy
   Parmesan

⅛ teaspoon freshly ground
   nutmeg

½ teaspoon salt

¼ teaspoon freshly ground
   black pepper

Tofu takes the place of the ricotta usually used in making these plump pasta dumplings. I particularly like them baked like gnocchi alla romana. Unlike the Italians, I heap these plump pasta dumplings with only a modest amount of melted butter and cheese before napping them with a light tomato sauce. If you wish, use olive oil in place of the butter and cheese, or skip both and use just your favorite tomato sauce.

1. Preheat the oven to 350°F. Coat a 9-inch square baking dish with the melted butter and set aside.

2. Bring a large pot of salted water to a boil, then reduce the heat until it is barely simmering.

3. Beat the egg yolks with the tofu until the mixture is creamy, and the tofu resembles small-curd cottage cheese.

4. Chop the spinach very finely and transfer it to a bowl. Add the egg mixture, Pecorino, nutmeg, salt, and pepper. Combine well, using a wooden spoon.

5. Place the flour on a dish or work surface. Form the gnocchi by rolling a tablespoon of the mixture into a small ball, then rolling it in the flour. There will be about 24 gnocchi.

Pecorino Cheese

Pecorino cheese is made from sheep's milk. It is sharper than Parmigiano-Reggiano, made from cow's milk. Sheep's milk cheeses are made in several regions of Italy. Pecorino Romano, the one most readily available in the United States, comes from the area in Lazio around Rome. Feel free to use any aged Italian Pecorino in this dish.

6. While forming the gnocchi, bring the water back to a boil. Drop them into the water, a few at a time. When they rise to the surface, about 2 minutes, remove them with a slotted spoon. Arrange the gnocchi in the baking dish, overlapping them to make one layer. Spoon the tomato sauce over the gnocchi. Sprinkle with the Pecorino Romano.

7. Bake for about 25 minutes, or until the gnocchi are heated through and the sauce bubbles.

½ cup all-purpose flour

1 cup marinara or other prepared tomato sauce

2 tablespoons freshly grated Pecorino Romano

PER SERVING, WITHOUT SAUCE: Calories 238 • Soy Protein 7.6 g • Total Protein 16.4 g • Carbohydrates 17.1 g • Fat 11.6 g • Saturated Fat 5.3 g • Cholesterol 157.5 mg • Fiber 2.6 g • Sodium 520.7 mg

stews, casseroles, and chilis

Simmering soy in stews and casseroles, you can create a veritable United Nations of dishes. Here is a feast of ethnic choices that circles the globe, from British cottage pie and Eggplant Manicotti in which eggplant replaces the pasta, to Piñon, a kind of Caribbean lasagne made with plantains, to an incendiary Ethiopian wat and tofu bathed in a tomato-based peanut sauce glowing with ginger and black pepper, from Benin in West Africa. From the American Southwest, Fifty-Fifty Chili, a combination of beef and soy crumbles, is the perfect introduction for anyone hesitant about using soymeat. Thirty-Minute Chili has big flavor without meat.

Using everything from familiar tofu and tempeh to various kinds of meat alternatives, including spicy chorizo soy sausage, these dishes include casual Beans and Franks (page 230), to elegant Quince and Tofu Pot Pie with Mushrooms and Chestnuts (page 233), a stunning variation of the boeuf bourguignon made at a three-star Parisian restaurant.

Spanish Chickpea Stew

Serves 4

Spanish cooking features many rustic dishes like this robust chickpea casserole, made here with soy chorizo. On a trip to Spain in 1998, I discovered meaty, roasted piquillo peppers. You can mail order them from ethnicgrocer.com. Serve the stew ladled over a slice of grilled, crusty peasant bread to soak up its saffron-scented juices.

1. Dissolve the saffron threads in 1 tablespoon of warm water in a small bowl, 15 to 20 minutes.

2. Heat the oil in a Dutch oven over medium-high heat. Add the onion and sauté 3 minutes. Add the garlic and cook until the onion is soft, about 5 minutes. Add 2 cups water (1½ if using canned beans), the chickpeas, potato, parsley, and saffron liquid. Reduce the heat and cover. Cook for 45 minutes if using soaked chickpeas, or until beans are tender, 20 minutes, if using canned. Add the sausage and chopped pepper. Simmer, uncovered, for 5 minutes.

3. Season to taste with salt and pepper and serve.

PER SERVING: Calories 275 • Soy Protein 1.8 g • Total Protein 12.3 g • Carbohydrates 39.6 g • Fat 8.5 g • Saturated Fat 0.9 g • Cholesterol 0 mg • Fiber 10.1 g • Sodium 121.2 mg

¼ teaspoon saffron threads

1 tablespoon extra virgin olive oil

1 medium onion, chopped

3 garlic cloves, chopped

1 cup dried chickpeas, quick soaked (see box), or two 15-ounce cans, drained and rinsed

1 medium yellow-fleshed potato, peeled and diced

2 tablespoons chopped flat-leaf parsley

¼ cup soy chorizo sausage

¼ cup chopped Spanish piquillo pepper, or roasted red bell pepper, (see page 177)

Salt and freshly ground black pepper

Quick Soaking Dried Beans

To shorten both the soaking and the cooking time of dried beans, place the beans in a deep pot. Add water to cover by 2 inches. Bring to a boil over high heat. Reduce the heat and simmer 2 minutes. Cover the pot and remove it from the heat. Let the covered beans stand 1 hour. Rinse and drain the beans.

Braised Cabbage with Tempeh and Cranberries

One 8-ounce package
tempeh made with
quinoa and sesame
seeds

2 tablespoons butter or
canola oil

1 large onion, halved and
cut into ½-inch slices

1 small savoy cabbage,
quartered, cored, and
cut into ¾-inch slices

½ cup dry white wine

1 Bosc pear, peeled,
quartered, cored, and
cut crosswise into
½-inch slices

1 cup chicken or
vegetarian chicken
broth

1 bay leaf

½ teaspoon caraway
seeds

⅛ teaspoon ground mace

Pinch of cayenne

1 cup fresh or frozen
cranberries

Salt and freshly ground
black pepper

You might not find this choucroute at Brasserie Lipp in Paris, but it is just as memorable, with its cranberries, pears, and caramelized cabbage. Charring the tempeh adds the smokiness sausages usually contribute to a traditional choucroute. Wine and caraway add Alsatian earthiness.

1. Cut the tempeh crosswise into 4 pieces. Slice each slab horizontally in half. Stack up 4 slices. Cut the stack diagonally in each direction, making 16 triangles. Repeat with the remaining tempeh, making 32 pieces of tempeh in all.

2. Heat a heavy, dry skillet over medium-high heat. When the pan is very hot, sear the pieces of tempeh until they smell fragrant and are charred in spots, about 30 seconds. Turn, using tongs, and sear the other side. You will have to do this in batches. (Searing the tempeh can be done up to 24 hours ahead; refrigerate the tempeh until it is to be used.)

3. Combine the batter, onion, and cabbage in a large Dutch oven over medium heat and cook until the vegetables start to wilt, about 4 minutes. Increase the heat to medium-high and cook, stirring often, until the onions and cabbage are browned, 12 to 15 minutes. There will be a crusty brown layer on the bottom of the pot.

4. Pour in the wine, scraping the bottom of the pot to dissolve the caramelized layer. When the wine is almost entirely evaporated, about 5 minutes, add the pear, broth, bay leaf, caraway seeds, mace, and cayenne. Mix in the cranberries and tempeh. Simmer until the cabbage and cranberries are soft, about 15 minutes. Remove the bay leaf.

5. Season to taste with salt and pepper and serve.

PER SERVING: Calories 271 • Soy Protein 10.5 g • Total Protein 15 g • Carbohydrates 35.7 g •
Fat 7.6 g • Saturated Fat 1.3 g • Cholesterol 15.5 mg • Fiber 10 g • Sodium 67.9 mg

Smoky Southwestern Stew

Pineapple gives this chunky stew an appealing balanced, natural sweetness. A touch of chipotle chile adds a kick of smoky heat. This dish comes together quickly, making it perfect for weeknight meals. Serve it accompanied by brown or white rice.

1. Heat the oil in a skillet over medium-high heat. Add the soymeat, turning the pieces so they are lightly browned and crisped on both sides, about 8 minutes. Remove the soymeat and set aside.

2. Add the onion to the pan. Sauté until golden, 6 to 7 minutes, stirring often. Add the garlic, tomatoes, and vegetable broth powder, stirring to mix them. Add the sweet potatoes, chipotle, raisins, cumin, oregano, and cloves. Cover and simmer for 20 minutes; the potato should slightly resist when pierced with the point of a knife in the center of a piece.

3. Add the vinegar, pineapple, and cilantro. Simmer, uncovered, until it has reduced to a thick sauce. Mix in the soymeat and heat through.

4. Season to taste with salt and pepper. Serve immediately. (Or cool and place in a covered container. The stew will keep for up to 3 days, tightly covered and refrigerated. Reheat gently but thoroughly before serving.)

PER SERVING: Calories 228 • Soy Protein 5.0 g • Total Protein 10.5 g • Carbohydrates 33.1 g • Fat 6.4 g • Saturated Fat 0.7 g • Cholesterol 0.1 mg • Fiber 4.2 g • Sodium 402.8 mg

2 tablespoons canola oil

7 ounces frozen soymeat nuggets (one package), defrosted

1 medium onion, halved and cut vertically into ¼-inch crescents

1 tablespoon minced garlic

One 28-ounce can diced tomatoes with their juice

1 tablespoon vegetable broth powder

1 medium sweet potato, peeled, halved, and cut into ¾-inch slices

1 canned chipotle chile, chopped, or ½ teaspoon ground chipotle powder

3 tablespoons golden raisins

1 teaspoon ground cumin

1 teaspoon dried oregano

⅛ teaspoon ground cloves

2 teaspoons white or red wine vinegar

1 cup 1-inch cubed fresh pineapple

½ cup loosely packed cilantro leaves, coarsely chopped

Salt and freshly ground black pepper

Korean Beef Stew

MARINADE

2 scallions (white and
green parts), thinly
sliced

3 garlic cloves, finely
chopped

2 tablespoons soy sauce

1 teaspoon brown sugar

1 teaspoon sesame seeds

¼ teaspoon roasted
sesame oil

¼ teaspoon freshly ground
black pepper

1 pound top round beef,
cut into 1-inch cubes

1 tablespoon peanut oil

2 tablespoons Korean
soybean paste, or
Japanese red miso

1 teaspoon roasted
sesame oil

2 garlic cloves, minced

1 medium onion, chopped

2 Korean green chiles, cut
diagonally into thin
slices, or 3 serrano plus
2 poblano chiles

1 medium potato, peeled
and cut into 1-inch
cubes

1 small zucchini, cut into
½-inch slices

1 scallion (white and green
parts), chopped

Koreans love beef. They make this lean beef stew, simmered in an earthenware pot. The bean paste used to enrich its flavor is similar to Japanese miso. Korean food is robust, featuring the strong flavors of garlic and chile peppers. Here, long, green Korean chiles add an appealing earthy quality, as well as heat. (If you cannot get them, a combination of serranos and poblanos works equally well.) Like most stews, this one tastes even better the next day. Serve it with rice, to soak up its savory sauce.

1. For the marinade: Combine the scallions, garlic, soy sauce, sugar, sesame seeds, sesame oil, and pepper in a medium bowl. Add the meat and toss to coat. Let it sit for 10 minutes.

2. Heat the peanut oil in a Dutch oven over medium-high heat. Sear the pieces of meat on all sides. Add the marinade. Stir in the bean paste, sesame oil, garlic, onion, and chiles. Cook, stirring occasionally, until the onion softens, 4 to 5 minutes.

3. Add 1½ cups boiling water and stir, scraping up any bits sticking to the bottom of the pot. Reduce the heat, cover the pot partially, and simmer for 40 minutes. Add the potato cubes and zucchini. Cook until the meat is tender, about 20 minutes. Transfer to a serving bowl, and garnish with the chopped scallion.

PER MAIN-COURSE SERVING: Calories 286 • Soy Protein 1.5 g • Total Protein 30.4 g • Carbohydrates 20.4 g • Fat 9.8 g • Saturated Fat 2 g • Cholesterol 62.3 mg • Fiber 3.1 g • Sodium 879.6 mg

Jamaican Cook-Up with Black Soybeans and Greens

Serves 6

This is one of the quickest meals I know, although I discovered it in one of the most leisurely places on earth. Strolling along the beach near Ocho Rios in Jamaica, I came across a man cooking creamy coconut rice, smoky-tasting greens, and velvety red beans, all in an iron kettle set over a charcoal fire in a shack. He ladled out this modest food onto a paper plate, and I ate it sitting on a log beside the sea. In our high-speed world, however, you can make this meatless dinner in 30 minutes thanks to frozen collards and canned beans.

1. Heat 2 tablespoons of the coconut milk in a large saucepan or small Dutch oven over medium-high. Add the onion and green pepper and sauté for 3 minutes, or until the onion softens.

2. Add 2 cups hot water, the remaining coconut milk, rice, collard greens, carrot, scallions, thyme, allspice, and red pepper flakes. Cover the pot, bring it to a boil, and reduce the heat. Simmer until the rice is done, 15 to 20 minutes.

3. Mix in the soybeans. Season to taste with salt and pepper. Let sit, covered, until you are ready to serve.

NOTE: To use fresh collards, remove the stems from a medium bunch of the greens, about ¾ pound. Cut the leaves crosswise into ½-inch strips. Boil the greens for 5 minutes and drain. There should be 3 cups cooked greens.

½ cup coconut milk

1 medium onion, chopped

1 medium green bell pepper, seeded and cut into ¾-inch pieces

1 cup long-grain white rice

One 10-ounce package frozen chopped collard greens (see Note)

1 large carrot, cut into ¾-inch pieces

⅓ cup sliced scallions (white and green parts)

1¼ teaspoons dried thyme

¼ teaspoon ground allspice

⅛ to ¼ teaspoon hot red pepper flakes

One 15-ounce can black soybeans, drained

Salt and freshly ground black pepper

PER SERVING: Calories 233 • Soy Protein 4.9 g • Total Protein 9.5 g • Carbohydrates 38.7 g • Fat 4.4 g • Saturated Fat 2.5 g • Cholesterol 0 mg • Fiber 7.0 g • Sodium 40.8 mg

2 small tomatillos,
    chopped

3 tablespoons canola oil

⅓ cup almonds, chopped

¼ cup sesame seeds

½ teaspoon aniseed

2 large garlic cloves,
    chopped

⅓ cup dried Turkish
    apricots, chopped
    (see Note)

1 slice white bread, darkly
    toasted

6 dried ancho chiles,
    stemmed and seeded

3 cups fat-free chicken
    broth or vegetarian
    chicken broth

1 tablespoon Dutch-
    processed cocoa
    powder

¼ teaspoon ground
    cinnamon

⅛ teaspoon freshly ground
    black pepper

Pinch of ground clove

2 tablespoons sugar

½ teaspoon salt

Two 8-ounce packages
    soy tempeh, each cut
    crosswise into 3 pieces

Tempeh with Apricot Mole

Mole, taken from the native word for sauce, refers to both Mexico's festive national dish and to the profound sauce that is the heart of all moles. Chef Rick Bayless describes mole as having "the silken fullness of a twenty-piece dance band." Preparing a mole, like scoring a song for an orchestra, requires time and attention, so it is usually a special occasion dish. I serve this mole with polenta. Any leftover sauce is also good served over rice and beans or sliced turkey breast.

1. Place the tomatillos in a cold nonstick skillet. Cook over medium-high until lightly browned and soft, 4 minutes. Scrape them into a bowl. Wipe out the pan.

2. Heat 1 tablespoon of the oil in the skillet over medium heat. Add the almonds, sesame seeds, aniseed, and the garlic and cook until golden, stirring constantly, 3 to 4 minutes. Add this to the tomatillo mixture. Add the apricots. Break the toast into the bowl. Set aside.

3. Tear the anchos into 1-inch pieces. Heat 1 tablespoon of the oil in the skillet. Cook half the chiles, turning them with tongs, until they soften and their inside is a lighter color, 30 seconds. Do not let them smoke. Transfer the chiles to a bowl. Repeat with the remaining chiles. Cover the chiles with hot water and soak until they are soft, 20 minutes. Drain, reserving 2 cups of the soaking water if it is not bitter.

4. Puree the chiles in a blender with the 2 cups chile soaking water (use fresh water if the soaking water was too bitter). Press the chile puree through the strainer back into their soaking bowl. Do not wash the blender.

5. Combine the tomatillo mixture in the blender with 2 cups of the chicken broth, cocoa, cinnamon, pepper, clove, sugar, and salt. Puree. Strain it back into its bowl.

6. Cook the chile puree in an ovenproof Dutch oven over medium heat until it has reduced to the thickness of tomato paste, 15 minutes. Add the tomatillo puree and cook until the mole thickens again, 15 to 20 minutes. Stir in the remaining cup of broth. Partially cover the pot and simmer until the mole coats a spoon well, 30 minutes.

7. Meanwhile, heat the remaining 1 tablespoon oil in a skillet over medium-high heat. Brown the tempeh for 2 minutes. Turn and brown the other side. Set aside.

8. Preheat the oven to 400°F. Place the tempeh in the mole, turning it once. Cover and bake for about 30 minutes, or until the sauce is hot and bubbly.

9. Let the tempeh rest in the mole for 20 minutes. Divide the tempeh among six plates with ⅓ cup mole on each plate.

NOTE: Turkish apricots are sweeter than those from California.

PER SERVING: Calories 374 • Soy Protein 16.1 g • Total Protein 24.7 g • Carbohydrates 30.2 g • Fat 19.1 g • Saturated Fat 2.8 g • Cholesterol 0 mg • Fiber 11.3 g • Sodium 293.9 mg

Ethiopian Wat

3 tablespoons Niter
  Kebbeh (recipe follows)

1½ cups chopped yellow
  onions

½ cup chopped red onion

¼ cup finely chopped
  shallots

2 teaspoons canola oil

7 ounces frozen bite-size
  soymeat (one package,
  defrosted)

1 tablespoon Berbere
  (page 220)

1 tablespoon minced garlic

1 cup tomato sauce

2 tablespoons tomato
  paste

4 hard-cooked eggs,
  shelled

1 pocket pita, plus
  additional bread, as an
  accompaniment

Ethiopian dishes tend to be ferociously hot, particularly the red pepper–based stews called wats. Here, the heat from Berbere, the aromatic mixture of ground red pepper and spices that dominates Ethiopian cooking, is used moderately, though you can add more to taste. *Niter kebbeh*, seasoned clarified butter, adds different spices to the flavor explosion. Sarah Selassie, the mother of an Ethiopian friend, showed me how to cook the onions so they melt into a soft confit, yet are barely colored. This slow, gentle method is essential to the flavor of many Ethiopian dishes. Use tofu or tempeh to replace the soymeat, if you wish.

1. Heat the niter kebbeh in a small Dutch oven or heavy pot with a tight-fitting cover over medium-high heat. Add the yellow and red onions and the shallots and sauté until soft, about 6 minutes. Cover the pot, reduce the heat, and cook the onions very slowly for 30 minutes, until they are very soft and wet. Add ½ cup water. Cover the pot. Cook the onions for an additional 30 minutes, reducing the heat as needed so they do not color. Uncover the pot, increase the heat, and cook, stirring, until the onions are barely moist. They will be shiny, like a soft onion marmalade.

2. Meanwhile, in a nonstick skillet, heat the oil over medium-high heat. Add the soymeat and sauté until the pieces are browned in places and slightly crisp, about 5 minutes, turning them occasionally. Set aside.

3. Stir the berbere and garlic into the onion mixture. Add the tomato sauce and tomato paste. Cover and simmer gently for 5 minutes, to let the flavors blend. Add the sautéed soymeat and the eggs. Cover and simmer gently for 5 minutes.

4. Split the pita bread into two rounds. Place them on a serving platter, with the insides facing up. Spoon the wat over the bread and serve. Accompany with additional pita breads, to tear apart and use for eating the wat.

PER SERVING: Calories 447 • Soy Protein 7.4 g • Total Protein 20.8 g • Carbohydrates 47.2 g • Fat 20.9 g • Saturated Fat 8.3 g • Cholesterol 236.1 mg • Fiber 5.0 g • Sodium 548.6 mg

Niter Kebbeh (Flavored Clarified Butter)

Makes ¾ cup

Ethiopian niter kebbeh, like Indian ghee, is butter that has been melted, then simmered gently until it is a warm gold. The spices, which vary according to the taste of the cook, infuse the butter, then are strained out. The flavor of this clarified butter is so concentrated that a mere teaspoon adds alluring accents to zucchini, spinach, vegetable soups, cooked lentils, and rice. Also, try it on grilled salmon.

½ pound (2 sticks) unsalted butter

½ inch fresh ginger, chopped

1 garlic clove, chopped

2 whole cloves

¼ teaspoon dried basil

¼ teaspoon ground fenugreek

⅛ teaspoon celery seeds

⅛ teaspoon ground coriander

⅛ teaspoon ground cumin

1. Melt the butter in a small, heavy saucepan over low heat. Add the ginger, garlic, cloves, basil, fenugreek, celery seeds, coriander, and cumin. Cook over low heat, barely simmering, for 30 minutes.

2. Strain through a fine sieve or cheesecloth and place in a glass jar. (Niter kebbeh will keep for 6 months or more, tightly covered, in the refrigerator.)

Berbere (Ethiopian Seasoning)

½ cup ground hot red
  pepper, such as
  cayenne

1 tablespoon garlic
  powder

1 tablespoon onion
  powder

1 teaspoon ground ginger

1 teaspoon ground cloves

1 teaspoon kosher salt

½ teaspoon ground cumin

½ teaspoon ground
  fenugreek

½ teaspoon ground
  cinnamon

¼ teaspoon freshly ground
  black pepper

In Ethiopia, families make this incendiary, aromatic seasoning once a year, after they harvest and dry the hot red peppers that are its base. Each cook varies the blend according to her preference. Ethiopian cooks use berbere by the cupful to add body to their dishes as well as spice. Next time you make chili or tomato sauce, try adding some of this flavorful heat.

1. Combine the hot red pepper, garlic and onion powders, ginger, cloves, salt, cumin, fenugreek, cinnamon, and pepper in a bowl and mix well.

2. Transfer to a glass jar. (This seasoning will keep for 2 months, tightly covered, in the refrigerator.)

Injera

Ethiopians eat *injera*, a flatbread that is folded to resemble a large, moist, beige dish towel. Eating with their hands, they tear off pieces of the *injera* and use it to scoop up the stewlike dishes typical of Ethiopian cooking. Teff, a tiny, high-protein grain which grows in Ethiopia is used to make the batter, which is then allowed to stand and ferment. (Each grain of teff is the size of a grain of sand.) Pocket pita breads split in half are a useful substitute for *injera*.

Tofu Benin with Tomato-Peanut Sauce

Harmony in the Kitchen is a program of multicultural cooking classes held a half dozen times a year in New York City. The classes feature chef Michel Nischan and artists like Geoffrey Holder and Ismael Merchant. While Nischan chats them up about their favorite dishes, these creative cooks serve up memorable surprises. Angélique Kidjo, a songwriter and performer from Benin, in West Africa, blew the audience away with this hot tomato- and onion-based peanut sauce. Simmering this stew takes some time, but not much attention, and the recipe makes a generous amount. Enjoy its incendiary sauce with tempeh, chicken, shrimp, and fish, as well as with tofu or over plain brown or white rice.

1. To make the paste, combine the ginger, garlic, crab boil seasoning, and pepper, making a thick rough mixture. Cut each tofu slab crosswise, making 4 pieces. Spread each piece of the tofu with the paste, covering it evenly on both sides. Set the tofu on a plate, cover it with plastic wrap, and refrigerate for 8 hours, or overnight.

2. Coarsely chop one of the onions. Combine the chopped onion with the tomatoes in a food processor and puree. Set it aside. Halve the other onion and cut it into ½-inch slices.

3. Heat the oil in a large skillet over medium heat. Add the sliced onion and sauté until it is golden and very soft, 8 to 10 minutes, reducing the heat, if necessary. Add the pureed mixture, the tomato paste, sugar, and salt. Simmer for 15 minutes over medium heat, stirring occasionally.

4. Dissolve the peanut butter in 1½ cups lukewarm water. Mix this into the tomato sauce. Simmer for 15 minutes.

SEASONING PASTE

- 2 tablespoons finely grated fresh ginger
- 2 tablespoons grated or pressed garlic
- 1 teaspoon ground crab boil or fish seasoning powder
- 1 teaspoon freshly ground black pepper

- 16 ounces firm or extra firm tofu, pressed in 2 slabs (see page 49)
- 2 Spanish onions
- 3 large tomatoes, seeded and chopped
- 2 tablespoons canola oil
- 2 tablespoons tomato paste
- 1 tablespoons sugar
- 1 teaspoon salt
- ¼ cup smooth unsweetened peanut butter

5. Add the tofu, with its seasoning paste, to the pan. Push each piece into the thick sauce so it is covered. Simmer, uncovered, over medium heat, for 15 minutes, so the spice paste coating the tofu has time to blend into and flavor the sauce.

6. Serve immediately. (Or cool and refrigerate for up to 3 days, tightly covered. Reheat in a 350°F oven, or in the microwave until heated through.)

PER SERVING: Calories 372 • Soy Protein 11.3 g • Total Protein 19.1 g • Carbohydrates 32.9 g • Fat 20.9 g • Saturated Fat 3.0 g • Cholesterol 0 mg • Fiber 5.5 g • Sodium 722.1 mg

Eggplant Manicotti

As a rule, manicotti is a stuffed pasta dish. Here, however, eggplant slices are used instead, making this casserole moderately low in carbohydrates and packed with protein. Touches of cinnamon and currants add a Sicilian note to the filling of tofu, mozzarella, and ricotta. The tomato sauce is particularly muscular, thanks to red wine and hot pepper flakes (which you can omit if you wish). Making Caponata (page 109) helps use the eggplant that is left over. Serve with a Caesar Salad (page 150). For dessert, Pistachio Orange Biscotti (page 306) and fresh fruit do nicely.

1. To make the tomato sauce, heat the oil in a large saucepan or small Dutch oven over medium-high heat. Add the onion and sauté for 3 minutes. Add the garlic and cook until the onion is soft, about 4 minutes. Add the tomatoes, basil, oregano, bay leaf, wine, and red pepper flakes, if using. Cook until the sauce is thick, about 30 minutes. Remove the bay leaf and season to taste with salt and pepper. (Cool and refrigerate the sauce if not using it immediately. The sauce will keep for up to 5 days, covered and refrigerated. Bring to room temperature before completing the dish.)

2. Preheat the oven to 350°F. Coat 2 baking sheets with non-stick cooking spray.

3. To make the filling, combine the tofu, 1½ cups of the mozzarella, ½ cup of the Parmigiano, the currants, if using, cinnamon, rosemary, and egg in a bowl. Mix in the scallions and parsley and set aside.

4. Cut off the tops and bottoms of the eggplants. Stand each on end and slice off the two opposite sides, reserving them for another use. Cut each eggplant vertically into four ½-inch-thick slices. Brush the slices lightly on both sides with the oil. Lay them on the baking sheets, in a single layer. Bake until the slices are soft and flexible, about 12 minutes. Set aside on

TOMATO SAUCE

1 tablespoon extra virgin olive oil

1 cup chopped onions

2 garlic cloves

One 28-ounce can diced tomatoes, with their liquid

2 tablespoons chopped basil

2 tablespoons chopped oregano

1 bay leaf

⅓ cup dry red wine

½ teaspoon hot red pepper flakes, optional

Salt and freshly ground black pepper

EGGPLANT

16 ounces soft tofu, squeezed (see page 48)

2 cups (8 ounces) shredded mozzarella

¾ cup (1½ ounces) freshly grated Parmigiano-Reggiano or soy Parmesan

¼ cup currants, optional

¼ teaspoon ground cinnamon

1 teaspoon chopped fresh rosemary

1 large egg, lightly beaten

2 scallions (green part only), chopped

2 tablespoons chopped flat-leaf parsley

2 large eggplants (about 1½ pounds each)

2 tablespoons extra virgin olive oil

the baking sheet until the eggplant is cool enough to handle, about 10 minutes. Leave the oven on.

5. Coat a baking dish large enough to hold the manicotti in one layer with olive oil or nonstick cooking spray. Cover the bottom of the baking dish with 1 cup of the tomato sauce. Place an eggplant slice on your work surface, with the narrow top of the neck side facing you. Place about ½ cup of the filling on the eggplant, about 2 inches in from the edge facing you. Fold it over, covering the filling, and roll up the eggplant, making sure the filling is firmly packed and spreads out to edges of the eggplant. Set the roll in the baking dish. Repeat, using all the eggplant, and nestling the rolls tightly next to one another. Spread the remaining sauce over the manicotti. Sprinkle with the remaining ½ cup of mozzarella and the remaining ¼ cup Parmigiano. Cover the dish with foil.

6. Bake until the eggplant is soft and the cheese on top is bubbling, about 30 minutes.

7. Uncover and let the manicotti sit for 10 minutes before serving; this gives the eggplant time to settle so it does not tear when you cut into it.

PER SERVING: Calories 265 • Soy Protein 5.0 g • Total Protein 19.3 g • Carbohydrates 12.3 g • Fat 15.2 g • Saturated Fat 5.8 g • Cholesterol 48.8 mg • Fiber 3.1 g • Sodium 613.8 mg

Piñon

This layered casserole, alternating sliced plantains with soy crumbles, is a kind of Caribbean lasagne. My version is inspired by Eddie Palmieri, the Latin jazz musician who prepared it at Harmony in the Kitchen, the cooking classes featuring artists who cook. I lightened up his recipe by combining whole eggs with whites and by frying the plantains in less oil. Piñon is ideal for a casual dinner party or a potluck as it can be made in steps and reheats well.

1. Preheat the oven to 400°F. Coat an 8-inch square baking dish with nonstick cooking spray and set aside.

2. Cut each plantain into quarters lengthwise to make eight long, flat slices.

3. Heat the oil in a nonstick skillet over medium-high heat. Fry the plantain slices until golden brown on both sides, about 3 minutes on each side, using tongs to turn them once. Lay the fried plantains on paper towels to drain. (This can be done several hours before assembling the dish).

4. If you are using fresh green beans, boil them in salted water for 4 minutes. Drain, then immediately plunge the beans into a bowl of ice water to stop the cooking and set the color. (This can be done up to 24 hours before assembling the dish.) If you are using frozen beans, boil just until defrosted, about 2 minutes, then plunge into ice water as for the fresh beans. Drain well.

5. Combine the soy crumbles with the cilantro and scallions in a medium bowl. In another bowl, whisk the eggs and whites with the cayenne, salt, and a generous amount of pepper.

6. To assemble the piñon, arrange four slices of plantain to cover the bottom of the baking dish. Cover with half the soy mixture. Spread half the green beans to cover evenly. Pour

2 large ripe plantains

3 tablespoons canola oil

¾ pound fresh green beans, halved lengthwise, or one 10-ounce package frozen French-cut beans

2 cups Enriched Soy Crumbles (page 43)

1 cup chopped cilantro

1 cup chopped scallions (white and green parts)

4 large eggs

4 large egg whites

Dash of cayenne

½ teaspoon salt

Freshly ground black pepper

half the egg mixture over the beans. Repeat, using up the remaining plantain, soy crumbles, beans, and egg. Cover the dish tightly with foil.

7. Bake for 45 minutes, or until a knife inserted in the center comes out clean.

8. Uncover and let it sit for 20 minutes before cutting and serving. (Or cool completely. It will keep for up to 2 days, tightly covered and refrigerated. Reheat in the oven at 400°F and serve.)

PER SERVING: Calories 304 • Soy Protein 7.9 g • Total Protein 18.0 g • Carbohydrates 34.5 g • Fat 12.0 g • Saturated Fat 1.9 g • Cholesterol 141.4 mg • Fiber 5.8 g • Sodium 527.4 mg

Plantains

Plantains look like big, tough bananas, but their flesh is firmer and drier. Plantains may be green (unripe), yellow (semiripe), or blacker than a ripe banana. Asian and Latin markets sometimes have them at all three stages. Yellow plantains, also called *amarillos*, have peach-tinged flesh. They taste tangy and sweet. For piñon, these are ideal.

To peel a plantain, cut off the top and bottom. Slit the skin down the curved inside and along the back. Using your fingers, pull off the skin by opening it along the slits.

Picadillo

In much of Latin America, each cook has a personal recipe for picadillo. Ingredients common to all of them are tomatoes, onions, garlic, and meat. Soy crumbles let you make a meatless picadillo that sambas with savory capers and olives, cinnamon and clove, plus the sweet-tart harmony of the fruit. Picadillo reheats well. You can also freeze it in individual portions for solo meals to reheat in the microwave and serve over rice.

1. Heat the oil in a skillet over medium-high heat. Add the onion, pepper, and garlic and sauté until the onion is soft, about 4 minutes.

2. Mix in the soy crumbles and tomatoes, breaking up the tomatoes with a wooden spoon. Add the cinnamon, oregano, cloves, bay leaf, and currants. Cook until the tomatoes begin to soften, about 5 minutes, stirring occasionally.

3. Mix in the apple, olives, and capers and cook for 2 minutes. Remove the bay leaf and season to taste with salt and pepper.

4. Make a bed of rice in each of 6 shallow, wide bowls. Spoon the picadillo over the rice and serve.

PER SERVING: Calories 358 • Soy Protein 11.9 g • Total Protein 19.2 g • Carbohydrates 56.6 g • Fat 5.6 g • Saturated Fat 0.6 g • Cholesterol 0 mg • Fiber 6.6 g • Sodium 1002.8mg

I tablespoon canola oil

¾ cup chopped onion

1 green bell pepper, chopped

1 garlic clove, chopped

1 recipe Enriched Soy Crumbles (see page 43) made with beef or vegetarian chicken broth

One 28-ounce can whole tomatoes, drained

½ teaspoon ground cinnamon

½ teaspoon dried oregano

⅛ teaspoon ground cloves

1 bay leaf

¼ cup dried currants

1 small Fuji apple, peeled, cored, and finely chopped

¼ cup pitted green olives, chopped

2 tablespoons salt-cured capers, soaked, drained, and chopped

Salt and freshly ground black pepper

6 cups hot cooked rice

Serves 6

2 tablespoons canola oil

1 large onion, chopped

2 garlic cloves, minced

One 8-ounce package soy
    tempeh, cut into ½-inch
    cubes

¼ cup chili powder
    (see Note)

1 teaspoon ground cumin

1 teaspoon dried oregano

One 28-ounce can diced
    tomatoes, with their
    liquid

One 4-ounce can whole
    green or jalapeño
    chiles, drained and
    chopped

1 cup chopped cilantro

Salt and freshly ground
    black pepper

Cooked brown rice

Thirty-Minute Chili

In Texas, using beans in chili gets you run out of town. But use tempeh made from soybeans, and even Lone-Star chili lovers will praise its meaty taste and texture. When you make this chili a day ahead, it develops a smoother flavor as it sits overnight. It freezes well, so make a double batch and save some for another day. Serve over brown rice.

1. Heat the oil in a Dutch oven over medium-high heat. Add the onion and sauté for 3 minutes. Add the garlic and cook until the onion is soft, about 4 minutes. Add the tempeh. Sauté until the mixture colors lightly, about 2 minutes.

2. Stir in the chili powder, cumin, and oregano, and cook until the seasoning is aromatic, about 1 minute. Add the tomatoes, chiles, and the cilantro. Simmer, uncovered, until the chili is thick, about 10 minutes.

3. Season to taste with salt and pepper and serve.

NOTE: Use a chili powder consisting of ground chile peppers, cumin, oregano, and salt. Avoid those containing garlic powder, which adds a bitter taste.

PER SERVING, WITHOUT RICE: Calories 161 • Soy Protein 8.0 g • Total Protein 10.6 g • Carbohydrates 13.2 g • Fat 7.6 g • Saturated Fat 1 g • Cholesterol 0 mg • Fiber 4.3 g • Sodium 338.9 mg

Fifty-Fifty Chili

This chili has the hefty flavor of an all-meat dish, but it combines beef with soy crumbles, so it has less fat and cholesterol. To increase the heat in this mildly warm chili, you can add fresh serrano or habanero chiles or hot red pepper flakes. Its flavor improves when it is refrigerated for 1 to 2 days and then reheated, and it freezes well. Serve ladled over pinto beans or cooked brown rice.

2 tablespoons canola oil

1 pound lean ground beef

1 large onion, chopped

3 garlic cloves, chopped

2 to 3 jalapeño peppers, seeded and chopped

One 12-ounce package refrigerated soy crumbles, or 2 cups frozen

¼ cup chili powder

1 tablespoon ground cumin

1 tablespoon dried oregano

One 28-ounce can whole tomatoes with their liquid

Salt and freshly ground black pepper

1. Heat 1 tablespoon of the oil in a Dutch oven or heavy pot over medium heat. Add the ground beef, stirring with a wooden spoon to break up the meat. Cook until the meat loses its red color, about 5 minutes. With a slotted spoon, transfer the meat to a bowl and set aside. Discard the liquid in the pot.

2. Heat the remaining 1 tablespoon oil in the pot over medium-high heat. Add the onion, garlic, jalapeños, and soy crumbles. Cook, stirring occasionally, until the onion is translucent, about 6 minutes. Return the cooked meat to the pot. Stir in the chili powder, cumin, and oregano and cook for 1 minute, until the seasoning is aromatic. Add the tomatoes, breaking them up with a wooden spoon. Bring the chili to a boil, reduce the heat, and simmer for 30 minutes, or until the chili is thick and the flavors are well blended.

3. Season to taste with salt and pepper and serve.

PER SERVING: Calories 353 • Soy Protein 8.5 g • Total Protein 24.5 g • Carbohydrates 17.3 g • Fat 21.6 g • Saturated Fat 6.8 g • Cholesterol 56.7 mg • Fiber 6.0 g • Sodium 468.6 mg

One 15-ounce can yellow
   soybeans, with jelled
   juices
¼ cup finely chopped
   onion
1 garlic clove, finely
   chopped
½ cup tomato sauce
2 packed tablespoons
   brown sugar
1 tablespoon unsulphured
   molasses
½ teaspoon ground ginger
½ teaspoon dry mustard
1 teaspoon Worcestershire
   sauce
2 turkey, beef, or meatless
   frankfurters, cut into
   ½-inch slices
Freshly ground black
   pepper

Beans and Franks

You may expect meatless hot dogs, but that is not where the soy is in this enlightened favorite. Instead I use soybeans, baked in tomato sauce with ginger and a touch of molasses. Vegetarians can use soy franks, too, but I prefer the snap—the hot dog lover's term for the firm bite of a good frank—of the preservative-free, uncured turkey franks from Applegate Farms. Leftovers reheat well.

1. Combine the beans, onion, garlic, tomato sauce, sugar, molasses, ginger, mustard, and Worcestershire sauce in a saucepan. Bring to a boil over medium-high heat. Reduce the heat and simmer, stirring occasionally, for 15 minutes.

2. Add the frankfurters. Simmer them with the beans until they are heated through, 10 minutes.

3. Season to taste with pepper and serve. (If you are not serving immediately, cool the beans and franks. They will keep for up to 3 days, in a tightly closed container, in the refrigerator. Reheat, using the microwave, stovetop, or oven.)

PER SERVING: Calories 364 • Soy Protein 23.5 g • Total Protein 28.2 g • Carbohydrates 36.6 g • Fat 14.5 g • Saturated Fat 2.5 g • Cholesterol 10.0 mg • Fiber 9.6 g • Sodium 421.3 mg

Cottage Pie

Serves 6

Cottage pie is made with beef, shepherd's pie with lamb. This is properly a cottage pie because, while meatless, its filling resembles beef more than lamb. Either way, it is comfort food so handsomely presented it deserves to be shared. Rather than using a pastry bag to pipe on the topping, I form the mashed potatoes into flattened disks and lay them over the filling.

1. Preheat the oven to 375°F. Coat a 2-quart baking dish with nonstick cooking spray and set aside.

2. To make the filling, heat 2 teaspoons canola oil in a skillet over medium-high heat. Add ½ cup of the onions and the shallots and sauté until they are soft, about 4 minutes. Add the soy crumbles and mushroom broth. Bring the liquid to a boil, reduce the heat, and simmer until the crumbles are almost dry, about 8 minutes. Turn the crumbles mixture into a bowl and wipe out the pan.

3. Heat the remaining 2 tablespoons oil in the skillet over medium-high heat. Add the remaining ¼ cup onion and sauté until soft, about 3 minutes. Mix in the flour and cook for 1 minute, stirring constantly. Whisk in the broth and thyme and bring to a boil. Reduce the heat and simmer until the sauce thickens, about 2 minutes. Add the carrot and celery and simmer for 2 minutes more. Remove the pot from the heat and mix in the reserved soy crumbles, the miso, peas, and parsley. Season to taste with salt and pepper and transfer the filling to the prepared baking dish.

4. To make the topping, combine the potatoes and garlic in a pot and cover them with cold water by 2 inches. Place over high heat, cover, and bring to a boil. Reduce the heat and cook for 20 minutes. Drain and return the vegetables to the pot until they are just cool enough to peel. Mash the peeled

FILLING

2 tablespoons plus 2 teaspoons canola oil

¾ cup finely chopped onions

3 tablespoons finely chopped shallots

2 cups frozen or one 12-ounce package refrigerated soy crumbles

1 cup mushroom broth

2 tablespoons all-purpose flour

1¼ cups chicken or vegetarian chicken broth

1 teaspoon dried thyme

1 small carrot, cut into ½-inch slices

½ cup sliced celery

1 tablespoon brown rice or barley miso

½ cup frozen baby green peas

¼ cup chopped fresh flat-leaf parsley

Salt and freshly ground black pepper

2 large baking potatoes, halved

3 large garlic cloves, unpeeled

3 tablespoons unsalted butter or margarine

Salt and freshly ground black pepper

potatoes and garlic in a bowl. When the mixture is smooth, blend in the butter. Season to taste with salt and pepper. Continue mashing until the topping is like a soft dough.

5. Scoop up ¼ cup of the topping. Pat this into a pancake 1 inch thick. Lay it on top of the filling. Repeat, making slightly overlapping rows, like roof tiles, to cover the filling. Drag the tines of a fork over the potato cakes, making ridges.

6. Bake the pie for 25 to 30 minutes, or until the filling is hot and bubbling and the ridges on the topping are browned.

7. Let the hot pie sit for 20 minutes before serving. Cottage Pie will keep for up to 2 days, covered and refrigerated. Simply bring it to room temperature, then slip it into a 400°F oven until it is heated through and browned on top.

PER SERVING: Calories 255 • Soy Protein 8.5 g • Total Protein 11.8 g • Carbohydrates 32.0 g • Fat 9.0 g • Saturated Fat 4.2 g • Cholesterol 15.0 mg • Fiber 3.5 g • Sodium 884.0 mg

Quince and Tofu Pot Pie with Mushrooms and Chestnuts

Serves 8

A particularly outstanding boeuf bourguignon was the inspiration for this sophisticated pot pie. When I apprenticed with Alain Senderens at L'Archestrate, his 3-star restaurant in Paris, we marinated cubed, lean fillet in fine wine with aromatic vegetables, then seared the meat and simmered it in the wine marinade. Applying this technique to firmly pressed tofu, I added quince and chestnuts to the final dish. Touches of dry French cider and Dijon mustard knit together the flavors in this savory dish. Its crowning glory is a golden cloud of crumpled phyllo. Serve with mashed potatoes or steamed new potatoes. It is also good topped with the mashed potatoes used on Cottage Pie (page 231) or simply ladled inside a ring of steamed rice.

1. To make the marinade, combine the wine, vinegar, onion, celery, shallots, garlic, thyme, and peppercorns in a nonreactive pot. Cut the tofu into 1-inch cubes and add them to the pot. Bring the marinade to a boil over medium-high heat. Remove the pot from the heat and let it cool to room temperature, about 1 hour. Transfer the tofu and marinade to a bowl with a tight cover or resealable plastic bag. Refrigerate for at least 2 hours, and up to 2 days.

2. Discard the marinade. Blot the tofu cubes dry, using paper towels. Fill a medium skillet with 1 inch oil and heat it over medium heat until the surface shimmers. Add the well-dried tofu, using tongs and taking care, as it will splatter. When the cubes darken and get slightly crusty, about 1 minute, turn them with the tongs, and crisp them on the other side. Drain the tofu on paper towels and set aside. Cool

MARINADE

3 cups dry red wine

½ cup red wine vinegar

1 small onion, chopped

1 celery rib, chopped

½ cup sliced shallots

2 garlic cloves, chopped

1 teaspoon dried thyme

1 teaspoon black
  peppercorns

FILLING

16 ounces firm tofu,
  pressed in 2 slabs
  (see page 49)

About 2 cups canola oil

8 pearl onions

3 tablespoons unsalted
  butter

2 tablespoons finely
  chopped shallot

1 garlic clove, finely
  chopped

1 tablespoon all-purpose
  flour

2 tablespoons tomato
  puree or paste

½ cup dry red wine

1 cup dry French-style
  cider

1 teaspoon dried thyme

4 juniper berries, chopped

1 bay leaf

2 teaspoons Dijon mustard

1 medium tomato, seeded and chopped

8 large white mushrooms, stemmed and cut into 6 to 8 pieces

½ large quince or 1 small Bosc pear, peeled, cored, and chopped

¾ cup cooked chestnuts, halved or in large pieces (see page 116)

CRUST

4 sheets phyllo pastry

1 tablespoon melted unsalted butter

the oil and discard it or strain it through cheesecloth to reserve for another use. Wipe out the skillet.

3. Boil the pearl onions in a medium pot of water for 3 minutes. Drain and peel. Set aside.

4. Preheat the oven to 400°F. Coat a 12-inch cazuela or other 6-cup, shallow, ovenproof serving dish with nonstick cooking spray. Set it aside.

5. Melt the butter in a large skillet over medium-high heat. Add the shallot and garlic and sauté until they are soft, about 3 minutes. Mix in the flour, reduce the heat to medium, and cook for 1 minute, stirring so the flour does not color. Stir in the tomato puree and add the wine, cider, thyme, juniper berries, and bay leaf. Simmer gently until the liquid has reduced to the thickness of tomato soup, about 15 minutes. Mix in the mustard.

6. Add the reserved tofu, onions, tomato, mushrooms, quince, and chestnuts to the sauce. Bring the filling just to a boil. Remove the bay leaf. Pour it into the prepared baking dish, filling it to within ½ inch from the top. Set aside.

7. To make the crust, one at a time, place a sheet of the phyllo on your work surface. Brush it lightly with some of the melted butter. Gently crumple the sheet into a loose ball about 4 inches in diameter. Place it on top of the pie filling. Repeat with the remaining phyllo, leaving about ½ inch between the crumpled sheets so the filling can bubble up during baking.

8. Bake the pot pie for 10 minutes. Reduce the heat to 325°F. Bake for 18 to 20 minutes, or until the edges of the phyllo are brown.

9. Serve hot.

PER SERVING: Calories 305 • Soy Protein 5.7 g • Total Protein 8.8 g • Carbohydrates 23.3 g • Fat 12.9 g • Saturated Fat 4.7 g • Cholesterol 15.0 mg • Fiber 2.7 g • Sodium 170.6 mg

steaks, chops, skewers, and meat loaf

Searing soyfoods over high heat, particularly on the grill, and roasting them in bold marinades adds crusty texture and unexpected interest to these meaty dishes. Slicing into hefty Chip's Chops (page 238), an aromatic, herb-roasted tofu cutlet spiked with tropical mango salsa (page 240), or tangy Hawaiian Kebabs (page 244) demonstrates what savor this easy cooking brings to a substantial slab of tempeh, tofu, or soymeat. Similarly, blending soy crumbles or tofu with ground meat makes meat loaf perfect for anyone making the transition to soy or who continues to enjoy meat as well as soy.

Glazed Tofu Steaks

1 tablespoon hoisin sauce

1 tablespoon soy sauce or tamari

1 teaspoon honey or brown sugar

1 teaspoon balsamic or rice vinegar

1 teaspoon Worcestershire sauce (see Note)

½ teaspoon ground ginger

¼ teaspoon Chinese five-spice powder

¼ teaspoon garlic powder

¼ teaspoon freshly ground black pepper

16 ounces soft, firm, or extra firm tofu

Tofu lovers find these generous crusty cutlets as appealing as the lamb chop or steak that tempts a carnivore. When these steaks cool, they become firm enough to slice or dice. Cut up, the tofu is good added to salads and stir-fries, including Broccoli with Black Bean Sauce (page 259).

1. To make the glaze, combine the hoisin sauce, soy sauce, honey, vinegar, Worcestershire sauce, ginger, five-spice powder, garlic powder, and pepper in a bowl.

2. Cut the tofu lengthwise into 4 slices. Place them on a couple of layers of paper towels to drain until the towels are soaked through, 2 minutes.

3. Heat a skillet large enough to hold the tofu in one layer over medium-high heat. Blot the top of the tofu well. Add it to the dry pan. Stir the glaze mixture and pour it over the tofu.

4. Turn the tofu to coat it all over with the glaze. Cook for 3 minutes; the glaze will thicken around the tofu, which will brown on one side. Turn the tofu and cook until the glaze in the pan is almost dry and the tofu is browned on the bottom.

5. Serve hot or lukewarm. (Glazed tofu will keep for up to 4 days, covered and refrigerated. Bring to room temperature or warm gently before serving.)

NOTE: Natural food stores have vegetarian Worcestershire sauce made without anchovies.

PER SERVING: Calories 140 • Soy Protein 11.3 g • Total Protein 11.7 g • Carbohydrates 6.7 g • Fat 7.4 g • Saturated Fat 1.0 g • Cholesterol 0.1 mg • Fiber 0.1 g • Sodium 263.6 mg

Smoked BBQ Tofu

Serves 4

1. Preheat the oven according to the directions for the smoker bag. Coat a baking rack with cooking spray. Set the baking rack on a plate which fits inside the smoker bag.

2. For the barbecue sauce, combine the hoisin sauce, teriyaki sauce, honey, Worcestershire sauce, and peanut oil in a bowl.

3. Blot the tofu well with paper towels. Place the slices on the rack. Brush them with the barbecue sauce. Turn the tofu over. Brush it generously again with the sauce.

4. Slip the plate with the tofu into the smoker bag. Seal it tightly by rolling the open end over three or four times. Carefully place the filled bag in the oven, following the instructions on the package. Smoke the tofu for 10 minutes. Wearing two oven mitts, remove the filled bag from the oven. Let it sit for 5 minutes. Cut the bag open, following the package directions.

5. Cool the tofu on the rack to room temperature, and transfer it to a covered container. Refrigerate the tofu for at least 8 hours before using to give the flavors time to meld and mellow. (This tofu will keep for up to 3 days in a plastic container in the refrigerator.)

BARBECUE SAUCE

1 tablespoon hoisin sauce

1 tablespoon teriyaki or soy sauce

2 teaspoons honey

1 teaspoon Worcestershire sauce

2 teaspoons peanut oil

One 16-ounce block firm tofu, or one 12-ounce block yaki dofu, cut lengthwise into 4 pieces

One foil smoker bag (light smoke) (see page 54)

PER SERVING: Calories 145 • Soy Protein 11.3 g • Total Protein 11.8 g • Carbohydrates 8.2 g • Fat 7.4 g • Saturated Fat 1.0 g • Cholesterol 0.1 mg • Fiber 0.1 g • Sodium 263.7 mg

Serves 6

16 ounces (two 8-ounce
    packages) soy tempeh

MARINADE

1 tablespoon tamari

1 garlic clove, minced

½ teaspoon onion powder

½ to 1 teaspoon dried
    thyme

¼ teaspoon freshly grated
    nutmeg

¼ cup canola or
    vegetable oil

1 large egg, lightly beaten

½ teaspoon salt

¼ teaspoon freshly ground
    black pepper

½ cup walnuts

1 cup dried bread crumbs

Rich Mushroom Gravy
    (recipe follows)

Chip's Chops

Pat Calhoun at White Wave suggested this hearty dish. The marinated tempeh, baked in a walnut and crumb crust, lived up to expectations. To prepare this dish on a weeknight, I make the tempeh in its marinade two to three days ahead, the crumb mixture the night before, and prepare the mushroom gravy while the chops are in the oven.

1. Preheat the oven to 350°F.

2. Cut the cakes of tempeh crosswise into 3 pieces. Place the tempeh in a baking dish just large enough to hold the 6 pieces.

3. To make the marinade, combine the tamari, garlic, onion powder, thyme, nutmeg, and oil in a small saucepan. Add ½ cup water. Bring the marinade to a boil over medium-high heat. Pour the hot marinade over the tempeh; it does not cover it.

4. Bake the tempeh, uncovered, for 15 minutes. Turn the pieces over and bake for another 15 minutes. Cool the tempeh in the marinade; it will absorb most of it. Use immediately, or wrap the tempeh in plastic and refrigerate for up to 3 days. If you are completing the dish, leave the oven on.

5. Place the egg in a dish. Mix in the salt and pepper. Place the walnuts in a food processor, along with 2 tablespoons of the bread crumbs. Pulse until the nuts are finely ground, taking care not to let them get warm and oily. Add the remaining bread crumbs to the food processor and process to combine them. Pour the mixture onto another dish. Dredge a piece of the tempeh in the egg, then roll it in the crumb mixture until well coated, pressing the crumbs to help them adhere. Place the breaded tempeh on a baking sheet. Repeat, coating all the tempeh.

6. Bake the tempeh for 15 minutes. Turn and bake for 10 minutes, or until the "chops" are golden brown. While the chops bake, make the gravy.

7. Place 1 chop on each of 6 dinner plates. Spoon about ⅓ cup of the gravy over each chop, and serve. The baked chops can be individually wrapped in aluminum foil and frozen for up to 1 month. Preheat in a 350°F oven for 30 minutes, wrapped in the foil.

Rich Mushroom Gravy

Makes 2 cups

Miso and mushroom broth contribute to the intense flavor of this gravy. Pureeing part of the gravy makes it quite thick. Try this gravy over mashed potatoes, cooked buckwheat, or kasha varnishkas.

1 tablespoon canola oil

1 cup chopped Spanish onion

1 small garlic clove, minced

2 cups thinly sliced white mushrooms

½ teaspoon dried thyme

1 cup mushroom broth

1 tablespoon red or barley miso

Salt and freshly ground black pepper

1. Heat the oil in a medium skillet over medium-high heat. Add the onion and garlic and sauté until the onion is soft, about 4 minutes. Add the mushrooms. Cook until they are browned, 6 to 8 minutes.

2. Remove ½ cup of the mushroom mixture from the pan and set aside. Add the thyme and ¾ cup of the broth. Bring the liquid to a boil, scraping up any browned bits from the bottom of the pan with a wooden spoon. Boil until the gravy thickens slightly, 1 minute. Remove from the heat.

3. Cream the miso with the remaining ¼ cup of broth in a small bowl. Mix this into the hot gravy. Transfer the contents of the pan to a blender. Whirl until the gravy is a pulpy puree. Pour it back into the pan. Mix in the reserved mushrooms and heat the gravy until it almost boils. Serve hot.

GRAVY: PER ⅓ CUP: Calories 66 • Soy Protein 2.7 g • Total Protein 3.9 g • Carbohydrates 4.3 g • Fat 4.0 g • Saturated Fat 0.5 g • Cholesterol 5.9 mg • Fiber 1.1 g • Sodium 129.5 mg

CHOPS ALONE: Calories 328 • Soy Protein 13.7 g • Total Protein 19.5 g • Carbohydrates 21.3 g • Fat 19.8 g • Saturated Fat 2.7 g • Cholesterol 29.5 mg • Fiber 5.5 g • Sodium 647.7 mg

CHOPS PLUS GRAVY: Calories 394 • Soy Protein 16.4 g • Total Protein 23.4 g • Carbohydrates 25.6 g • Fat 23.8 g • Saturated Fat 3.2 g • Cholesterol 35.4 mg • Fiber 6.6 g • Sodium 777.2 mg

Herb-Roasted Tofu Cutlets with Fresh Mango Salsa

½ cup lightly packed cilantro leaves

½ cup lightly packed mint leaves

½ cup lightly packed flat-leaf parsley

2 scallions (green and white parts), coarsely chopped

2 garlic cloves, coarsely chopped

½ teaspoon coriander seed, roughly chopped with a knife, in a mini chopper, or crushed in a mortar

Zest of 1 lime

¼ cup fresh lime juice

1 teaspoon salt

½ teaspoon freshly ground black pepper

6 tablespoons extra virgin olive oil

16 ounces extra firm tofu, pressed in 2 slabs (see page 49)

One of the most exciting meals I have had was lunch at the Herbfarm near Seattle, where Chef Jerry Traunfeld uses fresh herbs with unique artistry. For his Green-Roasted Fish Fillets, he combines cilantro, mint, and lime in a kind of pesto, then bakes the fish in this aromatic paste. I use tofu, letting it cool after baking until it is once again firm. Then I grill the verdant fillets and serve them with mango salsa. This recipe can be multiplied for parties.

1. Preheat the oven to 425°F. Coat an 8-inch square baking dish with nonstick cooking spray and set aside.

2. To make the seasoning paste, combine the cilantro, mint, parsley, scallions, garlic, coriander seed, lime zest, lime juice, salt, and pepper in a blender and puree. With the motor running, drizzle in the olive oil.

3. Cut each slab of tofu crosswise in half, making 4 pieces. Coat the tofu with the paste. Place the tofu in the baking dish. Bake for 15 minutes. Cool, cover with plastic wrap, and refrigerate overnight.

4. To make the salsa, combine the mango, jicama, onion, serrano chile, orange zest, and lime juice. Season to taste with salt and pepper. Let the salsa sit for 20 minutes to 2 hours before serving.

5. Lightly coat an outdoor grill or a grill pan with oil. Heat the grill to medium-high heat. Wipe most of the seasoning paste off the tofu. Grill until the tofu is heated through and well-marked from the grill, 3 to 5 minutes on each side, turning the tofu once.

6. To serve, place the tofu and ¼ cup of the salsa on each plate.

PER SERVING: Calories 335 • Soy Protein 11.8 g • Total Protein 12.8 g • Carbohydrates 11.7 g • Fat 28.3 g • Saturated Fat 4.0 g • Cholesterol 0 mg • Fiber 2.2 g • Sodium 492.0 mg

MANGO SALSA

½ cup chopped mango

¼ cup finely chopped jicama

¼ cup finely chopped red onion

1 serrano chile pepper, seeded and finely chopped

2 teaspoons grated orange zest

2 tablespoons fresh lime juice

Salt and freshly ground black pepper

Tofu Piccata

MARINADE

1 teaspoon grated lemon
  zest

Juice of 1 lemon

½ cup dry white wine

⅓ cup mellow white miso

1 small garlic clove,
  minced

1 tablespoon extra virgin
  olive oil

16 ounces firm tofu, cut
  and pressed in
  2 slabs (see page 49)

3 tablespoons all-purpose
  flour

1 tablespoon extra virgin
  olive oil

1½ tablespoons salt-cured
  capers, soaked and
  drained

Give tofu bold flavors like these to soak up, and it positively glows. Here, tofu pressed into a meaty cutlet is baked in a marinade made with the ingredients for a classic Italian piccata—plus a touch of miso. Then it is lightly floured and sautéed like a chicken breast. Adding the marinade to the pan lets you scrape up all the golden bits that help make a mouthwatering sauce.

1. Preheat the oven to 350°F.

2. To make the marinade, combine the lemon zest and juice in a small saucepan with the wine, miso, garlic, and olive oil. Add ¼ cup water. Bring to a boil over high heat. Cook for 1 minute.

3. Place the tofu in a glass baking dish just large enough to hold the 2 pieces side by side. Pour the hot marinade over the tofu, turning it once so it is well-coated with the liquid.

4. Bake for 30 minutes. Let the tofu cool in the pan in the marinade. (At this point, the tofu and its marinade can be stored for up to 24 hours, covered in plastic wrap and refrigerated.)

5. Remove the tofu from the baking dish, mixing the excess coating back into the marinade. Cut each slab of tofu crosswise. Reserve the marinade. Dredge the tofu in the flour, turning it so it is coated on all sides.

6. Heat the oil in a nonstick skillet over medium-high heat. Add the tofu and sauté until it is golden on one side, 1 to 2 minutes. Turn and brown on the other side. Add the reserved marinade and capers to the pan. Bring the liquid to a boil.

7. To serve, place the piccata on dinner plates, spoon the pan sauce over, and serve.

PER SERVING: Calories 243 • Soy Protein 14.2 g • Total Protein 15.1 g • Carbohydrates 15.0 g • Fat 12.6 g • Saturated Fat 1.6 g • Cholesterol 0 mg • Fiber 1.3 g • Sodium 956.7 mg

Thai Tofu Kebabs

Cucumber is an ingredient rarely used in cooked dishes. It is perfect on these simple kebabs. These kebabs need only to be heated through to take on the flavor of the fire and these skewers are ready to serve in a few minutes. They are a particularly good choice for family cookouts, since they appeal to children and grownups alike. Serve with Three-Bean Salad (page 165).

1. To make the marinade, combine the lime juice, soy sauce, garlic, basil, red pepper flakes, black pepper, and olive oil in a resealable plastic bag.

2. Cut the pressed tofu into 12 cubes. Add the tofu to the bag. Marinate in the refrigerator for at least 4 hours, up to 24 hours.

3. Soak four 10-inch bamboo skewers in water for 15 to 30 minutes. Preheat a grill to medium-high or a broiler.

4. Halve the cucumber lengthwise. Use a teaspoon to scoop out the seeds. Cut each piece crosswise into 1-inch crescents.

5. To assemble the kebabs, slip a cucumber piece almost to the bottom of a skewer. Add a tofu chunk. Slip on 2 or 3 onion crescents, followed by a tomato. Repeat, adding another piece of tofu, onion, and tomato. Finally, add a third tofu chunk, onion, and a cucumber crescent, turned toward the onion. Make up 3 more skewers in the same way.

6. Grill or broil the kebabs for 2 minutes. Brush them with some of the marinade. Cook another minute. Turn and cook until the tofu is hot and the vegetables lightly charred, 2 to 3 minutes, brushing them with marinade halfway through the cooking. Serve hot.

MARINADE

⅓ cup fresh lime juice (about 2 limes)

1 tablespoon soy sauce

1 garlic clove, chopped

2 tablespoons chopped Thai or Italian basil

½ teaspoon hot red pepper flakes

¼ teaspoon freshly ground black pepper

¼ cup olive oil

1 pound firm or extra firm tofu, pressed in one block (see page 49)

4-inch piece of cucumber, peeled

8 cherry tomatoes

1 medium red onion, halved vertically and cut into ½-inch crescents

PER SERVING: Calories 265 • Soy Protein 12.0 g • Total Protein 13.0 g • Carbohydrates 9.4 g • Fat 21.3 g • Saturated Fat 3.0 g • Cholesterol 0 mg • Fiber 1.7 g • Sodium 273.4 mg

1 medium sweet potato

1 medium green bell
    pepper, seeded and cut
    into 8 flat pieces

Eight 1-inch pieces sliced
    pineapple (see Note)

10 ½ ounces frozen
    soymeat nuggets (one
    package), defrosted

SAUCE

¼ cup apple juice

1 tablespoon soy sauce

2 tablespoons honey

1 tablespoon unsulphured
    molasses

Juice of ½ lime

1 teaspoon ground cumin

½ teaspoon onion powder

¼ teaspoon hot red
    pepper flakes, optional

1 tablespoon peanut oil

Hawaiian Kebabs

Green pepper and fresh pineapple are a familiar duo to fans of sweet-and-sour dishes. Here they are joined by sweet potatoes on skewers bathed in a honeyed sweet-and-sour glaze. The soy in these kebabs is an ideal introduction for anyone hesitant about meat replacements. For a colorful Asian buffet, offer platters of these skewers, together with Shrimp Balls (page 118), and Ginger Fried Rice (page 266).

1. Soak four 10-inch bamboo skewers in water for 15 to 30 minutes. Preheat the grill to medium-high or a broiler.

2. Cut the sweet potatoes into ¾-inch slices. Halve any slices that are larger than 1 inch in diameter. Combine the potatoes and 2 cups water in a saucepan. Cover and bring to a boil over high heat. Cook for 4 minutes after the water begins to boil. Drain and set the sweet potatoes aside until cool enough to handle. Using a small knife, cut away the peel. (This method is faster than peeling the potatoes before cooking.)

3. To make the sauce, combine the apple juice, soy sauce, honey, molasses, lime juice, cumin, onion powder, red pepper flakes, if using, and oil in a saucepan. Boil over medium-high heat for 5 minutes, until the sauce is reduced by a third and just slightly thickened. Set aside.

4. To assemble the kebabs, slip a piece of the pineapple almost to the bottom of a skewer, followed by a piece of the green pepper. Add a soy nugget. The pieces should be touching but not tightly packed, so some sauce can run between them. Slip on a piece of the sweet potato, another soy nugget, and a second piece of sweet potato. Add the third soy nugget and end with a second piece each of green pepper and pineapple. Repeat, making 4 skewers in all.

5. If you are grilling, brush each skewer generously with the sauce and place on the grill. If you are using the broiler, place

the kebabs in a shallow pan and brush them well with the sauce. Cook for 2 minutes. Brush the kebabs with more sauce, turn, and baste on the second side. Cook for 2 minutes, until the vegetables are cooked through and the kebabs are lightly charred in spots. Serve immediately.

NOTE: There is no need to buy a whole pineapple when making these kebabs. Just check the salad bar. The fruit section usually includes pineapple chunks that will be just the right size.

PER SERVING: Calories 401 • Soy Protein 11.4 g • Total Protein 20.1 g • Carbohydrates 68.9 g • Fat 7.3 g • Saturated Fat 1.3 g • Cholesterol 0 mg • Fiber 5.3 g • Sodium 275.5 mg

Green Pepper Tip

Here is a quick way to get slabs of pepper, ready to cut into strips or to dice. It is faster and neater then halving a pepper, pulling out the core and getting rid of any loose seeds. It also eliminates having to trim away the ribs. Ellen Fried, an intern who worked with me, showed me this technique.

Stand the pepper on its bottom on a cutting board. Place your knife vertically across the top of the pepper, about ½ inch from the outside of the pepper. Cut down, slicing off one side of the pepper. Turn the pepper 90 degrees and cut off the second side. Repeat, slicing off the third side. For the fourth side, lay the pepper on its side and slice off the last piece. This leaves the core, the top stem, and the bottom all in one piece. Cut off the bottom piece, if you want to use it.

Rockin' Moroccan Skewers

1½ cups 1-inch pieces textured soy protein (about 72)

5 tablespoons extra virgin olive oil

½ cup chopped onion

3 garlic cloves, sliced

1¼ cups fresh orange juice

¼ cup fresh lemon juice

1 inch fresh ginger, grated or minced

2 tablespoons dried oregano

2 tablespoons sweet paprika

1 tablespoon dried thyme

1 tablespoon ground turmeric

2 teaspoons ground cinnamon

1 teaspoon cayenne pepper

1 teaspoon salt

These unusual kebabs show off textured soy protein infused with the flavors of charmoula, the Moroccan-spiced vinaigrette usually used with seafood. A creation of Native Foods chef Tanya Petrovna, they appeal to vegetarians and meat-eaters alike. A few minutes on the grill or under the broiler heightens their golden color and rounds out the spices in these golden skewers. Serve with rice or in Full Dress (recipe follows).

1. Place the soy protein in a pot. Add 1 cup water. Bring to a boil over medium-high heat. Reduce the heat and simmer until the water is almost completely absorbed, about 5 minutes. Drain the hydrated soy in a colander. Spread the pieces on a plate to cool.

2. To make the marinade, heat 2 tablespoons of the oil in a skillet over medium-high heat. Add the onion and garlic and sauté until lightly browned, about 8 minutes. Transfer them to a blender.

3. Add the orange juice, lemon juice, ginger, oregano, paprika, thyme, turmeric, cinnamon, cayenne, and salt to the blender. Process to a puree. Add the remaining 3 tablespoons olive oil and blend.

4. Push 12 pieces of the soy onto each of six 10-inch skewers. Place the kebabs in a shallow glass or other nonreactive dish. Pour the marinade over them. Turn them once in the marinade to coat well. Cover the dish with plastic wrap and refrigerate for 2 hours, up to 24 hours.

5. Preheat the grill to medium-high or a broiler.

6. Remove the kebabs from the marinade and reserve the marinade for serving the kebabs with Full Dress (recipe fol-

lows). Grill the kebabs until grill marks show, turning the skewers 2 to 3 times so the soy colors on all sides, about 5 minutes in total. To broil, place the kebabs on a jelly-roll pan. Set the pan under the broiler. Turn the skewers 2 to 3 times, until they are golden and slightly crispy on all sides, 6 to 8 minutes.

PER SERVING: Calories 309 • Soy Protein 8.6 g • Total Protein 12.2 g • Carbohydrates 52.9 g • Fat 6.9 g • Saturated Fat 0.3 g • Cholesterol 0 mg • Fiber 6.2 g • Sodium 319.4 mg

Full Dress for Rockin' Moroccan Skewers

Serves 6

The eye-filling colors of crunchy carrots, succulent zucchini, tart dried cranberries, sweet potatoes, and creamy quinoase make a show-stopping setting and perfect foil for the kebobs. The recipe is easily multiplied, this is a good dish for feeding a group.

1 cup small broccoli florets

1 small carrot, halved lengthwise and thinly sliced

1 cup small cauliflower florets

1 cup thin sweet potato slices, cut in quarters

1 small zucchini, halved lengthwise and thinly sliced

4 cups cooked quinoa

1 medium red onion, halved and sliced into ¾-inch crescents

1 tablespoon dried cranberries

¼ cup toasted sliced almonds

1. Steam or boil the broccoli, carrot, cauliflower, sweet potato, and zucchini until tender-crisp, 2 to 3 minutes. Drain and immediately plunge the vegetables into a bowl of ice water. Drain well.

2. Place 1 cup of the quinoa in each of four wide, shallow soup bowls. Top the quinoa with a generous ½ cup of the cooked vegetables. Top with some of the onions. Sprinkle a quarter of the cranberries, almonds, and parsley over the quinoa and vegetables. Balance a skewer of the crisped soy kebabs on the edge of the bowl, or set it on top of the vegetables. Drizzle with 2 to 3 tablespoons of the marinade and serve.

2 tablespoons chopped
fresh flat-leaf parsley

Reserved marinade from
the kebabs (see Note)

NOTE: Refrigerate the leftover marinade until you are ready to serve. Discard what is not used.

PER SERVING: Calories 483.6 • Soy Protein 8.6 g • Total Protein 15.9 g • Carbohydrates 72.7 g • Fat 13.9 g • Saturated Fat 1.3 g • Cholesterol 10.6 mg • Fiber 13.0 g • Sodium 407.4 mg

Lemon Grill Tempeh

Serves 4

The first tempeh I ever tasted was White Wave's Lemon Broil. The interplay of its tart marinade and meaty texture were the perfect introduction to this exotic soyfood. When White Wave decided to stop making Lemon Broil, they published the recipe so its fans could continue enjoying this soy classic. This is my version, designed to work for home cooks. Enjoy these burgerlike squares, grilled or pan-seared and tucked into a bun and topped with all the fixings of a hamburger. Or, cut these patties into strips and serve on top of Spinach Salad, in place of the crisped tempeh bits (page 155).

Two 8-ounce packages soy or mild-flavored tempeh (see page 30)

2 large lemons

2 garlic cloves, minced

1 tablespoon tamari

1 teaspoon onion powder

¼ teaspoon freshly ground black pepper

½ teaspoon salt

¼ cup olive oil

1. Preheat the oven to 350°F.

2. Halve each cake of tempeh crosswise. Arrange the pieces in a baking dish just large enough to hold them in one layer.

3. To make the marinade, grate the zest from one of the lemons. Squeeze the juice from both; there should be ½ cup. Combine the juice and zest in a small nonreactive pot. Add ½ cup water. Mix in the garlic, tamari, onion powder, pepper, salt, and oil. Bring the marinade to a boil over medium-high heat. Pour the marinade over the tempeh. It should almost cover it.

4. Bake the tempeh, uncovered, for 15 minutes. Turn and bake for 15 minutes more.

5. Let the tempeh cool completely in the marinade. Remove the tempeh from the marinade and serve. (The tempeh will keep for up to 5 days, tightly wrapped and refrigerated. It will pick up even more flavor if it is refrigerated in the marinade for up to 24 hours. The tempeh can also be frozen.)

PER SERVING: Calories 322 • Soy Protein 24.6 g • Total Protein 24.7 g • Carbohydrates 13.3 g • Fat 20.0 g • Saturated Fat 4.0 g • Cholesterol 0 mg • Fiber 7.8 g • Sodium 502.3 mg

Florentine Meat Loaf

2 teaspoons extra virgin
    olive oil

¾ cup chopped onion

½ cup chopped leek
    (white part only)

1 garlic clove, minced

2 cups frozen or one
    12-ounce package
    refrigerated soy
    crumbles

¼ cup dry white wine

16 ounces ground turkey
    (7 percent fat)

One 10-ounce package
    frozen chopped
    spinach, defrosted and
    squeezed dry

1 large egg white

2 tablespoons tomato
    paste

½ cup Italian seasoned
    dried bread crumbs

1 teaspoon dried basil

½ teaspoon dried oregano

1 teaspoon salt

½ teaspoon ground black
    pepper

2 large plum tomatoes,
    thinly sliced

This is a perfect starter recipe for anyone hesitant about soy. Putting it together is the same as making your favorite meat loaf. The soy crumbles combine with the lean turkey like additional meat. "Don't ask, don't tell" describes the way they disappear in the baked loaf.

1. Preheat the oven to 375°F. Coat an 8½ × 4½-inch loaf pan with cooking spray, and set aside.

2. Heat the oil in a skillet over medium-high heat. Saute the onion and leek until the onion is translucent, about 4 minutes. Stir in the garlic and cook for 1 minute. Mix in the soy crumbles, breaking up any clumps. Pour in the wine and cook until it evaporates, 2 to 3 minutes. Turn the mixture into a large bowl.

3. Add the turkey, spinach, egg white, tomato paste, bread crumbs, basil, oregano, salt, and pepper to the cooked soy mixture. Using your hands or a wooden spoon, mix until all the ingredients are well combined. Pack the mixture firmly into the prepared pan. Smooth the top of the loaf, using the back of a fork. Cover the meat loaf with foil, sealing it well.

4. Bake for 30 minutes. Remove the meat loaf from the oven, uncover, and arrange the tomatoes to cover the top, overlapping the slices. Bake the meat loaf, uncovered, until the internal temperature measures 165°F on an instant-read thermometer, or until the juices run clear when a knife is inserted into the center of the loaf. The center should feel firm when pressed with your finger.

5. Cool the meat loaf in the pan for 20 minutes before slicing. Or cool it completely in the pan, unmold, and wrap it in foil. (It will keep for up to 4 days, covered and refrigerated.) Slice and reheat in the oven or microwave.

PER SERVING: Calories 199 • Soy Protein 5.2 g • Total Protein 19.3 g • Carbohydrates 14.9 g • Fat 6.6 g • Saturated Fat 1.5 g • Cholesterol 44.8 mg • Fiber 3.8 g • Sodium 726.9 mg

Chinese Meat Loaf

Serves 8

In Asia, dishes like Ants Climbing a Tree and Ma Po Tofu combine tofu with meat or seafood. Tofu and meat go together in Western dishes like this meat loaf, where the soy lowers the fat and cholesterol but does not impact the flavor. Ginger adds warm flavor that goes well with the orange-hoisin glaze. Serve this meat loaf with steamed Swiss chard, spinach, or other dark, leafy greens, and mashed potatoes.

1. Preheat the oven to 350°F.

2. Mash the meat and tofu together in a bowl, using a fork, until they are just combined. Mix in the ginger, sugar, pepper, soy sauces, sherry, cornstarch, and sesame oil. Mix in the egg white until the mixture is well combined. Pack the meat loaf into a 9 × 5-inch loaf pan, smoothing the top.

3. Mix the orange zest with the hoisin sauce. Spread it over the top of the meat loaf. Cover the pan with aluminum foil.

4. Bake the meat loaf for 45 minutes. Uncover, and bake for 15 to 20 minutes, or until the juices from the center run clear or an instant-read thermometer inserted into the center registers 180°F.

5. Remove the meat loaf from the oven. Cool it in the pan for 20 minutes before slicing. (Or cool it completely in the pan, unmold, and wrap it in foil. It will keep for up to 4 days, covered and refrigerated. Slice and reheat in the oven or microwave.)

NOTE: If you cannot get Chinese thin and dark soy sauces, use 2 tablespoons reduced-sodium soy sauce plus ½ teaspoon molasses.

1 pound lean ground beef

16 ounces firm tofu, squeezed (see page 48)

2 tablespoons peeled minced fresh ginger

½ teaspoon sugar

½ teaspoon ground white pepper

1 tablespoon thin soy sauce (see Note)

1 tablespoon dark soy sauce (see Note)

1 tablespoon dry sherry

1 tablespoon cornstarch

1 teaspoon roasted sesame oil

1 large egg white, lightly beaten

2 teaspoons grated orange zest

1 tablespoon hoisin sauce

PER SERVING: Calories 203 • Soy protein 5.7 g • Protein 16.9 g • Fat 12.9 g • Saturated Fat 4.3 g • Cholesterol 39.1 mg • Carbohydrates 3.9 g • Fiber 0.1 g • Sodium 323.4 mg

stir-fries and curries

These Chinese and Southeast Asian dishes are made mostly with traditional soyfoods—tofu, miso, tempeh, or edamame. They hew to true ethnic lines; each curry uses spices blended to create its particular character. Even the soymeat used in the Vietnamese salad is popular in Asia. I also share some of the Chinese-American dishes I fell in love with when I was growing up. At the time, Cantonese cooking was the only choice in restaurants and the chefs distorted authentic recipes to fit their conception of American taste. Today, more authentic Asian cooking is available and Chinese restaurants feature cooking from Shanghai, Fukien, and Taiwan as well as the provinces of Hunan and Sichuan, but I still enjoy chop suey and other dishes for their nostalgic resonance.

In our increasingly multicultural world, conventional supermarkets carry most of the Asian ingredients called for in the recipes which follow. Some of the soy products, though, do require shopping in an Asian grocery store.

Egg Foo Yong

Perhaps you must be a certain age to love this fried egg pancake, which is served blanketed in a thick savory brown sauce. In the 1950s, shrimp, diced chicken, or pork often studded these mini-omelets, but now I serve this Chinese-American dish using crumbled tofu instead. To experience complete nostalgia, eat any leftovers cold, standing in front of the open refrigerator.

1. Beat the eggs in a large bowl.

2. Heat 1 tablespoon of the oil in a skillet over high heat. Add the cabbage and onion and stir-fry for 2 minutes, using a pancake turner or wok paddle to keep the vegetables moving. Add the bean sprouts and stir-fry until the vegetables are soft, but not limp, about 1 minute. Add them to the beaten eggs, along with the tofu, salt, and pepper.

3. Wipe out the skillet. Add the remaining oil and heat over high heat until it is shimmering. Ladle 1 cup of the egg mixture into the pan, making a 6-inch pancake. If necessary, reduce the heat to medium-high. Cook until the bottom is browned and the center is just set enough to turn the pancake, about 2 minutes. Cook until the second side is browned and the center of the pancake is set. Use a large pancake turner to remove the pancake, gently shaking it to drain off any excess oil. Drain on a plate covered with a paper towel. Repeat, making 4 pancakes in all, and placing a paper towel between each to blot up any extra oil. Cool and carefully discard the oil remaining in the pan.

4. To make the sauce, dissolve the cornstarch in 1 tablespoon of the broth, leaving the spoon in the bowl. Heat the peanut oil in a saucepan over medium-high heat. Add the garlic and sauté for 10 seconds. Add the remaining broth, the oyster sauce, soy sauce, and sesame oil. When the liquid

4 large eggs

½ cup peanut oil

2 cups sliced napa cabbage (cut crosswise into ½-inch strips)

1 medium onion, cut into ⅜-inch slices

1 cup mung bean sprouts

7 ounces firm tofu (½ package), squeezed (see page 48) and crumbled

1 teaspoon salt

¼ teaspoon freshly ground white or black pepper

2 tablespoons chopped scallions (green part only)

SAUCE

1 tablespoon cornstarch

1 cup defatted chicken or vegetarian chicken broth

1 teaspoon peanut oil

1 teaspoon minced garlic

2 tablespoons oyster sauce (see Note)

1 teaspoon soy sauce (regular or reduced sodium)

½ teaspoon roasted sesame oil

boils, restir the cornstarch binder and add it to the sauce. Cook, stirring, until the sauce is slightly thickened and clear, 1 to 2 minutes.

5. To serve, place one pancake on each plate. Cover with the sauce and garnish with the scallions.

NOTE: Vegetarians can use oyster-free oyster sauce (see box).

PER SERVING: Calories 414 • Soy Protein 4.6 g • Total Protein 13.0 g • Carbohydrates 11.8 g • Fat 36.5 g • Saturated Fat 6.8 g • Cholesterol 212.5 mg • Fiber 2.8 g • Sodium 811.6 mg

Oyster Sauce

Originally, this savory, thick brown sauce was made only from oysters, water, and salt, but now it also contains caramel for color and cornstarch for thickening. Some brands also contain MSG, sugar, and other ingredients, so read the labels carefully. Lee Kum Kee and Hop Sing Lung are good brands. Wah Shan brand makes a vegetarian oyster sauce that uses mushrooms.

Chinese
Pepper Steak

At our local Cantonese restaurants, this dish was made with green peppers and colorful tomato wedges. To avoid the pallid flavor of today's cardboard tomatoes, I prefer using red and green bell peppers. Replacing the meat with frozen soymeat, such as Veat, or textured soy protein "chips," produces a dish so good meat-eaters take a minute to realize they are not eating steak. Vegans can use oyster-free oyster sauce (see page 254).

1. To make the marinade, combine the soy sauce, sherry, and sesame oil in a bowl. Mix in the cornstarch. Add the soymeat, mixing to cover the pieces well. Set aside to marinate for 10 minutes. Drain and set aside.

2. To make the seasoning sauce, mix together the soy sauce, sherry, sesame oil, oyster sauce, sugar, and ground pepper. Set aside.

3. Cut each pepper lengthwise into 1-inch strips. Cut each strip diagonally at 1-inch intervals, alternating the angle of the knife to make 1-inch triangles. There will be about 1 cup each of cut red and green pepper.

4. Place a wok over high heat. When it is hot, drizzle the peanut oil around so it flows down the sides of the wok. Add the garlic and ginger and stir-fry for 30 seconds. Add the onion, peppers, and soymeat and stir-fry for 1 minute. Pour in the broth, and cook until it has almost evaporated, 2 to 3 minutes. Pour in the seasoning sauce and stir-fry until all the vegetables are coated and the sauce thickens just slightly, 1 minute.

5. Transfer the pepper steak to a serving dish and serve at once.

PER MAIN-COURSE SERVING: Calories 139 • Soy Protein 12.9 g • Total Protein 14.1 g • Carbohydrates 14.4 g • Fat 4.3 g • Saturated Fat 0.7 g • Cholesterol 0 mg • Fiber 5.1 g • Sodium 591.3 mg

MARINADE

1 tablespoon soy sauce

1 tablespoon dry sherry

¼ teaspoon roasted sesame oil

1 tablespoon cornstarch

7 ounces bite-size frozen soymeat (one package) defrosted, or 1 cup 1-inch textured soy protein chips

½ large green bell pepper

½ large red bell pepper

1 tablespoon peanut oil

1 teaspoon chopped garlic

1 teaspoon minced peeled fresh ginger

1 medium onion, cut vertically into ⅜-inch slices

¼ cup chicken or vegetable broth

SEASONING SAUCE

1 tablespoon soy sauce

1 tablespoon dry sherry

¼ teaspoon roasted sesame oil

2 tablespoons oyster sauce (see page 254)

½ teaspoon sugar

¼ teaspoon freshly ground black pepper

Serves 4 as a main
course or 6 as part of a
multicourse meal

MARINADE

1 large egg white

1 tablespoon dry sherry

2 tablespoons cornstarch

½ teaspoon salt

¼ teaspoon freshly ground
white pepper

16 ounces extra firm tofu,
pressed in 2 slabs
(see page 49)

1 tablespoon dry sherry

2 tablespoons oyster
sauce (see page 254)

2 tablespoons plus ½ cup
chicken or vegetarian
chicken broth

2 teaspoons cornstarch

½ teaspoon sugar

⅛ teaspoon freshly ground
white pepper

1 cup peanut oil

1 teaspoon minced fresh
ginger

1 garlic clove, minced

1 large celery rib, cut
diagonally into ½-inch
slices

¼ cup sliced bamboo
shoots (½-inch strips)

Moo Goo Gai Pan

Once very popular, this Cantonese dish is seldom seen on Chinese menus anymore. Chinese chefs American-ized it by using canned mushrooms in place of fresh, so I use them, too. However, I do replace tinny-tasting canned water chestnuts with thinly sliced celery. White pepper, which tastes more authentic, is not essential. Toasted almonds are; their flavor and crunch set off the tenderness of the tofu and enhance all the other flavors in the dish. Velveting tofu (see page 257) has a remarkable effect, infusing it with flavor while giving it almost the same texture as marinated chicken.

1. Cut each tofu slab crosswise into 4 strips. Cut each strip into 4 triangles.

2. To make the marinade, whisk the egg white in a medium bowl until it is foamy. Whisk in the sherry, cornstarch, salt, and pepper. Add the cut tofu to the marinade, tossing it with your hands to coat the pieces. Set it aside to marinate for 15 minutes.

3. Combine the sherry, oyster sauce, 2 tablespoons broth, cornstarch, sugar, and pepper in a small bowl. Set aside, leaving the spoon in the bowl.

4. Lift the tofu from the marinade with a slotted spoon and drain it well. Discard the marinade. Heat the oil in a wok over high heat until it is shimmering. Fry the tofu just until the surface is crisped and lightly colored, 1 to 2 minutes. Remove the tofu, using a slotted spoon and set it on paper towels to drain. Pour off all but 1 tablespoon of the oil. (Discard or strain the oil to reuse.)

5. Return the wok to the heat. Add the ginger and garlic and stir-fry until fragrant, 30 seconds. Add the celery, bamboo shoots, and mushrooms. Stir-fry until the celery is tender-crisp, about 2 minutes. Add the tofu. Pour in the remaining

½ cup broth. Restir the cornstarch mixture and add it to the wok. Stir-fry until the sauce thickens and coats the tofu and vegetables, about 1 minute.

6. Transfer the moo goo gai pan to a serving dish, garnish with the toasted almonds, and serve immediately.

½ cup canned button mushrooms

2 tablespoons blanched almonds, toasted and coarsely chopped

PER MAIN-COURSE SERVING: Calories 241 • Soy Protein 11.8 g • Total Protein 14.7 g • Carbohydrates 11.9 g • Fat 16.2 g • Saturated Fat 2.4 g • Cholesterol 0 mg • Fiber 2.0 g • Sodium 549.0 mg

Velveting

This technique is used on chicken, meats, and seafood, particularly shrimp and scallops. It consists of marinating the food in a blend of beaten egg white and cornstarch. Together, they seal in the moisture and make the marinade cling. Then the food is deep-fried briefly, just to sear it. This process tenderizes and prevents the pieces of food from sticking to one another or to the pan when they are stir-fried, so you can use very little oil. Velveting tofu makes it like tender chicken breast.

Serves 4 as a main
course or 6 as part of a
multicourse meal

MARINADE

1 tablespoon soy sauce

2 teaspoons dry sherry

1 teaspoon salt

½ teaspoon freshly ground
    white or black pepper

1 teaspoon roasted
    sesame oil

2 teaspoons cornstarch

1 pound firm tofu, pressed
    in 2 slabs (see page 49)

2 tablespoons peanut oil

1 large onion, halved and
    sliced into thin
    crescents

1 garlic clove, minced

2 cups sliced bok choy,
    cut diagonally into
    ½-inch slices

2 cups mung bean sprouts,
    rinsed and well dried

1 rib celery, cut diagonally
    into ½-inch slices

½ teaspoon salt

½ cup chicken or
    vegetarian chicken broth

SEASONING SAUCE

1½ tablespoons soy sauce

1 tablespoon dry sherry

2 teaspoons cornstarch

1 tablespoon oyster sauce

Chop Suey

While chop suey is looked down on as a prostitution of refined Cantonese cooking, author Ken Hom separates the fiction of how it was created during the California Gold Rush from fact. In a poor rural area of China, *tsap sui* is a dish that uses up scraps of food. In his book, *Easy Family Recipes from a Chinese-American Childhood*, Hom gives recipes for the Chinese and the Chinese-American versions. This is a marriage of Ken Hom's recipe with bean curd. Serve with cooked long-grain rice.

1. Cut each piece of tofu crosswise into ¼-inch slices. Stack 3 to 4 slices and cut them crosswise, making thin strips about 1-inch long.

2. To make the marinade, combine the soy sauce, sherry, salt, pepper, sesame oil, and cornstarch in a bowl. Add the tofu strips to the marinade. With a fork, mix gently to coat the tofu with the marinade. Set aside to marinate for 20 minutes.

3. To make the seasoning sauce, combine the soy sauce, sherry, cornstarch, and oyster sauce in a small bowl. Set aside.

4. Place a wok or skillet over high heat. When it is hot, drizzle the peanut oil around so it flows down the sides of the wok. Add the onion and stir-fry for 2 minutes. Add the garlic, bok choy, bean sprouts, celery, and salt. Stir-fry for 2 minutes. Add the tofu with its marinade and stir-fry for 1 minute. Add the broth and cook until the vegetables are tender-crisp, about 2 minutes.

5. Quickly stir the seasoning sauce and drizzle it into the pan while stir-frying. As soon as the sauce thickens, transfer the vegetables to a platter and serve.

PER MAIN-COURSE SERVING: Calories 165 • Soy Protein 7.6 g • Total Protein 10.3 g • Carbohydrates 12.3 g • Fat 8.8 g • Saturated Fat 1.3 g • Cholesterol 0 mg • Fiber 2.1 g • Sodium 1034.1 mg

Broccoli with Black Bean Sauce

Serves 4 as a main course or 6 as part of a multicourse meal

This recipe comes from Sandy Sonnenfelt, chef at the Pasta Shop in Oakland, California. When she showed me how to make the spectacular marinated tofu she bakes and smokes she whipped up this dish as an example of how to use it. We then agreed plain tofu is fine because of all the pungent flavors already in the recipe. This dish is equally good served hot or at room temperature.

8 cups (16 ounces) broccoli florets

¼ cup soy sauce

1 teaspoon sugar

1 teaspoon hot red pepper flakes

2 teaspoons roasted sesame oil

1 tablespoon cornstarch

¼ cup peanut oil

3 tablespoons chopped garlic

1. Bring a large pot of water to a boil. Fill a bowl with cold water and ice cubes. Plunge the broccoli into the boiling water just to blanch it, 1 minute. Immediately transfer it to the bowl of ice water. Drain well and set aside.

2. Mix together the soy sauce, sugar, red pepper flakes, sesame oil, and ⅓ cup water in a small bowl. Set aside.

3. Dissolve the cornstarch in 2 tablespoons cold water in a separate bowl and set aside, leaving the spoon in the bowl.

Preserved Black Beans

Also called dried black beans and salted beans, these are small soybeans that have been fermented, then dried and salted. Some brands include ginger or dried orange peel. Typically they are used with seafood, meat, and poultry but they also go well with sturdy vegetables, such as asparagus and broccoli. Classically, black beans are combined with garlic and either ginger or chiles. Some cooks rinse them, others do not. I put them in a strainer and run cold water over them for a few seconds. Stored in a jar and refrigerated, these beans will keep indefinitely. The best brand is Yang Jiang, but Mee Chun and Koon Chun are also good.

3 tablespoons chopped
    peeled fresh ginger

4 tablespoons preserved
    black beans

16 ounces firm or extra
    firm tofu, pressed
    (see page 49) and cut
    into 1-inch cubes

4. Heat the peanut oil in a wok or skillet over high heat. Add the garlic and ginger, and stir-fry until they are fragrant, about 30 seconds. Add the fermented black beans and cook for 5 seconds. Add the tofu and soy sauce mixture and cook for 2 minutes. Restir the cornstarch mixture and add it to the wok. Cook until the sauce starts to thicken, about 1 minute. Add the broccoli and stir-fry just until it is coated with the sauce. Serve immediately.

PER MAIN-COURSE SERVING: Calories 324 • Soy Protein 12.8 g • Total Protein 18.7 g • Carbohydrates 14.4 g • Fat 23.7 g • Saturated Fat 3.7 g • Cholesterol 0 mg • Fiber 4.1 g • Sodium 964.7 mg

Kung Pao Edamame Rice Bowl

The only relation this dish has to authentic Chinese kung pao dishes is the hot pepper and sesame oil used liberally in Sichuan cooking. I invented this colorful stir-fry one night, using fresh orange juice and zest left over from another recipe. To complete a light supper, this stir-fry is served over cooked rice. A mug of Ginger Consommé with Silken Tofu (page 126) makes a nice accompaniment.

1. To make the sauce, combine the orange juice, soy sauce, cornstarch, zest, sugar, salt, red pepper flakes, and black pepper in a small bowl. Stir in the sesame oil and set aside.

2. In a wok or large skillet, heat the peanut oil over high heat. Add the onion, bell pepper, carrots, garlic, and ginger and stir-fry for 2 minutes. Add the edamame and corn and stir-fry for 3 minutes; the vegetables will be tender-crisp.

3. Stir the seasoning sauce and pour it into the pan. Stir-fry until it thickens, about 1 minute.

4. Serve at once over rice.

PER SERVING: Calories 512 • Soy Protein 16.6 g • Total Protein 21.1 g • Carbohydrates 79.3 g • Fat 13.0 g • Saturated Fat 1.7 g • Cholesterol 0 mg • Fiber 8.4 g • Sodium 587.0 mg

SEASONING SAUCE

3 tablespoons orange juice

1 teaspoon soy sauce

1 tablespoon cornstarch

2 teaspoons grated orange zest

1 teaspoon sugar

1 teaspoon salt

⅛ to ¼ teaspoon hot red pepper flakes

¼ teaspoon freshly ground black pepper

½ teaspoon roasted sesame oil

1 tablespoon peanut oil

1 medium red onion, cut into 1-inch pieces

1 small red bell pepper, seeded and cut into 1-inch pieces

8 baby carrots, halved crosswise

1 to 2 large garlic cloves, minced

1 inch fresh ginger, minced

2 cups frozen shelled edamame, defrosted

1 cup canned corn (about 8 baby corn ears)

4 cups hot cooked jasmine rice

Serves 4 as a main course or 6 as part of a multicourse meal

½ teaspoon baking soda

1 sheet dried bean curd

16 ounces Shanghai bok choy (see Note)

1 teaspoon cornstarch

1 tablespoon vegetable oil

1 garlic clove, minced

1 cup rich chicken broth or 1 teaspoon powdered vegetable broth dissolved in 1 cup warm water

Bok Choy with Soft Soy Sheets

This vegetarian dish, which I first tried at Evergreen, a Shanghai restaurant in New York City's Chinatown, sounds unusual, but people fall in love with it. Bean curd sheets are made by heating soymilk over hot water until it forms a skin, which is removed and dried in large sheets, then folded. They are sold at Asian groceries. Use either the hard, dry kind or the supple sheets sold in the refrigerator case.

1. Bring a large pot of water to a boil. Fill one bowl with cold water and ice cubes. Fill a second bowl with 6 cups water and add the baking soda.

2. Tear the hard edge off the bean curd sheet. Tear it into pieces 4 to 6 inches long. Soak them in the water with the baking soda for 5 minutes.

3. Meanwhile, cut the bok choy vertically into quarters, trying to keep the stems attached.

4. Plunge the bok choy into the boiling water just to blanch it, 1 minute. Immediately transfer it to the bowl of ice water. When it is completely cool, drain well.

5. Drain the bean curd sheets in a colander. Rinse under cold running water for 1 minute. Drain well and set aside.

6. Dissolve the cornstarch in 2 teaspoons of cold water. Set aside.

7. Set a wok or heavy skillet over high heat. Drizzle the oil into the hot wok. Add the bok choy and the garlic. Stir-fry for 1 minute. Add the bean curd sheets and the broth. Cook until the bok choy is tender-crisp, about 2 minutes. Restir the cornstarch mixture and add it to the wok. Cook just until the liquid has some body. It will not thicken.

8. Immediately turn the contents of the wok into a shallow serving bowl and serve.

NOTE: The leaves of Shanghai bok choy are spoon-shaped. The leaves and stems are both the same light green. It is often harvested as a baby plant of 6 inches or less.

PER MAIN-COURSE SERVING: Calories 79 • Soy Protein 2.5 g • Total Protein 3.7 g • Carbohydrates 3.5 g • Fat 5.3 g • Saturated Fat 0.3 g • Cholesterol 0.2 mg • Fiber 2.7 g • Sodium 246.2 mg

*Serves 4 as a main
course or 6 as part of a
multicourse meal*

Edamame with Bean Curd Noodles and Preserved Vegetable

PRESERVED
VEGETABLE

8 ounces bamboo mustard
   cabbage (also known as
   gai choy), or mustard
   greens
1½ teaspoons kosher salt

3 fresh bean curd sheets
   (see Note)
1 cup shelled frozen
   edamame, defrosted
1 teaspoon cornstarch
1 tablespoon peanut oil
1 teaspoon sugar
½ teaspoon salt, optional
⅓ cup rich chicken or
   vegetarian chicken
   broth

This Shanghai dish is a vibrant combination of pungent, salt-pickled greens, sweet edamame, and flat soy "noodles." This so-called pasta is actually a supple form of tofu in thin, ivory sheets. In China, this dish is made only when fresh soybeans are in season. Here, thanks to frozen edamame, you can enjoy it anytime you like.

1. To make the preserved vegetable, cut the greens and stems crosswise into ¼-inch strips and place them in a large bowl. Sprinkle with the salt. With your hands, toss to distribute the salt throughout the greens. Cover the bowl with a plate and set it aside in a cool place or in the refrigerator for 12 to 24 hours. Transfer the preserved vegetable to a container and cover tightly. The pickled greens will keep for up to 4 days, refrigerated. Rinse and drain well before using.

2. Stack the bean curd sheets. Place them with the narrow side facing you. Roll up the sheets, making a tube. Cut this tube crosswise into ½-inch strips. With a sharp knife, cut through one side of the rolled "noodles." Unroll, and place the strips in a medium bowl. Cover with cold water. Soak until the strips are ivory-colored and supple, 3 hours to overnight. (Refrigerate if they will soak for more than 4 hours.) These soaked noodles will keep for up to 3 days, stored in cold water, and refrigerated.

3. When you are ready to complete the dish, bring a large pot of water to a boil. Drain the noodles and add them to the boiling water, along with the edamame. Cook until just heated through, 3 to 5 minutes. Drain and set aside.

4. Dissolve the cornstarch in 1 tablespoon cold water and set it aside, leaving the spoon in the bowl.

5. Meanwhile, place a wok over high heat. When it is hot, drizzle the oil around so it flows down the sides of the wok. Add 1½ cups preserved vegetable and stir-fry until the greens soften but are still bright green, 2 minutes.

6. Drain the beans and noodles and add them to the wok. While stir-frying, add the sugar, and salt, if using. Add the broth and cook, tossing the ingredients in the wok to separate the noodles and evenly distribute them. Restir the cornstarch mixture and add it to the wok. Stir-fry until the juices in the pan thicken slightly, 30 seconds.

7. Transfer the dish to a serving platter. Serve hot or lukewarm.

NOTE: Use fresh bean curd sheets, not the brittle ones sold dried, or the kind sold frozen. These can be difficult to find. Start by asking at a local Shanghai restaurant, where you may find this dish on the menu.

PER MAIN-COURSE SERVING: Calories 222 • Soy Protein 16.0 g • Total Protein 16.8 g • Carbohydrates 10.5 g • Fat 12.7 g • Saturated Fat 0.8 g • Cholesterol 0.3 mg • Fiber 4.2 g • Sodium 377.1 mg

Ginger Fried Rice

3 tablespoons chicken or
   vegetarian chicken
   broth

2 tablespoons soy sauce

½ teaspoon sugar

½ teaspoon roasted
   sesame oil

3 tablespoons peanut oil

4 ounces soft tofu,
   chopped into ½-inch
   pieces

1 garlic clove, finely
   chopped

2 tablespoons finely
   chopped fresh ginger

½ small red bell pepper,
   chopped

½ cup chopped red onion

3 scallions (white and
   green parts), cut into
   ½-inch pieces

5 cups chilled or frozen
   cooked rice

2 cups mung bean sprouts

Salt and freshly ground
   black pepper

This recipe shows how Chinese prefer fried rice, using more rice and less "stuff." In place of pork, I use chopped bean curd fried in peanut oil until it is golden. Using chilled cooked rice is essential. Rice that is warm becomes gummy and sticks to the pan, making a mess. Add green peas and a scrambled egg, even shrimp, if you like.

1. To make the seasoning sauce, combine the broth, soy sauce, sugar, and sesame oil in a small bowl and set aside.

2. Place a wok over high heat. When it is hot, drizzle 1 table-spoon of the peanut oil around so it flows down the sides of the wok. Add the tofu and stir-fry until golden. With a slotted spoon, quickly transfer the tofu to a paper towel and drain.

3. Add the remaining 2 tablespoons oil to the wok. When it is almost smoking, add the garlic, ginger, red pepper, and onion and stir-fry for 1 minute. Add the scallions and stir-fry for 30 seconds. Add the rice, fried tofu, and bean sprouts. Stir the seasoning sauce and add it to the wok. Stir-fry until the ingredients are evenly combined and the fried rice is hot all the way through. Season to taste with salt and pepper.

4. Transfer the rice to a serving bowl. Serve hot or warm.

PER SERVING: Calories 118 • Soy Protein 2.3 g • Total Protein 3.8 g • Carbohydrates 11.6 g • Fat 6.7 g • Saturated Fat 4.2 g • Cholesterol 0 mg • Fiber 2.4 g • Sodium 82.0 mg

Burmese Curry

Serves 4 as a main course or 6 as part of a multicourse meal

Once called Burma, Myanmar is a diamond-shaped country bordered by China, India, Thailand, and the Indian Ocean. China's influence shows in the use of soyfoods, particularly tofu. The turmeric, cardamom, and ginger in this curry reflect Indian cooking. Like the Thais, the Burmese appreciate dishes that are hot and sharp. The fish sauce they use adds savory, smooth flavor though it smells nasty during cooking. If you wish, you can reduce the amount of red pepper in this golden curry. Serve it with lots of jasmine rice, to soak up its delicious sauce.

16 ounces firm tofu, cut into 2 slabs and pressed (see page 49)

1 teaspoon salt

½ teaspoon turmeric

1 inch fresh ginger, chopped

½ teaspoon hot red pepper flakes

2 large Spanish onions, thinly sliced vertically (about 5 cups)

3 tablespoons chopped garlic

¼ cup peanut or vegetable oil

1. Rub the tofu with the salt and turmeric and set it on a plate. Cover with plastic wrap and refrigerate for 1 hour.

2. Combine the ginger, red pepper flakes, 2 cups of the onions, and half the garlic in a food processor. Pulse the mixture until it is a coarse paste. Spread half this paste over the bottom of a baking dish or plate. Halve the pieces of tofu crosswise, making 4 "fillets." Set them on top of the onion

Fish Sauce

Fish sauce is a ubiquitous seasoning in Southeast Asian cooking, where it is used like the Chinese use soy sauce. This golden to dark brown liquid is drawn off from anchovies or other small fish that have been heavily salted and layered to ferment in barrels or jars. It is inexpensive and keeps forever. Every country in Southeast Asia makes its own brands. Many cooks recommend Three Crabs brand from Vietnam, but I prefer Thai Kitchen, Squid, or Tiparos, all from Thailand. Read the label, as MSG and other additives are showing up in some brands. To Thais, fish sauce is so integral to the taste of dishes that even vegetarians use it, according to cookbook author Nancie McDermott, who has lived in Thailand.

1 tablespoon fish sauce
  (see page 267)

2 inches lemongrass, very
  thinly sliced
  (see page 270)

Juice of 1 lime

3 medium tomatoes,
  peeled, seeded, and
  diced

½ teaspoon ground
  cardamom

paste. Coat the tofu fillets with the remaining paste; they should be thickly blanketed. Set aside.

3. Heat the oil in a heavy skillet over medium-high heat. Add the remaining 3 cups onions and garlic. Sauté until the onions are very soft and golden, about 15 minutes, reducing the heat, if necessary, so they do not brown. Add the coated tofu, scraping all the paste from the plate into the pan. Cover the pot, reduce the heat to medium-low, and simmer until the onions are brown, about 20 minutes.

4. Add the fish sauce, lemongrass, lime juice, tomatoes, cardamom, and ½ cup water. Cover and simmer until the tofu is swimming in an aromatic sauce, 10 to 15 minutes.

5. Serve hot.

PER MAIN-COURSE SERVING: Calories 293 • Soy Protein 11.3 g • Total Protein 14.0 g • Carbohydrates 19.0 g • Fat 19.2 g • Saturated Fat 3.0 g • Cholesterol 0 mg • Fiber 2.6 g • Sodium 846.0 mg

Laotian Lemon "Pork" with Green Beans

Serves 4 as a main course or 6 as part of a multicourse meal

This creamy dish is a perfect introduction to the seductive flavors of Southeast Asian cooking. It has the interweaving of sweet coconut, salty and pungent fish sauce, fried shallots, and tart citrus that is typical of the region. This dish is easy enough to make on a weeknight. Preparing it does not require a wok, and its most Asian ingredients, the fish sauce and coconut milk, are easily kept on hand in the pantry. If you can, use long beans as their firmness makes this dish more authentic, but green beans are fine. As with most Asian dishes, this one is best served with a fragrant white rice, such as jasmine.

1. Fill a bowl with ice water. Cook the beans in boiling water until they are tender-crisp, 3 to 4 minutes. Drain them and immediately plunge the beans into the bowl of cold water so they remain crisp and bright green. Drain and set the beans aside.

2. Heat the oil in a heavy skillet over medium-high heat and fry the shallots until they are golden brown and crisp, 2 to 3 minutes. Scoop the shallots from pan, using a slotted spoon, and drain them on paper towels. Do not empty the oil from the pan. (Steps 1 and 2 can be done several hours ahead, and the beans refrigerated. Let them come to room temperature before completing the dish.)

3. Stir-fry the soymeat slices in the oil remaining in the pan, until they brown in places and start to crisp, 3 to 4 minutes. While stir-frying, add the fish sauce, shallots, and coconut milk. Then add the lemon zest, lemon juice, and scallions. Reduce the heat and simmer for 2 minutes, until the scallions are wilted.

8 ounces long beans or green beans, cut into 3-inch pieces

3 tablespoons vegetable oil

1 cup thinly sliced shallots

7 ounces frozen soymeat fillet (one package), defrosted, and cut crosswise into ¼-inch slices

1 tablespoon fish sauce (see page 267)

1 cup coconut milk

1 teaspoon grated lemon zest

2 tablespoons fresh lemon juice

3 scallions (white and green parts), cut into 1-inch pieces

Cilantro sprigs

4. Arrange the soymeat on a serving platter and spoon the sauce over. Arrange the cooked green beans around the soymeat. Garnish with sprigs of cilantro and serve.

PER MAIN-COURSE SERVING: Calories 377 • Soy Protein 7.4 g • Total Protein 16.2 g • Carbohydrates 25.4 g • Fat 23.7 g • Saturated Fat 9.3 g • Cholesterol 2.6 mg • Fiber 7.6 g • Sodium 438.3 mg

Lemongrass

Tall, slender stalks of lemongrass provide the floral citrus flavor in many Southeast Asian curries, soups, and salads. Western chefs also infuse sweet syrups, custards, and sauces with this aromatic seasoning.

Fresh lemongrass is sold at Asian markets and, increasingly, at supermarkets. To use it, cut off the dry, grasslike top, leaving the 3- to 4-inch-long, ivory bottom. Peel away and discard the 2 to 3 tough outer layers. Cut each stalk lengthwise in quarters. Stack these pieces and cut them crosswise in fine slices, or chop them, according to the recipe.

Dried lemongrass is virtually tasteless. If fresh lemongrass is not available, use a combination of fresh lemon and lime zest in its place.

Thai Green Curry with Eggplant and Fried Tofu

Serves 4 as a main course or 6 as part of a multicourse meal

This curry offers a wonderfully complex and aromatic blend of sweet, pungent, and hot flavors. In Thailand, cooks often buy curry paste at a local market. When pressed for time, I do the same, using Thai Kitchen's Green Curry Paste, sold at the supermarket.

1. Heat the coconut cream in a medium heavy-bottomed skillet over medium-high heat. Simmer gently until oil glistens on the surface of the cream. Stir in the curry paste and cook until the paste is aromatic, 1 to 2 minutes.

2. Add the coconut milk, fried tofu, eggplant, bamboo shoots, and pea eggplants, if using. Stir in the fish sauce, sugar, ½ cup of the basil, 6 lime leaves, and salt. Boil gently, stirring occasionally, until the eggplant is tender but still holds its shape, 8 to 10 minutes. Taste and adjust the seasonings as needed.

3. Transfer the curry to a serving bowl. Garnish with the remaining ¼ cup basil and 2 lime leaves and the chiles. Serve hot or warm.

PER MAIN-COURSE SERVING: Calories 713 • Soy Protein 19.5 g • Total Protein 25.6 g • Carbohydrates 31.3 g • Fat 57.0 g • Saturated Fat 30.4 g • Cholesterol 0 mg • Fiber 11.1 g • Sodium 1735.0 mg

½ cup coconut cream (see page 273)

½ cup Thai Green Curry Paste (recipe follows)

3 cups coconut milk

16 ounces firm tofu, deep fried (see page 55)

8 Thai green eggplants, quartered lengthwise (about 2 cups)

1 cup sliced fresh bamboo shoots

¼ cup pea eggplants, optional

2 tablespoons fish sauce (see page 267)

1 tablespoon palm or brown sugar

¾ cup Thai basil leaves

8 kaffir lime leaves

1 teaspoon salt

3 Thai red chile peppers, thinly sliced on the diagonal

1½ teaspoons whole
   coriander seeds

1 teaspoon whole cumin
   seeds

3 black peppercorns

1½ stalks fresh
   lemongrass,
   thinly sliced
   (see page 270)

2 cups coarsely chopped
   cilantro leaves and
   stems

1 tablespoon coarsely
   chopped fresh
   galangal or ginger

2 garlic cloves, chopped

2 large shallots, chopped

3 to 6 Thai green or
   serrano chiles,
   stemmed and chopped

Zest from ½ lime or kaffir
   lime, chopped

½ teaspoon salt

½ teaspoon shrimp paste
   (see Note)

1 to 2 tablespoons
   peanut oil

Thai Green Curry Paste

The sweetness in this verdant seasoning comes from the coconut milk. Green curries are served for feasts and celebrations. Even with the shrimp paste, Thais use this paste for making vegetarian curries. Try this paste blended with coconut milk to accompany grilled tuna, chicken, or tofu.

1. In a small, dry skillet over medium-high heat, dry-roast the coriander and cumin seeds until they are fragrant and slightly darker in color, 3 to 5 minutes. Transfer the spices to a small bowl and cool to room temperature. Using a mortar, spice grinder, or clean coffee mill, grind the roasted spices and peppercorns, to a fine powder. Set aside.

2. Combine the lemongrass, cilantro, galangal, garlic, shallots, chiles, lime zest, and salt in a food processor and whirl until they are finely chopped. Add the shrimp paste and process the ingredients to a paste, scraping down the sides of the bowl two or three times. Add the oil and process until it is blended in. The final texture should be fairly smooth. The curry paste will keep for up to 5 days, tightly covered in a glass jar, and refrigerated.

NOTE: Vegans can omit this ingredient or substitute soy sauce.

PER TABLESPOON: Calories 11 • Soy Protein 0 g • Total Protein 0.5 g • Carbohydrates 2.0 g •
Fat 0.2 g • Saturated Fat 0 g • Cholesterol 0.7 mg • Fiber 0.5 g • Sodium 65.3 mg

Coconut Cream and Coconut Milk

For coconut cream, open a can of coconut milk without shaking it and spoon off the thick layer at the top. What remains in the can is coconut milk. If you make your own coconut milk from scratch, the cream rises to the top when you refrigerate it. I use Thai Kitchen's canned coconut milk, sold in natural food stores, because it is made without sulfites.

seafood

Asians often combine tofu and miso with nonvegetarian ingredients, for aesthetic as well as practical reasons. Delicate bean curd complements the sweetness of fresh crabmeat while helping this luxurious seafood go further.

Chefs from Australia to New York are using miso to deepen the flavor of marinades and sauces used with fish. When cooking with miso, they sometimes employ non-Asian techniques, such as boiling it. While this inactivates miso's enzymes, it also concentrates its complex flavors. Edamame have also caught the attention of chefs, as an enticing ingredient to combine with salmon and other fish.

Miso-Poached Salmon with Spinach

Serves 4

Miso takes the place of wine in flavoring the poaching liquid for the salmon. It is then reduced to a smooth sauce. A ring of spinach adds color to the plate. This recipe does take some time to prepare. The result is well worth it.

1. Toast the sesame seeds in a dry skillet over medium-high heat until they make a popping noise and smell fragrant, about 4 minutes. Set aside.

2. To make the court bouillon, combine the sake and miso in a nonstick skillet, using a fork to cream the miso into the liquid. Add the sugar, soy sauce, and vinegar. Bring the court bouillon barely to a simmer.

3. Add the salmon to the skillet, skin side up. Poach for 3 minutes, turn, and cook the salmon for 2 minutes more. Transfer the fish to a plate and cover to keep warm.

4. Increase the heat under the miso liquid and boil until it is reduced to the consistency of a creamy gravy, about 10 minutes. Set aside.

5. Heat 1 tablespoon of the canola oil in a large nonstick skillet. Add the spinach, turning it in the oil until it is wilted. Stir in the soy sauce and sesame oil.

6. Heat the remaining tablespoon of canola oil and the butter in a medium skillet. Add the salmon, skin side up, and cook until the fish is crisp and well-browned. Turn and continue cooking until the salmon has the desired degree of doneness.

7. Arrange the spinach in a ring on four warm dinner plates. Place a piece of salmon in the center of each spinach ring. Reheat the miso sauce and spoon around the spinach. Sprinkle some sesame seeds over the vegetable ring and serve.

1 tablespoon sesame seeds

One 1½-pound salmon fillet, with the skin, cut in 4 pieces

2 tablespoons canola oil

2 pounds fresh spinach, stemmed

2 teaspoons soy sauce

¼ teaspoon roasted sesame oil

1 tablespoon unsalted butter

MISO COURT BOUILLON

½ cup sake

¼ cup mellow white or sweet white miso

1 tablespoon sugar

2 tablespoons soy sauce

2 tablespoons rice vinegar

PER SERVING: Calories 453 • Soy Protein 2.1 g • Total Protein 44.2 g • Carbohydrates 29.8 g • Fat 21.6 g • Saturated Fat 3.3 g • Cholesterol 98.6 mg • Fiber 20.4 g • Sodium 1576.1 mg

Roasted Salmon with Edamame Sauce

Four 6-ounce salmon fillets

¼ cup sweet white or mellow white miso

1 teaspoon grapeseed or canola oil

2 teaspoons roasted sesame oil

4 cups sliced baby bok choy (cut crosswise into ⅜-inch slices)

Salt and freshly ground black pepper

EDAMAME SAUCE

3 large garlic cloves

⅓ cup plus 2 tablespoons shelled frozen edamame

1 tablespoon silken tofu, at room temperature

1 teaspoon mushroom soy sauce or tamari

Salt and freshly ground black pepper

At Heartbeat, the restaurant in New York City's Hotel W Midtown, executive chef Michel Nischan ministers to both body and soul with elegantly satisfying food. Here he uses three traditional soy foods—edamame, miso, and a touch of tofu—in one dish. Dredging the fish in miso is a Japanese technique. Turning edamame into a sauce, accented with the muted flavor of blanched garlic and velveted (see page 257) with tofu, fuses East and West. Like many chef's recipes, this one has multiple steps. All of them are simple, from boiling the garlic to stir-frying the bok choy that accompanies this dish.

1. Coat the salmon on both sides with the miso, using a tablespoon for each piece of fish. Set them on a plate, cover with plastic wrap, and refrigerate for 1 hour.

2. Preheat the oven to 350°F.

3. To make the sauce, combine the garlic in a small saucepan with 1 cup cold water and bring to a boil for 1 minute over medium-high heat. Drain the garlic and repeat this two more times, boiling the garlic for 3 minutes in all. It will have the texture of a boiled onion. Coarsely chop the garlic.

4. Boil the edamame until they are soft, 5 to 6 minutes. When the beans are cool enough to handle, squeeze to pop each one out of the thin skin covering the bean. Place ⅓ cup of the peeled beans in a blender. Reserve the remaining beans for a garnish.

5. Combine the blanched garlic, tofu, soy sauce, and 3 tablespoons warm water in a blender. Puree, adding more water if needed, a tablespoon at a time, to make a sauce that is smooth and spoonable. Season to taste with salt and pepper and set aside.

6. Heat a cast-iron skillet large enough to hold the salmon fillets in one layer over medium-high heat. Coat the pan with the grapeseed oil. Add the miso-coated salmon, skin side up. Cook until it is browned and has a crisp crust, 2 to 3 minutes. Turn the fish, using a pancake turner. Transfer the pan to the oven. Roast the salmon until it is pink and still translucent in the very center, 3 to 5 minutes, depending on the thickness of the fillets. (They will continue cooking after being removed from the oven.) Transfer the fish to a plate and let it sit for 5 minutes.

7. Heat 2 teaspoons of the sesame oil in a nonstick skillet over medium-high heat. Add the bok choy and sauté until it is tender-crisp, about 3 minutes. Season it to taste with salt and pepper.

8. Arrange 1 cup of the bok choy to make a bed in the center of each of four warm dinner plates. Top each with a piece of the salmon. Drizzle the edamame sauce generously on each plate around the dish. Garnish with a few of the cooked beans, sprinkled around the plate.

PER SERVING: Calories 371 • Soy Protein 6.4 g • Total Protein 40.8 g • Carbohydrates 9.9 g • Fat 17.1 g • Saturated Fat 2.4 g • Cholesterol 93.6 mg • Fiber 1.7 g • Sodium 634.2 mg

Tuna Spring Rolls with Edamame Coulis

COULIS

1 small bunch cilantro, with
    stems, about 3 cups

2 cups shelled frozen
    edamame

1 large garlic clove, halved

1 red Thai chile pepper or
    ¼ teaspoon hot red
    pepper flakes

1½ teaspoons Thai or
    Vietnamese fish sauce

1½ teaspoons salt

1½ teaspoons grapeseed
    oil or olive oil

SPRING ROLLS

4 large savoy cabbage
    leaves, from the outside
    of the head

12 ounces sushi tuna,
    preferably yellowfin, cut
    into four 4 × 1-inch
    fingers

3 tablespoons thinly sliced
    sushi ginger

4 spring roll wrappers

1 teaspoon coarsely
    ground black pepper

1 large egg yolk, beaten

1 cup vegetable oil

Salt

Green hot pepper sauce

Soy sauce

Chef Jean-Georges Vongerichten serves this dramatic warm sushi at Jo Jo, his elegant New York City bistro. It calls for savoy cabbage, but only the dark, sturdy outer leaves. Assembling these spring rolls is simple. The steps are described in great detail to assure your success. The most important thing is getting impeccably fresh sushi-grade tuna. Use any of the bright green edamame coulis that is left over to accompany salmon and any other seafood.

1. To make the coulis, plunge the cilantro in boiling water just to wilt it, 30 seconds. Transfer it with a slotted spoon to a bowl of ice water. When the cilantro is chilled, drain it and set aside.

2. Add the edamame to the boiling water. Cook just until the beans are defrosted, 1 to 2 minutes; then chill in the ice water. Drain well.

3. Place the cilantro in a blender. Add ½ cup cold water, the garlic, and the chile pepper. Blend to a dark green, pulpy puree. Add 1½ cups of the edamame to the blender, along with the fish sauce and salt. Blend to a velvety, bright green puree. With the motor running, blend in the oil. If necessary, add more water, 2 tablespoons at a time, to get a thick puree that easily plops from a spoon. It should be salty.

4. To make the spring rolls, plunge the cabbage leaves into boiling water until they are supple, about 1 minute. Quickly transfer them to ice water. Drain the leaves well. Trim each leaf into a square large enough to roll the tuna in, about 4 inches square, cutting away the tougher bottom part and rounded sides. Blot each square very well with paper towels.

5. Place a piece of tuna horizontally across one of the cabbage squares, just above the center. Place a spring roll wrap-

per on a work surface, to one side of the cabbage, with one point facing you. Blot the ginger dry on a paper towel. Arrange a quarter of the slices to cover the top of the tuna. Sprinkle ¼ teaspoon of the pepper over the ginger. Wrap the tuna in the cabbage, bringing up the bottom and folding it tightly over the ginger. Pulling toward you, roll the tuna away from you, so the edges of the cabbage just meet.

6. Place the wrapped tuna horizontally just below the widest point on the spring roll wrapper. Bring up the bottom point over the cabbage. Fold in the two sides of the wrapper. Roll just until the wrapper covers the cabbage. Brush the upper triangle of the wrapper above the sushi roll with egg yolk. Pulling toward you, tightly roll up the spring roll. Press to seal the wrapper. Repeat steps 5 and 6, making four rolls.

7. Pour the oil into a small skillet. Heat the oil to 375°F over medium-high heat. Fry the spring rolls, one at a time, just until the wrapper is crisp and lightly colored, turning them once—1 minute on the first side, and 30 seconds on the other. Drain the fried rolls on a paper towel.

8. To serve, cut the ends off each spring roll using a sharp knife. Cut each roll crosswise into 4 pieces. Most likely, the wrapper will shatter somewhat as you cut it. The fish should be raw except for a thin beige ring around the very edge. Stand the pieces in a row just below the center of a white dinner plate. Sprinkle each with a pinch of salt. For decoration, squirt a squiggle of the hot green pepper sauce from a plastic bottle in a line horizontally across the plate, or drizzle it from a spoon, then zigzag a line of soy sauce over the hot sauce. Place 2 tablespoons of the edamame coulis at the top of the plate, and sprinkle about 6 of the reserved beans randomly around it. Dip the tuna roll in the edamame coulis as you eat it.

PER SERVING, WITH SAUCE: Calories 379 • Soy Protein 16.6 g • Total Protein 38.6 g • Carbohydrates 23.7 g • Fat 15.5 g • Saturated Fat 2.2 g • Cholesterol 64.4 mg • Fiber 7.5 g • Sodium 1236.5 mg

Crab Cakes

15 shelled edamame
    beans, frozen or fresh

1 egg white

4 ounces soft tofu,
    squeezed
    (see page 48)

1 teaspoon grapeseed or
    vegetable oil

⅓ cup cornstarch

1 teaspoon soy sauce

½ teaspoon salt

⅛ teaspoon freshly ground
    black pepper

½ pound jumbo lump
    crabmeat, picked over
    to remove cartilage

2 cups vegetable oil

1 recipe Tadashi's Dipping
    Sauce (recipe follows)

Crab cakes are one of life's simple pleasures, particularly the way Tadashi Ono, chef at Sono restaurant in New York City makes them. A genius at combining Eastern and Western ingredients and techniques, he binds these crab cakes with egg white and tofu, which cuts out a lot of fat and showcases the sweet chunks of crab. He also sheds these ethereally light cakes with edamame. While top-quality crabmeat is costly, a half-pound is all you need to serve four people as a starter. For a main course, you could form four conventionally shaped crab cakes, instead of these elegant ovals.

1. Boil the edamame in salted water until tender, 2 to 3 minutes. Drain and rinse in a strainer under cold water until the beans are cool, about 2 minutes. Drain and set aside.

2. Combine the egg white, tofu, grapeseed oil, 1 teaspoon of the cornstarch, soy sauce, salt, and pepper in a food processor. Blend until you have a smooth puree, stopping to scrape down the sides of the bowl as needed. Transfer the puree to a bowl.

3. Add the crabmeat and edamame to the bowl. Gently combine them with the puree, using your hands or a rubber spatula, taking care to beak up the lumps as little as possible. Cover with plastic wrap and refrigerate for 1 hour. These crab cakes should be formed and cooked as soon as the mixture is thoroughly chilled; they will be drier and less delicate-tasting if you wait.

4. To form the crab cakes, scoop up about ½ cup of the mixture with a large soupspoon. Holding another soupspoon in your other hand, place it upside down over the crabmeat. To form the cake, scoop the crab onto the second spoon, twisting it with your wrist. Repeat this once or twice, firming and

smoothing the cake into a plump oval, like a French quenelle. Place the crab cakes on a plate as they are formed.

5. Heat the vegetable oil in a skillet to 325°F. Dust the crab cakes lightly with some of the remaining cornstarch. Turn and dust them on the other side.

6. Fry the crab cakes, a few at a time, until they are lightly colored and crisp on the outside, about 3 minutes, turning them once. Drain on paper towels. Serve at once, passing the dipping sauce on the side.

PER SERVING: Calories 208 • Soy Protein 4.3 g • Total Protein 17.3 g • Carbohydrates 12 g • Fat 10.5 g • Saturated Fat 0.7 g • Cholesterol 40 mg • Fiber 0.7 g • Sodium 223.5 mg

Tadashi's Dipping Sauce

Makes ⅓ cup

This dipping sauce is sharp and fresh, just right against the richness of the crab cakes. Use a good-quality soy sauce, such as Pearl River Bridge.

Combine the ingredients in a small bowl. Serve.

2 tablespoons soy sauce

2 tablespoons fresh lemon juice

1 tablespoon grated peeled fresh ginger

PER TABLESPOON: Calories 6 • Soy Protein 0.3 g • Total Protein 0.4 g • Carbohydrates 0 g • Fat 0 g • Saturated Fat 0 g • Cholesterol 0 mg • Fiber 0 g • Sodium 374.3 mg

mainly vegetables

Vegetables paired with soy can be the star of a meal, or enhance it from the side of your plate. In this collection of meatless dishes, Sicilian Stuffed Red Peppers (page 283) make delicious use of tempeh in place of prosciutto, the fluffiest mashed potatoes are made with soymilk, and soy coffee creamer produces blissfully rich, creamy spinach (page 290). Edamame and black soybeans stand on their own and meld into colorful ensembles like Brunswick-style Sweet Soybeans (page 288) and kale braised with tomatoes (page 285), while smoked tofu is an appealing surprise in Rösti (page 292), the Swiss potato pancake.

Stuffed Red Peppers

Serves 4

To reach author Mary Simeti's farm in Sicily, you must negotiate a dirt track up a steep hill. The rutted road, almost indistinguishable from the land on either side of it, makes it easy to end up in someone's field along the way. When I arrived, Mary apologized for having thrown together lunch using what was at hand, then served this delicious improvisation to which I have added tempeh. Serve with Mediterranean Lentil Soup (page 130).

2 large red bell peppers, halved lengthwise and seeded

2 tablespoons extra virgin olive oil

1 small onion, finely chopped

1 small green Cubanelle frying pepper, seeded and chopped

1 small garlic clove, minced

1 cup Crisped Tempeh (see page 181)

1½ cups cubed fresh semolina bread (1-inch pieces)

1 ounce caciocavallo cheese or provolone, cut into ¼-inch cubes

Salt and freshly ground black pepper

1. Preheat the oven to 375°F.

2. Place the pepper halves on a baking sheet, cut side up. Cut a thin slice off the underside, if necessary, to help the pepper halves sit flat.

3. Heat 1 tablespoon of the oil in a skillet over medium-high heat. Add the onion, pepper, and garlic and sauté until the onion is soft, about 3 minutes. Mix in the tempeh and remove the pan from the heat.

4. Whirl the bread in a food processor to make medium to fine crumbs.

5. Add the bread crumbs and cheese to the tempeh mixture, mixing until they are evenly combined. Season to taste with salt and pepper.

6. Fill the pepper halves with the stuffing mixture, pressing it lightly and making sure it gets into all the crevices. Drizzle the remaining 1 tablespoon of oil over the peppers.

7. Bake the stuffed peppers until the filling is lightly browned, about 15 minutes. Serve warm or at room temperature. (These peppers will keep for up to 3 days, lightly covered with foil and refrigerated. Bring to room temperature before serving.)

PER SERVING: Calories 227 • Soy Protein 5.3 g • Total Protein 10.5 g • Carbohydrates 24.4 g • Fat 10.4 g • Saturated Fat 2.5 g • Cholesterol 4.9 mg • Fiber 3.4 g • Sodium 197.2 mg

1 medium delicata squash
(about 1¼ pounds)

4 teaspoons sweet rice
miso

4 teaspoons tahini

2 teaspoons apple juice

Freshly ground black
pepper

Miso-Glazed Delicata Squash

Gaella and Christian Elwell served these beautiful miso-glazed squash rings when I had dinner with them at South River Farm, where they make artisinal, earthy misos in the most traditional way. Delicata squash look like big, ridged cucumbers striped in cream and dark green or orange.

1. Preheat the oven to 350°F. Lightly coat a baking sheet with nonstick cooking spray or oil and set aside.

2. Trim the ends of the squash. Cut it crosswise into 8 rings, each about 1-inch thick. With a teaspoon, scoop out the seeds and soft flesh in the center of each ring and discard. Arrange the squash on the prepared baking sheet.

3. Cream the miso, tahini, and apple juice in a small bowl, using the back of a spoon, until the mixture is evenly blended and has the thickness of stirred yogurt. Spread about a teaspoon of this miso mixture over the top of each squash ring, and around the edges of the inside opening.

4. Bake the squash until it is tender when pierced with the tip of a knife, about 20 minutes.

5. This squash is good served hot or warm. (It will keep for up to 2 days, tightly covered and refrigerated. Bring to room temperature before serving. Do not reheat, as this will destroy the live enzymes in the miso.)

PER SERVING: Calories 47 • Soy Protein 0.3 g • Total Protein 1.6 g • Carbohydrates 7.1 g • Fat 1.5 g • Saturated Fat 0.2 g • Cholesterol 0 mg • Fiber 1.1 g • Sodium 78.4 mg

Kale with Black Soybeans and Tomatoes

These dark greens, combined with protein-rich beans can be paired with a big baked potato for a complete vegetarian meal. In winter, they add earthy comfort served beside roast chicken or loin of pork. In summer, I add fresh corn kernels, then heap this colorful trio on top of farro or whole wheat pasta. Curly kale is my first choice, but you can also make this dish with long-leafed lacinata kale, which is sometimes called dinosaur kale.

1 medium bunch curly kale

2 tablespoons extra virgin olive oil

3 cloves Roasted Garlic (page 100), peeled and chopped

1 cup canned black soybeans, drained

1 cup canned diced tomatoes with their juice

¼ teaspoon hot red pepper flakes

Salt

1. To stem the kale, run a sharp knife up from the bottom along one side of the hard center stem. Run the knife up the other side until you can easily cut out the stem. Heap the stemmed kale in a colander, and rinse well.

2. Add the kale to a large pot of boiling water. Cook for 5 minutes. Drain well to eliminate most of the moisture clinging to the leaves.

3. Heat the oil in a large skillet over medium-high heat. Add the garlic and mash it using a fork. Add the kale, soybeans, tomatoes, and red pepper flakes, mixing to combine. Add salt to taste and simmer until the kale is tender, about 5 minutes. Cool slightly before serving.

PER SERVING: Calories 160 • Soy Protein 4.5 g • Total Protein 7.5 g • Carbohydrates 14.9 g • Fat 8.3 g • Saturated Fat 1.1 g • Cholesterol 0 mg • Fiber 4.6 g • Sodium 606.3 mg

1 cup short-grain white
  rice

2 teaspoons mirin, sake, or
  dry sherry

1 teaspoon low-sodium
  Japanese soy sauce

¼ teaspoon salt

¾ cup shelled frozen
  edamame

2 tablespoons black
  sesame seeds

Mame Gohan

The Japanese name of this dish translates as "beans and rice." When edamame are in season, during the summer, they are a favorite addition to steamed rice. Elizabeth Andoh supplied a recipe, which I have simplified, using water in place of a broth made by simmering the soybeans in dashi. If you use a rice cooker, add the edamame when it has finished the cooking stage. Mame gohan goes well with Glazed Tofu Steaks (page 236) and with grilled fish.

1. Rinse the rice in cold water in a bowl, changing the water until it runs clear. Drain it very well and place it in a heavy medium saucepan with a tight-fitting lid. Add 2 cups cold water, the mirin, soy sauce, and salt. Cover the pot and place it over high heat.

2. When the cover jiggles and foam begins to appear at the edges, in 3 to 4 minutes, reduce the heat to medium and cook for 10 minutes; the rice will be very moist but almost cooked. Raise the heat to high for 30 seconds. Turn off the heat and quickly add the edamame to the pot; do not stir. Cover the pot and let it stand, off the heat, for 10 minutes.

3. Fluff the rice while mixing the beans into it with a wooden paddle or fork. Scoop the rice into serving bowls.

Top each portion with a teaspoon of the sesame seeds and serve.

PER SERVING: Calories 281 • Soy Protein 6.3 g • Total Protein 10.6 g • Carbohydrates 46.8 g • Fat 6.0 g • Saturated Fat 0.8 g • Cholesterol 0 mg • Fiber 4.1 g • Sodium 172.2 mg

Japanese Rice

The Japanese use plump short-grain white rice because its grains cling together when cooked, making it easy to eat with chopsticks. This rice is used for sushi as well as dishes like mame gohan, for which it is prepared differently. Brands to look for include Kohuko Rose and Cal Rose.

Brunswick-style Sweet Soybeans

1 tablespoon canola oil

1 medium onion, chopped

½ medium green bell pepper, chopped

1 small celery rib, chopped

1 medium tomato, seeded and chopped

¾ cup shelled frozen edamame

¾ cup fresh, frozen, or canned corn kernels

2 tablespoons chopped flat-leaf parsley

½ cup vegetarian chicken broth or vegetable broth

½ teaspoon dried basil

½ teaspoon dried thyme

2 tablespoons soy bacon bits or 2 crumbled cooked soy bacon strips

Anyone with Appalachian roots knows Brunswick stew and is probably surprised to see it in a soy cookbook. Originally made with squirrel, then chicken, this regional American dish dates back to the 1820s. It is rumored that onions were the only vegetable used at first. Over time, other bounty from the late summer and fall harvest was added to the pot. What gives this meatless version authentic flavor is the smoky soy bacon bits. When you are in a hurry, this dish comes together quickly. It will also keep and reheat well. Serve over brown rice or beside roast chicken.

1. Heat the oil in a saucepan over medium-high heat. Add the onion, pepper, and celery and sauté until the onion is translucent, about 5 minutes.

2. Add the tomato, edamame, corn, parsley, broth, basil, and thyme. Simmer for 10 minutes, uncovered.

3. Mix in the soy bacon and serve.

PER SERVING: Calories 161 • Soy Protein 6.2 g • Total Protein 9.7 g • Carbohydrates 17.6 g • Fat 7.2 g • Saturated Fat 0.6 g • Cholesterol 0 mg • Fiber 3.8 g • Sodium 155.2 mg

Spinach and Edamame with Garlic

Firm green soybeans and tender leafy spinach might seem like an odd couple, but they make a delicious marriage, particularly with lots of garlic thrown in. Using frozen edamame and spinach, you can get this pleasantly unexpected dish on the table in less than 15 minutes. Equally good served hot or at room temperature, it is a fine choice for everyday dinners and as a party dish to serve at a buffet. Serve with salmon or halibut, or with a baked potato for a meatless meal.

1 tablespoon olive oil

3 large garlic cloves, thinly sliced

1½ pounds spinach leaves, trimmed of thick stems, or one 10-ounce box frozen chopped spinach, defrosted and squeezed dry

1 cup shelled frozen edamame

⅓ cup vegetarian chicken or vegetable broth

Salt and freshly ground black pepper

1. Combine the olive oil and garlic in a large skillet over medium-high heat and cook, stirring occasionally, until the garlic is soft but not colored, 3 to 4 minutes.

2. Add the spinach, edamame, and broth, and stir until the spinach is wilted. Cover the pan, reduce the heat to medium, and cook until the beans are al dente, about 5 minutes.

3. Season to taste with salt and pepper and serve immediately or at room temperature.

PER SERVING: Calories 168 • Soy Protein 8.3 g • Total Protein 13.4 g • Carbohydrates 14.1 g • Fat 8.5 g • Saturated Fat 1.1 g • Cholesterol 0 mg • Fiber 7.3 g • Sodium 200.1 mg

Serves 4

Two 10-ounce packages
   frozen chopped
   spinach, defrosted and
   squeezed dry
⅔ cup chopped scallions
   (white and green parts)
1¼ cups soy dairy creamer
¼ teaspoon freshly grated
   nutmeg
Salt and freshly ground
   black pepper

Braised Spinach

One of my favorite ways to enjoy spinach is *épinards en branche*. To make it, French cooks simmer the tenderest, just-picked spinach in cream and butter until the leaves and stems almost melt. Checking out what can be done with dairy-free soy creamer, I discovered that even frozen spinach, treated in this classic Gallic way, turns out as rich and soufflé-light, though virtually cholesterol-free. It is not, however, low in fat or calories, so save this soy-assisted showstopper for special occasions.

1. Combine the spinach, scallions, and creamer in a saucepan over medium-high heat. Add the nutmeg. When the liquid boils, reduce the heat and simmer, stirring the spinach occasionally. At first, all the liquid will be absorbed by the spinach. After 3 to 4 minutes, enough liquid re-emerges to keep it cooking. The spinach will swell as it cooks and become fluffy. Cook until the spinach melts in your mouth, about 20 minutes.

2. Season with salt and pepper to taste and serve immediately.

PER SERVING: Calories 434 • Soy Protein 2.5 g • Total Protein 7.2 g • Carbohydrates 53.2 g • Fat 23 g • Saturated Fat 5.6 g • Cholesterol 0.7 mg • Fiber 4.8 g • Sodium 239.5 mg

Champ

I never met a potato dish I did not like. Still, this Irish classic is one of my particular favorites. Yellow-fleshed spuds lend this version creamy richness. Work the potatoes while they are as hot as possible for the lightest results. A garnish of frizzled leeks crisped in oil turns this quick comfort food into a fine company dish.

1. Place the potatoes in a pot. Cover them with cold water by 2 inches. Place the pot over high heat and bring the water to a boil. Reduce the heat and cook until a thin knife pierces the potatoes easily, about 20 minutes. Drain the potatoes. Let them sit until they are just cool enough to handle, then peel them.

2. Mash the potatoes in a bowl, using a fork. When they are as smooth as you like (I *like* lumpy potatoes), work in the butter and scallions. Season the potatoes to taste with salt and pepper. Serve immediately.

1¼ pounds yellow-fleshed potatoes

¾ cup unsweetened soymilk

1 tablespoon unsalted butter or margarine

½ cup chopped scallions (white and green parts)

Salt and freshly ground black pepper

PER SERVING: Calories 163 • Soy Protein 1.3 g • Total Protein 3.7 g • Carbohydrates 27.0 g • Fat 3.9 g • Saturated Fat 1.8 g • Cholesterol 7.8 mg • Fiber 2.6 g • Sodium 61.3 mg

1 pound baking potatoes

4 ounces smoked or
   baked tofu

1 teaspoon salt

¼ teaspoon freshly ground
   black pepper

2 tablespoons unsalted
   butter or margarine

1 tablespoon canola oil

1 medium onion, finely
   chopped

Rösti

Someday, I hope to discover who created this irresistible version of the classic Swiss potato pancake by adding smoked tofu. The recipe for it simply arrived one day, in a fax written in German, thanks to my friend Martha Casselman. She sent it to me because she saw the word tofu in it. Then Judith Prince, whose family runs a chef's equipment business in New York City, translated it for me. Big enough to serve six, this giant pancake is so good that four people usually demolish it. I serve it for brunch, together with a green salad, or accompanying eggs; its smoky taste is a good alternative to bacon, while the potatoes stand in for home fries.

1. Place the whole potatoes in a pot. Cover them with cold water by 2 inches. Bring to a boil over high heat. Reduce the heat and cook the potatoes until a knife penetrates 1 inch into the potatoes, 10 minutes. Drain the potatoes and refrigerate them until chilled through. (This can be done 1 or 2 days ahead.)

2. Shred the unpeeled potatoes into a bowl, using the medium holes of a grater. Make the strands as long as possible by slanting the potato as you rub it over the grater. There will be about 3 cups shredded potato.

3. Shred the tofu, using the same medium holes of the grater; there will be a scant cup. Add the grated tofu to the potatoes. Toss together with the salt and pepper.

4. Heat the butter with the oil in a medium nonstick skillet over medium-high heat until the butter melts. Add the onion and sauté until it is soft, about 4 minutes. Add the shredded potato and tofu to the pan. Press the mixture with a pancake turner, making a 1-inch-thick pancake. Cook until the rösti is well browned on the bottom, about 5 minutes. Gradually

work the pancake turner in under the pancake in several places to loosen it in the pan. Press it firmly all over with the turner to compact the potatoes. Lift the skillet and shake it to be sure the pancake slides easily. Invert a dinner plate over the pan and, holding it in place with your hand, flip the two so the pancake drops onto the plate.

5. Slide the rösti back into the skillet, uncooked side down. Set the pan back over the heat. Cook until the bottom is well browned, 4 to 5 minutes, pressing on it occasionally.

6. Slip the rösti onto a plate. Cut it into wedges and serve.

PER SERVING: Calories 158 • Soy Protein 2.7 g • Total Protein 4.4 g • Carbohydrates 18.4 g • Fat 7.7 g • Saturated Fat 2.8 g • Cholesterol 10.4 mg • Fiber 2.0 g • Sodium 466.1 mg

desserts

f you have a sweet tooth, you are going to be very happy with all the desserts you can make with soy. Choose from old-fashioned shortcake, creamy cheesecakes, snappy gingersnaps, cream pies piled high, and the best chocolate mousse you have ever tasted.

Those who like chocolate can also indulge in Double-Chocolate Bread Pudding swimming in Caramel Sauce, Chocolate New York Cheesecake, Chocolate Spice Biscotti, and deep dark Chocolate Espresso Sorbet.

These sorbets are the easiest dessert you can make. Just heat the fruit with sugar and tofu, puree, and pour the base into a plastic bag. It goes directly into the freezer; no stirring or special equipment is needed because the tofu lets it freeze into a smooth sorbet without stirring.

For fun, how about Chocolate Surprise Cupcakes with creamy filling and a raspberry surprise? Or strawberries filled with rich chocolate ganache?

Including soy cuts down on the fat and cholesterol in these wickedly good desserts. By the time you have sampled most of them, you will also understand how to use soy in your own favorite dessert recipes, keeping them delicious while making them more healthful.

Lemon Tiramisù

I prefer this golden version to the traditional tiramisù made with espresso and chocolate. Its fresh flavors come from limoncello, an Italian lemon liqueur, plus lemon zest and fresh lemon juice. Most liquor stores carry either limoncello or some other lemon-flavored liqueur. Savoiardi are crisp, long Italian ladyfinger biscuits. Amaretti are intensely flavored almond cookies. Both are sold in Italian food stores.

1. To make the syrup, combine the sugar and lemon zest with 1¼ cups water in a deep saucepan. Bring to a boil, remove from the heat, and let it steep for 1 hour. Remove the strips of lemon zest, and stir in the limoncello. (The syrup can be made ahead up to this point. It will keep for up to 2 days, tightly covered and refrigerated.)

2. To make the cream, combine the tofu, cream cheese, sugar, limoncello, vanilla, and lemon zest in a food processor and whirl until well blended. Mix in 2 tablespoons of the lemon juice and set aside.

3. Set out an 8-inch square baking dish. Combine 1 cup of the lemon syrup with the remaining lemon juice in a shallow bowl. Turn the biscuits, one at a time, in the liquid, working quickly. They will just begin to soften. Line the baking dish with them as you go. Ten biscuits should cover the bottom of the baking dish completely.

4. Spread half the lemon cream over the biscuits. Sprinkle with half the amaretti. Repeat with the remaining ingredients. Sprinkle the toasted almonds over the top.

5. Cover and refrigerate for at least 2 hours before serving. Serve cold.

SYRUP

2¼ cups sugar

Zest of 1 lemon, removed in long strips

¼ cup limoncello or lemon-flavored liqueur

LEMON CREAM

16 to 19 ounces silken tofu, drained (see page 48)

½ cup soy cream cheese

½ cup sugar

3 tablespoons limoncello or lemon-flavored liqueur

1 teaspoon vanilla extract

Grated zest and juice from 1 lemon

20 savoiardi biscuits or ladyfingers

½ cup crushed amaretti

¼ cup toasted sliced almonds

PER SERVING: Calories 284 • Soy Protein 0.5 g • Total Protein 13.5 g • Carbohydrates 42.0 g • Fat 7.2 g • Saturated Fat 1.5 g • Cholesterol 22.0 mg • Fiber 0.9 g • Sodium 135.7 mg

16 to 19 ounces silken
   tofu, drained
   (see page 48)

½ cup soy cream cheese

⅓ cup superfine sugar

4 tablespoons dark rum

2 tablespoons brandy

2 teaspoons fresh lemon
   juice

1¼ cups cold espresso or
   strong coffee

20 savoiardi biscuits or
   ladyfingers
   (see Note)

1½ ounces dark chocolate

Tiramisù

This creamy dessert is what happens when the best chocolate is combined with tofu, savoiardi biscuits (Italian ladyfingers), and a bit of creativity. It is the perfect choice if you like luscious desserts that are not too sweet.

1. Combine the tofu, cream cheese, sugar, 1 tablespoon of the rum, the brandy, and lemon juice in a food processor and whirl until well blended. Set aside.

2. Set out an 8-inch square baking dish. Combine the coffee with the remaining 3 tablespoons rum in a shallow bowl. Turn the biscuits, one at a time, in the liquid, working quickly. They will just begin to soften. Line the baking dish with them as you go. Ten biscuits should cover the bottom of the baking dish completely.

3. Spread half the tofu mixture over the biscuits. Grate 1 ounce of the chocolate and sprinkle half of it over the tofu.

4. Repeat, making a second layer of biscuits and cream, topped with grated chocolate. Chop the remaining chocolate into small chunks. Sprinkle them over the top of the tiramisù.

5. Cover the dish with plastic wrap and refrigerate for at least 2 hours, up to overnight. (This dessert will keep for up to 3 days, covered and refrigerated.) Serve cold.

NOTE: Savoiardi are dry ladyfinger cookies. They are available at Italian food stores and some supermarkets.

PER SERVING: Calories 227 • Soy Protein 0.5 g • Total Protein 12.4 g • Carbohydrates 31.3 g • Fat 5.8 g • Saturated Fat 1.4 g • Cholesterol 21.9 mg • Fiber 0.3 g • Sodium 138.0 mg

Cannoli Cream

Italians often skip the cannoli shells and serve this creamy dessert in a small dish, like a pudding. It is elegant enough for a dinner party and easy enough to enjoy anytime.

1. Combine the tofu, cream cheese, sugar, and lemon juice in a food processor and whirl until well blended.

2. Pour the tofu mixture into a medium bowl and mix in the citron, orange zest, cinnamon, and chocolate.

3. Cover tightly and refrigerate for 2 hours before serving to let the flavors mellow. (The dessert will keep for up to 3 days, covered tightly and refrigerated.)

4. To serve, spoon into individual footed dessert dishes and sprinkle with the pistachios.

PER SERVING: Calories 397 • Soy Protein 11.1 mg • Total Protein 13.2 g • Carbohydrates 46.9 g • Fat 20.4 g • Saturated Fat 5.0 g • Cholesterol 0 mg • Fiber 1.6 g • Sodium 220.4 mg

16 to 19 ounces silken tofu, drained (see page 48)

½ cup soy cream cheese

1 cup confectioners' sugar

2 teaspoons fresh lemon juice

2 tablespoons chopped candied citron or golden raisins

1 teaspoon grated orange zest

1 teaspoon ground cinnamon

1½ ounces dark chocolate, chopped

¼ cup chopped pistachios

2 cups vanilla soymilk,
preferably refrigerated

1 packet (2 teaspoons)
unflavored gelatin

¼ cup sugar

2 teaspoons instant
espresso powder

1 cup heavy (whipping)
cream

Espresso Panna Cotta

This dessert turns soymilk into an ethereal pleasure, thanks to a trick I learned from Eileen Guastella. Former pastry chef at Felidia, New York City, she specializes in Italian desserts. Her trick is whipping the cream. Take care to chill the base well, or the cream will separate and float on top when the panna cotta sets. (The dessert still tastes sublime should this happen.) To go all out, spoon Pistachio Sauce (page 299) or Caramel Sauce (page 338) around the panna cotta.

1. Place eight pots de crème or 6-ounce ramekins on a baking sheet. Place them in the refrigerator to chill.

2. Pour 1 cup of the soymilk into a saucepan. Sprinkle the gelatin over it. Let it sit for 10 minutes to soften. It will become puckered-looking. Heat the mixture over medium heat until the gelatin dissolves and the milk forms bubbles around the edges, about 5 minutes. Add the sugar and espresso. Stir until the coffee dissolves, which takes about 3 minutes. Off the heat, mix in the remaining 1 cup soymilk.

3. Fill a large bowl with ice. Set a smaller bowl into it and add the soymilk mixture. Set aside to cool, stirring occasionally, until the mixture feels cool (60°F on an instant-read thermometer) and is almost starting to set, about 10 minutes.

4. While the milk mixture cools, whip the cream loosely; it should still jiggle in the center when the bowl is shaken. Remove the pan with the chilled cups from the refrigerator.

5. Whisk a quarter of the whipped cream into the cooled milk mixture. (If it is not sufficiently chilled, the whipped cream will melt rather than emulsifying with the mixture.) Continue whisking in the cream, a quarter at a time. Immediately pour the panna cotta mixture into the cold cups, whisking occasionally to keep it well mixed. Cover the pan with plastic wrap.

6. Refrigerate the panna cotta until it is set and well chilled, about 4 hours.

7. To serve, hold each cup in a bowl of hot water for 1 minute. Run a thin knife around the edge of the cup. Place a dessert plate over the cup. Invert the two, so the cream falls onto the plate. Serve immediately. While it will keep for several days, this dessert is best when served 4 to 12 hours after it is made.

PER SERVING, WITHOUT SAUCE: Calories 165 • Soy Protein 1.8 g • Total Protein 3.1 g • Carbohydrates 8.6 g • Fat 11.9 g • Saturated Fat 6.9 g • Cholesterol 40.8 mg • Fiber 0 g • Sodium 45.0 mg

Pistachio Sauce

Makes 1 cup

½ cup unsalted shelled raw pistachios

1 cup vanilla soymilk, preferably WestSoy, refrigerated

2 tablespoons sugar

1. Blanch the pistachios in boiling water for 30 seconds. Drain in a strainer. Taking the nuts from the strainer one at a time, slip off the tough outer skin.

2. Place the blanched, peeled pistachios in a saucepan. Add the soymilk and sugar. Bring the mixture barely to a boil and reduce the heat. Simmer the nuts in the soymilk for 5 minutes. Remove the pot from the heat and set aside until cool, about 30 minutes.

3. When the soymilk and nuts are lukewarm, puree the mixture in a blender.

4. Place a fine mesh strainer over a bowl. Strain the puree, using the back of a wooden spoon to press it, extracting as much liquid as possible. Discard the ground nuts. Chill the sauce. Serve chilled. (This sauce will keep for 1 day, tightly covered and refrigerated.)

PER TABLESPOON: Calories 34 • Soy Protein 0.4 g • Total Protein 1.2 g • Carbohydrates 3.2 g • Fat 2.0 g • Saturated Fat 0.2 g • Cholesterol 0 mg • Fiber 0.4 g • Sodium 6.1 mg

Chocolate Velvet Mousse

2 tablespoons powdered
   egg whites or 2 large
   egg whites

4 ounces dark chocolate,
   finely chopped

½ cup pureed silken tofu,
   (see page 51)

1 teaspoon orange-
   flavored liqueur, vanilla
   extract, or other
   flavoring

¼ cup sugar

Pairing top-quality chocolate with tofu, and using a classic culinary technique, results in the velvet mousse of your dreams. Sure to garner raves, this dessert is so simple that you can whip it up just for yourself when you have the craving for it.

1. In an impeccably clean bowl, sprinkle the egg white powder over 6 tablespoons of lukewarm water and stir for 1 minute. The powder will remain lumpy. Set aside for 20 minutes. Disregard this step if using fresh egg whites.

2. Meanwhile, melt the chocolate in a bowl over barely simmering water or in the microwave. Cool the chocolate to lukewarm. Stir the tofu and liqueur into the chocolate.

3. Beat the egg whites using a hand-held mixer, preferably fitted with a whisk attachment. When they resemble a firm foam, gradually add the sugar, beating until the whites are stiff and resemble soft marshmallow fluff, about 8 minutes in all.

4. Fold a third of the whites into the chocolate mixture. Fold the rest of the whites into this lightened mixture, just until blended.

5. Spoon the mousse into four dessert dishes or one large bowl, and refrigerate until chilled through, about 3 hours.

6. Let the mousse sit at room temperature for 15 minutes before serving. (The dessert will keep for up to 3 days, covered and refrigerated.)

PER SERVING: Calories 236 • Soy Protein 1.6 mg • Total Protein 5.7 g • Carbohydrates 30.6 g • Fat 9.8 g • Saturated Fat 5.7 g • Cholesterol 0.3 mg • Fiber 1.4 g • Sodium 48.1 mg

White Chocolate Mousse

Fans of white chocolate will swoon over this ethereal cream. Serve it with fresh berries or accompanying your favorite dark chocolate cake. For fun, I present it in a glass bowl, along with a platter of long-stemmed strawberries and have everyone dip the berries into the mousse.

Follow the directions for Chocolate Velvet Mousse, substituting 4 ounces white chocolate, using only 2 tablespoons sugar. Use 1 teaspoon fresh lemon juice in place of the liqueur or other flavoring.

PER SERVING: Calories 200 • Soy Protein 1.6 g • Total Protein 4.6 g • Carbohydrates 23.9 g • Fat 9.7 g • Saturated Fat 5.5 g • Cholesterol 6.0 mg • Fiber 0 g • Sodium 50.1 mg

Double-Chocolate Bread Pudding

⅓ cup dried cranberries

¼ cup apple juice

2 large eggs, plus 3 egg whites

1 cup lightly packed light brown sugar

2 tablespoons Dutch-processed cocoa powder

3 cups chocolate soymilk

1 teaspoon vanilla extract

1 loaf challah egg bread (about 16 ounces)

½ cup dried pitted prunes, chopped

Tart cranberries counterpoint the chocolate depth of this moist bread pudding, proving the affinity between chocolate and berries. It is also studded with prunes, another good partner for chocolate. To dress it up for company, serve this dessert in a pool of Caramel Sauce (page 338).

1. Set a rack in the center of the oven. Preheat the oven to 350°F. Coat a 10-inch tube pan with nonstick cooking spray.

2. Soak the cranberries in the apple juice until plumped, 20 minutes.

3. Whisk the eggs and egg whites with the brown sugar and cocoa in a large bowl. Mix in the soymilk and vanilla.

4. Tear the bread into 1-inch pieces (there should be about 12 cups). Add the bread cubes to the soymilk mixture. Drain the cranberries and add them to the bowl, along with the prunes. Mix with a fork until the bread is thoroughly moistened. Let the pudding mixture sit for 10 minutes. Pack it into the prepared pan.

5. Bake the bread pudding for about 50 minutes, or until it is puffed and browned; a bamboo skewer inserted into the center should come out clean.

6. Let the pudding sit in the pan for 20 minutes, then unmold, running a knife around the side and center, onto a cake plate. Serve warm, cutting the pudding into slices. (The pudding can be cooled completely. It will keep for up to 3 days, covered with foil and refrigerated. Wrap slices in foil and warm in the oven before serving.)

PER SERVING: Calories 240 • Soy Protein 1.2 g • Total Protein 7.7 g • Carbohydrates 43.0 g • Fat 3.6 g • Saturated Fat 1.1 g • Cholesterol 60.3 mg • Fiber 2.6 g • Sodium 235.4 mg

Fudge Brownies

Every sinful square happens to conceal 3 grams of soy protein, thanks to soy baking mix. They also contain the chocolate, eggs, and butter essential to a great brownie.

1. Set a rack in the center of the oven. Preheat the oven to 350°F. Coat an 8-inch square baking dish with nonstick cooking spray.

2. Melt the butter in a medium saucepan over medium heat and remove the pot from the heat. Mix in the chocolate until it is melted. Set aside to cool to lukewarm, about 5 minutes.

3. While the chocolate mixture cools, combine the flour, baking mix, cocoa, and salt in a bowl.

4. Whisk the sugar into the cooled chocolate mixture, then the eggs and vanilla. Add the dry ingredients to the pot. Mix with a rubber spatula until they are combined. Turn the batter into the prepared pan, smoothing it into an even layer. Sprinkle the nuts over the top, pressing them lightly into the batter with your fingers.

5. Bake for about 30 minutes, or until the brownies are slightly darker at the edge and pulling away from the sides of the pan. A bamboo skewer inserted into the center of the pan should come out clean.

6. Cool the brownies completely in the pan on a rack. Make four cuts across the pan in one direction. Turn the pan 90 degrees and make three cuts across the pan, making 12 brownies.

8 tablespoons (1 stick) unsalted butter, cut into 8 pieces

2 ounces unsweetened baking chocolate, chopped

½ cup unbleached all-purpose flour

½ cup soy baking mix

2 tablespoons Dutch-processed cocoa powder, sifted

¼ teaspoon salt

1 cup sugar

2 large eggs

1½ teaspoons vanilla extract

½ cup chopped walnuts

PER BROWNIE: Calories 236 • Soy Protein 3.0 g • Total Protein 6.0 g • Carbohydrates 24.2 g • Fat 14.0 g • Saturated Fat 7.4 g • Cholesterol 55.4 mg • Fiber 1.5 g • Sodium 128.1 mg

Floating Almond "Tofu" with Fresh Fruit

GEL

2½ tablespoons agar-agar
   flakes (see Note)

¼ cup sugar

1¼ cups unsweetened
   soymilk

1 teaspoon almond extract

FRUIT SALAD

1 cup sugar

1 cardamom pod

1 clove

2-inch cinnamon stick

½ Bartlett pear, peeled

½ pint fresh raspberries

1 peach, halved and cut
   into thin crescents

½ cup seedless green
   grapes, halved

2 kumquats, very thinly
   sliced, or ⅓ cup canned
   drained mandarin
   orange sections

1 teaspoon grated orange
   zest

Soupe de fruits exotiques was a signature dessert when I worked at L'Archestrate in Paris. It featured fresh fruits sliced paper thin, served floating in a liquid so lightly sweetened it could hardly be called a syrup. This refreshing variation includes almond "tofu" cubes that look like Jell-O made with milk. They are my take on a Chinese dessert known as almond float, which is usually served topped with canned fruit salad. Here I use soymilk, agar-agar, and almond flavoring, which is a nice compromise between the Asian and Western methods of making this gel. This is a nice dessert to serve at parties. In summer its cool allure is particularly appealing.

1. To make the gel, place 1¼ cups water in a saucepan over medium heat. Sprinkle the agar over it. Heat to dissolve the agar, reducing the heat so it does not boil. This can take up to 20 minutes; there must be no hard bits at all.

2. Mix the sugar with the soymilk and almond extract in a bowl. Mix this into the agar solution, heating until the sugar is dissolved.

3. Rinse a 9-inch square dish with cold water. Drain but do not dry. Pour in the almond mixture. Cool to room temperature, then refrigerate until set, about 3 hours. Cut into 1-inch cubes. (This gel will keep for up to 5 days in the refrigerator.)

4. To make the fruit salad, combine the sugar with 2 cups of water in a saucepan. Add the cardamom, clove, and cinnamon. Bring to a boil over medium-high heat. Cover, remove the pot from the heat, and let the spices steep for 20 minutes. Strain the syrup into a glass bowl and cool to room temperature.

5. Cut the pear in half lengthwise and core. Thinly slice each piece crosswise. Place the sliced pear in the glass bowl. Add the raspberries, peach, grapes, and kumquats. Add the cubed almond gel.

6. Refrigerate to chill completely, at least 2 hours before serving. Stir in the orange zest just before serving. (This dessert will keep for up to 24 hours, covered and refrigerated.)

NOTE: Eden Foods sells agar-agar flakes. Clear and tasteless, they are derived from a sea vegetable.

PER SERVING: Calories 220 • Soy Protein 1.9 g • Total Protein 2.5 g • Carbohydrates 52.9 g • Fat 1.1 g • Saturated Fat 0 g • Cholesterol 0 mg • Fiber 3.6 g • Sodium 3.1 mg

Pistachio Orange Biscotti

1¼ cups unbleached all-purpose flour

½ cup soy protein powder

1 teaspoon baking powder

½ teaspoon baking soda

½ teaspoon ground cardamom

¼ teaspoon salt

3 large eggs

1 cup sugar

1 teaspoon vanilla extract

2 teaspoons grated orange zest

1 cup (4 ounces) unsalted pistachios, chopped

⅔ cup chopped candied orange peel

These long, graceful cookies are truly irresistible. Of course, they include soy, as well as nuts and candied orange peel. They store well, making them perfect for sending as gifts.

1. Place a rack in the center of the oven. Preheat the oven to 325°F. Line a baking sheet with parchment paper or aluminum foil.

2. Whisk together the flour, protein powder, baking powder, baking soda, cardamom, and salt in a bowl.

3. In another bowl, whisk together the eggs and sugar until well blended. Mix in the vanilla and zest. Stir this mixture into the dry ingredients. Mix in the nuts and orange peel. The dough will be thick and sticky.

4. Divide the dough into four parts. With your hands, form 1 part into an 8-inch × 1½-inch log by rolling and patting it between your palms. Place the dough the long way on the prepared pan, setting it about 3 inches in from the side. Form another piece of the dough, and place it to make a log the length of the pan, smoothing the dough together where the pieces join. Scrape off any dough clinging to your hands and smooth it onto the log. Rinse and dry your hands. With the remaining dough, form a second log, leaving 3 inches between the 2 logs. Flatten each log slightly. Don't worry if the surface is rough-looking.

5. Bake for 30 minutes, or until golden. Remove from the oven and cool for 5 minutes. Meanwhile, reduce the oven temperature to 275°F. Peel the parchment or foil away from the logs. Replace it on the baking sheet, clean side up.

6. Place each log on a cutting board, and cut it diagonally into ½-inch slices, using a serrated knife.

7. Return the sliced biscotti to the lined baking sheet, standing them up about ½ inch apart. Bake for 20 minutes, or until the biscotti are crisp and lightly browned.

8. Cool completely on a wire rack. Store the biscotti in an airtight container for up to 2 weeks.

PER BISCOTTO: Calories 52 • Soy Protein 0.3 g • Total Protein 2.5 g • Carbohydrates 7.5 g • Fat 1.5 g • Saturated Fat 0 g • Cholesterol 10.6 mg • Fiber 0.3 g • Sodium 40.7 mg

1¼ cups unbleached
all-purpose flour

½ cup soy baking mix or
protein powder

⅔ cup Dutch-processed
cocoa powder

1½ teaspoons baking
powder

½ teaspoon baking soda

2 teaspoons ground
cinnamon

2 teaspoons aniseeds

½ teaspoon ground ginger

⅛ teaspoon ground cloves

⅛ teaspoon salt

1 cup granulated sugar

¼ cup packed light brown
sugar

1½ cups almonds
(6 ounces), coarsely
chopped

4 large eggs, beaten

1 teaspoon vanilla extract

Chocolate Spice Biscotti

I love blending chocolate with spices. Here, building on a recipe from Nick Malgieri's book *Chocolate,* I added five of my favorites, including cinnamon and anise. Ideally, you should let these biscotti sit overnight so their flavors can meld. Dunk these firm cookies in a cup of espresso, or enjoy them with a mug of peppermint tea.

1. Place a rack in the center of the oven. Preheat the oven to 325°F. Line a baking sheet with parchment paper or aluminum foil.

2. Whisk together the flour, baking mix, cocoa, baking powder, baking soda, cinnamon, aniseeds, ginger, cloves, and salt. Stir in the white and brown sugars, mix in the almonds, and add the eggs and vanilla. Using a fork and then your fingers, blend the ingredients until the last bits of dry ingredients have been worked into the claylike dough.

3. Divide the dough into four parts. With your hands, form 1 part into an 8 × 1½-inch log by rolling and patting it between your palms. Place the dough the long way on the prepared pan, setting it 3 inches in from the side. Form another piece of the dough, and place it to make a log the length of the pan, smoothing the dough together where the pieces join. Scrape off any dough clinging to your hands and smooth it onto the log. Rinse and dry your hands. With the remaining dough, form a second log, leaving 3 inches between the 2 logs. Flatten each log slightly.

4. Bake for 30 minutes, or until the logs are dry to the touch and almost firm. Cool them on the pan. Peel the parchment or foil away from the logs. Replace it on the pan, clean side up.

5. When the logs are completely cool, place them on a cutting board. Cut them each into ½-inch slices, using a serrated knife.

6. Return the sliced biscotti to the lined baking sheet, standing them up so they are close, but not touching. Bake for 20 to 30 minutes, or until the biscotti are dry and crisp.

7. Cool on the pan. Store them in an airtight container for up to 2 weeks.

_____

PER BISCOTTO: Calories 56 • Soy Protein 0.3 g • Total Protein 1.8 g • Carbohydrates 7.5 g • Fat 2.4 g • Saturated Fat 0.2 g • Cholesterol 14.2 mg • Fiber 0.8 g • Sodium 17.7 mg

Triple Ginger Snappers

1½ cups unbleached
    all-purpose flour

½ cup soy protein powder

2 teaspoons baking soda

¼ teaspoon salt

1 teaspoon ground ginger

1 teaspoon ground
    cinnamon

¼ teaspoon freshly ground
    nutmeg

12 tablespoons (1½ sticks)
    unsalted butter, at room
    temperature

¾ cup firmly packed dark
    brown sugar

¼ cup pure maple sugar
    (see Note)

1 large egg

¼ cup unsulphured
    molasses

1 teaspoon finely grated
    fresh ginger

¼ cup finely chopped
    crystallized ginger,
    preferably Australian

¼ cup granulated sugar

The combination of crystallized ginger, ground ginger, and fresh ginger puts these big cookies over the top for ginger-lovers. Crisp when just baked, these cookies become more cakelike when they sit for a few hours. This time also gives the flavors of mellow maple, muscular molasses, and all that ginger time to settle in together. These cookies keep particularly well.

1. Place a rack in the center of the oven. Preheat the oven to 375°F. Cover two air-cushioned cookie sheets with parchment paper or aluminum foil (see Note). If using foil, coat the foil with nonstick cooking spray.

2. Whisk together the flour, protein powder, baking soda, salt, ground ginger, cinnamon, and nutmeg in a bowl.

3. Beat the butter with the brown and maple sugars using an electric mixer, until the mixture is fluffy and no longer feels gritty, about 2 minutes. Beat in the egg, molasses, and fresh ginger. Add the dry ingredients all at once with the crystallized ginger. Beat on low speed, stopping several times to scrape down the sides of the bowl, until they are well combined, or stir with a rubber spatula. The dough will be soft but not sticky.

4. Place the granulated sugar in a bowl. Coat a ¼-cup measure lightly with nonstick cooking spray. Use it to scoop up 3 generous tablespoons of the dough if you want large cookies. For medium cookies, scoop up 2 generous tablespoons of the dough. With your hands, lightly form the dough into a flattened ball. Gently roll it in the sugar to coat it. Place the sugared dough on one of the prepared baking sheets. Flatten it with your fingers into a disk 1 inch thick. Space the cookies

at least 3 inches apart, placing 6 large or 8 medium cookies per pan. Put the filled baking sheet in the refrigerator while you form the remaining cookies.

5. Bake the cookies for 12 to 15 minutes, until they feel firm in the center, turning the baking sheet after 6 minutes so the cookies brown evenly.

6. Cool the cookies completely on the baking sheet. (They will keep for up to 1 week, sealed in an airtight container.)

NOTES: If you can't find maple sugar, use all brown sugar.

If you do not have air-cushioned baking sheets, the effect can be approximated by using two regular ones, stacked one on top of the other.

PER COOKIE: Calories 232 • Soy Protein 6.0 g • Total Protein 7.7 g • Carbohydrates 31.0 g • Fat 8.9 g • Saturated Fat 6.1 g • Cholesterol 35.8 mg • Fiber 0.3 g • Sodium 248.9 mg

Chocolate Surprise Cupcakes

6 large Chocolate
Cupcakes (page 313)

¾ cup Dream Cream
(page 336)

24 fresh raspberries

When was the last time you had a cream-filled Hostess cupcake? These devilishly good, divinely light cupcakes are a close copy. Their Dream Cream filling conceals more than soy. Bring these cupcakes to the office or to school for birthdays, or have them any time you want some sweet fun.

1. To hollow a space in the center of each cupcake, first cut a circle in the bottom of the cupcakes, using the tip of a small knife. Make it an inch in diameter and about ¾ inch deep. Working with the tip of the knife, lift out this round plug, and reserve it for later. Scoop out enough of the soft inside of the cupcake to make a space 1½ inches deep, using a teaspoon. Discard the scooped out crumbs.

2. One teaspoon at a time, spoon a tablespoon of the whipped topping into the cavity. Insert 2 raspberries. Fill the cavity with another tablespoon of the cream. Push the round plug from the bottom of the cupcake into place. Some cream will squeeze out around it. Wipe this away with the spoon. Repeat until all the cupcakes are filled.

3. These muffins can sit at room temperature for up to 1 hour before serving. (They will keep for up to 8 hours on a plate covered with foil and refrigerated.)

PER CUPCAKE: Calories 269 • Soy Protein 4.2 g • Total Protein 7.5 g • Carbohydrates 35.0 g • Fat 12.3 g • Saturated Fat 7.4 g • Cholesterol 65.8 mg • Fiber 2.0 g • Sodium 195.1 mg

Chocolate Cupcakes

*Makes 12 medium or
6 large cupcakes*

If you can make muffins, you will find making these cup-cakes just as quick and easy. Dark, moist, and light, they are good as is, with a surprise filling, or topped with Apple Cream Cheese Frosting (page 327).

1. Set a rack in the center of the oven. Preheat the oven to 350°F. Coat either one 12-cup standard (2¾-inch) muffin pan with nonstick cooking spray or one 6-cup pan for large (3½-inch) muffins.

2. Whisk together the flour, baking mix, cocoa, baking powder, and salt in a bowl.

3. Beat the sugar with the butter until fluffy, using an electric or hand mixer, about 2 minutes. Beat in the eggs, one at a time. Mix in a third of the dry ingredients, then a third of the soymilk. Repeat, until all the liquid and dry ingredients are mixed in. The batter will be quite thick.

4. Fill each cavity of the muffin pans three-quarters full.

5. Bake for about 30 minutes, or until the cupcakes feel springy when pressed in the center of the top and a bamboo skewer inserted into the middle comes out clean.

6. Cool for 1 minute in the pans, then remove the cupcakes, and cool completely on a wire rack.

1¼ cups unbleached
    all-purpose flour

½ cup soy baking mix

½ cup Dutch-processed
    cocoa powder

1¼ teaspoons baking
    powder

½ teaspoon salt

1¼ cups sugar

8 tablespoons (1 stick)
    unsalted butter

2 large eggs

1 cup unsweetened
    soymilk

PER LARGE CUPCAKE: Calories 158 • Soy Protein 3.0 g • Total Protein 4.6 g • Carbohydrates 22.5 g • Fat 6.2 g • Saturated Fat 3.7 g • Cholesterol 37.0 mg • Fiber 1.2 g • Sodium 127.6 mg

Chocolate New York Cheesecake

CRUST

1 cup chocolate graham cracker crumbs

¼ cup ground blanched almonds

3 tablespoons sugar

2 tablespoons unsalted butter, softened

FILLING

16 to 19 ounces silken tofu

1 cup (8 ounces) soy cream cheese

½ cup fudge sauce or chocolate syrup

¾ cup sugar

2 tablespoons Dutch-processed cocoa powder

1 teaspoon vanilla extract

1 teaspoon fresh lemon juice

Blending two kinds of chocolate gives this velvety cheesecake delicious depth. Cholesterol-free, it is an indulgence you can really enjoy. For best results, use Tofutti's soy cream cheese and Nasoya's or Mori-Nu's soft tofu. Do not use reduced-fat, fat-free, or enriched tofu. The thicker the fudge sauce you use, the creamier your cake will be.

1. Set a rack in the center of the oven. Preheat the oven to 350°F. Coat a 7-inch springform pan with nonstick cooking spray. Cover a baking sheet with foil.

2. To make the crust, break up the graham crackers. Pulse and whirl them in a food processor until they are crumbs, about 90 seconds. Transfer the crumbs to a bowl, and add the almonds, sugar, and butter. Blend the mixture with a fork, then your fingertips, until it is well combined. Sprinkle the mixture over the bottom of the pan. Press the crust lightly with your fingertips to compact it and make an even layer covering the bottom and partially up the sides of the pan. Refrigerate for 30 minutes.

3. To make the filling, puree the tofu in a food processor. Add the cream cheese and puree again. Pulse in the fudge sauce, sugar, cocoa, vanilla, and lemon juice. Pour the filling into the prepared pan, filling it almost to the top. Sharply tap the pan several times on the countertop to knock out any air bubbles.

4. Place the filled pan on the baking sheet and set it in the oven. Bake for 1 hour. The cake should be slightly puffed and the center wobbly. Turn off the heat, and leave the cake in the oven for another hour.

5. Remove the cake and set it on a rack. Let it cool completely, for 3 to 4 hours. Refrigerate the cake overnight, or for at least 8 hours. Before serving, if the top of the cake looks moist, blot it gently with a paper towel. (This cake will keep for up to 3 days, loosely covered with foil and refrigerated.)

PER SERVING: Calories 384 • Soy Protein 3.8 g • Total Protein 6.9 g • Carbohydrates 51.4 g • Fat 15.0 g • Saturated Fat 4.1 g • Cholesterol 0 mg • Fiber 1.6 g • Sodium 287.3 mg

Tropical Orange Cheesecake

CRUST

15 chocolate wafer cookies

¼ cup unsweetened dried coconut

1 tablespoon melted unsalted butter

FILLING

1½ cups (12 ounces) silken tofu

1 cup (8 ounces) soy cream cheese

¾ cup Orange Curd (recipe follows)

3 large eggs

⅓ cup sugar

2 teaspoons grated orange zest

Oranges are often used in cooking to complement and counterpoint other flavors, but their sharp sweetness is a knock-out when it gets the leading role. A bit of coconut in the crust adds a nice, tropical touch. Letting this cake mellow overnight before serving is difficult, but worth the wait.

1. Set a rack in the center of the oven. Preheat the oven to 350°F.

2. To make the crust, break up the cookies. Process them in a food processor until they are crumbs, about 90 seconds. Transfer the crumbs to a bowl and add the coconut and melted butter. Blend the mixture with a fork, then your fingertips, until it is well combined. Sprinkle the mixture over the bottom of a 9-inch springform pan. Press the crust lightly with your fingertips to compact it and make an even layer covering the bottom of the pan. Set aside. Rinse out and dry the bowl of the food processor.

3. To make the filling, combine the tofu, cream cheese, orange curd, eggs, sugar, and zest in the food processor and process just until they are blended. (Overprocessing mixes air into the filling; this causes bubbles in the finished cake.) Pour the filling into the prepared pan. Sharply rap the pan 3 or 4 times on the countertop to eliminate air bubbles.

4. Bake the cheesecake for 20 minutes. Reduce the heat to 325°F, and bake for 20 to 25 minutes, or until the cake is almost set in the center. Turn off the oven. Leave the cake in the oven, with the door open, for 20 minutes. This helps to reduce cracking as the cake cools.

5. Cool the cake completely on a rack.

6. Run the blade of a knife around the edge of the cake, releasing it from the sides of the pan. Cover the cake with foil. Refrigerate it for at least 12 hours, preferably for 24 hours before serving. This is essential to the creamy texture of this cake.

PER SERVING: Calories 237 • Soy Protein 2.7 g • Total Protein 6.0 g • Carbohydrates 20.5 g • Fat 10.4 g • Saturated Fat 5.7 g • Cholesterol 110.6 mg • Fiber 0.8 g • Sodium 208.2 mg

Orange Curd

Makes 2 cups

Lemon curd has the brilliance of morning sun, while oranges give this version the glow of late afternoon. Orange juice concentrate gives it an edge you cannot get from the juice. You will discover many ways of using orange curd beyond this cheesecake and the filling for Blueberry Phyllo Tartlets (page 322).

5 large egg yolks

½ cup defrosted frozen orange juice concentrate

½ cup sugar

3 tablespoons unsalted butter, cut in small pieces

1. Whisk together the egg yolks, juice concentrate, and sugar in a heavy saucepan. Cook over medium heat, whisking constantly, until steam starts to rise from the liquid and it starts to thicken. Reduce the heat to low, and stir with a wooden spoon until the curd coats the spoon. When you run your finger down the back of the spoon and the track it makes stays clear, the curd is done.

2. Remove the pot from the heat. Add all the butter and whisk until it is blended into the hot curd. Immediately transfer the curd to a bowl and place a piece of plastic wrap over the surface of the curd to prevent a skin from forming. Cool to room temperature before refrigerating. (Orange curd will keep for up to 5 days, covered and refrigerated.)

PER TABLESPOON: Calories 38 • Soy Protein 0 g • Total Protein 0.5 g • Carbohydrates 4.9 g • Fat 1.8 g • Saturated Fat 31.9 g • Cholesterol 1.0 mg • Fiber 0 g • Sodium 5.3 mg

One 9-inch pie crust

2 large barely ripe bananas

1 cup sugar

¼ cup cornstarch

2 large egg yolks

3 cups vanilla soymilk

2 teaspoons fresh lemon
   juice

1 teaspoon vanilla extract,
   optional

TOPPING

⅓ cup sweetened
   shredded coconut

8 vanilla wafer cookies

Banana Cream Pie

Unless you tell, no one will even dream there is soy in this unbelievable update of everybody's favorite dessert. Use a creamy refrigerated soymilk for the most attractive result. Blending the traditional toasted coconut topping with crushed vanilla wafers cuts down on the fat.

1. Bake the pie crust according to package directions and set aside.

2. Cut the bananas into ¼-inch slices, holding the knife at a 45° angle to the banana to make each slice as long as possible. Set aside.

3. To make the filling, combine the sugar and cornstarch in a deep saucepan. Beat the egg yolks in a bowl and whisk in the soymilk. Whisk ½ cup of the milk mixture into the pan until it is smooth. Whisk in the rest of the liquid. Bring the mixture to a boil over medium-high heat, stirring constantly with a whisk or wooden spoon. Immediately lower the heat, and boil the filling for 1 minute. Remove it from the heat and stir in the lemon juice and vanilla, if using. Mix in the bananas. Pour the filling into the baked pie shell. Let it sit for 10 minutes to cool slightly.

4. Place the pie in the refrigerator and chill completely, 3 to 4 hours.

5. To make the topping, preheat the oven to 350 °F. Spread the coconut in an even layer on an air-cushioned baking sheet or two regular baking sheets stacked one on top of the other. Bake for about 5 minutes to toast the coconut, stirring occasionally to ensure the coconut colors evenly to a light brown.

6. Place the cookies in a plastic bag. Crush them to coarse crumbs, using a rolling pin. Combine the coconut and crumbs in a small bowl, and set aside.

7. Sprinkle the coconut-cookie topping evenly over the chilled pie, reserving any extra for another use. Serve the pie the day it is made.

PER SERVING: Calories 253 • Soy Protein 1.7 mg • Total Protein 3.4 g • Carbohydrates 42.4 g • Fat 8.2 g • Saturated Fat 3.0 g • Cholesterol 42.5 mg • Fiber 1.1 g • Sodium 139.5 mg

Sweet Potato Pie

One frozen 9-inch whole
   wheat pie crust
   (see Note)

FILLING

2¼ pounds Garnet or
   Jewel yams

1 cup unsweetened
   soymilk

2 large eggs

½ cup firmly packed dark
   brown sugar

2 tablespoons unsulphured
   molasses

2 tablespoons unsalted
   butter, melted

½ teaspoon ground
   cinnamon

¼ teaspoon freshly grated
   nutmeg

¼ teaspoon Chinese five-
   spice powder

¼ teaspoon salt

This stunningly delicious pie has attracted a mate, helped seal a deal, even cured a case of the mean reds that made the blues look like a mere headache. My secrets include roasting moist Jewel or Garnet yams until their natural sugars caramelize, then adding a touch of five-spice powder with star anise to enhance their natural sweetness.

1. Set the oven rack in the center of the oven. Preheat the oven to 400°F. Defrost the pie crust out of the freezer, according to package directions.

2. Pierce each yam with a fork in several places. Roast the yams on a baking sheet until they feel very soft, 45 to 60 minutes, depending on their size. When the yams are cool enough to handle, peel them, scooping the flesh into a bowl. Mash the flesh with a fork until it is creamy. Measure 3 cups. Reserve any leftover mashed yams for another use.

3. Combine the warm mashed sweet potatoes, soymilk, eggs, brown sugar, molasses, butter, cinnamon, nutmeg, five-spice powder, and salt in the bowl of a food processor. Process just until smooth; overprocessing adds air which makes bubbles in the baked pie.

4. Place the pie crust on a baking sheet. Scoop the potato filling into the pie crust. Bake for 15 minutes. Reduce the oven temperature to 350°F. Bake for 30 to 40 minutes, until a thin bamboo skewer inserted in the center of the pie comes out clean.

5. Cool the pie for 15 minutes on the baking sheet. Transfer it to a rack and cool completely. Cover with foil and refrigerate overnight.

6. Let the pie sit at room temperature for at least 20 minutes before serving.

NOTE: Maple Cedar makes a snappy whole wheat pie crust. Its mild flavor is a perfect match with the filling.

PER SERVING: Calories 251 • Soy Protein 0.7 g • Total Protein 3.7 g • Carbohydrates 35.1 g • Fat 10.2 g • Saturated Fat 4.9 g • Cholesterol 64.5 mg • Fiber 1.9 g • Sodium 169.5 mg

Yams and Sweet Potatoes

Garnet, Jewel, and Beauregard yams make the best sweet potato pie. Their deep orange flesh is so moist that mashing it with a fork turns it into a puree.

Shopping for these sugar-sweet tubers is confusing because, while we call them yams, they are actually sweet potatoes. This mix-up dates back several centuries. It began when African slaves in the Caribbean dubbed locally grown tubers "nyami" because these sweet potatoes, members of the morning glory family, reminded them of the true yams (of the genus Dioscorea), they had known in Africa. The tubers we properly call sweet potatoes have drier, denser flesh that ranges in color from golden yellow to ivory white.

Blueberry Phyllo Tartlets

5 sheets phyllo dough

2 tablespoons unsalted butter, melted

⅓ cup drained and pureed silken tofu (see page 51)

⅓ cup Orange Curd (page 317)

2 tablespoons finely chopped mint

1¼ cups blueberries

¼ cup peach jam

These rustic-looking tartlets are so good you will think they came from a pâtisserie in the French countryside. You can assemble these tartlets in a snap.

1. Set a rack in the center of the oven. Preheat the oven to 350°F.

2. To make the tart shells, spread 1 sheet of the phyllo on a work surface, with the long side facing you. Brush the dough lightly with the butter. Cover it with a second sheet of the phyllo. Repeat, using up all the dough. Brush the top of the last sheet with butter. Trim the edges so they are even. Cut the phyllo vertically into four strips. Cut each strip crosswise into 3 squares, trimming off any excess dough. Fit the squares, buttered side down, into the cavities of a standard 12-cup muffin pan. Bake the tart shells for about 10 minutes, or until golden brown along the edges. They will continue to bake when removed from the oven, so do not worry if they are pale inside and at the bottom. Set aside to cool. These shells will keep for up to 3 days, in the muffin pan, loosely covered with foil.

3. Whisk together the tofu and Orange Curd with the mint in a bowl. Mix in ¾ cup of the blueberries. (This mixture can be refrigerated for up to 4 hours.)

4. Melt the peach jam in a small saucepan or in the microwave.

5. To assemble the tartlets, spoon 1 generous tablespoon of the filling into each phyllo shell. Cover with a layer of plain blueberries. To glaze the tartlets, spoon about ½ teaspoon of the melted peach jam over the berries.

6. Serve within 1 hour, while the phyllo is crisp.

PER TART: Calories 85 • Soy Protein 0.4 g • Total Protein 1.3 g • Carbohydrates 13.5 g • Fat 3.3 g • Saturated Fat 1.9 g • Cholesterol 21.0 mg • Fiber 0.9 g • Sodium 44.9 mg

Peach Shortcake with Raspberries

Shortcake is a dessert even more American than apple pie. After all, the colonists brought pie recipes with them, while the biscuit on which shortcake is based is an American invention. Soy flour helps make these buttery, golden biscuits crusty outside with a big crumb inside. They soak up the juices from the fruit without getting soggy. Dream Cream, a blend of freshly whipped cream and pureed tofu that seems even richer than plain cream, is ideal with this homespun dessert. Feel free to substitute whatever fruit is in season.

6 cups sliced fresh peaches or 5 cups partially defrosted frozen sliced unsweetened peaches

⅓ cup sugar

1 recipe Old-Fashioned Biscuit Shortcakes (recipe follows)

1½ cups Dream Cream (page 336)

1½ cups fresh raspberries

1. If you are using frozen peaches, cut the slices in half lengthwise. Toss the peaches with the sugar in a bowl. Set aside for 1 hour, until the fruit is moist, and a light syrup collects in the bottom of the bowl.

2. Split the shortcakes, using the tines of a fork, as you would an English muffin. Place the bottom of each shortcake in the center of a dessert plate. Cover each with a sixth of the peaches. Spoon the syrup from the bowl over the fruit.

3. Set the top of the shortbread over the fruit, tipping it at an angle so it touches the plate. Sprinkle one-sixth of the raspberries over the exposed peaches on the shortbread and on the plate around it. Dollop one-sixth of the whipped topping onto the plate next to the filled shortcake. Serve immediately.

PER SERVING: Calories 392 • Soy Protein 2.9 g • Total Protein 7.5 g • Carbohydrates 55.3 g • Fat 16.8 g • Saturated Fat 10.6 g • Cholesterol 44.7 mg • Fiber 4.3 g • Sodium 195.8 mg

Old-Fashioned Biscuit Shortcakes

1 cup unbleached
all-purpose flour

½ cup soy flour

¼ cup sugar plus
1 tablespoon

1½ teaspoons baking
powder

¼ teaspoon baking soda

⅛ teaspoon salt

6 tablespoons (¾ stick)
cold unsalted butter,
diced

½ cup low-fat buttermilk

1 large egg white, beaten
until frothy

1. Set a rack in the center of the oven. Preheat the oven to 425°F.

2. Combine the flour, soy flour, ¼ cup sugar, baking powder, baking soda, and salt in a bowl. Cut in the butter, using a pastry cutter or a fork, then your fingertips, until the mixture resembles coarse meal.

3. Lightly flour a work surface. Add the buttermilk to the dry ingredients. Stir with a fork just until the dough comes together. It will be soft and moist. Turn the dough out onto the floured surface. Knead it just until the dry bits are absorbed and the dough is fairly smooth, about 30 seconds. Do not overwork, or the shortcakes will be tough.

4. Roll out the dough to a rectangle ¾-inch thick. Dip the edge of a 2½-inch biscuit cutter, round cookie cutter, or drinking glass into your sack of flour. Cut 2½-inch rounds from the dough. Gently press the scraps together and reroll until you have 6 shortcakes. Brush the tops with some of the egg white. Sprinkle to coat them evenly with the remaining 1 tablespoon of sugar. Place the shortcakes on a baking sheet.

5. Bake the shortcakes for 13 to 15 minutes, or until they have risen to about 1½ inches and are golden brown on top.

6. Transfer the shortcakes to a rack and cool completely. (These shortcakes will keep for 24 hours, wrapped tightly in foil. After that, they lose some of their buttery flavor.)

PER SHORTCAKE: Calories 275 • Soy Protein 3.6 g • Total Protein 5.6 g • Carbohydrates 21.2 g • Fat 19.0 g • Saturated Fat 12.5 g • Cholesterol 47.0 mg • Fiber 1.0 g • Sodium 286.0 mg

Vermont Apple Cobbler

After an extended stay in France, I returned home with renewed appreciation for traditional American cooking and native ingredients, including maple syrup. This cobbler quickly became a favorite, with its golden brown topping, tart apple filling, and smoky maple syrup. To take it over the top, add a scoop of vanilla frozen dessert or a dollop of Dream Cream (page 336).

1. Set a rack in the center of the oven. Preheat the oven to 375°F. Coat an 8-inch baking dish generously with nonstick cooking spray.

2. Cut each apple into quarters. Cut each quarter into 4 slices. Toss the sliced apples with the maple syrup in the prepared baking dish, and set aside.

3. To make the cobbler batter, combine the flour, soy baking mix, baking powder, and salt in a bowl. Cream together the butter and sugar in another bowl. Beat in the egg. Add half the milk and half the flour mixture, mixing just to combine them. Add the rest of milk, then rest of the flour mixture, making a thick batter. Spread the batter over the apples.

4. Bake the cobbler for 20 to 30 minutes, until a toothpick comes out of the batter clean and the apples are soft enough to enjoy.

5. Let it sit about 15 minutes. Serve warm.

6 medium tart apples, peeled and cored

½ cup dark (Grade B) pure maple syrup

½ cup unbleached all-purpose flour

½ cup soy baking mix

2 teaspoons baking powder

½ teaspoon salt

4 tablespoons (½ stick) unsalted butter, softened

½ cup sugar

1 large egg

¼ cup unsweetened soymilk

PER SERVING: Calories 323 • Soy Protein 6.4 g • Total Protein 8.9 g • Carbohydrates 55.8 g • Fat 8.5 g • Saturated Fat 5.6 g • Cholesterol 55.4 mg • Fiber 3.4 g • Sodium 401.0 mg

Applesauce Cake with Apple Cream Cheese Frosting

1 cup unbleached
all-purpose flour

½ cup soy baking mix

½ teaspoon baking
powder

½ teaspoon baking soda

1 teaspoon ground
cinnamon

¼ teaspoon ground
nutmeg

¼ teaspoon salt

8 tablespoons (1 stick)
unsalted butter, at room
temperature, or
margarine

1 cup sugar

1 large egg, at room
temperature

1 teaspoon vanilla extract

2 teaspoons grated lemon
zest

1 cup unsweetened
applesauce, at room
temperature

½ cup raisins

½ cup golden raisins

1 recipe Apple Cream
Cheese Frosting
(recipe follows)

Popular through the 1930s, applesauce-based cakes sur-
faced again in the health-conscious sixties as a way of
making appealing cakes using less butter and fewer eggs.
Crammed with raisins and spice, the unfrosted cake is a treat
to carry in a backpack or enjoy in the car.

1. Place an oven rack in the lower third of the oven. Preheat
the oven to 325°F. Coat an 8-inch square baking pan with
nonstick cooking spray. Dust the pan with flour and set aside.

2. Sift the flour with the baking mix, baking powder, baking
soda, cinnamon, nutmeg, and salt into a bowl. In another
bowl, beat the butter and sugar with a hand mixer until they
are fluffy and light. Mix in the egg, vanilla, and lemon zest.
Mix in a third of the dry ingredients just until they are
blended, followed by half of the applesauce. Repeat, ending
with the dry ingredients. Stir in the raisins. Spread the batter
evenly in the prepared pan.

3. Bake for 30 minutes, or until the cake springs back when
lightly pressed in the center and a bamboo skewer inserted in
the center comes out clean.

4. Cool in the pan on a rack for 10 minutes. Turn the cake
out onto the rack. Cool the cake to lukewarm. If you are not
icing the cake, let it cool completely.

5. Spread the Apple Cream Cheese Frosting over the lukewarm cake. Refrigerate to set the frosting. Let the cake come
to room temperature before serving.

PER SERVING UNFROSTED CAKE: Calories 361 • Soy Protein 4.5 g • Total Protein 7.6 g •
Carbohydrates 58.1 g • Fat 11.9 g • Saturated Fat 8.3 g • Cholesterol 56.6 mg • Fiber 1.9 g •
Sodium 292.3 mg

Apple Cream Cheese Frosting

The fresh fruit in this frosting is unusual. I confess the idea was not mine but I cannot recall where I saw it in order to share the credit. Remarkably, the shredded apple remains white and delicious against the tangy cream cheese for 2 to 3 days. Spread this frosting on Chocolate Cupcakes (page 313) too.

1. Toss the grated apple with the lemon juice in a bowl.

2. Cream the cheese together with the sugar in another bowl, using a hand mixer or the back of a wooden spoon. Mix the apple into the cheese mixture, using a rubber spatula.

1 medium Golden Delicious apple, peeled and coarsely grated (about 1 cup)

1 tablespoon fresh lemon juice

½ cup soy cream cheese

¼ cup confectioners' sugar

PER SERVING FROSTED CAKE: Calories 440 • Soy Protein 4.8 g • Total Protein 8.1 g • Carbohydrates 68.7 g • Fat 15.9 g • Saturated Fat 9.3 g • Cholesterol 56.6 mg • Fiber 15.9 g • Sodium 292.5 mg

PER 2 ²/₃ TABLESPOONS FROSTING: Calories 79 • Soy Protein 0.3 g • Total Protein 0.5 g • Carbohydrates 10.6 g • Fat 4.0 g • Saturated Fat 1.0 g • Cholesterol 0 mg • Fiber 0 g • Sodium 45 mg

2⅓ cups unbleached
all-purpose flour

⅔ cups soy protein
powder

2 teaspoons baking
powder

¼ teaspoon baking soda

1 tablespoon Dutch-
processed cocoa
powder

1 tablespoon ground
ginger

1 teaspoon ground
cinnamon

½ teaspoon freshly ground
black pepper

1 teaspoon ground allspice

½ teaspoon ground cloves

½ teaspoon freshly grated
nutmeg

1 teaspoon salt

1½ cups sugar

½ cup blackstrap
molasses

1 teaspoon grated peeled
fresh ginger

8 tablespoons (1 stick)
unsalted butter, melted
and cooled

1 cup canola or
vegetable oil

Fresh Ginger Layer Cake with Caramelized Apples

As a child, I watched my mother make old-fashioned layer cakes, like Lady Baltimore and triple-tiered devil's food, which were the stars of school bake sales. This showpiece is as special as her towering cakes, but making it takes only modest skill. The spicy gingerbread layers should be made a day ahead to allow their flavor and texture to settle. Putting the cake together is simple.

1. Place one rack in the top third of the oven and a second in the bottom third. Preheat the oven to 350°F. Butter and flour two 9-inch round cake pans.

2. Combine the flour, soy powder, baking powder, baking soda, cocoa, ginger, cinnamon, pepper, allspice, cloves, nutmeg, and salt in a medium bowl.

3. Combine the sugar, molasses, fresh ginger, melted butter, oil, soymilk, and eggs in a large bowl and use a hand mixer to mix thoroughly.

4. Fold the dry ingredients into the wet ones, mixing just until they are blended. Pour the batter into the prepared pans.

5. Set the pans in the oven, one pan on each rack. Bake for 30 minutes, until the cake pulls away from the sides of the pan and feels firm in the center when lightly pressed.

6. Let the gingerbread layers cool in the pans for 5 minutes. Turn them onto racks to cool. (Wrapped in foil, they will keep for up to 3 days at room temperature.)

7. When you are ready to assemble the cake, prepare the caramelized apples. Cut each apple quarter into ¾-inch slices. You should have 12 slices per apple.

8. Melt the butter in a large skillet over medium-high heat. Add the apples in one layer. Sprinkle them with 1 tablespoon of the sugar and cook until brown, 2 to 3 minutes. Turn the slices, sprinkle with the remaining 1 tablespoon sugar, and brown, another 2 to 3 minutes. Set aside.

9. Place one gingerbread layer on a serving plate. Spread with half the Dream Cream, letting it spill over the side. Arrange half the caramelized apples over the cream. Drizzle on the liquid from the pan. Set the second gingerbread layer on top of the apples. Cover with the remaining Dream Cream, again letting it flow over the sides. Arrange the remaining apples in a ring on top of the cake. Serve immediately.

PER SERVING: Calories 757 • Soy Protein 4.7 g • Total Protein 20.1 g • Carbohydrates 72.9 g • Fat 44.3 g • Saturated Fat 15.4 g • Cholesterol 105.1 mg • Fiber 1.8 g • Sodium 448.0 mg

1 cup unsweetened soymilk, at room temperature

2 large eggs, at room temperature, beaten

1½ cups chilled Dream Cream (page 336)

CARAMELIZED APPLES

2 Golden Delicious apples, peeled, cored, and quartered

2 tablespoon unsalted butter

2 tablespoons sugar

Pineapple Ginger Sorbet

2 cups chopped fresh pineapple (about ½ medium pineapple)

¾ cup (6 ounces) silken tofu

½ cup sugar

1 tablespoon grated fresh ginger

2 teaspoons fresh lemon juice

Nature has a way of leading us to foods that are perfect partners by encouraging them to grow together. Pineapples and ginger both grow in Hawaii and other tropical spots. Using a sugar-sweet golden pineapple and yellow Hawaiian ginger increases the brilliance of this pairing. You will find golden pineapples at the supermarket. Most of Hawaii's golden ginger is organically grown, so you are most likely to find it at natural food stores. Enjoy this bold, bright sorbet after Fajitas (page 187) or Quince and Tofu Pot Pie (page 233).

1. Combine the pineapple, tofu, sugar, and ginger in a stainless steel or other nonreactive pot. Bring to a boil over medium heat, cover, reduce the heat, and simmer until the sugar dissolves, about 4 minutes. The tofu will look curdled at first. Continue cooking, uncovered and stirring often, until the tofu blends with the liquid, about 3 minutes.

2. Puree the pineapple mixture with the lemon juice in a food processor.

3. Pour the puree into a 1-quart, freezer-weight, resealable plastic bag. Freeze, laying the bag flat so the sorbet is an even slab when it solidifies, 3 to 4 hours.

4. To serve, remove the sorbet from the freezer bag and place it on a cutting board. Chop the sorbet into 2-inch chunks. Place the chunks in a food processor and pulse just until they are chopped up. Immediately spoon the sorbet into dessert dishes and serve.

PER SERVING: Calories 159 • Soy Protein 1.6 g • Total Protein 2.0 g • Carbohydrates 36.7 g • Fat 0.7 g • Saturated Fat 0 g • Cholesterol 0 mg • Fiber 1.0 g • Sodium 7.5 mg

Cranberry Lime Sorbet

I believe cranberries should be enjoyed year-round. In winter, I load extra bags of them into the freezer so I can serve this bracing sorbet at holiday dinners and also enjoy it on a hot summer day, served with Pistachio Orange Biscotti (page 306).

1. Combine the cranberries, apple, sugar, and tofu in a saucepan and stir in ½ cup water. Cover the pot tightly and set over medium heat. Cook until the cranberries and apple are soft, 8 to 10 minutes.

2. Puree the cooked mixture with the lime juice in a food processor.

3. Pour the puree into a 1-quart, freezer-weight, resealable plastic bag. Freeze, laying the bag flat so the sorbet is an even slab when it solidifies, in 3 to 4 hours.

4. To serve, remove the sorbet from the freezer bag and place it on a cutting board. Chop the sorbet into 2-inch chunks. Place the chunks in a food processor and pulse just until they are chopped up. Immediately spoon the sorbet into dessert dishes and serve.

2 cups cranberries, fresh or frozen

1 medium Fuji apple, peeled, cored, and diced

1 cup sugar

¾ cup (6 ounces) silken tofu

2 tablespoons fresh lime juice

1 teaspoon lime zest

PER SERVING: Calories 203 • Soy Protein 1.3 g • Total Protein 1.5 g • Carbohydrates 49.8 g • Fat 0.7 g • Saturated Fat 0 g • Cholesterol 0 mg • Fiber 2.1 g • Sodium 3.5 mg

Chocolate Espresso Sorbet

2 cups unsweetened soymilk

½ cup sugar

3½ ounces top-quality dark chocolate, chopped

¼ cup Dutch-processed cocoa powder

1 teaspoon instant espresso powder

½ cup (4 ounces) silken tofu

The first time I tasted chocolate sorbet was at Berthillon, the legendary Parisian *glâcier*. Here, my hommage to this genius ice-cream maker combines a full-bodied blend of cocoa and dark chocolate with espresso. A touch of creaminess comes from the unobtrusive presence of tofu. Serve this in a pool of Pistachio Sauce (page 299) or sneak it by the spoonful right from the freezer when you want something sinful in the middle of the night.

1. Combine the soymilk, sugar, chocolate, cocoa, and espresso powder in a saucepan. Slowly bring the mixture to a boil, whisking to combine all the ingredients. When the mixture boils, remove the pot from the heat and add the tofu.

2. If you have an immersion blender, use it to puree the tofu into the hot chocolate mixture. If not, pour the contents of the pot into a blender and carefully puree.

3. Pour the puree into a 1-quart, freezer-weight, resealable plastic bag. Freeze, laying the bag flat so the sorbet is an even slab when it solidifies, in 3 to 4 hours.

4. To serve, remove the sorbet from the freezer bag and place it on a cutting board. Chop the sorbet into 2-inch chunks. Place the chunks in a food processor and pulse just until they are chopped up. Immediately spoon the sorbet into dessert dishes and serve.

PER SERVING: Calories 216 • Soy Protein 4.0 g • Total Protein 7.2 g • Carbohydrates 32.1 g • Fat 8.8 g • Saturated Fat 3.7 g • Cholesterol 0.8 mg • Fiber 5.7 g • Sodium 6.1 mg

Coconut Cream Sorbet

Looking at the cup of coconut milk left over after making a Thai curry led me to make up this creamy sorbet. It is the perfect finish after any fiery dish, including Ethiopian Wat (page 218). For a tropical trio, serve with Pineapple Ginger Sorbet (page 330) and Chocolate Espresso Sorbet (page 332).

¾ cup (6 ounces) silken tofu

½ cup sugar

2-inch cinnamon stick

1 cup coconut milk

1. Combine the tofu, sugar, and cinnamon stick in a saucepan and add ½ cup water. Bring just to a boil over medium-high heat. Reduce the heat and simmer until the sugar is dissolved and the tofu is heated through, about 3 minutes. Set aside to cool to room temperature.

2. Remove the cinnamon stick. Puree the cooled tofu mixture with the coconut milk in a food processor or blender.

3. Pour the puree into a 1-quart, freezer-weight, resealable plastic bag. Freeze, laying the bag flat so the sorbet is an even slab when it solidifies, in 3 to 4 hours.

4. To serve, remove the sorbet from the freezer bag and place it on a cutting board. Chop the sorbet into 2-inch chunks. Place the chunks in a food processor and pulse just until they are chopped up. Immediately spoon the sorbet into dessert dishes and serve.

PER SERVING: Calories 106 • Soy Protein 1.2 g • Total Protein 1.7 g • Carbohydrates 13.5 g • Fat 5.0 g • Saturated Fat 3.5 g • Cholesterol 0 mg • Fiber 0.6 g • Sodium 5.5 mg

Serves 6 (Makes 1 quart)

Honeydew and Green Chile Granita

4 cups diced ripe honeydew melon

¾ cup sugar

¾ cup (6 ounces) silken tofu

1 medium jalapeño pepper, seeded and chopped

1 cup green salsa, drained to ½ cup solids

1 tablespoon fresh lime juice

1 lime, cut in wedges

Cool and sweet, with just a touch of heat, this icy granita is especially good after a bowl of incendiary chili. For the green salsa, I always use Frontera's Tomatillo Salsa, created by chef Rick Bayless. If you cannot find it at your local supermarket, it can be mail ordered (see page 351).

1. Combine the melon, sugar, and tofu in a saucepan. Bring to a boil over medium-high heat, cover, and reduce the heat. Simmer for 5 minutes, until the sugar is dissolved and the melon slightly softened.

2. Place the melon mixture in the bowl of a food processor. Add the jalapeño, drained salsa, and lime juice, and process to a pulpy puree.

3. Pour the puree into a 1-quart, freezer-weight, resealable plastic bag. Freeze, laying the bag flat so the sorbet is an even slab when it solidifies. Freeze until it solidifies, in 4 to 6 hours, or overnight.

4. Spoon the granita into champagne flutes or other tall, narrow glasses. Perch a lime wedge on the edge of the glass and serve.

PER SERVING: Calories 160 • Soy Protein 1.6 g • Total Protein 2.5 g • Carbohydrates 37.6 g • Fat 0.8 g • Saturated Fat 0 g • Cholesterol 0 mg • Fiber 0.9 g • Sodium 130.0 mg

Chocolate-Filled Strawberries

Rather than dipping strawberries into chocolate, I prefer stuffing them with trufflelike ganache. As you bite in, the smooth chocolate cream blends with the succulent berry. Use big, long-stemmed berries, Driscoll's are best; their large cavity lets you spoon in the soft ganache. Chilling hardens the filling, so stuff the berries only an hour or two before serving them.

20 large long-stemmed
   strawberries
1½ cups (double recipe)
   thick Chocolate
   Ganache (page 337)
32 small mint leaves

1. To cut the hull and stem from the strawberries, insert the tip of a small paring knife at a 45° angle where the shoulder of the berry curves in. Working in a circle, remove the top of the berry, with the hull. To enlarge the opening inside the berry, holding the knife vertically, work it around the inside of the berry, cutting away the flesh of the berry around the top.

2. Spoon about 2 teaspoons of the soft ganache into the berry. Add more ganache until it mounds nicely at the top of the berry. Insert 2 mint leaves at one side of the ganache. Set the filled berry on a plate. Repeat, until all the berries have been filled.

3. Serve within 2 hours of making. Or refrigerate for up to 8 hours, uncovered. Bring to room temperature before serving.

PER STUFFED BERRY: Calories 43 • Soy Protein 0.3 g • Total Protein 0.6 g • Carbohydrates 5.7 g • Fat 2.6 g • Saturated Fat 1.8 g • Cholesterol 0 mg • Fiber 0.6 g • Sodium 16.0 mg

Dream Cream

½ cup heavy (whipping)
  cream, preferably not
  ultrapasteurized, chilled

½ cup (4 ounces) silken
  tofu, pureed
  (see page 51)

1 tablespoon
  confectioners' sugar

¼ teaspoon vanilla extract

Good news. Whipped cream plus tofu equals a luxurious, natural topping. For dairy lovers, it offers all the pleasures of whipped cream with only a quarter of the fat and a third of the calories. Use it as a topping, icing, or filling. It also keeps for a couple of days, so you can whip it up ahead of time.

1. Place a bowl and a whisk or the beaters from an electric mixer in the freezer to chill.

2. Whip the cream in the chilled bowl until it is stiff. Take care not to overbeat or the cream will become grainy. Fold the tofu, sugar, and vanilla into the cream thoroughly, using a rubber spatula.

3. Cover with plastic wrap and refrigerate. When chilled, in about 3 hours, it will thicken to the consistency of a frozen nondairy whipped topping. (Dream Cream will keep for up to 2 days, tightly covered and refrigerated.)

PER 2 TABLESPOONS: Calories 31 • Soy Protein 0.4 g • Total Protein 0.6 g • Carbohydrates 0.7 g • Fat 2.9 g • Saturated Fat 1.7 g • Cholesterol 10.2 mg • Fiber 0 g • Sodium 3.6 mg

If ultrapasteurized cream is the only choice at your market, don't worry. It whips well enough to enjoy Dream Cream. The main difference is that regularly pasteurized cream tastes brighter and less "cooked." It also gives a bit more volume when whipped.

Chocolate Ganache

French pastry chefs use velvety ganache, made from chocolate melted with warm cream, as a frosting, for filling cakes and cookies, and to make truffles. The kind and quality of chocolate you use determines the sweetness and intensity of the ganache. The smaller amount of chocolate produces a creamy ganache useful for frosting Chocolate Cupcakes (page 313). The larger amount of chocolate makes fudgy ganache for stuffed strawberries (page 335).

½ cup (4 ounces) silken tofu, pureed (see page 51)

3 ounces dark chocolate, chopped

1. Place the tofu in a small bowl.
2. Melt the chocolate in a small bowl in the microwave or set it over a pan of barely simmering water until it just melts. Stir to make the chocolate creamy. Mix the chocolate into the tofu. (The ganache will keep for up to 4 days, tightly covered and refrigerated.) Bring to room temperature before using.

PER TABLESPOON: Calories 38 • Soy Protein 0.4 g • Total Protein 0.9 g • Carbohydrates 4.4 g • Fat 2.1 g • Saturated Fat 1.4 g • Cholesterol 0 mg • Fiber 0.5 g • Sodium 15.5 mg

FOR THINNER GANACHE, use 1½ ounces dark chocolate, chopped. This makes ½ cup ganache.

PER TABLESPOON: Calories 32 • Soy Protein 0.6 g • Total Protein 0.8 g • Carbohydrates 3.4 g • Fat 1.7 g • Saturated fat 1.1 g • Cholesterol 0 mg • Fiber 0.4 g • Sodium 12.4 mg

½ teaspoon cornstarch

1 cup vanilla soymilk

¼ cup sugar

Caramel Sauce

Given the choice, I prefer caramel to chocolate desserts. Better yet, serve this sauce with chocolate desserts. When making this sauce, always wear a long oven mitt and tilt your head away when adding liquid to the hot caramel. A bit of cornstarch gives the sauce just enough body. The thicker version has the consistency of chocolate sauce. Try this sauce with a baked apple as well as with Espresso Panna Cotta (page 298). Serve the thicker one with Double-Chocolate Bread Pudding (page 302) and Fresh Ginger Layer Cake (page 328).

1. Mix the cornstarch into the soymilk in a small bowl. Set aside on a baking sheet.

2. Put the sugar in a heavy, deep, small saucepan. Add 1 tablespoon water. Holding the pot by the handle, tip it so the water swirls around, wetting the sugar completely.

3. Set the pot over medium heat. Cook until the sugar bubbles and becomes crusty, then turns golden, beginning around the edges, about 10 minutes. Do not stir. When the sugar is evenly honey-colored and smells like it is just beginning to burn, place the pot on the baking sheet.

4. Stir the soymilk mixture. Pour it into the pot, standing back to avoid splatters. Stir carefully so that it does not splash. Keep stirring until the hardened sugar dissolves into the milk. Place the pot over medium heat. When the sauce comes to a boil and thickens slightly, pour it into a bowl to cool.

5. Serve at room temperature, stirring to mix in the darkened top.

PER 2 TABLESPOONS: Calories 36 • Soy Protein 0.8 g • Total Protein 1.0 g • Carbohydrates 7.7 g • Fat 1.0 g • Saturated Fat 0 g • Cholesterol 0 mg • Fiber 0 g • Sodium 0 mg

sources

Includes information for non-soy foods and ingredients.

soyfoods organizations and information resources

Soy Information Clearing House
4816 N. Pennsylvania St.
Indianapolis, IN 46205
Phone: (800) TALKSOY
(825–5769)
Website: *www.soybean.org*,
www.soyfoods.com

Soyfoods Association of North America
1723 U St., N.W.
Washington, D.C. 20009
Phone: (202) 986–5600
Fax: (202) 387–5553
Email: *info@soyfoods.org*
Website: *www.soyfoods.org*

Soyatech, Inc.
7 Pleasant St.
P.O. Box 84
Bar Harbor, ME 04609
Phone: (800) 424–SOYA; (207) 288–4969
Fax: (207) 288–5264
Website: *www.soyatech.com*

soyfoods companies

American Food Company
4738 Valley Blvd.
Los Angeles, CA 90032
Phone: (213) 223–7738
Fax: (213) 223–8450
Makes tofu and/or tofu products
Sold nationally in supermarkets

American Miso Company
Maple Creek Road
Rutherfordton, N.C. 28139
Phone: (800) 334–5809; (828) 665–7790
Fax: (828) 667–8051
Website: *www.great-eastern-sun.com*
Makes Miso Master Miso
Sold nationally in natural food stores

American Natural Snacks
P.O. Box 1067
St. Augustine, FL 32085–1067
Phone: (904) 825–2039
Fax: (904) 825–2024
Website: *www.ans-natural.com*

Makes Soya Kaas soy cheese and fat-free soy cheese
Sold nationally, mainly in natural food stores

American Prairie. *See* Mercantile Foods Company

Amy's Kitchen Inc.
P.O. Box 449
Petaluma, CA 94953
Phone: (707) 578–7188
Website: *www.amyskitchen.com*
Makes Amy's organic frozen entrees and canned foods
Sold nationally in supermarkets and natural food stores

Arrowhead Mills, Inc.
110 S. Lawton
P.O. Box 2059
Hereford, TX 79045
Tel: (806) 364–0730
Fax: (806) 364–8242
Produces organic dried soybeans and soy flour

Azumaya. *See* Vitasoy

The Baker's Catalogue
P.O. Box 876
Norwich, VT 05055

Phone: (800) 827–6836
Website: *www.KingArthurFlour.com*
offers soy flour

Bob's Red Mill Natural Foods, Inc.
5209 SE International Way
Milwaukie, OR 97222
Phone: (503) 654–3215
Fax: (503) 653–1339
Makes soy flour and soy grits
Sold in supermarkets and by mail order

Boca Burger Inc.
1660 N.E. 12th Terrace
Ft. Lauderdale, FL 33305
Phone: (954) 524–1977
Fax: (954) 524–4653
Website: *www.bocaburger.com*
Makes Boca Burger, Sausage Patties, Sausage Links, Recipe Basics, Tenders and other products
Sold nationally in supermarkets and natural food stores

The Bridge
598 Washington St.
Middletown, CT 06457
Phone: (860) 346–3663
Makes tofu
Sold regionally in natural food stores

Cedar Lake Foods–MGM Foods
5333 Quarter Rd.
P.O. Box 65
Cedar Lake, MI 48812
Phone: (517) 427–5143

Fax: (517) 427–5392
Makes Cedar Lake frozen entrees and meat alternatives, including burgers and hot dogs
Sold nationally in supermarkets and natural food stores

Celantano
225 Bloomfield Ave.
Verona, NJ 07044
Phone: (602) 857–0865
Fax: (602) 917–6826
Email: *bob@celentano.com*
Makes frozen pasta and vegetable entrees with tofu
Sold nationally in supermarkets and natural food stores

Cheeseland Inc.
2 Arthurs Way
Spring Valley, NY 10977
Phone: (800) 542–6625
Distributes soy cheeses, including gouda, smoked gouda, mozzarella, pepper Jack and American Swiss
Sold in specialty food stores in the New York City and San Francisco areas

China Tofu
3222 Whipple Rd.
Union City, CA 94587
Phone: (510) 489–7288
Makes tofu and soymilk
Sold regionally in Asian food stores

Colonel Sanchez Foods
P.O. Box 5848
Santa Monica, CA 90940
Phone: (303) 805–8089

Fax: (213) 732–2271
Makes Red Chili tofu tamales
Sold nationally in supermarkets and natural food stores

Country Life Natural Foods
P.O. Box 489
Pullman, MI 49450
Phone: (616) 236–5011
Fax: (616) 236–8357
Email: *clnf@accn.org*
Makes meat alternatives, organically grown soybeans, soy flour, soy grits, soymilk, soynuts, and textured soy protein
Sold nationally by mail order

Dixie USA, Inc.
P.O. Box 55549
Houston, TX 77255
Phone: (800) 233–3668
Fax: (713) 688–4881
Email: *info@dixieusa.com*
Website: *www.dixiediner.com*
Offers Dixie Diner's Club meat alternatives, soynut butter, tofu powder, soynuts, Nutlettes soy breakfast cereal, Beanut butter, Quick Fix mixes
Sold nationally in supermarkets, natural food stores, and by mail order

DoubleRainbow, Inc
275 S. Van Ness Ave.
San Francisco, CA 94103
Phone: (800) 489–3580
Website: *www.doublerainbow.com*
Makes Soy Cream frozen dessert
Sold nationally in Trader Joe's and natural food stores

Dr. Soy.com, LLC
15375 Barranca Parkway
Suite B101
Irvine, CA 92618
Phone: (949) 585–9393
Fax: (949) 585–9396
Email: *drb@drsoy.com*
Website: *www.drsoy.com*
Makes soynut snacks, breakfast
cereal, protein bars, drink powder
Sold nationally in natural food
stores

Earth Island
P.O. Box 9400
Canoga Park, CA 91309–0400
Phone: (818) 347–9946
Website:
www.followyourheart.com
Makes Follow Your Heart
chicken alternative, soy cheese
Sold nationally in natural food
stores

Eddie's Pasta. *See* Mrs. Leeper's

Eden Foods, Inc.
701 Tecumseh Road
Clinton, MI 49236
Phone (517) 756–7424; (800)
248–0320
Fax: (517) 456–6075
Email: *sales@eden-foods.com*
Website: *www.ener-g.com*
Makes Edensoy soymilks, misos,
shoyu, tamari, dried tofu, canned
black soybeans
Sold nationally in supermarkets
and natural food stores

El Burrito Food Products, Inc.
P.O. Box 90125
Industry, CA 91745

Phone: (800) 933–7828
Fax: (626) 369–6972
Makes Soyrizo meatless soy
chorizo, and soy taco filling
Sold nationally in supermarkets
and natural food stores

Elite Foods
489 Cabot Rd.
South San Francisco, CA 94080
Phone: (800) 376–5368
Makes Easy Tofu flavored,
smoked tofu, and Elite meat
alternatives
Sold regionally in natural food
stores

Ener-G Foods, Inc.
5960 1st Ave., South
Seattle, WA 98108
Phone: (800) 331–5222
Fax: (206) 764–3398
Email: *heidi@ener-g.com*
Website: *www.ener-g.com*
Makes soymilk drinks, soynuts,
tofu powder, soyquik lacto-free
beverage
Sold nationally in supermarkets,
natural food stores, and by mail
order

Ethnic Gourmet Foods
190 Fountain St.
Framingham, MA 01702
Website:
www.ethnicgourmet.com
Makes Taj Gourmet frozen Asian
entrees
Sold nationally in supermarkets
and natural food stores

FarmSoy Company
96C The Farm
Summertown, TN 38483
Phone: (931) 964–2411
Fax: (931) 964–2411
Email: *farmsoy@usit.net*
Makes soy yogurt, tempeh, tofu,
tofu products
Sold regionally in supermarkets
and natural food stores

Fearn Natural Foods
6425 W. Executive Dr.
Mequon, WI 53092
Phone: (414) 242–2400
Fax: (414) 242–2751
Makes meat alternatives, isolated
soy protein, lecithin, soy flour,
soy protein concentrate, soymilk
powder
Sold nationally in supermarkets
and natural food stores

Follow Your Heart. *See* Earth
Island

Franklin Farms
P.O. Box 18
931 Route 31
N. Franklin, CT 06254–0018
Phone: (860) 642–3014
Fax: (860) 642–3017
Website: *www.franklinfarms.com*
Makes veggie burgers
Sold nationally in natural food
stores

Fresh Tofu, Inc.
P.O. Box 1125
Easton, PA 18044
Phone: (610) 258–0883
Fax: (610) 258–1592
Email: *tofu@fast.net*

Makes soy products, fresh tofu, baked tofu, La Bella Burger, tofu no-egg salad with herbs, tofu turkey, bulk organic tofu
Sold regionally in natural food stores

Frieda's
4465 Corporate Center Dr.
Los Alamitos, CA 90720–2561
Phone: (714) 826–6100
Fax: (714) 816–0277
Email: mail@friedas.com
Website: www.friedas.com
Distributes Soyrizo and Soytaco meat alternatives, refrigerated edamame, soynuts, and other products
Sold nationally in natural food stores

Frontier Natural Products Coop
2990 Wilderness Blvd.
Suite 200
Boulder, CO 80301
Phone: (319) 227–7996
Fax: (319) 227–7417
Website: www.frontiercoop.com
Makes Buc'uns bacon bits
Sold nationally in natural food stores

Galaxy Foods Company
2441 Viscount Row
Orlando, Fl 32809
Phone: (407) 855–5500; (800) 441–9419
Fax: (407) 855–7485
Website: www.galaxyfoods.com/soyco.html
Produces Lite & Less and Soyco

grated Parmesan, Soymage dairy alternative, Veggy Lite & Less soy cheeses and other dairy alternatives
Sold nationally in supermarkets and natural food stores

Garden of Eatin'
5300 Santa Monica Blvd.
Los Angeles, CA 90029
Phone: (310) 886–8200
Makes Little Soy Blues all-natural tortilla chips with soybeans
Sold nationally in natural food stores

G.E.M. Cultures
30301 Sherwood Rd.
Ft. Bragg, CA 95437
Phone: (707) 964–2922
Makes tempeh and cultures for homemade tempeh
Sold nationally in natural food stores and by mail order

General Nutrition Corporation
Pittsburgh, PA 15222
Phone: (888) 462–2548
Customer Service Dept.
300 Sixth Ave
Pittsburgh, PA 15213
Website: www.gnc.com
Makes Soy Baking Mix
Sold nationally in natural food stores

GeniSoy Products Co.
2300 S. Watney Way, Suite D
Fairfield, CA 94533
Phone: (888) 436–4769

Website: www.genisoy.com
Makes Genisoy protein drink mixes, soymilk powder, soynut, and isolated protein bars and other products
Sold nationally in supermarkets and natural food stores

GFA Brands, Inc.
P.O. Box 397
Cresskill, NJ 07626
Phone: (201) 568–9300
Fax: (201) 568–6374
Makes Earth Balance soy margarine and Smart Balance Non-Hydrogenated Vegetable Shortening
Sold nationally in natural food stores

Glenn Foods, Inc.
181 South Franklin Ave.
Valley Stream, NY 11581
Phone: (888) 864–1234
Website: www.glennys.com
Makes Soy Crisps snacks
Distributed nationally in natural food stores

Global Protein Foods, Inc.
707 Executive Blvd.
Valley Cottage, NY 10989
Phone: (914) 268–8100
Fax: (914) 268–9601
Makes tofu, yakidofu, and other Asian soy products
Sold regionally in Asian food stores

Gloria's Kitchen
P.O. Box 2071
Burlingame, CA 94011

Phone: (650) 579–0638
Fax: (650) 579–1483
Makes frozen entrees with soy
Sold in supermarkets in the
western half of the U.S.

Gold Mine Natural Food Co.
3419 Hancock St.
San Diego, CA 92110–4307
Phone: (800) 862–2347
Fax: (619) 296–9756
Email: *goldmine@ix.netcom.com*
Distributes soymilk, hydrolyzed
vegetable protein, miso, organic-
ally grown soybeans and tamari
Sold nationally by mail order

The Hain Celestial Group
50 Charles Lindbergh Blvd.
Uniondale, NY 11533
Phone: (800) 434-HAIN
Websites: *www.westbrae.com* and
www.thehainfoodgroup.com
Makes WestSoy soymilk,
Westbrae canned soybeans
Sold nationally in supermarkets
and natural food stores

Harmony Foods Corporation
P.O. Box 1191
Santa Cruz, CA 95061
Phone (831) 457–3200
Fax: (831) 460–9407
Makes chocolate covered soynuts
Sold nationally in natural food
stores

Harvest Direct
P.O. Box 988
Knoxville, TN 37901–0988
Phone: (423) 523–2304; (800)

835–2867
Fax: (423) 523–3372
Email: *monty@harvestdirect.com*
Website: *www.harvestdirect.com*
Distributes Harvest Direct
Protean (dry soy burger mixes),
TVP, ground beef, strip beef,
chunk beef, ground or chunk
poultry, Solait instant soy drink
Sold nationally in natural food
stores

Health Trip Foods, Inc.
50 Beharrell St.
Concord, MA 01742
Phone: (888) 270–9688
Fax: (978) 371–8911
Makes soynut butter
Sold nationally in natural food
stores

Hearty & Natural. *See* SunRich,
Inc.

Hinoichi. *See* House Foods
America Corp.

Hodgson Mill
1203 Niccum Ave.
Effingham, IL 62401
Phone: (800) 525–0177
Fax: (217) 347–0198
Website: *www.hodgsonmill.com*
Makes Hodgson Mill soy flour
and bulgur wheat with soy grits
hot cereal
Sold regionally in supermarkets
and natural food stores

House Foods America Corp.
7351 Orangewood Ave.
Garden Grove, CA 92841
Phone: (714) 901–4350

Fax: (714) 901–4235
Makes Hinoichi tofu, yakidofu,
age, and other Japanese tofu
products
Sold nationally in supermarkets,
natural food stores, and Asian
food stores

Imagine Foods, Inc.
350 Cambridge Ave., Suite 350
Palo Alto, CA 94306
Phone (800) 333–6339
Email: *info@imaginefoods.com*
Website: *www.imaginefoods.com*
Makes Soy Dream soymilk, Ken
and Robert's veggy burgers
Sold nationally in natural food
stores

Island Spring Inc.
P.O. Box 747
Vashon, WA 98070
Phone: (206) 463–9848
Fax: (206) 463–5670
Email: *Lukoskie@wolfnet.com*
Makes Island Spring soymilk,
tofu burgers, traditional firm
tofu, silken firm tofu,
Delicious steamed tofu, and
smoked baked tofu cubes
Sold regionally in supermarkets,
natural food stores, and Asian
food stores

Jaclyn's Food Products, Inc.
P.O. Box 1314
Cherry Hill, NJ 08034
Phone: (609) 354–2267
Fax: (609) 354–8335
Email: *dsaver@hlthmall.com*
Website: *www.hlthmall.com/
healthmall/jaclyns/*
Makes Jaclyn's cheese pizza,

grilled tofu in peanut sauce, and grilled tofu in black bean sauce
Sold nationally in natural food stores

Jarrow Formulas, Inc.
1824 South Robertson Blvd.
Los Angeles, CA 90035–4317
Phone: (310) 204–6936
Fax: (310) 204–5732
Website: *www.jarrow.com*
Makes soy protein powder
Sold nationally in natural food stores

JFC International, Inc.
540 Forbes Blvd.
South San Francisco, CA 94080
Phone: (650) 871–1660
Fax: (650) 952–3272
Imports and distributes Kikkoman tofu and Asian soy products, Hinoichi tofu, Mori-Nu tofu, and other products
Sold nationally in supermarkets and Asian food stores

Kashi Company
P.O. Box 8557
LaJolla, CA 92038–8557
Phone: (858) 274–8870
Fax: (858) 274–8894
Website: *www.kashi.com*
Makes GoLean soy protein cereal
Sold nationally in supermarkets and natural food stores

Kikkoman Foods, Inc.
50 California Street, Suite 3600
San Francisco, CA 94111
Phone: (415) 956–7750
Website: *www.kikkoman.co.jp*
Makes tofu, soy sauce, and soy

cooking sauces
Sold nationally in supermarkets, natural food stores, and Asian food stores

Lifeway
6431 W. Oakton Ave.
Morton Grove, IL 60053
Fax: (847) 967–6558
Email: *Iway@linkom.net*
Websites: *www.soytreat.com*; *www.kefir.com*
Makes soy kefir
Sold in natural food stores

Lightlife Foods
153 Industrial Blvd.
Turners Falls, MA 01376
Phone: (413) 863–8500
Fax: (413) 863–8502
Email: *info@lightlife.com*
Website: *www.lightlife.com*
Makes Smart Dogs, Tofu Pups, Lean Links, Smart Deli meat alternatives, including cold cuts, Foney Baloney, Lightburgers, Wonderdogs, Gimme Lean, Ground Round Smart Bacon, tempeh
Sold nationally in supermarkets and natural food stores

Lisanatti. *See* P. J. Lisac & Associates, Inc.

Local Tofu
203 Main St.
Nyack, NY 10960
Phone: (914) 358–2309
Email: *localtofu@juno.com*
Makes Local tofu, Sam's herbal tofu spreads, chunky tofu, veggie dip
Sold regionally in natural food stores

Lumen Foods, Herbologics LTD.
409 Scott St.
Lake Charles, LA 70601
Phone: (318) 436–6748; (800) 256–2253
Fax: (318) 436–1769
Email: *support@soybean.com*
Website: *www.soybean.com*
Makes Heartline meat alternatives and textured soy protein
Sold nationally in supermarkets, in natural food stores, and by mail order

The Mail Order Catalog
P.O. Box 180
Summertown, TN 38483
Phone: (800) 695–2241
Fax: (931) 964–3518
Email: *catalog@usit.net*
Website: *www.healthy-eating.com*
Distributes wide range of meat alternatives, soymilk, textured soy protein, and isolated soy protein
Sold by mail order

Marburger Foods
P.O. Box 387
Peru, IN 46970
Phone: (765) 473–3086
Fax: (765) 473–8554
Email: *custser@netusal.net*
Website: *www.baconbits.com*
Makes bacon bits
Sold nationally by mail order

Melissa's World Variety Produce, Inc.
P.O. Box 21127

Los Angeles, CA 90021
Phone: (800) 588–0151
Fax: (323) 588–9774
Email: *hotline@melissas.com*
Website: *www.melissas.com*
Distributes Melissa's soynuts,
Soyrizo, Mori-Nu tofu,
edamame, meat alternatives, and
tofu products
Sold nationally in supermarkets,
in natural food stores, and by
mail order

Mercantile Food Company
P.O. Box 55
Philmont, NY 12565
Distributes American Prairie
Organic Black Soybeans

Miyako Oriental Foods, Inc.
4287 Puente Ave.
Baldwin Park, CA 91706
Phone: (626) 962–9633
Fax: (626) 814–4569
Distributes Cold Mountain miso,
Yamajirushi miso
Sold nationally in natural food
and Asian food stores

Morinaga Nutritional Foods, Inc.
See Mori-Nu Tofu

Mori-Nu Tofu
2050 W. 190th St., Suite 110
Torrance, CA 90504
Phone: (310) 787–0200; (800)
NOW–TOFU
Fax: (310) 787–2727
Email: *morinaga@aol.com*
Website: *www.morinu.com*

Produces and distributes
Mori-Nu silken, "Lite" and
organic tofu and Mori-Nu Mates
pudding & pie mixes
Sold nationally in supermarkets,
natural food stores, and Asian
food stores

Morningstar Farms
Kellogg Company
One Kellogg Square
P.O. Box 3599
Battle Creek, MI 49016
Phone: (616) 961–3989
Website:
www.morningstarfarms.com

Mrs. Clark's Foods LC
740 SE. Dalbey Dr.
Ankny, IA 50240
Phone: (515) 964–8100
Fax: (515) 964–8397
Email: *Bspurloc@mrsclarks.com*
Website: *www.mrsclarks.com*
Sells Mrs. Clark's LoSatSoy
mayonnaise and salad dressing
Sold nationally in supermarkets
and natural food stores

Mrs. Leeper's
12455 Kerran St., Suite 200
Poway, CA 92064–6855
Phone: (858) 486–1101
Fax: (858) 486–5115
Email: *mlpinc@pacbell.net*
Website: *www.mrsleeperspasta.com*
Makes Eddie's Organic Soy Pastas
Sold nationally in supermarkets
and natural food stores

Nancy's Cultivated Soy Yogurt.
See Springfield Creamery

Nasoya Foods
1 New England Way
Ayer, MA 01432
Phone: (978) 772–6880
Fax: (978) 772–6881
Email: *nasoya@aol.com*
Website: *www.nasoya.com*
Makes Nasoya tofu; Nayonaise,
Nasoya salad dressings, New
Menu burgers and hot dogs,
TofuMate seasoning mixes
Sold nationally in supermarkets
and natural food stores

Native Foods
1775 E. Palm Canyon Dr.
Palm Springs, CA 92264
Website: *www.nativefoods.com*
Makes tempeh
Sold by mail order

Naturade, Inc.
14370 Myford Rd., Suite 100
Irvine, CA 92606
Phone: (800) 421–1830
Website: *www.naturade.com*
Makes soy protein drink
Sold in natural food stores

New Paradigm Foods, LLC
931 W. Liberty
Wheaton, IL 60187
Phone: (800) 848–2769
Makes soy cereal
Sold regionally in natural food
stores

Northern Soy, Inc.
545 West Ave.
Rochester, NY 14611
Phone: (716) 235–8970
Fax: (716) 235–3753

Email: *soyboy@frontiernet.net*
Makes SoyBoy tofu, tempeh, ravioli, Not Dogs, burgers
Sold nationally in supermarkets and natural food stores

Nutra Nuts, Inc.
8033 Sunset Blvd., Suite 780
Los Angeles, CA 90046
Phone: (818) 761–6502
Fax: (818) 761–7592
Website: *www.nutranuts.com*
Makes soynut snack with popcorn
Sold nationally in natural food stores

Oregon Chai
17455 NW Marshall St.
Portland, OR 97209
Phone: (503) 221–2424
Fax: (503) 796–0980
Email: *nirvana@oregonchai.com*
Makes Black Tea Chai with soymilk
Sold nationally in natural foods stores

The Organic Garden
3990 Varsity Dr.
Ann Arbor, MI 48108
Phone: (734) 677–5570
Fax: (734) 677–5574
Email: *info@theorganicgardenfood.com*
Makes breakfast cereal, soynut snacks
Sold nationally in natural food stores

P. J. Lisac & Associates, Inc.
9001 S. E. Lawnfield Rd.
Clackamas, OR 97015
Phone: (503) 652–1988
Fax: (503) 653–1979
Makes Lisanatti Premium Soy-Sation and Lite Soy-Sation soy cheese products
Sold nationally in natural food stores and by mail order

Pacific Foods of Oregon Inc.
19480 SW 97th Ave.
Tualatin, OR 97062
Phone: (503) 692–9666
Fax: (503) 692–9610
Makes Pacific Foods soymilk and soy drinks
Sold nationally in supermarkets and natural food stores

Perrith Farms
33012 Highway #2
Newport, WA 99156
Phone: (509) 447–5146
Website: *www.smallplanettofu.com*
Makes plain and flavored tofu
Sold regionally in supermarkets and natural food stores

Phipps County
P.O. Box 349
Pescadero, CA 94060
Phone: (800) 279–0889
Fax: (650) 879–1622
Grows dried yellow and black soybeans (organic and conventional)
Sold nationally by mail order

Quong Hop & Company
161 Beacon St.
South San Francisco, CA 94080
Phone: (650) 553–9900
Fax: (650) 952–3329
Makes Soy Deli tofu and tofu entrees, Quong Hop & Co. tofu products, Gold Mountain, Pacific tempeh, Soy Fresh
Sold regionally in supermarkets, natural food stores, and Asian food stores

Rella Good Cheese Co.
P.O. Box 5020
Santa Rosa, CA 95402–5020
Phone: (707) 576–7050
Fax: (707) 545–7116
Email: *richard@rella.com*
Website: *www.rella.com*
Makes Soyrella cheese products
Sold nationally in supermarkets and natural food stores

Rising Moon
1432 Willamette
Eugene, OR 97401
Phone: (541) 342–1183
Email: *sales@risingmoon.com*
Website: *www.risingmoon.com*
Makes fresh ravioli with tofu
Sold regionally in natural food stores and by mail order

Robert's American Gourmet
P.O. Box 67
Roslyn Heights, NY 11577
Phone: (800) 626–7557
Website: *www.RobGourmet.com*
Produces soy pretzels and enriched potato chips
Sold nationally in supermarkets and natural food stores

Rosewood Products, Inc.
738 Airport Blvd.
Ann Arbor, MI 48108
Phone: (800) 466–2254; (734)

665–2222
Fax: (734) 668–8430
Email: *rosewood@cac.net*
Website: *www.mi-way.com/soy-cheese*
Makes China Rose products, Rosewood Farms tofu
Sold nationally in supermarkets, natural food stores, and Asian food stores

San Diego Soy Dairy
1330 Hill St., Suite B
El Cajon, CA 92020
Phone: (619) 447–8638
Makes tofu, soymilk, salad dressings
Sold regionally in supermarkets and natural food stores.

San-J International, Inc.
2880 Sprouse Dr.
Richmond, VA 23231
Phone: (804) 226–8333
Fax: (804) 226–8383
Email: *SanJ@Richmond.infi.net*
Website: *www.san-j.com*
Makes tamari and shoyu soy sauces; miso soup; Thai peanut, sweet-and-sour, Szechuan, and SJ grilling sauce
Sold nationally in supermarkets, natural food stores, and Asian food stores

Seapoint Farms
19022 Bayhill Lane
Huntington Beach, CA 92648
Phone: (888) 722–7098
Fax: (714) 960–8324
Website: *www.seapointfarms.com*
Distributes frozen edamame and ready-to-eat frozen entrees
Sold nationally in natural food stores

Shiloh Farms, Inc.
P.O. Box 97
Sulphur Springs, AR 72768–0097
Phone: (501) 298–3297
Fax: (501) 298–3359
Website: *www.user.hwark.com/shilohf*
Distributes organically grown dried soybeans and soy flour
Sold regionally in natural food stores and by mail order

Skeet & Ikes's
216–2323 Quebec St.
Vancouver
British Columbia,
Canada V5T 3A3
Phone: (604) 879–9100
Fax: (604) 879–9164
Email: *skeetike@istar.ca*
Website: *www.skeetike.com*
Makes flavored soynuts
Sold nationally in natural food stores

Smoke and Fire Natural Foods, Inc.
P.O. Box 743
Great Barrington, MA 01230
Phone: (413) 528–6891
Fax: (413) 528–1877
Email: *tofu@smokeandfire.com*
Website: *www.smokeandfire.com*
Makes flavored smoked tofu
Sold regionally in natural food stores

Sno Pac Foods, Inc.
521 W. Enterprise Dr.
Caledonia, MN 55921
Phone: (800) 533–2215; (507) 724–5281
Fax: (507) 724–5285

Email: *info@snopac.com*
Website: *www.snopac.com*
Produces Sno Pac Sweet Beans and frozen organic edamame
Sold nationally in natural food stores

Something Better Natural Foods
614 Capital Ave. N.E.
Battle Creek, MI 49017
Phone (616) 965–1199
Fax: (616) 965–8500
Sells soybeans, soy flour, soy grits, soymilk, soynuts, textured soy protein, and isolated soy protein
Sold nationally by mail order

South River Miso Company
888 Shelburne Falls Rd.
Conway, MA 01341
Phone: (413) 369–4057
Fax: (413) 369–4299
Email: *mail@southrivermiso.com*
Website: *www.southrivermiso.com*
Makes miso and tamari
Sold regionally in natural food stores and by mail order

Sovex Foods, Inc.
P.O. Box 2178
Collegedale, TN 37315
Phone: (800) 227–2320
Fax: (423) 396–3402
Makes "Better Than Milk" soymilk
Sold nationally in supermarkets and natural food stores

Soya World Inc.
312–19292 60th Ave.
Surrey (BC)
V3S 8E5 Canada
Phone: (604) 514–5292

Fax: (604) 514–8564
Website: *www.soyaworld.com*
Makes SoNice soymilk
Sold nationally in natural food stores

SoyBoy. *See* Northern Soy, Inc.

The SoyNut Butter Company
102 North Cook Street
Barrington, IL 60010
Phone: (800) 288–1012
Fax: (847) 635–6801
Makes soynut butters
I. M. Healthy soynut butter
Sold nationally in natural food stores

Springfield Creamery
29440 Airport Rd.
Eugene, OR 97402
Phone: (541) 689–2911
Fax: (541) 689–2915
Makes Nancy's Cultured soy yogurt
Sold nationally in natural food stores

Summercorn Foods, Inc.
1410 West Cato Springs Rd.
Fayetteville, AR 72701
Phone: (501) 521–9338; (888) 328–9473
Fax: (501) 443–5771
Email: *summercorn@straw.com*
Website: *www.straw.com/summercorn*
Makes Savory Soysage, tofu, onion dip, tofu garden patty (frozen), Smoke BBQ tofu
Sold regionally in supermarkets and natural food stores

SunRich, Inc.
P.O. Box 128
3824 SW 93rd St.
Hope, MN 56046
Phone: (800) 342–6976
Fax: (507) 451–2910
Email: *sunrich@11.net*
Produces Hearty & Natural Sweet Beans, edamame, burgers, ground meat alternatives, and SunRich Supreme soymilk
Sold nationally in supermarkets, natural food stores, and Asian food stores

Tofutti Brands, Inc.
50 Jackson Dr.
Cranford, NJ 07016
Phone: (908) 272–2400
Fax: (908) 272–9492
Email: *tofutti@nac.net*
Website: *www.tofutti.com*
Produces Tofutti premium and low-fat frozen desserts, Better Than Cream Cheese, Sour Supreme sour cream, and frozen prepared entrees
Sold nationally in supermarkets and natural food stores

Trader Joe's
P.O. Box 3270
South Pasadena, CA 91031
Phone: (800) SHOPTJS
Website: *www.traderjoes.com*
Sells soymilk, tofu, meat alternatives, soy pasta, and other soyfoods at over 160 stores around the U.S.

Tree of Life, Inc.
P.O. Box 410
St. Augustine, FL 32085–0410

Phone: (904) 825–2026
Fax: (904) 825–2009
Distributes Tree of Life and Harmony Farms meat alternatives, soy and tofu products, and soymilk
Sold nationally in supermarkets and natural food stores

Tumaro's Homestyle Kitchens
5300 Santa Monica Blvd., Suite 311
Los Angeles, CA 90029
Phone: (323) 464–6317
Fax: (323) 464–7063
Email: *info@tumaros.com*
Website: *www.tumaros.com*
Makes Homestyle Kitchen soy cheese burritos
Sold nationally in supermarkets and natural food stores

Turtle Island Foods, Inc.
P.O. Box 176
Hood River, OR 97031
Phone: (541) 386–7766
Fax: (541) 386–7754
Email: *info@tofurkey.com*
Website: *www.tofurky.com*
Makes meat alternatives including Tofurky, Deli Slices, and meatless burgers
Sold nationally in natural food stores

Turtle Mountain, Inc.
P.O. Box 70
Junction City, OR 97448
Phone: (541) 998–6778
Fax: (541) 998–6344
Email: *mark@turtlemountain.com*
Website: *www.turtlemountain.com*
Makes Sweet Nothings, organic

Soy Delicious, and conventional nondairy soy frozen desserts
Sold nationally in natural food stores

Veat Gourmet, Inc.
4690 E. Second St. #9
Benicia, CA 94510
Phone: (888) 321-VEAT
Fax: (707) 746–7767
Website: *www.veat.com*
Makes Vegetarian Gourmet-Bites, Nuggets, and Breast frozen soymeat
Sold nationally in natural food stores

Vegeking Corporation
877 Azusa Ave.
City of Industry, CA 91745
Phone: (626) 965–0889
Fax: (626) 965–8780
Email: *info@vegeking.com*
Website: *www.vegeking.com*
Makes VeggieMaster meat alternative entrees
Sold nationally in natural food stores

Vitasoy USA Inc.
400 Oyster Point Blvd., Suite 201
South San Francisco, CA 94080
Phone: (800) VITASOY (848–2769); (650) 583–9888
Fax: (650) 583–8881
Email: *custsrv@vitasoy/-usa.com*
Website: *www.vitasoy-usa.com*
Makes Azumaya tofu, Nasoya tofu, Nasoya Nayonaise, Nasoya Vegi-Dressings, Vitasoy soymilk, New Menu seasoning mixes
Sold nationally in supermarkets, natural food stores, and Asian food stores

Westbrae Natural Foods
P.O. Box 48006
Gardena, CA 90248
Phone: (310) 886–8200
Fax: (310) 886–8219
Website: *www.westbrae.com*
Makes Westsoy soymilks, tamari, soy sauce, Westbrae miso, canned organic soybeans
Sold nationally in supermarkets and natural food stores

White Wave, Inc.
1990 N. 57th Ct.
Boulder, CO 80301
Phone: (303) 443–3470
Fax: (303) 443–3952
Email: *questions@whitewave.com*
Website: *www.whitewave.com*
Makes Silk soymilk, yogurt and dairy creamer, White Wave tofu, baked tofu, soy cheese, tempeh, deli soymeats, and refrigerated entrees
Sold nationally in supermarkets and natural food stores

Whole Foods Market
601 N. Lamar #300
Austin, TX 78703
Phone: (512) 477–5566
Fax: (512) 322–9688
Website: *www.wholefoods.com*
Sells soy protein powder, tofu, soymilk, and other soyfoods, nationally under their own label (Also in Bread & Circus, Fresh Fields and other stores owned by Whole Foods)

The WholeSoy Company
49 Stevenson Street # 1075
San Francisco, CA 94105

Phone: (415) 495–2870
Fax (415) 495–3060
Website: *www.wholesoycom.com*
Makes soy yogurt and frozen dessert
Sold in supermarkets and natural food stores

Wildwood Natural Foods, Inc.
1560 Mansfield St.
Santa Cruz, CA 95062
Phone: (813) 476–4448
Fax: (813) 479–3764
Makes tofu, baked and smoked tofu, tofu cutlets, fresh soymilk, prepared tofu salads, veggie burgers
Sold regionally in supermarkets and natural food stores

Worthington Foods, Inc.
900 Proprietors Rd.
Worthington, OH 43085–3194
Phone: (614) 885–2594
Fax: (614) 885–2594
Website: *www.wfds.com*
Makes Morningstar Farms (Prime Patties; Vege-patties; Chik Patties; Deli Franks; breakfast links, patties, and strips; Grillers), Worthington Food products, Loma Linda products and Natural Touch Okara frozen patties, Harvest Burgers (original, flavored, southwestern), Harvest Burgers For Recipes (precooked crumbled meat alternative), breakfast patties and links
Sold nationally in supermarkets and natural food stores

Yves Veggie Cuisine, Inc.
1638 Derwent Way
Delta (Vancouver) BC
Canada V3M 6R9
Phone: (800) 667–9837
Email:
stayintouch@yvesveggie.com
Website: *www.Yvesveggie.com*
Makes Ground Round, Veggie
Pepperoni and Pizza Pepperoni,
Canadian Veggie Bacon and
other meat alternatives, and the
Good Slice soy cheese
Sold nationally in supermarkets
and natural food stores

Zöe Foods
P.O. Box 2014
Brookline, MA 02446
Phone: (617) 739–1269
Fax: (617) 739–3176
Website: *www.zoefoods.com*
Produces Flax & Soy Clusters
granola
Sold nationally in natural food
stores

Zendon
155–04 Liberty Ave.
Jamaica, NY, 11433
Phone: (718) 291–3333
Fax. (718) 291–0560
Email: *blaeevalley@aol.com*
Makes Zen Don soymilk drinks
and ready-to-eat organic soy
puddings
Sold nationally in supermarkets,
natural food stores, and Asian
food stores

**companies producing
ingredients for soyfoods**
ADM (Archer Daniels Midland)

4666 Faries Parkway
Decatur, IL 62525
Phone: (217) 424–2593
Fax: (217) 362–3959
Website: *www.admworld.com*
Makes meat alternatives, isolated
soy protein, soy fiber, soy flakes,
flour, grits, protein concentrate,
textured soy protein and other
products

Cargill Foods
P.O. Box 9300
Minneapolis, MN 55440
Phone: (800) 227–4455
Email: *dennis-
andrews@cargill.com*
Website: *www.cargillfoods.com*
Manufactures soybean, oil, flour,
textured soy protein, grits, flakes,
bacon bits

Central Soya
1946 W. Cook Rd.
Fort Wayne, IN 46818
Phone: (219) 425–5100
Produces soy flour, soy protein
concentrate, lecithin for other
manufacturers

Central Soyfoods
11 W. 14th St.
Lawrence, KS 66044–3415
Phone: (785) 843–0653
Manufactures soymilk, tempeh,
and tofu for other companies

Protein Technologies,
International
Checkerboard Square
P.O. Box 88940
St. Louis, MO 63188
Phone: (800) 325–7108

Fax: (314) 982–2461
Website: *www.suprosoy.com*
Makes Suprosoy protein isolate,
soy flakes, soy flour, and
soybean oil

US Soy
2808 Thomason Drive
Mattoon, IL 61938
Phone: (217) 235–1020
Fax: (217) 235–1006
Email: *ussoy1@advant.net*
Website: *www.ussoy.com*
Produces soybeans, soy flour,
textured soy protein, flax oil and
meal

non-soy companies
Bascom Maple Farms
RR1, Box 137
Alsted, NH 03602
Phone: (603) 835–6361
Email: *sales@bascommaple.com,
prichards@bascommaple.com*
Produces organic maple sugar
and maple syrup

Cystern Inc.
1104 Ohio Street N.
Arlington, VA 22205
Phone: (888) 297-8376;
(703) 536-5555
Fax: (703) 533-3661
Website: *www.cystern.com*
Distributes Savu Smoker Bags

Deb El Foods Corp.
2 Papetti Plaza
Elizabeth, NJ 07207
Phone: (800) 421–3447
Fax: (908) 351–0330

Produces Just Whites dried egg whites
Sold in supermarkets and natural food stores

Flavorganics
280 Doremus Ave.
Newark, NJ 07105
Phone: (973) 344–8014
Fax: (973) 344–5880
Website: *www.flavorganics. com*
Produces organic vanilla and other flavorings
Sold nationally in natural food stores, specialty food stores, and some supermarkets

Frontera Foods, Inc.
445 North Clark St.
Chicago, IL 60610
Phone: (312) 661–1434
Website: *www.FronteraKitchens.com*
Makes salsa
Sold in supermarkets and natural food stores

Liberty Richter, Inc.
400 Lyster Ave.
Saddle Brook, NJ 07663
Phone: (201) 843–8900

Fax: (201) 368–3575
Distributes Morga Saturated Fat-free Vegetable Broth powder and bouillon cubes
Sold nationally in natural food stores

Royal Pacific Foods, Inc.
2700 Blvd., Suite G
Monterey, CA 93940
Phone: (408) 645–1090
Fax: (408) 645–1094
Website: *www.gingerpeople.com*
Distributes Ginger People Crystallized Australian Ginger Bits
Sold in supermarkets, specialty food stores, and natural food stores

Spectrum Naturals
133 Copeland St.
Petaluma, CA 94952
Phone: (707) 778–8900
Fax: (707) 765–1026
Website: *www.spectrumnaturals.com*
Produces Spectrum Spread non-hydrogenated spread with butter flavor
Sold nationally in natural food stores

Thai Kitchen
229 Castro St.
Oakland, CA 94607
Phone: (510) 268–0209
Fax: (510) 834–3102
Website: *www.thaikitchen.com*
Distributes Thai Kitchen natural coconut milk, lite coconut milk, rice noodles and other Thai ingredients
Sold nationally in supermarkets and natural food stores

Tom Telliard Foods
254 West B Street
Colton, CA 92324
Phone: (909) 825–2773
Makes whole wheat ready-to-bake pie crust
Sold nationally in natural food stores

U.S. Mills, Inc.
200 Reservoir St.
Needham, MA 02494
Phone: (781) 444–0440
Fax: (781) 444–3411
Produces Erewhon Aztec Crunch Corn and Amaranth Cereal
Sold nationally in natural food stores

bibliography

Anderson, E. N. *The Food of China*. New Haven, Conn.: Yale University Press, 1988.

Anderson, Jean. *The American Century Cookbook*. New York: Clarkson N. Potter, 1997.

Arndt, Alice. *Seasoning Savy: How to Cook with Herbs, Spices and Other Flavorings*. Binghampton, N.Y.: The Haworth Herbal Press, 1999.

Bayless, Rick. *Rick Bayless's Mexican Kitchen*. New York: Scribner, 1996.

Bhumichitr, Vatcharin. *Vatch's South East Asian Cookbook*. New York: St. Martin's Press, 1997.

Bloom, Carole. *The International Dictionary of Desserts, Pastries and Confections*. New York: Hearst Books, 1995.

Chang, K. C., ed. *Food in Chinese Culture*. New Haven, Conn.: Yale University Press, 1977.

Cost, Bruce. *Asian Ingredients: A Guide to the Foodstuffs of China, Japan, Korea, Thailand, and Vietnam*. New York: HarperCollins, 2000.

Davidson, Alan. *The Oxford Companion to Food*. New York: Oxford University Press, 1999.

Hsiung, Deh-Ta. *The Chinese Kitchen*. New York: St. Martin's Press, 1999.

Hyman, Gwendal. *Cuisines of Southeast Asia*. New York: John Wiley, 1993.

Jones, Dorothea van Gundy. *The Soybean Cookbook*. New York: Arco Publishing Company, Inc., 1973.

Liu, KeShun. *Soybeans: Chemistry, Technology and Utilization*. Gaithersburg, Md.: Aspen Publishers, 1999.

London, Sheryl and Mel. *The Versatile Grain and The Elegant Bean*. New York: Simon & Schuster, 1992.

Madison, Deborah. *Vegetarian Cooking for Everyone*. New York: Broadway Books, 1997.

Malgieri, Nick. *Chocolate*. New York: HarperCollins, 1998.

———. *Cookies Unlimited*. New York: HarperCollins, 2000.

Margen, Sheldon, M.D., and the Editors of the University of California at Berkeley Wellness Letter. *The Wellness Encyclopedia of Food and Nutrition*. New York: Rebus, 1992.

Mariani, John F. *The Dictionary of American Food and Drink*. New York: Hearst Books, 1994.

Marks, Copeland. *The Korean Kitchen*. San Francisco: Chronicle Books, 1993.

McDermott, Nancie. *Real Thai: The Best of Thailand's Regional Cooking*. San Francisco: Chronicle Books, 1992.

McLaughlin, Michael. *The Back of the Box Gourmet*. New York: Simon & Schuster, 1990.

Mowe, Rosalind., ed. *Southeast Asian Specialties: A Culinary Journey*. Cologne: Culinaria Könemann, 1998.

Ortiz, Elisabeth Lambert. *The Complete Book of Japanese Cooking*. New York: Galahad Books, 1976.

Owen, Sri. *Indonesian Regional Cooking*. New York: St. Martin's Press, 1994.

Paino, John and Messinger, Lisa. *The Tofu Book: The New American Cuisine*. Garden City Park, N.Y.: Avery Publishing Group, 1991.

Passmore, Jacki. *The Encyclopedia of Asian Food and Cooking*. New York: William Morrow, 1991.

Patten, Marguerite. *Classic British Dishes*. London: Bloomsbury Publishing, 1994.

Purdy, Susan G. *As Easy as Pie*. New York: Collier Books, 1984.

Rombauer, Irma S., Marion Rombauer Becker, and Ethan Becker. *Joy of Cooking*. New York: Scribner, 1997.

Ross, Rosa Lo San. *Beyond Bok Choy*. New York: Artisan, 1996.

Schneider, Elizabeth. *Uncommon Fruits & Vegetables*. New York: Harper & Row, 1986.

Shaw, Diana. *The Essential Vegetarian Cookbook*. New York: Clarkson Potter, 1997.

Shurtleff, William, and Aoyagi Akiko. *The Book of Miso*. Berkeley, Calif.: Ten Speed Press, 1976.

———. *The Book of Tempeh*. New York: Harper & Row, 1979.

———. *The Book of Tofu*. Berkeley, Calif.: Ten Speed Press, 1975, 1998.

Simonds, Nina. *A Spoonful of Ginger*. New York: Alfred A. Knopf, 1999.

Tantillo, Tony, and Sam Gugino. *Eat Fresh, Stay Healthy*. New York: Macmillan, 1997.

Taylor, John Martin. *The Fearless Frying Cookbook*. New York: Workman Publishing, 1997.

Tropp, Barbara. *The Modern Art of Chinese Cooking*. New York: William Morrow, 1982.

Tsuji, Shizuo. *Japanese Cooking: A Simple Art*. New York: Kodansha International, 1980.

Villas, James. *Stews, Bogs, and Burgoos*. New York: William Morrow, 1997.

Warren, Olivia. *Taste of Eritrea*. New York: Hippocrene Books, 2000.

Watanabe, Tokuji. *The Book of Soybeans: Nature's Miracle Protein*. New York: Japan Publications, 1984.

Waters, Alice. *Chez Panisse Pasta, Pizza & Calzone*. New York: Random House, 1984.

White Wave. *Soyfood Recipes for the American Table*. Summertown, Tenn.: Book Publishing Co., 1998.

Wittenberg, Margaret, M. *Good Food: The Complete Guide to Eating Well*. Freedom, Calif.: The Crossing Press, 1995.

Williams-Heller, Annie, and Josephine McCarthy. *Soybeans From Soup to Nuts*. New York: Vanguard Press, 1944.

Wood, Rebecca. *The New Whole Foods Encyclopedia*. New York: Penguin Books, 1999.

Young, Grace. *The Wisdom of the Chinese Kitchen*. New York: Simon & Schuster, 1999.

index

braised:
  cabbage with tempeh and
    cranberries, 212
  spinach, 290
bread, 123, 140–48
  big dill loaf, 145–46
  curry flatbread, 143–44
  injera, 220
  pesto herb, 140–41
  pudding, cappuccino, 72
  pudding, double-chocolate, 302
  pumpkin caraway, 147–48
  salad, blankit Tunisian, 156
  see also muffins
breakfast, 58–81
  blintzes, 80–81
  buckwheat brûlée, 63–64
  cappuccino bread pudding, 72
  cranberry-ginger granola, 60
  ginger date scones, 65
  lemon loaf, 67
  maple yogurt sprinkles, 61
  migas, 71
  oat bran muffins, 66
  oatmeal and carrot jumbles, 68
  oatmeal porridge, 62
  onion and pepper scrambler, 70
  see also egg(s), egg dishes;
    pancakes; toast
broccoli:
  with black bean sauce, 259–60
  fusilli with sun-dried tomatoes,
    black soybeans and, 207
  and mustard dip, 99–100
  velvet, 135
brownies, fudge, 303
Brunswick-style sweet soybeans,
  288
buckwheat brûlée, 63–64
burgers, 182
  green bean and tempeh, 188
  pinto bean, with cumin
    mayonnaise, 189–90

Burmese curry, 267–68
burrito, Swiss chard, poblano,
  potato, and baked tofu,
  192
butter:
  flavored clarified, 219
  soynut, 28

cabbage with tempeh and
  cranberries, braised, 212
Caesar salad with Parmesan
  croutons, 150
cakes:
  applesauce, with apple cream
    cheese frosting, 326–27
  fresh ginger layer, with
    caramelized apples,
    328–29
  lemon loaf, 67
  see also cheesecake; cupcakes,
    chocolate; shortcake
calcium, 3, 26
California "bacon" and avocado
  wrap, 183
cannoli cream, 297
cantaloupe, in creamy orange
  smoothie, 85
caponata, 109
"cappuccino," mushroom and
  miso, 139
cappuccino bread pudding, 72
caramel sauce, 338
caraway pumpkin bread,
  147–48
carrot:
  and oatmeal breakfast jumbles,
    68
  and red lentil pâté, 112
  soup, tangy, 136
casseroles, 210, 223–27, 231–34
  cottage pie, 231–32
  eggplant manicotti, 223–24
  picadillo, 227

piñon, 225–26
quince and tofu pot pie with
  mushrooms and chestnuts,
  233–34
chai, supercharged, 96
champ, 291
cheese, see goat cheese; Parmesan
  croutons; Pecorino cheese
cheese, soy, 4, 11
cheesecake:
  chocolate New York, 314–15
  tropical orange, 316–17
cherry sauce, dark, 79
chestnut(s):
  pâté, 115–16
  quince and tofu pot pie with
    mushrooms and, 233–34
chicken salad, Chinese un-, 152
chickpea stew, Spanish, 211
chile, green, and honeydew
  granita, 334
chilis, 210, 228–30
  beans and franks, 230
  fifty-fifty, 229
  thirty-minute, 228
chili soynuts, hot, 122
Chinese (Chinese-American):
  bok choy with soft soy sheets,
    262–63
  chop suey, 258
  edamame with bean curd
    noodles and preserved
    vegetable, 264–65
  egg foo yong, 253–54
  ginger fried rice, 266
  kung pao edamame rice bowl,
    261
  meat loaf, 251
  moo goo gai pan, 256–57
  pepper steak, 255
  spiced nuts, 121
  tofu, 36–37
  un-chicken salad, 152

about the author

Dana Jacobi's four cookbooks include *The Best of Clay Pot Cooking* and *The Joy of Soy*, a James Beard Award Finalist (previously titled *The Natural Kitchen: SOY!*). She contributed the soy section to *The New Joy of Cooking*. "Something Different," her weekly food column, appears in national newspapers. She has also written for *Food & Wine*, *Vegetarian Times*, and the *New York Times*. A passionate knitter, Dana lives in New York City.